EP90

The Cambridge Series on Electronic Publishing

Managing Editor: P. HAMMERSLEY

The purpose of this new series is to publish books in the exciting and topical field of electronic printing and publishing. The series will attempt to cover all aspects of electronic publishing including:

• Matters relating to hardware, software and standards concerned with transferring authors' words and images to the printed page;

• Screen-based documents — hypertext and its implications for authors and readers;

• Document delivery — electronic methods of reader access to publications, full-text database publishing, CD-ROM delivery systems and the impact for libraries;

• On-line publishing systems and distributed publication systems — the impact of networks on the publication process;

• Human factors relating, for example, to document structures for readability, editing aids, expert-system based interfaces, and type and page design.

While there will be some overlap with other areas of computer science (such as information retrieval, HCI and computer graphics), the series will concentrate primarily on books concerned with publishing, and so should provide a scholarly and specific survey of developments in this subject area.

Titles will range from advanced textbooks to multi-author works.

Already Published:

EP88, Document Manipulation and Typography; J.C. van Vliet (ed).
Structured Documents; J. André, R. Furuta & V. Quint (eds).
Raster Imaging and Digital Typography 89; J. André & R. Hersch (eds).

EP90
Proceedings of the International Conference on Electronic Publishing,
Document Manipulation & Typography
Gaithersburg, Maryland, September 1990

Edited by
R. Furuta
University of Maryland

CAMBRIDGE UNIVERSITY PRESS

Cambridge

New York   Port Chester   Melbourne   Sydney

Published by the Press Syndicate of the University of Cambridge
The Pitt Building, Trumpington Street, Cambridge CB2 1RP
40 West 20th Street, New York, NY 10011, USA
10, Stamford Road, Oakleigh, Melbourne 3166, Australia

© Cambridge University Press 1990

First published 1990

Printed in the United States of America

Library of Congress cataloguing in publication data available

British Library cataloguing in publication data available

ISBN 0 521 40246 8

Table of contents

EP90 Organization   viii

Preface   ix

Issues and Tradeoffs in Document Preparation Systems   1
Brian W. Kernighan

Towards Document Engineering   17
Vincent Quint, Marc Nanard, and Jacques André

Managing Properties in a System of Cooperating Editors   31
Donald D. Chamberlin

A Logic Grammar Foundation for Document Representation and Document Layout   47
Allen L. Brown, Jr. and Howard A. Blair

Structured Editing—Hypertext Approach: Cooperation and Complementarity   65
Anne-Marie Vercoustre

An ODA Page Planner for Professional Publishing   79
Giovanni Guardalben and Mosé Giacomello

flo—A Language for Typesetting Flowcharts   93
Anthony P. Wolfman and Daniel M. Berry

Design of Hypermedia Publications: Issues and Solutions   107
Paul Kahn, Julie Launhardt, Krzysztof Lenk, and Ronnie Peters

Strengths and Weaknesses of Database Models for Textual Documents   125
B. N. Rossiter and M. A. Heather

A Structured Document Database System   139
Pekka Kilpeläinen, Greger Lindén, Heikki Mannila, and Erja Nikunen

The Integration of Structured Documents into DBMS   153
José Valdeni De Lima and Henri Galy

Electronic Publishing—Practice and Experience   169
David F. Brailsford, David R. Evans, and Geeti Granger

ADAPT: Automated Document Analysis Processing and Tagging   183
John Handley and Stuart Weibel

Recognition Processing for Multilingual Documents   193
A. Lawrence Spitz

Editing Images of Text   207
Gary E. Kopec and Steven C. Bagley

Automatic Generation of Gridfitting Hints for Rasterization of Outline Fonts or Graphics   221
Sten F. Andler

Chinese Fonts and their Digitization   235
Y. S. Moon and T. Y. Shin

The Role of a Descriptive Markup Language in the Creation of Interactive Multimedia Documents for Customized Electronic Delivery   249
Gil C. Cruz and Thomas H. Judd

An Extensible, Object-Oriented System for Active Documents   263
Paul M. English, Ethan Jacobson, Robert A. Morris, Kimbo B. Mundy, Stephen D. Pelletier, Thomas A. Polucci, and H. David Scarbro

Documents as User Interfaces   277
Eric A. Bier and Aaron Goodisman

Colophon	291
Author index	295
Keyword index	297

Electronic Publishing '90
International Conference on Electronic Publishing,
Document Manipulation, and Typography

National Institute of Standards and Technology
Gaithersburg, Maryland USA
September 18-20, 1990

Conference Committee

Conference Chair:	Peter King, University of Manitoba, Canada
Program Chair:	Richard Furuta, University of Maryland, USA
Exhibition Chair:	Debra Adams, Xerox Palo Alto Research Center, USA
Local Arrangements and Publicity Chair:	Larry Welsch, National Institute of Standards and Technology, USA

Program Committee

Jacques André, INRIA/IRISA—Rennes, France
Patrick Baudelaire, Digital Paris Research Laboratory, France
Richard J. Beach, Xerox Palo Alto Research Center, USA
Charles Bigelow, Stanford University, USA
David F. Brailsford, University of Nottingham, UK
Heather Brown, University of Kent at Canterbury, UK
Donald D. Chamberlin, IBM Almaden Research Center, USA
Giovanni Coray, École Polytechnique Fédérale de Lausanne, Switzerland
R. W. Davy, Chelgraph Limited, UK
Irene Greif, Lotus Development Corporation, USA
Vania Joloboff, Open Software Foundation, USA
Brian Kernighan, AT&T Bell Laboratories, USA
Dario Lucarella, Universita degli Studi di Milano, Italy
Pierre MacKay, University of Washington, USA
Norman Meyrowitz, Brown University, USA
Robert A. Morris, Interleaf and UMASS/Boston, USA
Jurg Nievergelt, ETH, Zurich, Switzerland
Vincent Quint, INRIA/IMAG, France
Brian Reid, DEC Western Research Laboratory, USA
Richard Rubinstein, Digital Equipment Corporation, USA
Alan Shaw, University of Washington, USA
Andries van Dam, Brown University, USA
Hans van Vliet, Free University, Amsterdam, The Netherlands
Jan Walker, Digital Equipment Corporation, USA

EP '90 Sponsor:	National Institute of Standards and Technology
EP '90 Co-Sponsors:	ArborText Inc., EPSIG/American Association of Publishers, INRIA, University of Maryland Institute for Advanced Computer Studies, Xerox Palo Alto Research Center
In Co-operation With:	Association for Computing Machinery, IEEE Computer Society/Technical Committee on Office Automation, TEX Users Group

Preface

EP90, "Electronic Publishing '90," is the third in a series of international conferences dedicated to all areas of electronic publishing, document manipulation, and digital typography, and is sponsored this year by the United States Department of Commerce, National Institute of Standards and Technology. The series began in 1986 with EP86, held in Nottingham, England, and sponsored by the British Computer Society. Two years later, EP88 was held in Nice, France, and was sponsored by INRIA.[1]

"Electronic publishing" remains a wide-ranging area of interest, encompassing all aspects of computer-assisted preparation, presentation, transmittal, storage, and retrieval of documents. Research in the area is found happily housed both in academic institutions and also in industrial laboratories. As the ultimate goal of the work is quite practical and tangible, researchers in the area tend to show a distinct preference for work that is supported by experience. The topics found in this year's program include traditional paper-based documents; hypertexts and hypermedia; font design (both latin and non-latin alphabets); experience with structured document preparation systems; the intersection with and application of database systems and software engineering environments; the theoretical foundations for document models and systems; character, text and document recognition and manipulation; experience with standards; and documents with actively-computed content.

The papers you see in this volume were, for the most part, selected through the hard work of the program committee. Fifty-three paper submissions were received. Each paper was distributed to each member of the conference committee, and many of the committee members read all or almost all of the submissions. I received between 10 and 19 initial rankings on each paper. Final selections were made in a full-day-long program committee meeting in which each submission was discussed individually in which seventeen of the submissions were selected. An additional three papers were invited, primarily to provide perspective on what

---

[1] The proceedings of the earlier conferences were also published by Cambridge University Press. EP86's proceedings are listed as: J. C. van Vliet, editor, *Text Processing and Document Manipulation*, Cambridge University Press, April 1986. EP88's proceedings are listed as: J. C. van Vliet, editor, *Document Manipulation and Typography*, Cambridge University Press, April 1988.

has been accomplished in the area and on what directions should be taken in the 90's.

Many papers also received readings by additional experts, recruited by members of the program committee. We would like to take this opportunity to thank these readers for their efforts: Al Aho, Henry Baird, Bruno Borghi, Claude Chrisment, Fred Cole, Andre Cousquer, Daniel Dardailler, Kate Ehrlich, Chris Fraser, Michel Gangnet, Henri Gouraud, R. Hersch, John Hobby, Rolf Ingold, Martin Jourdan, Solange Karsenty, J. A. Latone, Allen W. Luniewski, Victor Ostromoukov, Dieter Paris, Jacques Pasquier-Boltuck, Thierre Pudet, John Puttress, Richard Southall, Howard Trickey, Chris Van Wyk, Christine Vanoirbeek, A. M. Vercoustre, Brad Wade, and Mitch Zolliker.

We also would be remiss if we failed to acknowledge the following people for the assistance they have given to the conference committee: Patrice Boulanger and Sharon Wentling of NIST, John Gourlay of Arbortext, P. David Stotts of the University of Maryland, and Rick Beach, Steve Wallgren, and Dan Murphy of XEROX PARC.

RICHARD FURUTA
College Park, Maryland
June 15, 1990

Issues and Tradeoffs in Document Preparation Systems

Brian W. Kernighan

AT&T Bell Laboratories
Murray Hill, NJ 07974, USA

ABSTRACT: Users of document preparation systems must balance how much effort they put into producing their documents against how close their output is to what they want. The evolution of document preparation systems is a history of how users and implementers have dealt with this tradeoff as technology improves and as the user population itself evolves.

1 Problem: What You Get is Less Than What You Want

Computerized document preparation systems are not yet forty years old. People, on the other hand, have some thousands of years of accumulated tradition about how documents should be printed to satisfy utilitarian and esthetic criteria. With that much history, there is a rich collection of examples, and people are just as prolific at inventing new styles now as they ever were, so there seems to be no limit to the expectations for document preparation systems.

Furthermore, every user of a document preparation system is an "expert" in what his or her document should look like. The output is visible, so it can be readily compared against some mental or physical ideal, and the shortcomings will be immediately apparent. It is much harder to satisfy the casual user of a document preparation system than, for example, the casual user of a compiler.

Since the user's ideal of perfect output with no work cannot be reached, there is always a tradeoff. How much time or effort or money is the user willing to put into learning or using or buying a system? How much is the user willing to compromise output quality so as to spend less effort or time or money?

The history of document preparation systems is a history of how people have dealt with this tradeoff — balancing the expense and effort of production against the suitability of the output — as changes occur in hardware and software technology, costs, user expectations, the user population, and our understanding of what we are doing.

In the rest of this paper, I will discuss some of these tradeoffs. This is likely to seem like revisionist history; I am not trying to be complete, but only to give a sense of how this notion has affected the growth of our particular field. I am also likely to be provincial, if not parochial, in the choice of topics and examples, especially by focusing on what might be called the "academic" side of document preparation, systems like TROFF, TEX, and Scribe. The positive side of this is that by speaking on topics where I have first or second hand experience, I hope to reflect more accurately on what happened and why. (An excellent survey of document preparation systems up to 1981 can be found in [Furuta 1982].)

2 In The Beginning

In the late 1950's and early 1960's, interactive computing was in its infancy. When Jerry Saltzer wrote RUNOFF, the standard document preparation system of the day was a secretary with a typewriter. The great attraction of RUNOFF and programs like it was the ability to produce a clean new version of a document after a few changes had been made without having to type the whole thing over. This advantage was and is so compelling that people are willing to suffer severe hardship in preparation and ugly output to obtain it. Of course, when the output medium was just a typewriter, and the formatting program could be controlled with a handful of obvious commands like "leave a space" or "set the line length," the usage was easy and the output entirely adequate.

Programs that come directly from RUNOFF, of which the TROFF family is the most widespread, share a common heritage. They were originally intended to drive typewriter-like devices; the more elaborate mechanisms needed for typesetting were grafted on. And they were designed by pragmatic computer programmers, not typographers or typists; their syntax and semantic model reflect a programmer's view of the world.

Around the same time, the first electronic typesetting machines were developed. These remained largely tools of professional typographers, although programmers were needed to write programs that would control them. The proprietary typesetting programs that come from this period, for example PAGE-1 [Pierson 1972], seem to share the characteristic that they are linguistically even more irregular than the ones developed by non-typographers. Few have been described in the literature.

3 Affordable Typesetters

In 1972, the late Joe Ossanna, who had been interested in text formatting since the advent of RUNOFF, acquired for the Computing Science Research Center at Bell Laboratories a typesetter made by Graphic Systems, for the modest sum of about $12,000. This was the first typesetter that had a reasonable set of features at a price that a small group could justify for purely experimental purposes. The great novelty, at least as far as Graphic Systems was concerned, was that the machine was connected directly to a computer, instead of reading its input from paper tape.

This typesetter became the target of Ossanna's TROFF formatter. Much maligned, but still very much with us, TROFF was the base on which a remarkable number of document preparation tools were built. Technically, TROFF was not a lot different from a commercial system like PAGE-1, although its syntax and style were unrelated. TROFF shared with RUNOFF the basic notion that users decorated their input with commands that would control the formatting process. The richer set of operations permitted by the typesetter meant that a richer set of commands was needed, including in-line sequences for size and font changes, local motions, and non-ASCII characters. In addition, certain operations were sufficiently complicated that ordinary users were not expected to use them directly. Thus Ossanna provided a macro processor with some programming capability so that complicated sequences of operations could be defined and then used without knowledge of their details. Page makeup, for example, was not built in, but was handled by a "trap" mechanism that caused a specified macro to be invoked when a specified amount of output text had been produced. This made it possible to program any desired form of page layout, but only the most dedicated TROFF programmers could do this. This led Mike Lesk to create ms, a package of macros that handled the standard page formats in use at Bell Labs. Both ms and the much larger mm that followed are still widely used, in part because it is easier to put up with their shortcomings or make small changes and additions to them than to write one's own package from scratch.

The combination of TROFF and a typesetter that could print Greek letters, mathematical symbols, and a variety of sizes and fonts was tantalizing in a group that included a fair number of mathematicians. It was clearly possible to print mathematics, but it required heroic measures to force TROFF through the motions, and no one had the stamina for any but the most trivial examples.

How could mathematics be handled more conveniently? One might hope to modify TROFF, but this was impractical. Ossanna took a strongly proprietary view of the program, although he was always willing to add features for his users. The program was at that time written in assembly language, which made it hard to work with. And it was already dangerously close to the maximum program size on the PDP-11; it could not have grown much anyway.

So Lorinda Cherry and I were forced into a good idea: instead of modifying TROFF, we designed a separate program, EQN, that translated a separate language into TROFF commands. Fortunately, this coincided with the early flowering of the Unix operating system, including the notion of pipes, and with the creation of the YACC parser-generator. YACC encouraged a regular grammatical structure and made implementation easy, and the pipeline

```
eqn | troff
```

was completely natural.

It was only a short time later than Mike Lesk took the same idea, though with a very different syntax, and wrote TBL, a language for typesetting tables. Since then, there have been many other preprocessor programs, as people have attacked specialized areas of document preparation.

The TROFF model, with or without preprocessors, remains "open-loop control." The document contains commands that are meant to control its appearance. The commands are changed until the appearance is close enough or the user gives up. The specialized languages help because they make some parts of this much easier to control, but they are still based on embedded commands where the only way to be sure of the effect is to try it.

For in-house use the combination of a standard macro package and some preprocessors proved to be extremely effective, since the only competition was traditional typewriters, perhaps with a special symbol font. Output from TROFF was faster and much better looking, and many people were willing to pay the price of learning the system. (Unexpectedly, one of the greatest advantages of typeset output was that it was compact; judicious use of small sizes and two-column layouts produced legible output in half the space of typewritten text.)

For external use — conference and journal papers, for instance — the case was less clear. From the standpoint of professional typographers, the output quality was inferior, although good enough that authors were occasionally asked if their papers had been previously published. One group of professionals, however, did become interested, because external economics were changing too. The American Physical Society, which at the time used mechanical typewriters to produce 30,000 journal pages per year of complicated mathematics, was searching for a way to reduce their costs. They were willing at least to consider lower-quality appearance in return for lower costs. In 1975 Mike Lesk and I arranged an experiment in which a typist at Bell Labs typed five papers using TROFF, EQN, and TBL; the APS already had measurements of how long their typists had taken. To their surprise, and our delight, the Unix-based system was nearly $2\frac{1}{2}$ times faster. It took many further discussions, experiments, and software fixes, but the APS today produces more than 50,000 pages per year with fewer typists than they used to have. (The AT&T Technical Journal switched from a commercial printer to TROFF in mid-1989. "A prophet is not without honour, save in his own country, and in his own house." [Matthew *XIII*, v. 57])

TROFF was used for book publication as early as 1974, for *The Elements of Programming Style*. Although commercial printers did (and still do) produce better output than any "academic" document preparation system, the process of re-keyboarding into galleys was (and still is) painfully slow and prone to errors.

Since one of the messages of the book was the importance of presenting error-free computer programs, it was mandatory to avoid the errors caused by ordinary composition. The *Style* book was typeset directly from machine-readable source; the programs in it contained no errors from typesetting (although there were a couple of the traditional kind). The book went from conception to camera-ready form in six months and was published two months later. The whole process was so much faster than the norm that almost a year after the book appeared, it was still possible to be told by the publisher's representatives that no such book existed.

4 The Search for Quality

Certainly the major achievement in document preparation systems of the late 1970's and 1980's is Don Knuth's TEX and the web of programs that support it. The high value that Knuth places on the visual appearance of his books is the origin and continuing touchstone of TEX. "The genesis of TEX probably took place on 1 February 1977, when I first chanced to see the output of a high-resolution typesetting machine. [...] I could see no difference between the digital type and 'real' type." [Knuth 1989].

TEX carries the notion of embedded controls far beyond anything envisaged in TROFF. The TEX language has more than 250 basic commands and at least 60 parameters that can be interrogated and set; this is about three times as many commands and parameters as TROFF has. The language syntax is more regular and includes notions of nesting and scope.

TEX makes up pages by combining "boxes" containing individual characters into larger boxes; boxes are positioned relative to each other by adjustable spacing called "glue." Formatting decisions (where to break words into lines, where to break lines into pages, etc.) are expressed in a "penalty function." Minimizing this function by dynamic programming yields the set of breaks that best satisfies conflicting criteria. The boxes and glue model is one of several innovations in TEX; it unifies a number of apparently unrelated processes in a single mechanism. Horizontal justification, vertical justification, and centering, for example, can all be done by adjusting glue.

One sign that the model is not perfect is the number of cases where a box, once built, has to be taken apart again. This shows up in hyphenation and footnote processing. (The original version of TEX strongly discouraged footnotes, and would not split a footnote across a page boundary. Unfortunately, authors want footnotes to work, so the current TEX handles them properly.) Objects that are naturally larger than a page, like program listings and giant tables, are also not gracefully handled.

The elegant dynamic programming algorithm makes it hard to nail down the contents of an individual line, since some change later on in a paragraph can ripple back to the current line. Most typesetting systems set text a line at a time with a greedy algorithm; once the line has been set, future text has no effect on it. The penalty function minimization performed by TEX, however, can change an entire paragraph when a small change is made anywhere. The result is a better layout according to the rules, but in a production environment it is essential to have a convenient way to make changes that have only a local effect. More generally, any document preparation system needs ways to defeat automatic mechanisms, no matter how well-intentioned.

Knuth's work on TEX has had several interesting spinoffs. The perceived inadequacy of existing character sets led to the development of METAFONT, with which families of stylistically related characters can be created. METAFONT has not caught on to nearly the same degree as TEX has, perhaps because there is less compelling a need for new character shapes, and perhaps because it is very difficult to create characters with the right appearance.

What of TEX's facilities for handling special kinds of text processing? The experience with TROFF preprocessors showed the value of separate languages, each focused on and especially suited to a particular area. Separate programs are easier to write and maintain, and it is much easier for anyone with a good idea to contribute a new program than to modify an existing one. There are drawbacks too, however, notably the one-way flow of information, at least in the pipeline model.

TEX takes a monolithic approach: processing of mathematics and, to a lesser degree, tables is integrated into the language. In general, the more integrated a component, the more it will be required to match the rest of its environment. Thus mathematical constructions follow the basic syntax of the rest of TEX; keywords are all prefixed with \, although there are special rules about token parsing, the significance of blanks and newlines, and the use of certain commands and characters. As a result, TEX mathematics looks more cluttered than EQN, but it is more regular. As a simple example, consider this continued fraction:

$$a_0 + \cfrac{1}{a_1 + \cfrac{1}{a_2 + \cfrac{1}{a_3}}} \qquad (1)$$

in EQN:

`a sub 0 + 1 over {a sub 1 + 1 over {a sub 2 + 1 over a sub 3}}`

and in TEX:

```
a_0+{1\over\displaystyle a_1+
    {\strut 1\over\displaystyle a_2+
        {\strut 1\over a_3}}}
```

The commands \strut and \displaystyle force sizes and spacings to remain constant instead of shrinking automatically.

Of course this comparison is unfair; it happens to be one where EQN's choices of defaults is closer to "right." EQN does not shrink fraction numerators and denominators automatically, nor does it generally take account of the different heights of characters; TEX does both. To over-simplify, EQN tries to make the easy cases easy, and provides relatively few mechanisms for tuning, except for explicit local motions. TEX provides many more parameters that can be adjusted to produce a better appearance.

One of the major failings of TROFF is the degree to which the supposedly abstract notion of a formatting language has been compromised by irrelevant details of the output device it was originally aimed at, and also the idiosyncrasies of the first machine it was implemented on. As Edsger Dijkstra said [Dijkstra 1976], "It is not unusual to find anomalies in existing machines truthfully reflected in programming languages." Dijkstra's remark was made in the context of programming languages, but it is just as valid for formatters. Most document preparation systems are biased by the output device or devices that the builder is familiar with. The output device model can have an inordinate effect on everything else. As an egregious example, the point sizes on a long-vanished mechanical typesetter are enshrined in the input syntax of TROFF. (I pass over the syntax limitations, such as two-character command names, that are a legacy from the original implementation on a PDP-11.)

TEX has similar problems. The most significant is perhaps the fact that TEX believes that fonts are generated by METAFONT, and this has made it complicated to use TEX effectively on most commercial typesetters. For instance, one of the reasons why TEX sets mathematics so well is that it defines what characters are available and it knows accurately what their critical dimensions are. This is a by-product of using METAFONT. Unfortunately, few devices support the model that TEX requires. On most typesetters, fonts, especially math fonts, are a wild collection of ill-assorted characters, and few typesetters support the math characters that TEX assumes it can use. The internal representation of characters is often carefully protected proprietary information. It is difficult or even impossible to create new characters, and it is rare to have any more information about letter shape than some nominal set width. As a result, quality mathematical typesetting requires a lot of tuning, and sometimes legal negotiations with the manufacturer of one's typesetter. The job can be done if the environment is stable enough and the effort is deemed worthwhile; as mentioned above, the American Physical Society has been publishing with TROFF, EQN, and TBL for many years. More recently, the American Mathematical Society, which has used TEX for some years, switched from Knuth's Computer Modern font to fonts from a typesetter manufacturer; their experience is described in [Youngen 1989].

The graphics model in TROFF is primitive (lines, arcs, circles, ellipses, splines) but richer than the non-existent one in TEX. The LATEX notion of doing graphics by line segments at funny angles is a woefully inadequate substitute. It makes great demands on scarce memory, and it is a terrible input language for people. Neither TEX nor TROFF can do the kinds of graphical transformations of the Postscript model, not even something as simple as setting type at a 90 degree angle for graph labels, (unless a rotated font is used). Part of the reason is that most graphics operations were beyond the capabilities of typesetters when these languages were designed; it is also true that there was no suitable standard for graphics.

5 Affordable Near-Typesetters

The most significant change in document preparation systems in the 1980's has been the development of the affordable laser printer. Everyone can have an output device that, although not of typesetter quality, is superior to anything else.

The first widely available laser printers provided reasonable resolution and speed at a reasonable price, about the same as a typesetter a decade earlier. It is doubtful that TEX would be as successful as it has been if it had not been for the development of such printers. TEX was originally aimed at the Alphatype typesetter, an amazing but slow mechanical wonder. Early non-commercial laser printers were used as proofing devices, and for technical reports. But it was only with the broad availability of the laser printer that people began to take advantage of the capabilities of formatters, especially TEX.

Today, output technology is laser-printer based, but the important change is the emergence of Postscript as a *de facto* standard language for printers and even typesetters. Postscript provides a much richer graphics model than did any typesetter of the past, with arbitrary curves and transformations, area filling, clipping, half-toning, and the like. It also provides a different model of character generation from the linear scaling of early typesetters and the "everything is just a bitmap" view of TEX and METAFONT.

There is no integrated way to get at these richer facilities from within TEX, and only the most primitive way in bare TROFF. The current trend is electronic cut-and-paste, the inclusion of separately prepared Postscript in holes left by formatting commands. But this does not handle, for example, pictures that contain mathematical expressions. Another option is to use what amounts to an assembly-language window in the formatting language: `\special` in TEX, `\X'...'` in TROFF. Such escapes, though necessary, have all the undesirable properties of assembly language coding. TROFF preprocessors like PIC and IDEAL, and similar ones for TEX (e.g., [Olejniczak 1989]) provide somewhat more integrated access to graphics, but they too have only limited graphics capabilities. But user expectations for graphics are now far beyond the descriptive capabilities of these formatting languages, even when augmented with special languages.

6 User Interfaces: What Does the User Have to Face?

The user interface for the major document preparation systems remains a batch system, a form of remote control or action-at-a-distance. Furthermore, at the level of the built-in primitive operations of these programs, one has to be a programmer of considerable sophistication and experience to control them.

How does one arrange an interface so that users need not be programmers to get something done? And how does one arrange that users need not be programmers to accomplish something different from what the designer allowed for?

The Scribe formatter was the first serious attempt to address this problem. The idea was to specify a document in terms of its logical components — title, abstract, paragraph, list of items, reference, quotation — and have those logical components interpreted according to a style sheet that caused them to be printed with the desired appearance. A family of style sheets permits much the same input to be printed in a variety of physical appearances; in addition there are facilities for making modest changes of style parameters. This notion was implicit in Mike Lesk's ms macro package for TROFF, but it was not stated very explicitly, and it was never enforced: it was always possible to escape to TROFF. (The MONK formatter [Murrel 1989] provides a Scribe-like TROFF interface.) Standards like SGML and ODA (see, for example, [Brown 1989]) are meant to support logical descriptions of documents.

LATEX, by Leslie Lamport, is a macro package for TEX. Like Scribe, it strongly encourages a logical model of use, but it permits easy and even inadvertent access to the underlying TEX commands, which users are advised to use cautiously.

LATEX and ms suffer from the fact that the extension mechanism in the underlying formatter is a macro processor. Unfortunately, macro processors, although the easiest extension languages to build, are also the worst of programming languages. A trivial (but perpetual) problem is how to protect embedded commands against premature evaluation. In TROFF, the symptom is a plethora of additional \'s. In LATEX it is a "fragile" command, which is a command that can fail to work because of unwanted evaluation of a macro argument. The remedy is to have the user add \protect commands at judicious points. These are exactly the equivalent of adding an extra level of backslashes in TROFF, and are about as hard to understand and get right. Error recovery in a macro environment is difficult as well: everything is valid input, so if something goes wrong, commands may be converted into text and vice versa.

As an aside, one of the most challenging tests of a formatter's programmability is to simulate the format of APS journals, which affect an alternation of one- and two-column material on a single page, apparently to pack in as much text as possible. Mike Lesk wrote a TROFF macro package for APS format in the mid-1970's; a recent somewhat less complete version for TEX is described in [Benson 1989]. (The APS still does page layout by hand.)

Postscript is an interesting advance. Postscript recognizes the need for a language as an extension mechanism, and supports the elegant idea of sending a program instead of just data. The Postscript language is stack-based; operands are pushed onto and popped off a stack by operators. Linguistically, stack languages are probably the second-easiest extension mechanism, and are an improvement on macro languages. But they suffer almost as much from being hard to understand, and are just as prone to disintegration when something goes wrong. (See, for instance, [Gonczarowski 1989].) The problem in Postscript is not so much that data turns into program, but that the wrong kind of data appears on the stack. Because Postscript associates types with data, errors can often be caught quickly, but recovery remains difficult.

Even if a language starts out declarative, there is an inexorable pressure to add programmable features to it. For example, PIC was originally rather simple, but people wanted loops and conditionals; when they were added to PIC, people wanted them in GRAP as well.

Whether or not the basic tool is programmable, there is always a need for escape, because people want to do things that are simply not possible in the underlying process. For example, TROFF includes a command .sy that executes any operating system command; output from the command can be collected and inserted into the document if desired. This provides a trivial way to do "active documents." Its use is routine for complicated formatting processes, and it is often used to fetch text like program listings that must be processed before being formatted. (The .sy command is a potential security problem — an unscrupulous person could send a document that does something untoward when the victim runs it through TROFF. It's easy enough to defend against this if one plans ahead, but few would.)

There is no corresponding mechanism in TEX; if one wants to perform other operations as part of formatting, they have to be done before (in some kind of preprocessing) or after (in the DVI processor, for example).

Both TROFF and TEX have mechanisms that cause some piece of text to be passed to the output uninterpreted. TROFF's \X is used mainly for *ad hoc* extensions like sending small amounts of embedded Postscript, although it is also used extensively by the PM page makeup postprocessor [Kernighan & Van Wyk 1989]. TEX's \special is the basis of several tools, particularly graphics processors. In Postscript, job and page control features that don't fit into the primitives of the language are added through structured comments [Adobe 1985]. The problem with all such mechanisms is precisely their *ad hoc* nature — there are no standards for what gets passed through and thus such documents tend not to be portable.

Macro packages like LATEX or ms are valuable for encapsulating complicated sequences of commands, but they are limited to the syntax rules of the base language, and they cannot do more than what the base language can express. The former may be limiting to the user; the latter is limiting to the implementer.

Cooperating but separate processors provide an alternative that avoids these problems, at the price of some others. The family of TROFF processors is the most notable example; these separated components can be combined in ways that weren't thought of in the original design, and new ones can be added as people think of them. The advantages and drawbacks of the preprocessor approach have been spelled out before [Kernighan 1989]. Here I would like to stress a few of the lessons that we have learned.

One is that people will abuse tools in remarkable ways, far beyond anything that the author ever thought of. For example, Figure 1 is a version of the classic map that shows attrition during Napoleon's march to Moscow and his subsequent retreat. Remarkably, this PIC version, 270 lines of source, was created by hand.

If a program accepts textual input, then one can write a program to produce that output. It soon becomes apparent that machine-generated input stresses programs much harder than people do, and in very different ways. For instance, a complicated PIC picture drawn by hand might have a few hundred components; a picture generated by a program (a graph produced by GRAP, perhaps) can easily have 50,000. Fixed-size limits in programs are always too small. Regularity of input syntax is also important for machine-generated input. For example, during the development of GRAP, I discovered to my embarrassment that GRAP was producing numbers in scientific notation and PIC would not accept them.

Another lesson is the often inordinate difficulty of getting the target program to play dumb. For example, in early work getting TROFF to drive other typesetters, I usually found it hard to convince the typesetter-resident formatting program to turn off its own hyphenation and justification, or to place characters exactly where I requested them. This same problem occurs in TEX and TROFF, of course, where it is sometimes hard to force these programs to put output at specific positions.

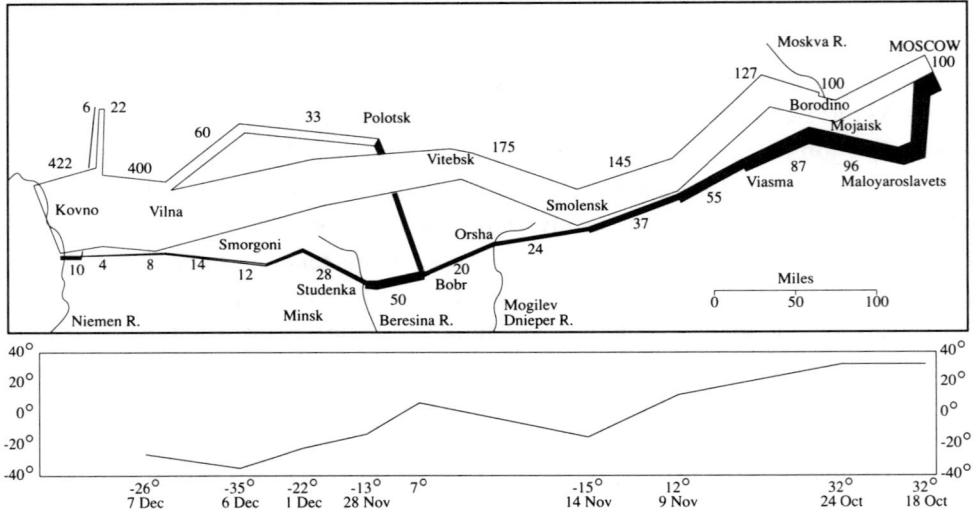

Figure 1: Napoleon Visits Moscow

TROFF, for example, treasures up horizontal and vertical motions and puts them out as late as possible. This makes it difficult to include embedded Postscript, since there is no guarantee that the logical position that TROFF has computed is reflected at the right time in the output that the Postscript postprocessor sees.

Another observation is that, just as people write programs to generate input, they write programs to process output further. Many of the same issues arise here, and some new one. As a trivial instance, it helps to have readable output; TROFF's ASCII output can be processed by any standard tool, while TEX's more compact binary DVI cannot.

Most important, it is necessary to preserve information so that subsequent programs can use it for things not thought of in the original design. As one instance, the family of programs that handle multi-directional text process text an output line at a time. This is not possible in TEX: "Because there are no end-of-line markers in TEX's DVI output format, the system structure adopted in this paper cannot be applied to make a tri-directional version of TEX. Instead one must make modifications to TEX either to have it do the reorganization or to have it emit end-of-line markers [Becker 1989]." On the other hand, even though TROFF output marks line boundaries, it does not reliably include the height and baseline for each line; this oversight leads to inordinately complicated code in PM that attempts to infer the missing information.

Another lesson is that although error reporting and recovery can often be primitive in such programs, and can always be primitive in the early stages, ultimately reporting and recovery have to be good. One trivial observation: we have had to add to TROFF and each preprocessor a command to reset its internal idea of the line number and source filename so that diagnostics are reported in terms of the user's input, not the result of multiple steps of processing. (The latest revision to TEX adds a new parameter called \inputlineno but makes it read-only; this precludes some future TEX preprocessor from setting it to give a true line number.)

7   What You See Is . . .

Another major hardware advance of the late 1980's, the widespread availability of bitmap screens, has made possible an entirely new style of formatter. Rather than embed commands and hope for the best, one can interact with a reasonably faithful display of what the document will look like and change it to taste in real time. The appeal is obvious and, for many kinds of documents, a WYSIWYG system is just what people want and need.

There is no gainsaying the advantages, but the disadvantages should also be noted. First, there is a significant sacrifice in facilities; a survey [Walter 1988] of commercial technical publication systems covering the gamut from simple desktop publishing to professional quality indicates that none is really up to the mark. Similar results are noted in a smaller review [Gruman 1987].

It is important to realize that interactive systems are not a panacea. It is frustrating to be forced to interact with a system when all one is doing is telling it the same thing that it has already been told repeatedly in the past. Once a task is well understood, it should be relegated to batch processing. The interface needed by experts may be baffling to novices, but experts can be hobbled by an interface aimed at novices.

It is also hard to augment the set of tools at the user's disposal when the only interface is through an interactive system. Interactive systems are generally closed: an interactive system represents a dead end in the use of a program. If a program has to be run by a person, then that program can not serve as the target of other programs. For example, if TROFF were only an interactive formatter, there would be no PIC language for drawing pictures; similarly, if PIC were an interactive picture editor, there would be no GRAP program for drawing graphs.

There is a strong tendency for interactive systems to concentrate on the visual aspects of preparing documents, at the price of the logical structure; indeed, it may be impossible to capture the logical structure that the user has in mind as the document is being entered. Leslie Lamport suggests that interactive systems are "good for serious document production only to the extent that they act like logical systems" (that is, that they work in terms of the logical structure of the document, not its visible representation) [Lamport 1988]. Clearly what is needed are systems that combine the best of interactive and batch. This is an active area of research and increasing commercial success, but it remains difficult, and no current system is more than an approximation.

8   Conclusions

What of the future? It is easy to imagine that the future will be more of what we are seeing now: our productivity and the quality of our output will increase as the sophistication of our tools increases, yet we will always face the same kinds of problems and the same tradeoffs between what is possible and what we are willing to pay for.

Many of the same problems still exist. Although our tools for plain black and white two-dimensional typography are better than they were, they remain too hard to use, especially by novices, and as programs are far too hard to extend. We need more work on comprehensible and flexible batch user interfaces.

Large multi-author documents such as manuals for complicated systems present document preparation issues beyond mere formatting: document management, on-line retrieval, electronic distribution, and the like.

There are new areas that will demand new tools and new ways to deal with their inclusion in documents. For example, we are in the earliest stages of widespread use of color. How will we provide access to color in an effective way?

Character sets and fonts will continue to proliferate, and if we hope to have our systems used elsewhere in the world, we will have to learn to handle different and often very large character sets.

How will we cope with "active documents"? Just because a document is active, I may not want to react to it. We will still need specialized languages to deal with particular aspects of such complicated documents: to access data bases, to play music, to show video, to control scripts.

We will continue to need good work in algorithms and data structures, if we are to be able to make our programs work at all, let alone be efficient and easy to evolve. Most of the existing programs are large and complicated. What can we do to make them more manageable?

How will we deal with the continuing tension between standards, whether *de facto* like TEX and Postscript, or *de jure* like SGML and ODA, and the necessity for evolution?

In spite of these puzzles, we will continue to make progress. A decade or two from now, today's problems will seem minor, and today's systems will seem as primitive as those of twenty years ago seem now.

9 Acknowledgements

I am very grateful to John Hobby, Doug McIlroy, Peter Nelson, Rob Pike, Howard Trickey, and Chris Van Wyk for helpful comments on this paper.

References

[Adobe85] Adobe Systems, Inc., *PostScript Language Reference Manual*, Addison-Wesley, 1985, pp. 265ff.

[Becker89] Zeev Becker and Daniel Berry, "TRITROFF, An Adaptation of the Device-Independent TROFF for Formatting Tri-directional Text," *Electronic Publishing*, vol. 2, no. 3, October 1989, pp. 119–142.

[Benson89] Gary Benson, Debi Erpenbeck, and Janet Holmes, *TUGboat*, vol. 10, no. 4, December 1989, pp. 727–742.

[Brown89] Heather Brown, "Standards for Structured Documents," *Computer Journal*, vol. 32, no. 6, December, 1989, pp. 505–514.

[Dijkstra76] Edsger W. Dijkstra, *A Discipline of Programming*, Prentice-Hall, 1976, p. 8.

[Furuta82] Richard Furuta, Jeffrey Scofield, and Alan Shaw, *Document Formatting Systems: Survey, Concepts, and Issues Computing Surveys*, vol. 14, no. 3, September 1982, pp. 417–472.

[Gonczarowski89] Jakob Gonczarowski and On G. Paradise, *Electronic Publishing*, vol. 2, no. 3, October 1989, pp. 157–167.

[Gruman87] Galen Gruman, "Software Reviews: Desktop Publishing," *IEEE Software*, vol. 4, no. 3, May 1987, pp. 70–77.

[Kernighan89] Brian W. Kernighan, "The Unix System Document Preparation Tools: A Retrospective," *AT&T Technical Journal*, vol. 68, no. 4, July/August, 1989, pp. 5–20.

[Kernighan & Van Wyk89] Brian W. Kernighan and Christopher J. Van Wyk, "Page Makeup by Postprocessing Text Formatter Output," *Computing Systems*, vol. 2, no. 2, Spring, 1989, pp. 103–132.

[Knuth89] Donald E. Knuth "The Errors of TEX," *Software—Practice & Experience*, vol. 19, no. 7, July 1989, pp. 607–685.

[Lamport88] Leslie Lamport, "Document Production: Visual or Logical?" *TUGboat*, vol. 9, no. 1, April 1988, pp. 8–10.

[Murrel89] Sharon L. Murrel and Thaddeus J. Kowalski, "Monk: A High-level Text Compiler," *AT&T Technical Journal*, vol. 68, no. 4, July/August 1989, pp. 45–60.

[Olejniczak89] Rolf Olejniczak-Burkert, "*texpic*—Design and Implementation of a Picture Graphics Language in TEX à la pic," *TUGboat*, vol. 10, no. 4, December 1989, pp. 627–638.

[Pierson72] John Pierson, *Computer Composition using PAGE-1*, Wiley-Interscience, 1972.

[Walter88] Mark E. Walter, Jr., *Technical Documentation Systems*, Seybold Publications, 1988.

[Youngen89] R. E. Youngen, W. B. Woolf, and D. C. Latterner, "Migration from Computer Modern Fonts to Times Fonts," *TUGboat*, vol. 10, no. 4, December 1989, pp. 513–519.

Towards Document Engineering

Vincent Quint[†], Marc Nanard[‡], and Jacques André[*]

[†] INRIA/Imag, 2, rue de Vignate, 38610 Gières, France
[‡] CRIM, 860 rue de Saint Priest, 34090 Montpellier, France
[*] INRIA/Irisa, Campus de Beaulieu, 35042 Rennes, France

ABSTRACT: This article compares methods and techniques used in software engineering with the ones used for handling electronic documents. It shows the common features in both domains, but also the differences and it proposes an approach which extends the field of document manipulation to document engineering. It shows also in what respect document engineering is different from software engineering. Therefore specific techniques must be developed for building integrated environments for document engineering.

KEY WORDS: software engineering, document engineering, structured editing, integrated environments.

1 Introduction

Software engineering and document manipulation have strong resemblances. Several attempts have been made to use software engineering tools for processing documents. Some of them have been fruitful, others have shown some inadequacies of the tools to the function. In this paper, we try to evaluate the contributions that software engineering concepts and techniques can offer to document processing, but also the limits of these contributions. Because of these limits, we think that specific techniques must be developed for building integrated environments that would allow documents to be produced with all the necessary features. These reflections are based on our experience with different types of systems, especially Grif [Quint86] and MacWeb [Nanard88].

The next section shows the resemblances between the domains of software engineering and document manipulation. Section 3 points out the main differences, considering the semantics of documents and programs, their logical structures, their graphical aspect and the way to use tools for producing documents and programs. Section 4 presents some contributions of software engineering to document manipulation and conversely, and section 5 tries to indicate what an integrated environment would be for professional publishing and desktop publishing.

2 From software engineering to document engineering

Software engineering[1] is concerned with commercial software production (as opposed to programming as an academic exercise or a recreational hobby). In the same way, document manipulation is concerned with the production of real documents, such as technical documentation, books or magazines. In both cases, the writing of small pieces of programs or texts, for personnal use, does not require any software factory or any writer workbench. So, such programs or texts are not relevant of the corresponding domains. On the other hand, small pieces of programs or texts generated during research into program production or during research into writing process are concerned with the present paper.

Document manipulation follows, with a 10 years delay, the same story as programming languages. First, exotic codes (similar to machine languages) were used to drive phototypesetters. Then, some higher level formatters (such as Troff or even TeX) were designed with the same goal as Fortran: to allow machine independency. Going further in abstraction, as Algol 60, Pascal or Ada did earlier, new formatters such as Scribe (and later on, LaTeX) used structuration concepts as well as compiling techniques. However, note that WYSIWYG systems have no immediate equivalents in programming languages. At a lower level, one can compare the C language which behaves like a machine independent language and PostScript which becomes a printer independent page description language.

As software engineering is not restricted to the use of programming languages, neither is document manipulation restricted to the use of formatters. Editing large documents requires the same matter as producing large programs. Many of the key words apply to both domains, for instance modularity, configuration management, user interface, reuse, life cycle or integrated environment. Even an aspect such as security (or reliability) is relevant to document manipulation[2]. All of these considerations make it useful to extend to "Document Engineering" what is usually called document manipulation.

Because software engineering is in advance of document engineering, obvious and fruitful proposals have been made to use software techniques and tools for text production. The type and structure concepts are the most commonly used[3]. Among most promising techniques are the methods of stepwise refinement and iterated enhancement, and the use of an integrated environment [Hamlet86].

---

[1] This term seems to have been first employed in 1969 [Buxton69] with a more pragmatic meaning than the one used, e.g., in *IEEE Transactions on Software Engineering*.

[2] A train crash has been quoted as caused by a typographic layout error [André89].

[3] However, note that often so called "structured" editors are actually only "typed" editors: saying in some style sheet that "a section is formatted in 12pt Helvetica, left justified, etc." has nothing to do with a hierarchical structure.

Syntax driven editors, such as *The Synthesizer* [Reps89], Mentor [Donzeau83] or Centaur [Borras87], accept a formal description of the syntax and the semantics of programming languages and handle programs written in the specified language. The abstract syntax allows an abstract representation of the program to be built, from which one or more graphical representations may automatically be constructed. This technique applies similarly to a class of documents. Relevant concepts such as views, annotations, links, gates, etc. fit both program models and text models.

Many other examples of reuse of software engineering techniques by document engineering experts show that this is a good way to follow.

3   Document engineering beyond software engineering

Even if tools for handling documents and programs have much in common, they also show many differences. One of these differences lies in the semantics, which is not the same for documents and for programs. Other differences are related to the logical structure and to the graphical aspect of documents and programs. User interfaces of editors for documents and programs also are very different. All these differences are presented in the next sections.

3.1   Different semantics

From a certain point of view, one can consider programs as a particular type of document. Like other documents, programs are made of lines and characters. They can be edited with text editors and be displayed and printed on the same devices as other documents. But this comparison cannot be continued much further, because the final uses of documents and programs are not the same. A program is intended to be executed by a computer; a document is intended to be read by a human reader, and that makes an important difference.

As stated above, until a certain step in the processing of a document by computer, the analogy between a document and a program is obvious. But, after the document has been printed, there is another step, with no equivalent for programs: the document is processed by human readers, and all the semantics of the document must be accessible during that step.

A document represented in electronic form may not only be formatted and read. It has also often to be processed by several applications. A structured document can be stored in a data base, it can be retrieved easier by information retrieval systems, it can be transformed into several formalisms, it can be reorganized, different forms can be extracted from it. etc. This is one of the reasons why a logical (or abstract) structure is important for a document. If a document is represented in an abstract form, this abstraction allows other applications to process that document. Because of these many uses of a document, its semantics are not as well defined as the semantics of a program, which is essentially defined for its execution by a computer.

Semantics of a program may be represented in a computer. In addition, it is often elicited by the programmer during the specification phase, before the program is written. It is not the case for documents, except for very rare exceptions.

3.2 Logical structure

Logical structures for documents [Furuta89] are different from those for programs. The syntactical structure of a program is represented by a tree and most syntax driven editors use only this structure, although some structural aspects of programs are not strictly hierarchical, like relationships between modules.

Documents need more complex structures. At a first glance, their logical structure can be considered as a tree: a book contains chapters, a chapter contains sections, a section contains paragraphs, and so on. But documents also use many non hierarchical relationships: all kinds of cross references, indexes, etc. The experience shows that the most interesting features of a document production system like Grif come from the non hierarchical structures. They allow the system to compute and automatically update all numbers, not only section or chapter numbers but also references to sections and chapters. They are very useful for browsing through a document. They allow users to establish relationships between documents or to share some (parts of) documents.

Another type of structure, very important for documents, is represented by hypertexts, where tree structures are less important than non herarchical links. As an example, the primary structure of Concordia [Walker88a] is made of hypertext links.

Documents need more various structures than programs. A tree structure may be used for representing the higher level structure (or primary structure), but some components of a document cannot be represented that way. A table, for instance, is a two-dimensional object that is better represented by a matrix than by a tree.[4] Therefore, several systems use a special structure for tables [Cameron89]. Structured graphics cannot be naturally described by tree structures and need a non hierarchical representation.

The structure of a program is completely defined by a grammar and it must be strictly consistent with that grammar. On the contrary, the structure of a document must tolerate an incomplete definition and must allow some flexibility with respect

---

[4]Nevertheless, some proposals have been made for representing a table as a tree, but with very strong constraints [Furuta88].

to the model. All types of documents cannot be completely defined in a formal way. Some parts, which are not supposed to be computed, may be less precisely defined.

3.3 Limitations of a logical structure

In a program, the separation between syntactical structure, graphical aspect (sometimes called pretty printing) and free text (comments, identifiers,...) is very clear and stable. In a structured document, logical structure, physical structure and contents can be considered as equivalent to syntactical structure, graphical aspect and free text respectively, but the boundaries between these levels of representation are not so well defined as they are in programs. There are interactions between the three representations [Southall89]. So, a long paragraph, originally written with small characters, is often divided into two paragraphs when it is displayed in large characters: the logical structure is modified for physical reasons. Another example is given by footnotes: in order to limit the number of pages, an author can transform some parts of a paragraph into footnotes.

When defining a generic logical structure for documents, the difference between contents and logical structure is not easy to make. Depending on the document type or the intended use of the document, one can consider a paragraph either as a terminal in the logical structure or as a structured component containing sentences, phrases or words playing different roles (key word, entry in the index or in the glossary, reference to a figure or to a section...). This shows that the boundary between logical structure and contents is not fixed and must be set in accordance with requirements.

A program follows basically one grammar, that which defines the programming language in which it is written. If it contains parts written in different languages, it follows different grammars, but all are of same type. A document follows at least two grammars, very different from each other: the grammar defining its logical structure and the grammar defining the natural language in which it is written. This paper, for instance, follows both the LaTeX grammar (article style) and the grammar of English (it is supposed to...). That implies that a document processing system should be able to handle at the same time computer languages and natural languages, or at least some aspects of natural languages, like spelling, punctuation, style, etc.

For reasons related to semantics (see section 3.1), the process followed by an author when writing a document leads him to often change the logical structure or even to add the logical structure after the contents has been written. This raises problems which are not often encountered when editing programs. Syntax driven editors generally provide parsers for automatically structuring text when it is typed without structure. The structuring of a document is somewhat different, since it is done manually by the user who indicates the structural components which organize a text that has already been entered in the system.

3.4 Graphical aspect

The graphical structure of programs is usually made up of a sequence of indented lines with some variations of character style for indicating key words, variables or comments. Actually, programs have a linear graphical structure which is divided into lines.

Documents, or at least some of their parts, have more complex, really bidimensional graphical structures. Examples of these complex structures are newspapers, tables, mathematical or chemical formulae and drawings. Formatting languages used in most syntax driven editors usually cannot describe this kind of graphical structures.

As a consequence of the importance of the graphical aspect, document production systems usually have two types of users: a graphic designer and an author. The former is responsible for the graphical appearance of documents, the latter for the logical structure and contents. These two users use the system in completely different ways, and take advantage of different functionalities. In software engineering, a single type of user, "the programmer", is involved in writing a program.

The essential purpose of a document is to be read, what puts a strong emphasis on its visual aspect. The importance of this aspect leads many writers to consider the graphical appearance of a document before its abstract or logical representation. Therefore many document production systems handle a document as a graphic object rather than a logical object.

In order to illustrate the importance of the graphical aspect in a document production system, some figures are given, taken from Grif. The grammar of the language for describing graphical structures is twice the size of the grammar of the language for describing logical structures. In the Grif editor, the part of the code handling the graphical structure is about three times the size of the code handling the logical structure. This indicates that, in a system using a direct manipulation style of interaction, the most important and complex part is dedicated to handling the physical appearance of documents. Manipulating the logical structure, even with a sophisticated model, is much simpler than generating and handling the graphical aspect of a complex document. As programs do not contain the most complex objects encountered in documents, the graphical part of syntax driven editors is not suited for handling these objects.

3.5 The process of writing

Not only are uses of programs and documents different, but so are design methods. Most programs are designed in a top-down manner, with successive refinements. Very few documents can be written that way. Even when the final form of a document must be strongly structured, the author starts often with unstructured text, just for capturing his thoughts. The structuring phase comes later.

On the other hand, some techniques of software engineering may be transposed to documents. Modularity is an example: generic structures of documents can be defined in small, self-contained modules rather than in large monolithic programs. This approach gives to documents the same advantages as to programs: clarity, reusability, maintainability, sharing, etc. Nevertheless, it is difficult to specify modules as rigorously as for programs and encapsulation cannot be as complete [Quint89].

Another approach to modularity is presented in [Walker88b]. Here, modularity is not considered at the generic level, where formal languages are used, but at the specific level: documents themselves are built from modules. That approach has also been taken in MacWeb [Nanard88]. These two examples of modularity in document production systems show that the concepts of software engineering can be transposed in different ways to document engineering.

3.6 User interface

In this section only a direct manipulation interface is considered, as it seems to be the only style of interface users want to use. Concerning the user interface, the basic difference between editors for documents and editors for programs comes from the users themselves. In the case of a program editor, the user is a programmer. That means that he knows about the syntactic structure of the program and that the notion of a tree structure representing the program is familiar to him. Then it is natural to propose commands that explicitly make reference to that structure, for instance for moving across the tree. For a document editor, the situation is completely different. As it must be supposed that the user does not know what an abstract tree is, a different style of interface is needed. The logical structure is useful for enabling the system to make computations on the document, but it must not burden the user with an unnatural model. For that reason, user interface issues in structured document manipulation systems have to be studied further.

Users of systems for the production of structured documents do not only see the user interface under the form of editing commands. They are also faced with the languages that define the logical structure and the graphical appearance of documents. The style of these languages must be adapted to non programmers.

Declarative languages seem to be better accepted by users than procedural ones: they allow the user to express what is required rather than the way to get it. But most users ask for no language at all, at least for describing the appearance of documents. So a graphical language would certainly be the best choice.

Most document production systems use extensively modern user interface techniques, especially direct manipulation. Moreover, many user interface techniques have been developped according to the requirements of these systems. On the other hand, the part dedicated to logical information is often less developped.

4 Cross fertilization

Because of the differences presented in the previous section, tools designed for programs are generally not usable for producing documents, even logically structured documents. It is then necessary to develop tools specifically adapted to documents. Nevertheless, programs and structured documents have common features that suggest that some concepts and techniques used in software engineering could be used in document production too, and conversely.

Programming environments are used for producing not only programs, but also many types of documents related to programs, like specifications, documentations, manuals, helps. All these documents are generally structured according to some well defined model and therefore they are good candidates for structured document editors. Instead of trying to combine in a unique tool all of what is needed for handling programs and documents at the same time, it seems more interesting to use complementary tools: some dedicated to programs, others to documents. That leads to light tools, well suited to the function they have to perform.

Separating programming tools and documentation tools also allows to use the latter in various applications, not only in programming environments. Actually, software engineering is only one of the possible fields of application for structured document systems. Among other fields are technical documentation or specialized publishing (law, medicine, teaching, dictionaries and encyclopediae, etc.).

A typical use of document processing tools in software engineering is the display of complex pictures. Like many document production systems, Grif contains an important component that allows it to display the graphical appearance of a logical structure according to a set of presentation rules. In addition, this component maintains the correspondance between the logical structure and the graphical appearance, so that each change made on one representation is immediately reflected on another. This mechanism has been extracted from the document editor and it is now used by various graphical tools in programming environments. An example is given by the debugging tool presented in [Seze89].

In a programming environment, tools handle abstract objects (in that case the control paths of an ADA program) and use the display component for handling the graphical representation of these objects (trees and graphs in that case) and the interaction with the user on the picture.

A concept of software engineering worth being considered for documents is reusability. In software engineering this concept poses two problems: (1) how to find existing pieces of codes that can be reused in new applications, or even how to know that they exist, and (2) how to integrate these pieces in different contexts. Concerning the first problem, information retrieval tools are available for documents [Salton89], but there is no equivalent tool specifically designed for programs. In documents, a logical structure is a help for solving this problem. The types of components, the attributes (in the SGML sense), the structure itself help to locate the parts that one wants to reuse. In hypertexts, links are also useful for locating pieces of text. Concerning the second problem, the situation is exactly the opposite: programs take advantage of techniques such as object oriented or modular programming. With these techniques, reusing some parts of a program in new programs is made easier. Documents, on the other hand, cannot so easily be reused in different contexts, except for some types of documents, such as technical manuals [Walker88b]. In general, pieces written independently can rarely be merged in a new consistent document without rewriting some parts. But the logical structure may help. Numbers of sections, figure, notes, etc, are computed by the system, based on the logical structure. They can be updated automatically according to the new context. References can also be updated if they are part of the logical structure.

5 Document engineering environments

The previous section has shown that the technology of software engineering is not directly usable for producing documents. This section focuses on some of the functionalities a document engineering environment must provide the user with.

Due to the specificity of document life cycle, the design of such an environment should be task driven. That is a consequence of the non sequential structure of writing, which has been studied in [Hayes80]. For documents, there is no equivalent to the well known specification step, or to the classical sequential approach of software development. Producing a document results in free, non ordered (and often unpredictable) commutations between a set of processes. The most important of them are: producing sentences and paragraphs, gathering ideas and data, reviewing, organizing ideas at semantic level, formatting, logically structuring the document, managing the produced documents.

Another important point the design has to take into account is that the target of a document is twofold: both the reader who perceives it through its visual structure, and the machine which manages the document base and makes its retrieval possible.

Thus, the design of an efficient document engineering environment is today more concerned with integration problems than with the development of new elementary tools for document manipulation.

Environments for professional publishing and environments for desktop publishing have slightly different typical problems. The firsts are concerned with a problem of amount of data, and of long life of these data. The others are more concerned with a problem of user friendliness and of immediate efficiency. Each of these two areas have their own economic interest and scientific problems. In each of them, the amount of produced texts and the number of users concerned make it impossible to ignore their specificity.

An exhaustive list of suitable functionalities for a document engineering environment is of no interest here. Only some of them will be considered. In particular, the importance of structured editors and formatters has already been discussed [Furuta88] and will no longer be considered here.

5.1 *Professional publishing*

When producing large quantities of documentation (technical documents, price lists, travel brochures, etc.), some part of the information is already available. The most important problems are to access it, to convert it, to adapt it to the context of the intended document and to organize it. Even when a document is produced by a single professional writer, the information handled often has several sources and several authors. For instance, a technical document includes pictures, data collected from databases and shared portions of texts. A given piece of information may be shared by many documents such as preliminary specifications, an implementation reference book and a user's guide.

In that context, information retrieval tools are needed for reusing texts as well as programs. Compatibility between information sources and document engineering environment is also necessary. Standards are the key for this compatibility. Automatic structure recognition is an important complement to document recognition systems. Structure recognition is needed when dealing with old documents which have been produced out of any standard. For instance, most of the documentation of nuclear power plants was produced in the seventies and is unstructured. Even tables have often been typed line by line in a typewriter like style! Restructuring this documentation is an important challenge for making its evolution more efficient.

Flexible approaches make it possible to express at low cost the access path and the structure and type conversions which are needed. As a consequence, the major problems when producing large documents concern the automatic integration of various data sources.

Professional publishing is often a collaborative work. It requires the collaboration of various human expertises (authors, specialists of specific domains, professional writers, typographers, reviewers...). The system is responsible for the ease of communication between these partners and should provide tools for ensuring the consistency of their work.

A document engineering environment should allow the user to "work on" as well as to "edit" a document. Adding and consulting private notes is one of these useful features. A note dynamically linked to some part of a document is fundamentally different from a comment present in a source program. It is a typical problem for hypertext technique. Some software development environments such as HyperCentaur [Vercoustre90] also use hypertext approaches for managing the documentation attached to programs.

Another important part of a document engineering environment should concern the help to the reviewing process too. The most classical of these helps is the spelling checker. Tools such as IBM Critique also provide some simple style checking. The main problem remains that semantics of text are rarely explicit, thus making far more difficult the automatic checking of documents than the checking of programs specifications. Only very specific applications such as deeds produced by sollicitors can take advantage of their strong and explicit semantic. The semantic structure of such documents can be processed and makes their automatic generation possible.

5.2 Desktop publishing

Most desktop publishing systems are today designed for dealing only with the editing and formatting steps. But they actually are being used from the flow of ideas through the production of the camera ready copy. Since desktop publishing users are not professional writers, it is very important both to provide them with simple and efficient tools and to take into account their own natural behavior. A user centered design is required for these tools and their level of integration into a coherent system is the key issue of such environments.

End users rarely are used to deal with abstractions: they "think as they see" and it is not possible to change this fact! This is the reason for the success of WYSIWYG systems. There is, of course, no basic opposition between WYSIWYG and structuration or abstraction. It is just a matter of man-machine interface and of incrementally computing the relevant information to be provided to the user with a correct feedback [Chen88]. A page editor fully integrated with a structured document editor is still the basic need of most users.

A document engineering environment cannot be a collection of independent tools, but must be integrated as much as possible. The fast, frequent and unpredictable commutation between the various tasks involved when producing a document requires a very fast commutation time between the facilities provided. For instance, the capability of handling personal notes linked to document parts is of no help if the notes cannot be added on the fly when working on a document, or if they cannot be reused by other components.

In document manipulation systems, the friendliness of the user interface is more important than anything else. A feature would not be helpful if the cognitive load for its use is not very low compared with its benefit. It is not surprising that much progress in human computer interaction have been initiated by document manipulation problems. Many scientists working in one area are today interested in the other.

Anyhow, there is no fundamental difference between desktop publishing oriented environments and professional publishing oriented environments. In the long term, the professional document engineering environment will surely focus more on integration and desktop publishing will integrate more concepts and abstractions.

6 Conclusion

Although there are some resemblances between documents and programs, we have put the emphasis on the differences. Pointing out these differences will help in designing new tools, better suited to their role and offering more and more services to users.

References

[André89] J. André, "Can structured formatters prevent train crashes?", *Electronic Publishing – Origination, Dissemination and Design*, vol. 2, no. 3, October 1989, pp. 169–173.

[Borras87] P. Borras, D. Clément, Th. Despeyroux, J. Incerpi, G. Kahn, B. Lang, and V. Pascual, *Centaur: The system*, Research Report 777, INRIA, December 1987.

[Buxton69] J.N. Buxton and R. Randell, *Software Engineering Techniques*, Report on a Conference sponsored by the Nato Scientific Committee, Rome, Italy, 27th–31st October 1969, published by Nato, Brussels, 1970.

[Cameron89] J. P. Cameron, *A Cognitive Model for Tabular Editing*, Research Report no. OSU-CISRC-6/89-TR 26, The Ohio State University, Colombus, Ohio, June 1989.

[Chen88] P. Chen, M.A. Harrison, and I. Minakata, "Incremental Document Formatting", *Proceedings of ACM Conference on Document Processing Systems*, ACM Press, December 1988, pp. 93–100.

[Furuta88] R. Furuta, V. Quint, and J. André, "Interactively Editing Structured Documents", *Electronic Publishing – Origination, Dissemination and Design*, vol. 1, no. 1, April 1988, pp. 19–44.

[Furuta89] R. Furuta, "Concepts and Models for Structured Documents", *Structured Documents*, J. André, R. Furuta, and V. Quint, eds., Cambridge University Press, 1989, Elsevier Science Publishers B. V., 1983, pp. 7–38.

[Donzeau83] V. Donzeau-Gouge, G. Kahn, B. Lang, B. Mélèse, and E. Morcos, "Outline of a tool for document manipulation", *IFIP 83*, R. F. A. Mason, ed., pp. 615–620.

[Hamlet86] R. Hamlet, "A Disciplined Text Environment", *Text Processing and Document Manipulation*, J.C. van Vliet ed., Cambridge University Press, 1986, pp. 78–89.

[Hayes80] J. R. Hayes and L. S. Flower, "Identifying the Organization of Writing Processes", *Cognitive Process in Writing*, L. W. Greeg and E. R. Steinberg, ed., Lawrence Erlbaum Associates Publishers, 1980.

[Nanard88] J. Nanard, M. Nanard, and H. Richy, "Conceptual Documents: a Mechanism for Specifying Active Views in Hypertext", *Proceedings of ACM Conference on Document Processing Systems*, ACM Press, December 1988, pp. 37-42.

[Quint86] V. Quint and I. Vatton, "Grif: An Interactive System for Structured Document Manipulation", *Text Processing and Document Manipulation*, J.C. van Vliet ed., Cambridge University Press, 1986, pp. 200–213.

[Quint89] V. Quint and I. Vatton, "Modularity in structured documents," *Woodman'89*, J. André & J. Bézivin, eds., Bigre num. 63–64, IRISA, Rennes, May 1989, pp. 170–177.

[Reps89] T. W. Reps and T. Teitelbaum, *The Synthesizer Generator: A System for Constructing Language-Based Editors*, Springer Verlag, New York, 1989.

[Salton89] G. Salton, *Automatic text processing*, Addison-Wesley, Reading, Mass., 1989.

[Seze89] P. de Seze, C. Bonnet, J.-F. Caillet, and B. Raither, "A Graphical Trace Analysis Tool for Ada Real-Time Embedded Systems", *Proceedings of the Sixth Washington Ada Symposium*, Washington D. C., June 1989, pp. 47–52.

[Southall89] R. Southall, "Interfaces Between the Designer and the Document," *Structured Documents*, J. André, R. Furuta, V. Quint, eds., Cambridge University Press, 1989, pp. 119–131.

[Vercoustre90] A.-M. Vercoustre, "Structured Editing—Hypertext Approach: Cooperation and Complementarity", *EP90*, R. Furuta ed., Cambridge University Press, (these proceedings), 1990, pp. 65–78.

[Walker88a] J. H. Walker, "Supporting Document Development with Concordia," *Computer*, vol. 21, no. 1, January 1988, pp. 48–59.

[Walker88b] J. H. Walker, "The Role of Modularity in Document Authoring Systems," *Proceedings of ACM Conference on Document Processing Systems*, ACM Press, December 1988, pp. 117–124.

Managing Properties in a System of Cooperating Editors

Donald D. Chamberlin

IBM Research Division
Almaden Research Center
San Jose, California 95120

ABSTRACT: Today's workstations make it possible for users to create and interact with many types of objects. It is desirable that a document creation tool allow all these types of objects to be mixed and nested without restriction in documents, that each type of object be treated uniformly wherever it is found, and that the tool be extensible to new types of objects. The Quill document creation system addresses these requirements by providing an extensible family of specialized editors, coordinated by a Shell that provides common services and presents a consistent user interface. The Shell manages a database that records the *properties* of various objects in the document, allows objects to inherit properties from other objects, and allows users to override properties when desired. Quill generalizes the concept of properties to include user-supplied procedures that specify the active behavior of an object during WYSIWYG editing.

KEYWORDS: document systems, editors, markup, properties, inheritance, extensibility

1 Introduction

Today's personal workstations make it possible for users to create and interact with a wide variety of complex data types: text, graphics, images, tables, forms, mathematical and chemical formulae, music, etc. It is highly desirable that a document creation tool allow all these types of data to be mixed and nested without restriction in documents, and that each data type be treated uniformly wherever it occurs. On the other hand, each type of data may have complex semantics and require specialized manipulations. It is difficult for a single editor to provide a robust set of commands for editing disparate data such as mathematics and music while providing a reasonably manageable user interface. Furthermore, any editor that attempts to be all-inclusive will surely fail to anticipate some useful data types or manipulations.

The Quill document creation system is an attempt to resolve the dilemma of breadth vs. specialization in an open-ended way. Quill is a family of cooperating, specialized editors, coordinated by a *Shell* that provides common services to the editors and maintains a consistent user interface. At present, the Quill family consists of four editors, which can manipulate text, graphics, tables, and mathematical formulae. Each editor has specialized knowledge and commands. Quill is extensible in that a new editor can be added to the family if it conforms to a set of well-defined rules. The Quill editors are independent of each other, and addition of a new editor does not impact the existing editors in any way.

All Quill editors must subscribe to the model that a document consists of a hierarchy of *elements*. Each editor may have its own types of elements—e.g., text elements may include lists, headings, and footnotes; graphic elements may include lines, curves, and filled areas; etc. Some editors may have fixed sets of element-types, and others may permit users to create new types of elements. This document model is taken from ISO Standard 8879, the Standard Generalized Markup Language (SGML) [ISO86], and permits a mixed-type Quill document to be stored as a self-contained SGML file.

Quill is a WYSIWYG editing system, and its user interface presents an accurate representation of formatted pages to the user for direct manipulation. The user can select an object in the document by clicking on it with the mouse; this causes the editor for the selected object to become the *active editor*. The Shell is responsible for Quill's user interface—it presents a menu of commands of the active editor, and permits the user to scroll over the pages of the document and to control the "zoom" (magnification level) of the document view. The Shell also presents a *Tag Display* that represents the current position in the document and the logical hierarchy of elements in the neighborhood of this position, as shown in Figure 1.

It is basic to the Quill design that any kind of material can be nested inside any other kind of material, to any number of levels. Therefore, each Quill editor is required to implement an object called a *frame*, which denotes a rectangular space that the editor makes available to another editor in which to lay out a lower-level nested object. Each editor must also be prepared to format its own objects within the boundaries of a frame provided by a higher-level editor. The highest level of frame, which contains the whole document, is owned by the Shell.

In order to participate in the Quill system, each editor must meet the following requirements:

- It must register its commands with the Shell, so the commands can be presented on menus when the editor is active.

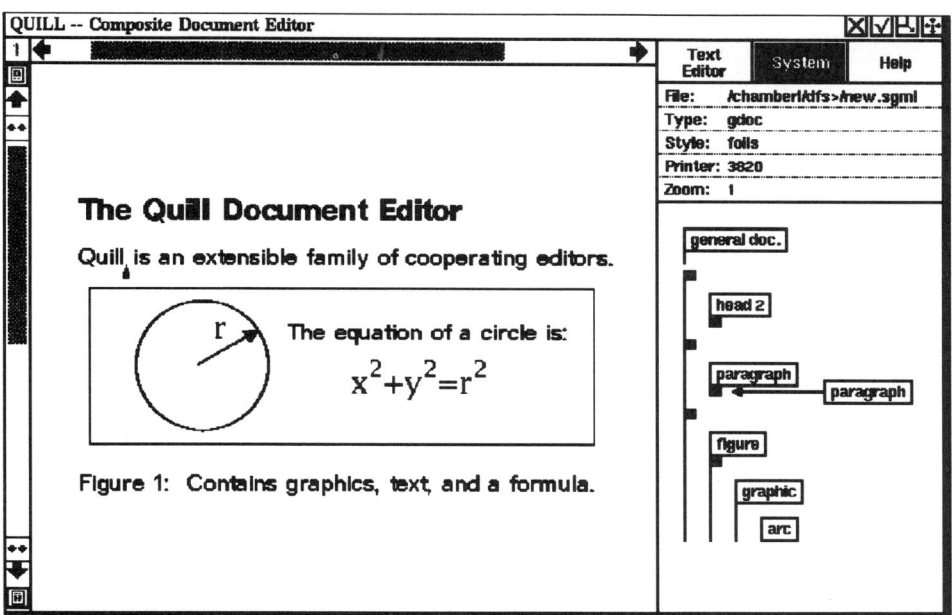

Figure 1: Appearance of a Quill window during editing of a document

- It must represent its objects as nodes in a hierarchic data structure called the *Logical Tree*. The basic connectivity of this data structure is mandated by the Shell, which needs to understand the hierarchic structure in order to parse incoming documents and manage the Tag Display. The content of the individual nodes in the Logical Tree, however, is controlled by the various editors.
- It must be able to draw its objects on the screen, in the position and size as directed by the Shell.
- It must be able to save its objects in a revisable SGML file, and in a printable PostScript file.
- It must communicate with the editors above and below it in the element hierarchy, to manage the frames which represent the boundaries between editors. For any given frame, the editor above the frame determines its placement and its maximum allowed size, while the editor below the frame determines its actual current size. Whenever one of the editors changes the size or placement of a frame, or damages the frame's content (e.g., by erasing an overlapping object), it is required to notify

the other editor with which it shares the frame. Each editor must also implement a *creation action*, by which it creates a new frame, at user request, and activates another editor to provide the content of the frame. Communication between editors is accomplished via calls to a set of procedures that each editor is required to provide. This inter-editor interface has been described in more detail in an earlier paper [Cham88a].

2 DocPaks and Properties

The idea that objects in a document can possess formatting "properties" such as font and size, and that these properties can be inherited when objects are nested inside each other, has been implemented in a number of non-interactive document formatters including Scribe [Reid79] and L^AT_EX [Lamport86, Knuth84]. More recently, a number of WYSIWYG systems have allowed users to define their own logical "elements" and to specify the formatting properties of these elements by interacting with "style sheets." The idea of deriving the physical appearance of a document from its logical elements under the control of "properties" can be found in commercial WYSIWYG editors such as Ventura Publisher [Ventura86], Interleaf [Interleaf86], and Microsoft Word [Micro89], and in research systems such as Grif [Quint86], which supports inheritance of properties by nested elements.

Quill builds on the idea of property-based logical-to-physical mappings in the following ways:

- Rather than a single editor, Quill is a family of specialized editors, each of which implements its own set of logical elements and properties. Nested elements may inherit properties from elements belonging to other editors.
- In addition to inheriting property values directly (e.g., "same font as my parent"), an element can inherit a value that is computed in a more complex way, e.g., "my size is two points smaller than that of my parent", or "my baseline is raised by an amount equal to 80 percent of my parent's size."
- In addition to a fixed set of properties, an element can invoke a user-supplied procedure that specifies an active role for the element, e.g., generating a figure number or resolving a reference.

- End-users are allowed to override the properties of individual elements in a document in order to create special effects or to "fine-tune" the appearance of the document.

Each of the Quill editors must implement a bi-directional mapping between logical and physical objects—i.e., given a logical element, it must be possible to generate its physical appearance; and when the user selects a physical object, it must be possible to find the logical element that it represents. For some editors, this mapping is straightforward. For example, the logical objects of the Graphic Editor, such as polylines and arcs, are one-to-one with physical objects, and the algorithms for generating these physical objects are fixed and known to the Graphic Editor.

For other editors, however, the mapping between logical and physical objects is much more complex. The best example of such an editor in Quill is the Text Editor. The Text Editor does not have a fixed set of logical elements, but allows users to define new types of elements and to specify their appearance and behavior. Furthermore, logical text elements are not one-to-one with physical objects. For example, a <heading> element may correspond to several physical objects, including the heading itself, a "running footer" on many subsequent pages, and an entry in the Table of Contents. There may be dependencies among logical elements; for example, a <figure reference> element may need to generate some text that depends on the placement and content of a <figure> element. Finally, users may wish to specify several different logical-to-physical mappings, called *styles*, so that a given logical element may have a different appearance in each style.

In Quill, the rules for generating physical objects from logical elements are held in a file called a *DocPak*. There is a DocPak for each different *type* of document, such as a Technical Report or Business Letter. The DocPak consists of an SGML *Document Type Definition*, which lists the types of logical elements and rules for combining them into documents, and one or more *style specifications*. For example, a Technical Report might be formatted in different styles for publication in *Communications of the ACM* and in *IEEE Computer*.

The elementary parts of a DocPak, which control the details of the formatting process, are called *properties*. Properties are interpreted by the various editors that use the DocPak; for example, the Text Editor might have properties to control fonts and justification, while the Graphic Editor might have properties to control line style and thickness.

During a Quill editing session, the various editors need to retrieve properties from the DocPak in order to make formatting decisions. Editors may also wish to allow a user, during editing, to examine and override the properties of an individual element or of a type of element. For these purposes, the Shell provides a set of services called DocPak Services. Since the Shell is independent of the various editors and does not understand their properties, the Shell is simply serving as a database manager, managing a repository of properties, and retrieving and updating them on demand from the editors.

The Quill system also includes a specialized *Design Editor* for creating and maintaining DocPaks. The Design Editor provides a set of property-specification tools which is independent of any specific editor but sufficient for the needs of many editors. The Design Editor also cooperates with other Quill editors to manage objects nested inside a DocPak.

3 PGroups

The management of properties in DocPaks is organized around the concept of a *PGroup*, which is a group of related properties. Each PGroup in a DocPak has a name which consists of four parts: an editor-name, a style-name, a PGroup-type-name, and a PGroup-instance-name. The first two parts indicate the editor that "owns" and interprets the PGroup, and the document style to which the PGroup applies. The last two parts of the name are interpreted by the owning editor. A PGroup-type names a set of PGroups which all have the same set of properties (though some of the properties may be defaulted in a given PGroup-instance).

Quill does not place any restrictions on how individual editors use PGroups, and the usage is quite different among the existing Quill editors. Some editors may adopt a convention that part of the PGroup-name is derived from the type of element to which the PGroup applies. For example, the PGroup named `(Text.Foils.Look.Paragraph)` is owned by the Text Editor, it applies to the Foils Style, and by a Text Editor convention it might control the "Look" of the `<paragraph>` element.

PGroups are encoded in the DocPak using SGML syntax. The DocPak consists of a collection of *style segments*, each of which contains the specification for a particular style of document as understood by a particular editor (e.g., the Letter Style of the Text Editor). The beginning of a style segment is denoted by a <STYLE> tag. Within a style segment, each PGroup is denoted by a tag that specifies the Type-name and Instance-name of the PGroup, followed by its properties. For example, the following fragment of a DocPak encodes a PGroup whose full name is (Text.Report.Look.Paragraph), and which contains four properties:

```
<STYLE name = Report>
   <LOOK name = Paragraph
      break   = line
      font    = roman
      size    = 10
      align   = justified >
```

Often, the creator of a DocPak may wish two styles, or two PGroup-instances, to be similar, and intend that changes to one style or PGroup apply to the other as well. For this purpose, a PGroup-instance may be declared to be *LIKE* another PGroup-instance of the same type, and a style-segment may be declared to be *LIKE* another style-segment of the same editor. In both cases, *LIKE* means "this object is the same as the named object, with the following exceptions." LIKE-declarations are applied to the evaluation of individual properties. For example, suppose that we need to find the value of a property P in PGroup-instance G1 of Style S1. If G1 contains no property P but G1 is declared "LIKE G2", the search for the property P continues in group G2 of Style S1. If a needed PGroup (G1 or G2) does not exist in S1 but S1 is declared "LIKE S2", the search for the missing PGroup continues in Style S2. The use of LIKE-declarations is illustrated by the following example:

```
<STYLE name = Report>
   <LOOK name = Paragraph
      break   = line
      font    = roman
      size    = 10
      align   = justified >
   <LOOK name = Example   like = Paragraph
      font    = courier
      align   = left >
<STYLE name = Foils   like = Report>
   <LOOK name = Paragraph
      size    = 18 >
```

The above example is equivalent to declaration of the following four PGroup-instances (only three of which are explicitly present):

PGroup-name: (Editor.Style.Type.Instance)	Break Prop.	Font Prop.	Size Prop.	Align Property
(Text.Report.Look.Paragraph)	line	roman	10	justified
(Text.Report.Look.Example)	line	courier	10	left
(Text.Foils.Look.Paragraph)	line	roman	18	justified
(Text.Foils.Look.Example)	line	courier	18	left

In addition to its properties, a PGroup may optionally have a *body*, which is an unnamed character string that follows the PGroup's tag in the DocPak. The body of a PGroup is typically used to contain a procedure; for example, each Text element in Quill has a semantic procedure, written in the REXX programming language [Cowl85], and these procedures make up the bodies of LOOK-type PGroups.

4 Shell Services for Managing Properties

As noted above, the Quill Shell provides a collection of services to help the individual editors with management of properties. In order to use these services, each editor must *register* its properties with the Shell. The Shell makes an initialization call to each editor at the beginning of a session, and each editor returns a data structure identifying all its PGroup-types, and the properties that are contained in each. For each property, the editor declares a range of values, a default value, and whether the property is *computable*. A computable property is a property whose value in the DocPak requires further computation to turn it into an absolute value. The commonest kind of computable properties are those which involve inheritance from a higher level of the document hierarchy. For example, the "font size" property of an element may have the value "same", meaning "my font size is the same as that of my logical parent".

As the Shell and the editors cooperate to manage properties, the general rule is that the Shell serves as a database manager and provides certain user interface services, but all interpretation of the semantics of the properties must be done by the editors. Each editor is required to provide two functions that can be called by the Shell. The first of these editor-supplied functions, which we will call ValidateProp, is called during the initial loading of a DocPak to test property values for validity and to replace invalid values with valid ones. This function enables the Quill editors to protect themselves against errors in user-supplied DocPaks.

The second function that must be provided by each editor is the ComputeProp function, which converts a *computable* property-value into an absolute value. This conversion is performed in the context of a specific position in the document; it may involve inheritance from higher-level elements, or any other computation desired by the editor. The ComputeProp function is called by the Shell when it has a need to present both the computable and the absolute value of a property to a user (e.g., when displaying a property-sheet for an element in the document.)

In exchange for the ValidateProp and ComputeProp functions provided by editors, the Shell provides two general kinds of property-related services to the editors: services for retrieving the values of properties, and services for displaying property-sheets for user interaction. In both of these services, the concept of *property override* plays a major role.

A Quill DocPak contains a complete specification for the physical appearance of each type of logical element in the DocPak. Therefore, a user need only specify the logical elements (e.g., paragraphs, footnotes, headings, etc.) to be used in a given document, and the name of the formatting style to be used, and the appearance of the document can be derived from the DocPak. Indeed, the creator of a Quill DocPak can ensure that the DocPak exercises complete control over the appearance of documents, by placing a *lock* on each property to prevent end users from altering it. However, in many applications it is desirable to allow users to override the properties in the DocPak, for a particular element or for all elements of a given type. For example, a user may wish to override the font property of an individual paragraph, or of all paragraphs in the document. A user may also wish to override properties that are not related to a specific element, such as the width of the page margins.

In Quill, editing commands are provided to the user by the individual editors, such as the Text Editor and the Table Editor. As a service to the editors, the Shell implements a function called SysPropSheet which provides a uniform and convenient implementation for property-override commands. SysPropSheet is called by an editor, with a four-part PGroup-name and optionally a pointer to an element in the document hierarchy. The Shell displays a property sheet to the user, containing all the properties of the given PGroup, and allows the user to edit the properties on the sheet. If any of the properties on the sheet are computable, SysPropSheet displays both their computable and absolute values (calling ComputeProp of the owning editor to obtain the absolute values). The properties displayed to the user take into account any existing document-level overrides, and if an element-pointer is passed to SysPropSheet, the instance-level overrides for that element are reflected in the sheet also. For each property on the sheet, SysPropSheet provides a suitable form of user dialog (menu of tokens, prompter for string, etc.) based on the definition of the property provided by the editor at initialization time.

If, after interacting with the property sheet, the user confirms his changes, SysPropSheet creates a new set of property overrides. The new overrides apply either to the document as a whole or, if an element-pointer was passed, only within the scope of that element. The overrides are recorded by the shell and made effective in later calls to SysPropSheet and in calls to services that retrieve property values. Property overrides are also written out in the form of SGML "Processing Instructions" when the document is saved.

The Shell service for retrieving a property value is called SysGetProp. SysGetProp is called by an editor, with a four-part PGroup-name, the name of the property to be evaluated, and an optional pointer to an element in the document hierarchy. SysGetProp returns the value of the property, at the first of the following levels that applies:

1. An instance-level override for this property within the scope of the given element.
2. A document-level override for this property.
3. The value of this property in the DocPak. Finding this value may require following *LIKE*-chains from one PGroup to another and from one Style to another.
4. If the value is not resolved at any lower level, the default value for this property, declared by the editor at initialization time.

For computable properties, SysGetProp returns a computable value. It is up to the editor to turn the computable value into an absolute value (possibly by calling its own ComputeProp function).

For some properties, declared at initialization time, the value of the property is the name of one or more PGroups. For example, the (Text.Book.Look.Chapter) **PGroup might contain a** Pagedef **property whose value is the names of two PGroups containing the page templates to be used for odd and even-numbered pages. These types of properties are presented by SysPropSheet in the form of "buttons" on the property** sheet which the user can invoke by a mouse-click. Pressing one of these buttons results in a recursive call to SysPropSheet, "popping up" another property sheet for the named PGroup (selected by menu, if there is more than one.) Overrides applied to this "second-level" PGroup (or to lower-level PGroups arrived at in the same way) are made effective either at the document level or at the instance-level within the scope of the element for which SysPropSheet was originally called.

5 Property Inheritance

As noted above, interpretation of property semantics is left to the individual editors. An important semantic feature that many editors need is that of *inheritance*, which means that the value of a given property is derived in some way from the properties of the parent element. The simplest form of inheritance might be expressed by a property value such as "`same`", meaning "same as the equivalent property of my parent." More complex forms of inheritance might involve arithmetic expressions, such as "`*-2`", meaning "two points smaller than my parent." In some cases, a property may be inherited from a different property of the parent, as in "`shift=superscript`", meaning, "shift my baseline upward an amount appropriate to make a superscript within my parent's content." In this example, the `shift` property of an element is inherited from the parent's `size` property, via a computation provided by the editor.

Inheritance of properties is extremely common in Quill—in fact, most elements inherit most of their properties from their parents. In order to implement inheritance efficiently, an editor may attach to each node in the Logical Tree a *resolved property list*, containing the absolute value of each property of the element represented by that node, after all overrides, inheritance, and computation. Then if a call to SysGetProp returns a value that calls for inheritance, the value of the parent element's properties can be efficiently retrieved from the parent's resolved property list.

Although the semantics of inheritance are defined by the individual editors, it is sometimes necessary for a property to be inherited from one editor to another. For example, the Math Editor may wish a mathematical formula to be set in the same size as the surrounding text, which belongs to the Text Editor. For the purpose of cross-editor inheritance, Quill has defined a small set of *universal properties*. If an editor finds that one of its elements needs to inherit the value of a universal property, and the parent element belongs to a different editor, the desired value may be obtained by calling a function called InheritProperty, which is part of the standard interface between editors.

At present, the universal properties defined by Quill consist of font properties such as typeface and size. It is important to note that not all Quill editors are required to implement or understand the universal properties. If an editor that has no fonts, such as the Graphic Editor, receives a call from a lower-level editor to inherit a font property, it can simply call the InheritProperty function of the next-higher editor. In this way the call will propagate up the Logical Tree until it reaches an editor that can provide a value for the font to be inherited.

6 The Quill Text Editor

As an illustrative example, we will describe how the Quill Text Editor uses PGroups to control the process of formatting text. Since the Text Editor serves as the "flow editor" for Quill, it needs to create the pages on which materials from the various editors will flow. Each page is a collection of nested *blocks* that can hold columns of text or other objects such as footnotes, floating figures, or page numbers. The blocks can grow or shrink to accommodate the content of each individual page. Each different type of page is described by a PGroup of type "Pagedef". Some of the properties in the Pagedef PGroup are used to name other PGroups that describe the blocks nested on the page. Each Style in a DocPak can have many named Pagedef's; for example, the page template for the title page of a book might have the name (Text.Book.Pagedef.Titlepage).

The Text Editor also has a PGroup-type called "Look", which controls the appearance of a given type of element in the document, such as a heading or footnote. All elements of the same type (e.g., all footnotes) share the same Look, unless the user applies property overrides. If an element (e.g., a <chapter>) needs to introduce a new type of page, one of its Look-properties is used to name the Pagedef-type PGroups containing templates for its odd, even, and first pages.

As noted previously, each type of element in a Quill document has an associated semantic procedure, written in the REXX programming language, that controls its formatting. The semantic procedures can be written and modified by users, and are contained in the DocPak. The semantic procedures make use of a set of formatting primitives, implemented by Quill and described in an earlier paper [Cham88b]. The primitive function that causes material to appear in the document is the Output function, which takes three arguments:

1. The *content string* to be placed in the document. This string may be generated by the semantic procedure, and/or it may contain a code that represents the *natural content* of the element—i.e., the content that is typed by a user and which may be revised during a WYSIWYG editing session. The natural content of each element is saved in an SGML file at the end of the session, whereas generated content is regenerated in each session (and may vary from one Style to another.)
2. The *stream* into which the string is to be placed. The current page template indicates how streams are mapped onto the various blocks on the page, for main text, footnotes, floating figures, etc.
3. The *look* to be used for the content string. This is the name of a Look-type PGroup, which defaults to the element-type (e.g., `foot-note`.) The *look* parameter may also apply final overrides, called *output overrides*, to the individual properties. An output override might be used, for example, if an element wishes its generated content to appear in bold but its natural content to appear in normal weight.

We can now summarize the complete process of resolving the formatting properties of a text string placed into the document by the `Output` function of the Text Editor. Text formatting is controlled by the properties found in `Look`-type PGroups. Each of these properties is resolved by the earliest of the following steps that applies:

1. An output-override (a property-value specified in the Output function itself) takes first precedence.
2. A call to SysGetProp searches for a property-value at four levels: instance-level overrides, document-level overrides, the DocPak, and the default value for this property defined by the Text Editor. Within the DocPak, *LIKE*-chains may be followed at the PGroup-level and the Style level.
3. If the result of Step 1 or 2 is an inheritable value (e.g., "SAME" or "*+2"), the Text Editor applies the inheritable value to the value recorded in the *resolved property list* of the parent element. If the parent element is not a text element, the Text Editor calls the InheritProperty function of the editor that owns the parent element. If inheritance is called for and there is no parent element, the Text

Editor uses the absolute property value found in a special PGroup-instance named "Topmost".

7 The Design Editor

As noted previously, the Design Editor is the tool provided by Quill for creating and modifying DocPaks. The Design Editor is intended for use by a relatively sophisticated user, who needs to create a new document type or style. We will refer to the user of the Design Editor as the Designer.

The Design Editor interacts with the Quill Shell and with other editors in the usual way, editing a DocPak as though it were a document whose elements are Styles and PGroups. When the Designer wishes to create or edit a PGroup, the Design Editor calls the SysPropSheet service of the Shell, causing a property sheet to appear and interact with the user to collect the desired properties.[1] The Design Editor also allows the Designer to control the *LIKE*-links between PGroups and between Styles, and to place *locks* on individual properties to prevent them from being overridden by end users during editing of a document.

The Design Editor has the ability to call another Quill editor to edit the content of a *frame* nested inside a DocPak, using the standard interface between editors. For example, those parts of the DocPak that consist of text, such as REXX programs, are edited by the Text Editor.

8 Conclusions

Quill is organized as an extensible collection of editors and a Shell which provides common services to all the editors. The system presents a consistent user interface, and permits unlimited nesting of objects of mixed type. A standard interface between editors permits new editors to be added without impacting the existing ones. Quill thus combines the advantages of seamless integration of mixed-type objects, specialized editing operations for each data type, and extensibility to new types of objects. Use of the ISO Standard SGML syntax permits documents containing many types of objects to be stored in self-contained files.

Quill builds on the direction of modern WYSIWYG systems which operate on logical *elements* whose appearance is defined in a separate *style*

---

[1] Of course, when SysPropSheet is called by the Design Editor, it cannot display the absolute values of computable properties, since they do not yet apply to a specific element in a document.

definition. To this base, Quill adds the following innovations:

- Multiple styles defined for the same set of elements, with sharing of common parts between the styles.
- Inheritance of properties through a hierarchy of elements, including relative inheritance such as "two points larger", and inheritance of common properties between elements belonging to different editors.
- End-user overrides of properties for individual elements or for all similar elements in a document.
- Integration of style-sheets with semantic routines, allowing each element to have a procedural definition as well as a set of predefined properties.
- A set of Shell services, common to all editors, for resolving properties and displaying property sheets.
- A specialized Design Editor for creating and editing style definitions, and Designer-specified *locks* that control user overrides to the style definitions.

9 Acknowledgements

Important contributions to the design and implementation of Quill have been made by a number of people at Almaden Research Center, including Helmut Hasselmeier, Joe Latone, Allen Luniewski, Dieter Paris, Brad Wade, Yaron Wolfsthal, and Mitch Zolliker. The Quill team has also benefitted from interactions with other workers in IBM, including Ken Borgendale, Joe Czyszczewski, Bob Hinkle, and Ken Nolan.

References

[Cham88a] D.D. Chamberlin, H.F. Hasselmeier, A.W. Luniewski, D.P. Paris, B.W. Wade, and M.L. Zolliker, "Quill: An Extensible System for Editing Documents of Mixed Type," *Proceedings of the 21st Hawaii International Conference on System Sciences,* IEEE Computer Society Press, 1988, 317-326.

[Cham88b] D.D. Chamberlin, "An Adaptation of Dataflow Methods for WYSIWYG Document Processing," *Proceedings of the ACM Conference on Document Processing Systems,* Santa Fe, NM, December 1988, 101-109.

[Cowl85] M.F. Cowlishaw, *The REXX Language: A Practical Approach to Programming,* Prentice-Hall, Inglewood Cliffs, NJ, 1985, 176 pages.

[Interleaf86] *Interleaf Workstation Publishing Software User's Guide,* Interleaf, Inc., 1986.

[ISO86] *Information Processing—Text and Office Systems—Standard Generalized Markup Language (SGML),* Standard ISO 8879, International Organization for Standardization, 1986, 155 pages.

[Knuth84] D.E. Knuth, *The T$_E$Xbook,* Addison-Wesley, Reading, MA, 1984, 483 pages.

[Lamport86] L. Lamport, *L^{A}T$_E$X: A Document Preparation System,* Addison-Wesley, Reading, MA, 1986, 242 pages.

[Micro89] *Using Microsoft Word,* Microsoft Corp., 1989, 635 pages.

[Quint86] V. Quint and I. Vatton, "GRIF: An Interactive System for Structured Document Manipulation," in J.C. van Vliet (ed.), *Text Processing and Document Manipulation,* Proceedings of the EP86 Conference, Cambridge University Press, 1986, 200-213.

[Reid79] B.K. Reid and J.H. Walker, *SCRIBE Introductory User's Manual,* Computer Science Dept., Carnegie-Mellon University, 1979, 332 pages.

[Ventura86] *Xerox Ventura Publisher Edition Reference Guide.* Xerox Corp. and Ventura Software, Inc., 1986, 332 pages.

A Logic Grammar Foundation for Document Representation and Document Layout

Allen L. Brown, Jr.[†‡] and Howard A. Blair[‡†]

[†] *Xerox Corporation*
Webster Research Center
800 Phillips Road 128-29E
Webster, New York 14580, USA
[‡] *Syracuse University*
School of Computer and Information Science
Center for Science and Technology 4-116
Syracuse, New York 13244-4100, USA

ABSTRACT: We present a powerful grammar-based paradigm for electronic document markup: coordinated definite clause translation grammars. This markup is of a declarative character, being, in effect, a collection of constraints on the logical and physical structure of documents. To the best of our knowledge, coordinated grammars and their parsers can accommodate all of the descriptive and layout processing functionality enjoyed by extant electronic markup languages. We describe an operational prototype that demonstrates the feasibility of a syntax-directed basis for formalizing and realizing document layout.

KEYWORDS: document description language, layout processing, logic grammar.

1 Introduction

Our aim is to formulate an electronic markup language with an unambiguous formal semantics within which one can specify documents in a declarative fashion. We contrast our goal with the reality of popular electronic markup languages such as TEX, LATEX, Scribe, SGML and ODA. While the casual user's view of some of these markups (*e.g.* LATEX and Scribe) would *appear* to be declarative[1], the actual meanings of user issued directives are to be understood through underlying imperative languages. This is evident when a user needs to comprehend the "style" defining mechanisms of these markups.

The technical point of view that we have adopted regarding document representation and document processing is aggressively syntax-oriented. While our

---

[1] In complete fairness to the designers of SGML, we should point out that it is clearly their *intent* to be declarative. The problem that they leave unresolved is the formal interpretation of their declarations.

methods are related to both syntax-directed translation of programming languages and to syntax-directed natural language processing, our approach is novel in that it uses multiple grammars for the same document. Specifically, these grammars separately represent the logical and layout views of the document represented. The layout grammar is said to be *coordinated* with the logical grammar, and the two are allowed to interact through a narrowly defined interface.

In the remainder of this essay we shall demonstrate that the syntax-directed methods we have developed provide a natural and powerful framework for document representation and document processing. Our main vehicle for arriving at this conclusion is the embedding of ODA-like document representation/processing capabilities in a logic grammar framework. Presuming the reader to have some acquaintance with Prolog, we sketch a direct embedding of ODA structures and processing in that language. We introduce a particular logic grammar: the definite clause translation grammar (DCTG). We then provide a comprehensive exposition of DCTG's and parsing applied to document representation and document processing by considering the detailed specification of the layout process (realized in our operational prototype) for a simple ODA-like document. We show how to pass from the definition of the document layout process based on *total* parsing that is declarative but impractically inefficient to one based on *partial* parsing that is equally declarative and potentially quite efficient. We briefly discuss the adaptations of efficient context free parsing and incremental attribute evaluation techniques that we plan for our second phase of research. We close by sketching the future phases of research that follow from our operational prototype and its associated semantical framework.

2 ODA and Prolog

ODA [Weisz *et al.*, 1988] expresses a syntactically well-defined collection of *document constituents* of which the principal sorts are content portions (*e.g.* graphic characters, raster graphic elements and geometric graphic elements), logical objects and logical object classes, layout objects and layout object classes, and attributes. A logical (layout) structure is a tree-like arrangement of logical (layout) objects and object classes, with the trees' being "foliated" with content portion constituents.

The logical structure of an ODA document is a partitioning of the document's content based on meaning. In that context, logical object classes are elements of generic logical structure from which a set of logical objects with common characteristics may be derived (*e.g.* composite logical objects representing sections), while logical objects are elements of a document having specific interpretations (*e.g.* particular chapters, sections and paragraphs).

The layout structure of an ODA document is a partitioning of the document's content based on presentation. In that context, layout object classes are elements of a generic layout structure from which a set of layout objects with common characteristics may be derived (*e.g.* pages with common headers and footers), while layout objects are elements of a specific layout structure of a document having specific geometric properties (*e.g.* particular pages and blocks). An attribute is an element of a document constituent that has a name and a value, and that expresses a characteristic of that constituent or relationship with one or more other constituents (*e.g.* the "presentation style" attribute establishes the relationship between a basic component description and a presentation style). Document constituent attributes can be viewed as decorating the ODA structure trees in much the same way as semantical attributes decorate parse trees in the attribute grammar paradigm.

The ODA language allows the composition of the above-mentioned constituents into *document descriptions*, each of the latter being composed of a *document profile* and a *document body*. A document profile is a collection of predefined (and preinterpreted) attributes that apply globally to the document description. The document body consists of a generic logical structure, a generic layout structure, specific logical structure, specific layout structure, and style constituents. The last are predetermined (and preinterpreted) collections of attributes that explicitly and implicitly link logical constituents with layout constituents.

We initially attempted to formalize ODA by a direct Prolog translation of ODA document constructs. We translated particular ODA document descriptions into particular Prolog fragments. Certain ODA constituents correspond to particular Prolog-defined predicates.[2] The real utility of ODA, however, comes only through the descriptive interpretations of various attributes (*e.g.* presentation style) and processes (*e.g.* document layout). The interpretation of these attributes is the main task of *document processing* as exemplified by the layout process. These interpretations are given in [Weisz *et al.*, 1988] in an informal fashion. The main task of formalizing ODA is to define these interpretations *rigorously*. The interpretations turn out to be other Prolog fragments relative to which we define *each* (and every) Prolog translation of an ODA document description. Hereafter, we shall refer to the translation of an ODA structural document description into a logic program as the *data* description and to the Prolog interpretation of

---

[2]In our various ODA translation efforts we have ignored the document profile and all of the details encoded in ODA's document content representations. To elucidate the core document layout process it suffices to view content portions of a document as atomic constructs with certain externally apparent attributes.

attributes (in the document processing context) as the *process* description. The latter rendering can be thought of as defining *interpreters* for various document processors.

The recipe for generating the data description is as follows: Generic (logical and layout) objects are represented as unary predicates. We may think of these generic objects as *types* whose *tokens* are specific (logical and layout) objects. In particular, tokens are individual terms in the Prolog language. Generic attributes, *i.e.* attributes of generic logical or layout objects, are represented as binary predicates. For example, the fact (part of the data description) that the generic letter has a presentation style attribute with value 'letter_layout' is represented by

```
presentation_style(X,V) :- letter(X), letter_layout(V).
```

which says that the presentation_style of the generic letter is the generic letter_layout. That a specific letter object #Letter had the specific presentation style #Letter_Layout would result from asserting the fact

```
presentation_style(#Letter,#Letter_Layout).
```

Specific (logical and layout) structures, on the other hand, are realized as Prolog terms whose nesting structure follows the hierarchy of the Prolog rules representing the related generic structures.

For the most part the translation recipe above leaves undefined the attributes that are part of the process description. For example, what does it *mean* for the logical class summary_paragraph to have an alignment attribute of justified (*i.e.* alignment(X,justified) :- summary_paragraph(X).)? The real definition for this attribute lies in its intended interpreter, in this case the *layout process*. The gist of ODA's layout model is as follows: Each ODA content portion is mapped on to one or more (layout) blocks (having geometric extents constrained by ODA layout attributes such as alignment having a value of justified) where the blocks may be generated "on the fly". The content portions are totally ordered and it is in that order that blocks for content objects are generated. The order derives from the depth-first (pre-)ordering of the tree implicit in a document's specific logical description. To capture the layout process we defined the Prolog predicate layout_process(X,Y,U,V) where V is the specific layout structure resulting from laying out the specific logical structure U (an instance of the generic logical structure whose user visible name is X) according to the generic layout structure whose user visible name is Y. The layout_process predicate can be (and has been) sufficiently Prolog-defined to handle the ODA specimen document of [Weisz *et al.*, 1988, Annex B]. We find the definition is fundamentally flawed in that layout occurs mainly by side-effect, and its definition mimics the traditional procedural style of document layout. In the sections that follow we address these flaws by substantially raising the level of abstraction of the logic programming account of ODA data descriptions. We thereby enable an declarative account of layout process description.

3 Logic grammars and documents

Definite clause grammars are a version of context-free grammars [Harrison, 1978] that have particularly straightforward translations into definite clauses (Prolog facts and rules), yielding parsers for those grammars. There are, however, many features of languages that are either inconvenient or impossible to capture by context-free grammars. Subject-verb agreement in English is such a feature. To address the problem, investigators of logic-based parsing formalisms [Abramson and Dahl, 1989, Shieber, 1986] have borrowed liberally from researchers in attribute grammars [Deransart et al., 1988]. One result of this confluence of interests is the definite clause translation grammar. This particular logic grammar provides a logic programming setting with both the context-sensitive expressive power and structuring discipline of attribute grammars. In our particular version of DCTG's (a variant of that described in [Abramson and Dahl, 1989]) we present the following context-sensitive grammar to handle noun-verb agreement:

```
sentence ::=
    meta(seq([noun_phrase^^T1,verb_phrase^^T2])) <:>
  num(Num) ::- T1^^num(Num),T2^^num(Num).
noun_phrase ::=
    meta(seq([determiner^^T1,noun_phrase2^^T2])) <:>
  num(Num) ::- T1^^num(Num),T2^^num(Num).
noun_phrase ::= meta(seq([noun_phrase2^^T1])) <:>
  num(Num) ::- T1^^num(Num).
noun_phrase2 ::=
    meta(seq([adjective,noun_phrase2^^T2])) <:>
  num(Num) ::- T2^^num(Num).
noun_phrase2 ::= meta(seq([noun^^T1])) <:>
  num(Num) ::- T1^^num(Num).
verb_phrase ::= meta(seq([verb^^T1])) <:>
  num(Num) ::- T1^^num(Num).
verb_phrase ::= meta(seq([verb^^T1,noun_phrase^^T1])) <:>
  num(Num) ::- T1^^num(Num).
determiner ::= [the] <:> num(sing).
determiner ::= [the] <:> num(plur).
determiner ::= [a] <:> num(sing).
determiner ::= [some] <:> num(plur).
```

```
adjective ::= [decorated].
noun      ::= [pieplate]  <:> num(sing).
noun      ::= [pieplates] <:> num(plur).
noun      ::= [surprise]  <:> num(sing).
noun      ::= [surprises] <:> num(plur).
verb      ::= [contains]  <:> num(sing).
verb      ::= [contain]   <:> num(plur).
```

To understand the DCTG, consider the first rule of the grammar. This rule has two parts separated by the token <:>. The first part is a syntactic constraint indicating that a sentence is composed of a noun_phrase followed by a verb_phrase. Two Prolog variables, T1 and T2, are introduced. In the course of parsing these will be bound respectively to the parse tree generated for noun_phrase and that generated for verb_phrase. The second part of the rule is zero or more (one in this case) *semantic* constraints. These semantic constraints govern the values that can be taken on by attributes associated with parse trees (and therefore with nonterminals). The parse trees associated with each of sentence, noun_phrase and verb_phrase have num attributes and the value of that attribute for a parse tree generated from sentence is constrained to be the same as the values of that attribute for the parse trees generated from noun_phrase and verb_phrase. The nonterminals of the grammar such as determiner that rewrite to terminals such as [the] have the values of their num attributes fixed at particular constants (either sing or plur). The translation (to definite clauses) of the DCTG yields yes on queries such as ?- sentence([some, pieplates, contain, a, surprise]). and no on ?- sentence([some, pieplates, contains, a, surprise])..

An ODA document can be embedded in the DCTG formalism in the following way: Generic logical and generic layout structures are each encoded as grammars. Nonterminals will correspond to generic objects and terminals will correspond to individual content portions. Attributes in the ODA sense will be directly mapped into attributes in the DCTG sense. Specific logical and layout structures are simply the parse trees generated by their respective grammars.

The layout structure grammar is *coordinated* with the logical structure grammar. Roughly speaking, this means that any "string" of content portions generated by the logical structure grammar is also generated by the layout structure grammar, and that certain subtrees of the parse tree of the logical structure grammar will correspond to subtrees of the parse tree of the layout structure grammar. The parse trees with respect to the two grammars for that string are distinct. The logical structure grammar for a fragment of the ODA specimen document's [Weisz et al., 1988, Annex B] generic logical structure (with some of its attributes defined) is as follows[3]:

```
letter ::= meta(seq([header,body])) <:>
   object_class(root), user_visible_name("Letter").
header ::= meta(seq([date,addressee,subject,summary])) <:>
   object_class(composite), user_visible_name("Header").
summary ::= meta(rep(summary_paragraph)) <:>
   object_class(composite), user_visible_name("Summary").
```

No parse tree variables appear in this DCTG because none of the nonterminals of this fragment has attributes dependent upon the attributes of other nonterminals appearing in the same production.

4 Representing and laying out a simple ODA-like document

A full recounting of our logic grammar/parsing treatment of the data/process descriptions of the ODA specimen document would be inappropriately complex for a report of this length. Instead, we shall illustrate the essential details of our approach by appealing to an ODA representable document of considerably simpler structure. The generic logical structure of our simple document will consist of arbitrarily long sequences of paragraphs. (We shall take a paragraph to be a simple text portion.) Similarly, the generic layout structure for our simple document consists of arbitrarily long sequences of plates (pages), which in turn are arbitrarily long sequences of paragraph blocks. Below we present DCTG's simple[4] and simple_layout that correspond to the generic logical and layout document structure diagrams illustrated in (respectively) figures 1 and 2. We begin by declaring simple_layout and para_block to be the styles corresponding respectively to simple and para:

```
styles(simple_layout,simple).
styles(para_block,para).
```

Were simple and para ODA logical objects, these declarations would correspond to asserting that the values of the "layout style" attributes of these two objects respectively have as values the generic layout objects simple_layout and para_block.

Below is the DCTG representing the generic logical structure of the simple document:

---

[3]Simple concatenation of phrase structures is indicated in our DCTG's by use of the metasyntactic constructor seq, such constructors being introduced by the indicator meta. We also make use of the metasyntactic constructor rep indicating arbitrary repetition of the phrase structure(s) in its scope. Readers familiar with ODA should note the analogy with the ODA content generator operators SEQ and REP.

[4]We identify a grammar with its root nonterminal. Hence we speak of the simple DCTG.

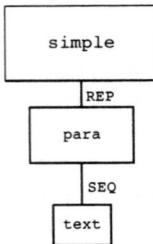

Figure 1: Simple generic logical structure.

```
simple^^T0 ::= meta(rep(para^^T1)),
   {T0^^content_interval(U,V)} <:>
  logical_type(root),
  (style(X) ::- styles(X,simple)),
  (countent(Z) ::- sum_countent_from(T1,Z)),
  (content_interval(M,N) ::-
    M is 1, sum_countent_from(T1,N)).
para ::= meta(seq([text^^T1])) <:>
  (style(X) ::- styles(X,para)),
  (countent(Z) ::- T1^^countent(Z)),
  (content_interval(M,N) ::-
    number(M), T1^^countent(U), N is (M + (U - 1))).
text ::= ["TEXT1"] <:>
  (countent(Z) ::- Z is 1),
  (content_interval(N,N) ::- number(N)).
text ::= ["TEXT2"] <:>
  (countent(Z) ::- Z is 1),
  (content_interval(N,N) ::- number(N)),
  layout_directive_req(apart).
text ::= ["TEXT3"] <:>
  (countent(Z) ::- Z is 1),
  (content_interval(N,N) ::- number(N)).
```

The DCTG has root nonterminal simple, intermediate nonterminals para and text, and terminals "TEXT1", "TEXT2", and "TEXT3" (which expressions are Prolog text terms). The syntactic part of the simple DCTG production asserts that a simple is any nonempty finite sequence of para's. Similarly, para is syntactically specified to be a text and text is syntactically specified to be one of the three terminals, "TEXT1", "TEXT2", or "TEXT3".

In addition to the syntactic characterization of nonterminals provided by productions, there is the semantic characterization provided by *guards* and attributes. The guard of the simple production (the expression embraced by {}) guarantees that the production can be used successfully only if the countent_interval

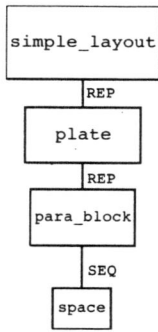

Figure 2: Simple generic layout structure.

attribute can be given a value consisting of the ordered pair whose first and second components are the values of U and V respectively (*i.e.* the indices of the content portions spanned by simple). simple has attributes logical_type, style, countent, and content_interval. The first attribute asserts that simple names a logical structure grammar (*i.e.* a "root object" in the parlance of ODA). The second says that the style of simple is X if X styles simple, *i.e.* X = simple_layout. The countent attribute asserts that the number of content objects spanned by simple is the sum of the numbers of content objects spanned by each of the immediate descendants (*i.e.* the para's) of simple. The content_interval attribute indicates that the interval of indices of content portions spanned by simple includes the first through last content portions.

The style attribute of para is X if X styles para, *i.e.* X = para_block. The countent attribute of para is the same as the countent attribute of the object (*i.e.* text) that is the immediate descendant of para. The content_interval attribute of para is the same as the content_interval attribute of the object (*i.e.* text) that is the immediate descendant of para.

Finally, the second occurrence of text has a layout directive request of apart. That is, the content associated with no previous logical object will be placed on the same layout object (a plate in this case) as the content associated with that occurrence of text. This attribution corresponds to the ODA layout directive "new layout object". This particular content object is to be placed in a layout object distinct from that which receives the previous (in the layout order) content object. The countent attributes of all the occurrences of text have values of 1. The content_interval attributes of all the occurrences of text have values that are intervals of length 1 beginning at an index 1 greater than the upper bound of the previously indexed object (in the layout order).

Below is the DCTG representing the generic layout structure of the simple document:

```
simple_layout^^T0 ::= meta(rep(plate^^T1)),
    {T0^^content_interval(1,V)} <:>
  layout_type(root),
  (page_count(PC) ::- sum_page_count_from(T1,PC)),
  (out_trees(TTI,TTO) ::-
      styles(simple_layout,X),
      find1_node(node(X,STT,Sem),TTI,TTO1,true),
      propagate_trees(T1,TTO1,TTO)),
  (countent(Z) ::- sum_countent_from(T1,Z)),
  (content_interval(M,N) ::-
      number(M), sum_countent_from(T1,U),
      N is (M + (U - 1))).
plate^^T0 ::=
    meta(rep(para_block^^T1)),
    {T0^^set_depth(X),
     sum_set_depth_from(T1,S), X >= S} <:>
  layout_type(page), (page_count(PC) ::- PC is 1),
  (set_depth(X) ::- X is 1.0),
  (out_trees(TTI,TTO) ::- propagate_trees(T1,TTI,TTO)),
  (countent(Z) ::- sum_countent_from(T1,Z)),
  (content_interval(M,N) ::-
      number(M), sum_countent_from(T1,U),
      N is (M + (U - 1))),
  layout_directive_ack(apart,text).
para_block ::= meta(seq([space^^T1])) <:>
  layout_type(block),
  (out_trees(TTI,TTO) ::-
      styles(para_block,Y),
      find1_node(node(Y,STT,Sem),TTI,[T|TTO],true)),
  (countent(Z) ::- T1^^countent(Z)),
  (content_interval(M,N) ::-
      T1^^countent(U), N is (M + (U - 1))),
  (set_depth(X) ::- T1^^set_depth(X)).
space ::= ["TEXT1"] <:>
  (set_depth(X) ::- X is 0.5), (countent(Z) ::- Z is 1),
  (content_interval(N,N) ::- number(N)).
space ::= ["TEXT2"] <:>
  (set_depth(X) ::- X is 0.5), (countent(Z) ::- Z is 1),
  (content_interval(N,N) ::- number(N)).
space ::= ["TEXT3"] <:>
  (set_depth(X) ::- X is 0.5), (countent(Z) ::- Z is 1),
  (content_interval(N,N) ::- number(N)).
```

The guard of the `simple_layout` production guarantees that the production can be used successfully only if the `countent_interval` attribute can be given a value consisting of the ordered pair whose first and second components are the values of U and V respectively. `simple_layout` has intermediate nonterminals `plate`, `para_block`, and `space`. The syntactic part of the `simple_layout` rule asserts that a `simple_layout` is any nonempty finite sequence of `plate`'s, that a `plate` is any nonempty finite sequence of `para_block`'s, that a `para_block` is a `space`, and that a `space` is one of the terminals "TEXT1", "TEXT2" and "TEXT3". Consistent with our earlier remarks that the layout structure grammar is coordinated with the logical structure grammar, the terminals of `simple_layout` subsume those of `simple`. Turning now to the semantic attributes of the `simple_layout` DCTG, we shall explain all but the `out_trees` attribute. We shall postpone its explanation until our description of the layout process.

`simple_layout` has a `layout_type` of root, indicating that `simple_layout` names a layout structure grammar. The value of the `page_count` attribute is constrained by its rule to be the reckoning of the number of layout objects spanned by `simple_layout` having a `layout_type` attribute with value `page`. The `countent` attribute asserts that the number of content objects spanned by `simple_layout` is the sum of the numbers of content objects spanned by each of the immediate descendants (*i.e.* the `plate`'s) of `simple_layout`. The `content_interval` attribute indicates the interval of indices of content objects spanned by `simple_layout` includes the first through last (in layout order) content objects.

`plate` has a `layout_type` attribute with value `page` and a `page_count` attribute with a fixed value of unity. (Naturally, an object of `layout_type` of `page` counts as a single page!) The value of the `set_depth` attribute of an object indicates an object's vertical extent, and, in the case of a `plate`, has a value of 1.0. The `layout_directive_ack` attribute for `plate` indicates the type and the source of `layout_directive_requests` to which a `plate` is willing to respond. In this case `plate` responds to `apart` requests from (logical) objects of type `text`. As the request indicates that requesting content object is to be placed in a layout object distinct from that which received the previous content object, the acknowledgement of the request leads to the creation of a new `plate` object to receive the requesting content object. The `countent` attribute asserts that the number of content objects spanned by `plate` is the sum of the numbers of content objects spanned by each of the immediate descendants (*i.e.* the `para_block`'s) of `plate`. The value of the `content_interval` attribute of `plate` is the pair consisting of the index of the first content object spanned by the left-most (in layout order) of the `plate`'s immediate descendants, and the index of the last content

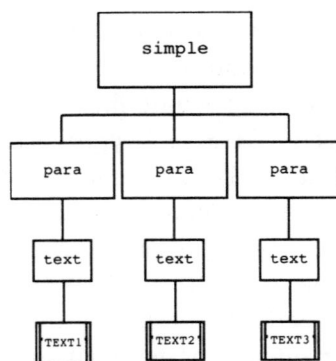

Figure 3: Simple specific logical structure.

object spanned by the right-most (in layout order) of the plate's immediate descendants. The guard of the plate rule admits only those applications of the production in which the sum of the set_depth's of the para_block's is no larger than the set_depth of the plate.

A para_block has a layout_type attribute with value block and "synthesizes" the value of its set_depth attribute from the value of the same attribute of the space object below. A para_block's countent attribute asserts that the number of content objects spanned by the para_block is the same as that spanned by its immediate descendant (*i.e.* the space). The value of the content_interval attribute of para_block is the pair consisting of the index of the first content object spanned (left-most in layout order) by the para_block's immediate descendant, and the index of the last content object spanned (right-most in layout order) by the plate's immediate descendant.

All three space objects have set_depth attributes with values of 0.5. As indicated by the values of their countent attributes, each spans precisely one content object. As a consequence, their content_interval attributes are unit intervals whose boundaries are the indices (in layout order) of the single content objects spanned.

Considering ["TEXT1" , "TEXT2" , "TEXT3"] to be the input string of content portions, the logical structure grammar simple (figure 1) yields only one context free parse, that of figure 3. On the same input list of content portions, the layout structure grammar simple_layout (figure 2) yields four context free parses, figures 4-7. The main task of the layout process is to "disambiguate" the latter parses by using the context-sensitive information provided primarily by the attributes in the layout structure grammar. A collection of preference criteria is applied to the set of context free parses (of the layout structure grammar on

Logic Grammar Foundation for Documents

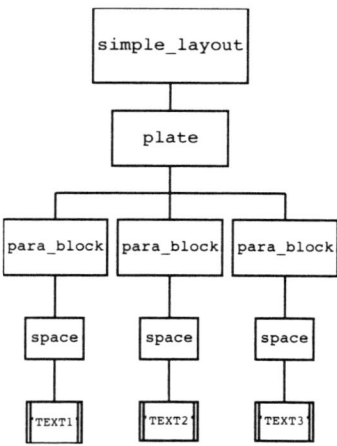

Figure 4: First simple specific layout structure.

a particular input string of content portions). These criteria induce a preference ordering on the parses. With respect to that ordering the "best" parses are chosen. A parse tree P1 is preferred to a parse tree P2 if

1. P1 satisfies the guards (the literals embraced by {}) on all the productions used in its construction, but P2 does not;

2. P1 and P2 are unordered by the previous criterion, but P1 is coordinated with the parse of the input list according to the logical structure grammar while P2 is not;

3. P1 and P2 are unordered by the previous criteria, but P1 spans fewer page objects than does P2; and

4. P1 and P2 are unordered by the previous criteria, but some content portion X appears on an earlier page in P1 than it does in P2, while no content portion before (in the layout ordering) X appears on an earlier page in P2 than it does in P1.

We define a Prolog predicate layout

```
layout(CG,FG,L,FTT) :-
  bagof(
    FT,
    (parse([CG],[CT|CTT],L,[]),
     parse([FG],[FT|FTT1],L,[]),
     FT^^out_trees([CT],OTT), reqs_ackd(CG,CT,FG,FT)),
    FTT2),
  min_pages(FTT2,FTT3), min_place(L,FTT3,FTT).
```

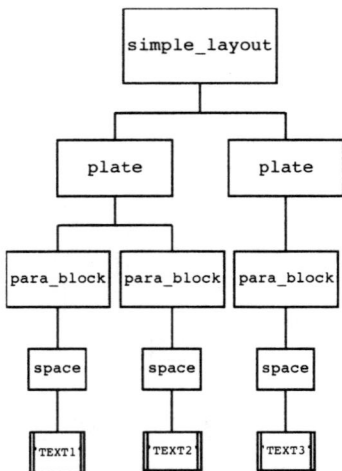

Figure 5: Second simple specific layout structure.

that guarantees an ordering under these criteria by means of other Prolog defined predicates that we shall describe presently.

parse([CG],[CT|CTT],L,[]) parses the input list of content portions L (bound to ["TEXT1", "TEXT2","TEXT3"]) according to the logical structure grammar CG (bound to simple), binding CT to the resulting parse tree. Similarly, parse([FG],[FT|FTT1],L,[]) parses the input list of content portions L according to the layout structure grammar FG (bound to simple_layout), binding FT to the resulting parse tree. The success of FT^^out_trees([CT],OTT) guarantees that the appropriate stylistic correspondences obtain between elements of the specific logical structure represented by CT and the specific layout structure represented by FT (*i.e.* they are coordinated). Recall that in the discussion above we mentioned the apart "request" and "response". The reqs_ackd predicate assures that for each request in the logical structure there is indeed a respondent in the layout structure. Successful acknowledgement demands (among other things) the rejection of any context-free parse that does not have the content associated with the requesting text object appearing in a plate distinct from that receiving the content associated with the previous text object. Among the parse trees of figures 4-7 then, only those of figures 6 and 7 are acceptable. Figure 4 is rejected by the guard of the plate rule and figure 5 is rejected by reqs_ackd. FTT2 is now bound to a list of parse trees (bindings of FT) for which all the foregoing conditions obtained, that is, those of figures 6 and 7. min_pages(FTT2,FTT3) succeeds just in case FTT3 is bound to those parse trees FT (on the list FTT2) having the least number of pages, (pages being those subtrees having an attribute

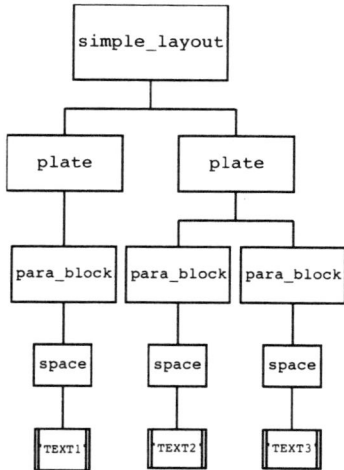

Figure 6: Third simple specific layout structure.

layout_type with value page). In this instance, that means exactly the parse tree of figure 6. Finally, min_place(L,FTT3,FTT) guarantees that FTT is bound to those FT's on the list FTT3 such that the content items appear as early as possible in the layout order (when compared with other members of FTT3) among the subtrees having an attribute layout_type with value page. Again, that means exactly the parse tree of figure 6.

5 Partial parsing

We have shown how the logic grammar representation of documents together with attributed parsing can give a declarative account of document layout. Our approach as described thus far would be hopelessly inefficient as a *practical* basis for document layout. In part this inefficiency is due to casting layout as an optimization problem in which we generate *all* of the candidate context-free parses, evaluate their attributes, and compare the various parses to find the optimal ones. We have remedied this particular inefficiency by resorting to *partial parsing*. We represent ordinary parse trees as Prolog terms. Each grammar generates a certain well-defined set of such terms. These trees are *total* in that they are always variable-free (ground). A partial parse tree for a grammar is (essentially) a term that unifies with some total parse tree of that grammar. We can define a preference ordering on the partial parse trees analogous to the one we defined on the total parse trees in such a way that any maximally preferred parse tree among the *total* parse trees also happens to be maximally preferred among the partial parse trees.

We can greatly restrict the parse trees that we need to consider in our

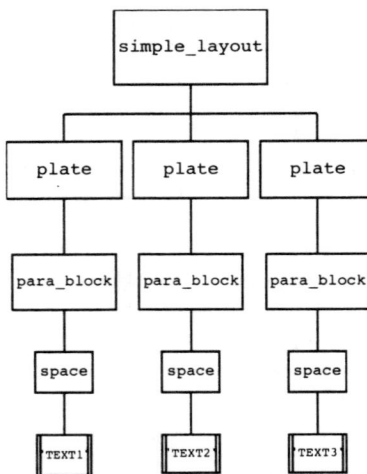

Figure 7: Fourth simple specific layout structure.

optimization problem. This follows from the fact that *layout* is the assignment of content items to pages in a manner consistent with the layout order of the content items. Thus, we are interested in the partial parses that correspond to having filled the first n pages with some initial segment of the input list of content portions. For a particular layout structure grammar and input list of content portions we define the n-page partial parse trees to be those partial parse trees generated by the grammar, each of which has n disjoint subtrees that are variable-free and whose root nodes all number among their valued attributes layout_type(page), and each of which spans an initial segment of the input list of content portions. For *these* partial parse trees we define the following preference ordering: An n-page partial parse tree P1 is preferred to an n-page partial parse tree P2 if

1. P1 satisfies the guards on all the productions used in its construction, but P2 does not;

2. P1 and P2 are unordered by the previous criterion, but P1 is stylistically consistent (coordinated) with the portion of the logical grammar (total) parse tree spanning the same initial segment of the input list as P1 while P2 is not; and

3. P1 and P2 are unordered by the previous criteria, but P1 spans a longer initial segment of the input list than does P2.

These partial parse trees can be generated in a top-down or bottom-up fashion, and in the order of increasing n. Straightforward modification of virtually any context-free grammar parsing algorithm and associated attribute valuation algorithms will provide a framework that will facilitate the early rejection of partial parses of which the eventually rejected total parses are substitution instances.

6 Future directions and conclusions

In order to address other sources of inefficiency in our prototype, we shall redesign and reimplement our parsers to exploit the classes of efficient context-free parsers and incremental attribute evaluators described in [Graham *et al.*, 1980] and [Reps, 1984]. Our current parsers take as input a coordinated pair of grammars and an input string of content items and produce a coordinated pair of parse trees. It is possible to compile the coordinated pair of grammars so as to generate a Prolog program specific to parsing according to those grammars. We intend to implement such a compilation stategy and thereby make additional gains in efficiency.

We have alluded to the fact that coordinated grammars (and hence document descriptions) have a declarative formal semantics. We are exploring a mathematical abstraction called a *markup scheme* [Brown and Wakayama, 1990], a formal framework modeled after program schemes [Greibach, 1975]. Markup schemes admit a least fixed point semantics derived from that of logic programs [Lloyd, 1987]. Moreover, within this framework it is possible to abstract away the details of various electronic markup languages and compare their expressive power according to the presence or absence of various features. We intend to carry out such a comparison among selected markups, examining their expressive power with respect various features of those representations.

In addition to making analytic use of markup schemes, we shall employ them in a synthetic fashion. The logic grammar formulation of document representation that we have presented is not particularly specialized to the representation of documents. We should like to conceive such a specialization, both for reasons of efficiency of document processing and to enhance the usability of the description language. To that end we hope to formulate a constraint logic programming language whose domain of discourse includes certain tree structures that describe particular documents, and whose constraints govern the admissibility of these tree structures according to structural or functional considerations.

We have offered here a powerful logic grammar-based paradigm for electronic document markup. This markup is of a declarative character, being, in effect, a collection of constraints on the logical and physical structure of documents. Moreover, this logic grammar representation admits a formal semantics that can be used directly to compare and contrast a variety of extant (and possible) electronic markup languages. To the best of our knowledge, coordinated grammars and their parsers can accommodate all of the descriptive and layout processing functionality enjoyed by extant electronic markup languages. We have demonstrated the possibility of syntax-directed basis for formalizing and realizing document layout. We recognize that substantially more work is needed to make a syntax-directed document layout a practical reality within the coordinated grammar framework. We have embarked upon an effort to achieve that reality.

References

[Abramson and Dahl, 1989] Harvey Abramson and Veronica Dahl. *Logic Grammars*. Springer-Verlag, New York, 1989.

[Brown and Wakayama, 1990] Allen L. Brown, Jr. and Toshiro Wakayama. Assigning meaning to markup. Manuscript to be submitted for publication, 1990.

[Deransart et al., 1988] Pierre Deransart, Martin Jourdan, and Bernard Lorho. *Attribute Grammars: Definitions, Systems and Bibliography*, volume 323 of *Lecture Notes in Computer Science*. Springer-Verlag, New York, 1988.

[Franchi-Zannettacci and Arnon, 1989] Paul Franchi-Zannettacci and Dennis S. Arnon. Context-sensitive semantics as a basis for processing structured documents. In Jacques André and Jean Bézivin, editors, *Proceedings of the Workshop on Object-Oriented Document Manipulation*, pages 135–146, 1989.

[Graham et al., 1980] Susan L. Graham, Michael A. Harrison, and Walter L. Ruzzo. An improved context-free recognizer. *ACM Trans. on Programming Languages and Systems*, 2(3):415–462, July 1980.

[Greibach, 1975] Sheila A. Greibach. *Theory of Program Structures: Schemes, Semantics, Verification*. Springer-Verlag, Berlin, 1975.

[Harrison, 1978] Michael A. Harrison. *Introduction to Formal Language Theory*. Addison-Wesley, Reading, Massachusetts, 1978.

[Lloyd, 1987] John W. Lloyd. *Foundations of Logic Programming*. Springer-Verlag, Berlin, second edition, 1987.

[Reps, 1984] Thomas W. Reps. *Generating Language-Based Environments*. MIT Press, Cambridge, Massachusetts, 1984.

[Shieber, 1986] Stuart M. Shieber. *An Introduction to Unification-Based Approaches to Grammar*, volume 4 of *CSLI Lecture Notes*. Center for the Study of Language and Information, Stanford, California, 1986.

[Weisz et al., 1988] Henri C. Weisz, Ian R. Campbell-Grant, Roy Hunter, Roy Pierce, L.J. Zeckendorf, and Barry J. Woods. Information processing, text and office systems, office document architecture (ODA) and interchange format. Technical Report DIS 8613, International Standards Organization (ISO), March 1988.

Structured Editing - Hypertext Approach: Cooperation and Complementarity

Anne-Marie Vercoustre

INRIA
B.P.105, 78153 Le Chesnay, France
e-mail: vercous@inria.inria.fr

ABSTRACT: As Hypertext systems are now widely available, many technical and conceptual problems have been identified. We argue here that such systems could take advantage of the proven technology of structured editors in order to provide both the user and the system with a conceptual document model providing a sound basis for the hierarchical links. A prototype combining structured editing and hypertext facilities proposes two approaches to implementing non-hierarchical links to subtrees: the first one uses the *paths* from the tree root as anchorage mechanism, while the second one uses tree pattern matching as a first step towards semantic and more manageable links.

KEYWORDS: structured editing, syntax directed editors, hypertext, scripted documents, anchor.

1 Introduction

Electronic Publishing currently involves different aspects of document production ranging from page setting and document formatting to editing and writing tasks, which are often supported by an information base.

Early tools were mainly printing systems, including either batch tools (text formatting systems like Troff and TEX) or else WYSIWYG text editors (such as FrameMaker, Macwrite, Macdraw, etc.). Although these tools may be concerned with the structuring of a document, they only address the layout structure of the document [Joloboff 1987].

On the other hand, syntax directed editors were designed to manipulate structured documents. They take full advantage of their structure for editing and navigation commands. These editors, such as Mentor [Donzeau 1980], the Cornell Program Synthesizer [Teitelbaum 1981], Mentor-Rapport [Mélèse 1984], and Grif [Quint and I.Vatton 1986; Furuta 1988], represent the documents using a tree structure that is built up according to the generic structure of the model (abstract syntax) rather a flat text.

Hypertexts provided a new approach to document organization and data base navigation. Hypertext systems are based on the various relationships between different document components and allow the user to navigate from one component to another by activating links. Such an approach extends the notion of **indexing** by giving access to information both within and between documents (references to another section, bibliographic references, etc.).

Hypertext may provide a promising framework for document design and writing activities (which are different from editing). These tasks involve the assembly and organization of ideas according to certain methodologies that remain to be studied in greater depth [Nanard 1985; Bisseret 1987].

However, just as structured and non-structured editing can be complementary [Mélèse 1984], it is the intention of this paper to show that *structured editing and hypertext approaches can also cooperate in order to benefit from the respective advantages of each.*

Structured editing is based on a single structure for a class of documents. This structure is formally described and allows a consistent structure of the documents to be maintained according to certain data models. Moreover, the reader may be made well aware of this model (by some meta display) and keeps it in mind when navigating in the system. So many hypertext problems vanish as far as hierarchical links are concerned.

While hypertext systems are beginning to be used widely and the size of the involved data increases, many problems are beginning to appear and to be clearly identified [Conklin 1987; Brown 1988 b,c], due to the great number of links, which makes the system unmanageable and the user quickly lost. The need for high-level abstractions is strongly set down to provide both the system and the user with sound underlying models of the manipulated documents [Garg 1988; Fiderio 1988; Brown 1988 b]. We believe that the Abstract Syntax used in structured editors can offer good support for solutions.

The complementarity of these approaches has been demonstrated through an experimental implementation with the Centaur system in which we have extended the Centaur structured editor towards a hypertext system using Centaur's annotation mechanism [Donzeau 1984; Borras *et al.* 1987]. The implementation uses annotations written in Lisp code as executable links to documents that are stored separately. *Access Paths* into trees are used as *anchoring* mechanism, as defined by Halasz and Schwartz [1990], for addressing locations within structured documents. Moreover, a HyperCard-like interface [Apple87] has been implemented with buttons showing the existing links.

After a short review of the characteristics and advantages of structured editors and hypertext systems (in section 2 and 3), section 4 presents the annotation and access path mechanisms used in Centaur. Section 5 describes the hypertext application and its user interface.

2 Hypertext Approach

The main characteristic of hypertext systems is their capacity to allow a certain number of documents and information sources to be consulted by following links. There are basically two types of link:
- **Hierarchical** (sometimes called organizational) links, which allow the user to study a document in greater or lesser "depth" and which are often associated with a zoom mechanism.
- **Non-hierarchical links,** which are used for specific applications such as cross-referencing within one document or between several documents, or links to collaborating authors' comments. Links may also be used to manage different versions of the documents or archive parts of them.

The links are generally typed, at least by their name, and can be displayed by means of a link marker (a button or an highlighted string acting as a button). This "button" allows the user to select the link he wants to follow.

Apart from the predefined types of links, hypertext systems often provide the user with the possibility of adding his own links and types of links.

The advantages of hypertext are now well agreed upon. Basically they are:
- Management of internal and intertextual references and facilities to access all the linked documents. The hypertext approach allows a non-linear reading of a document as well as a non-hierarchical organization of the material.
- Modularity of information: The same text can be referenced from several places, thus making duplication of the text unnecessary. Because of this, the information content is always coherent.
- Dynamic structuring of information: Through the use of links, it is possible to reorganize all (or part) of the information either hierarchically or non-hierarchically.

Even if this flexibility in organizing hypertext documents is very attractive, the need for structuring is apparent from several viewpoints:
- Structured documents are still the main kind of documents to be produced and read, at least on a paper support, with numbered sections, subsections, title, introduction and conclusion. Most hypertext systems involve nodes containing small units but provide tools for building hierarchies of units like in Concordia [Walker 1988]. Some systems allow several nodes to be aggregated in *composite units* (hierarchical or not) or the creation of structured nodes using templates (like in IDE built on NoteCards [Jordan 1989]). This addition of composite nodes proves the need for associating related information in higher

level structures. Meta models of such structures facilitate the rapid and accurate creation of regular network patterns in hypertexts.
- Creating documents with linearized structure from hypertext documents. It deals with the provision of a structured view of a part of the hypertext data base, according to some relevant selection criteria, using either the nodes' content [Engelbart 1968], or the semantics of the links [Nanard 1988].
- Providing the user with a structured display of the answers to his queries. Indeed, in information retrieval, the system often finds many answers because of imprecise queries. So, it has either to choose the most appropriate answer, or to present all the answers in a structured and summarized display and let the user choose.
- Enforcing the intention of the author: display of the topics hierarchy (for example the detailed table of contents) is a natural way of making explicit the structure of the author's mind. Following predefined paths through the hypertext network may be another approach for guiding the reader [Zellweger 1988], but does not exploit the reader's cognitive model (the Book Metaphor) that could help him to memorize the information.

3 Structured Editing

Structured document editors separate the logical structure of the documents handled from their display and their printing. The interactive and structured editors such as Mentor, the Cornell Program Synthesizer, Gandalf [Medina 19882], Pecan [Reiss 1984], were primarily developed for a particular class of documents: programs. Mentor-rapport was one instance of Mentor for writing technical documents, while Interleaf [Morris 1987] and Grif [Quint 1986] were designed to manipulate only documents (text with formulas, tables or graphics).

These systems represent the documents using a tree structure that is built up according to the generic structure of the model. The atoms in this structure are generally the line or the paragraph that are edited by a classical text editor.

Some systems (such as Grif or Interleaf) allow the handling of documents that contain references to another part of the document or intertextual references, which may be seen as a first step towards non-linear documents.

The advantages of structured editing were highlighted by Nanard [1987] and Furuta [1988] through comparison with classical text editing. The main advantages are:
- Separating the internal representation of the document from its presentation results in increased flexibility and reusability.

- The use of a presentation model allows a standard presentation of the documents and relieves the user of page-setting tasks during the authoring phase.
- The documents' structure reflects the legal relationships between the objects that make up the documents and contains more information than flat text. Maintaining the consistency of the documents is ensured by their conformity to a formal description. Compared to the hypertext approach, the hierarchical links are automatically and consistently updated. Moreover the user may be aware of the document models when browsing around using a natural and simple cognitive model of documents.
- The types represent supplementary constraints on the objects that allow each object to be processed appropriately and increase the power of the commands available to the user. Types may reduce the scope of commands like searching. Information retrieval methods, which, up to now, have mainly used keyword or string pattern matching [Brown 1988 b; Rijsbergen 1986; Frisse 1988; Lucarelli 1988], could take advantage of the tree structure and the abstract syntax for improving searching mechanisms.
- Browsers, graphical views, outlines with dynamic changing of detail level may be mechanically generated using reliable formal specifications. Outgoing and incoming links may be displayed at any level of detail, using a link inheritance mechanism like in [Feiner 1988].

The disadvantages of structured editing [Bisseret 1987; Nanard 1985] are the following:
- The hierarchical model of the document is too restricting for the user and does not correspond to the actual authoring activity. It is a fact that the authoring of a document implies the availability of a large quantity of information and other (small) documents that have no hierarchical links between them.
- Document models are too rigid: even if it is possible to select or define one's own model, it is often (too) difficult to switch from one model to another. Better modularity in the document model definition [Quint and I.Vatton 1989] will improve the situation.

These drawbacks are also expected to be overcome by adding hypertext facilities.

One of well known problems in hypertext is the management of the large number of links that are created. Frank Halasz, one of the developers of NoteCards, points out that the hierarchical structure is widely used in hypertext documents and that non-hierarchical reference links are much less frequent.

High level abstractions are therefore necessary to formalize the hierarchical links: Hierarchical hypertext links could be usefully replaced by a formal description of the hierarchical structure of the document. This description could be used by the system to ensure the validity of these links.

4 Centaur System

The Centaur system is a generic interactive environment [Borras *et al.* 1987]. When provided with the description of a particular language (including its syntax and semantics) it produces a language specific environment that includes a structured editor. Centaur is a second generation version (in Lisp) of the Mentor system [Lang 1985], which has been in use for several years as a program development environment.

Mentor-Rapport was one of the first experimental systems for editing technical documents combining both structured and textual editing.

Centaur uses an internal representation of the documents in the form of an abstract syntax tree structure. The abstract syntax defines the legal trees in the edited language. The Centaur kernel (a virtual tree processor or VTP) defines and implements a protocol to support the creation, handling and storing of the abstract syntax trees. It may be read as a collection of abstract data types corresponding to the various entities handled by the system. Moreover the VTP ensures the modularity and extension capacities of the system by using an object oriented approach. The annotation mechanism allows the system to be extended through the dynamic addition of new object types.

4.1 The annotations

Most documents contain references to information situated in another part of the document or in another document (footnotes, references to another chapter or bibliographic references, etc.). This information takes the form of annotations, which are included without altering the structure of the main document.

Annotations were originally introduced in Mentor as a means to handle program comments in a structured way. They gradually evolved into a more general mechanism to enrich the abstract representations for various purposes. In Centaur the annotations are now organized according to their specific role and the formalism in which they must be expressed. Hence the annotation mechanism allows non hierarchical combinations of documents belonging to different formalisms into so-called **multi-formalism documents.** Indeed multi-formalism documents, as used for example in software ingineering [Donzeau *et al.* 1984] may be seen as hypertext structures.

In the VTP, the roles of annotations have to be "declared" in advance and are embodied as objects in a class called *decor*. The definition of a decor includes its name, the type of objects that may be annotated and the type of objects that may be used as annotations characterized by this decor.

As the annotations are strongly typed by the definition of their decor, a specific display and selection of each decor may be provided in an object-oriented approach. This is an important property in hypertext applications where the links are often characterized by buttons that activate an action according to the type of link.

4.2 Locations in a tree

A designation inside a structured object may actually designate either the sub-object that is placed at the designated location, or the location of that sub-object within the larger one.

The usual method for designing subtrees of a given tree uses pointers towards nodes of the tree. This solution is simple and easy to use. Most of the centaur primitives work with the pointers. However, when we want to do more complex things, we are too strictly limited by this method. Centaur is now provided with a new method for designating subtrees [Clément 1988]. This method designates any subtree, or any collection of subtrees of a given tree, by the notion of access path. We call *Path*[1]. the link from the top of the tree to the top of any designated subtree. With the paths, we can consider the relationship between two trees, more independently from the implementation technique used for the tree. We can answer questions like "are these two subtrees children of this third" more easily than when using pointers.

The path mechanism may be used to extend the application domain of the annotations and improve their management.

Originally introduced as a generalization of the property lists (introduced by the Lisp language), the annotations were firstly used as values attached to the subtree. The annotations, like the comments, were edited and saved at the same time as the annotated object. The need then arose to consider not only the annotation values, but also the location of the annotations. When an annotation is hooked at a location, the annotation value is not affected by editing the object at this location.

When the annotation locations are implemented using the above path mechanism, the paths are updated when the corresponding location is changed. For example, for the "insert before" command, there corresponds an increment of 1 on all the paths with the same "left-hand factor" as the path associated to the current position. When the annotation locations are **inside** the modified subtree, the updating may be a little more difficult, because the new subtree may have a

---

[1] The word path is used instead of access path for short. It should not be confused with the concept of path as "ordered traversal of some links" used in some Hypertext systems [Zellweger 1988]

completely different structure. In this case, *Diff* algorithms [FRI89] on trees could be of some use for establishing the mapping between old and new positions.

On the same way, the link destination (subtree) may be referred to by an access path into the target document. Indeed paths provide a **relative naming** of objects inside a larger one, that will be used as **anchorage value** according to the definition given in [Halasz and Schwartz 1990]. Of course paths have to be updated when the target document is being edited. Link destination could be dynamically updated (when the target is trying to be accessed), using paths as a *cache* on the set of locations: all target positions in a document will be memorized in a *path variable* (a list of paths) with a name for each position. As it was mentioned earlier, while the document is edited, path variables are kept consistent. When a position is being accessed through a path, names are compared. If they are different, the old path stored in the link will be replaced by the one in the path variable.

While giving a fast access within structured document, we believe than paths offer a more tractable anchorage value than pointers towards subtrees. More advanced examples of the use of access paths may be found in [Clément88].

4.3 Hypercentaur mechanisms

Hypercentaur prototype is a multi-language, multi-decor environment to facilitate the implementation of hypertext applications. It uses a particular class of decor corresponding to annotations written in Le_Lisp, which is the implementation language of Centaur.

The Hypercentaur annotations have the following characteristics:
- All the functions are generic with regard to the decor to which they belong. The decor is generally characteristic of the application concerned. In hypertext-like applications, the decors, as webs in Intermedia [Yankelovitch87], provide the means to separate the links according to their application context.
- It is possible to dynamically define "subtypes" of decor within an application. This allows a better structure of the hypertext application and facilitates the creation of new types of "links" by the user.
- Executable code is attached to the annotation. A partition of the code is provided by the subtype mechanism. When a subtype is selected (by program or user action), the specific code is selected by a filtering process in the Lisp annotation tree.
- Buttons can be interactively created and associated to a decor subtype. When clicked down, the corresponding code will be executed.

```
example :
```

```
(selectq arg1
    (eval-in-package
        (setq #:sys-package:colon 'interface))
    (printp (ecrirep (current-tree-k)))
)
```

This example is taken from the Le_Lisp environment. The above Lisp code is the annotation content. The type of this annotation has been pre-declared by the declaration of its decor as annotation in Lisp of Lisp trees.

Looking at the annotation content (a Lisp *selectq* function), we can identify two selectors: "eval-in-package" and "printp". The code associated to the "eval-in-package" label was designed to be activated by program (namely the Lisp evaluator). The code associated to "printp" will be activated by clicking on a "printp" button, displaying to the user an internal tree view (whereas the current one is a linearized text view).

5 Hypertext Application

To add the advantages of a hypertext approach to those of a structured editor for document production, we have used the above Hypercentaur mechanisms. We defined a specific decor named "hyperlink" that is used to implement non-hierarchical links.

5.1 Links Implementation

The names of links are implemented as sub-types of the "hyperlink" type that characterizes this application. A specific link is activated by evaluating the Lisp code associated to the corresponding sub-type.

```
example :

(selectq arg1
    (source (#:interface:goto
                "/u/croap/vercous/rapport/hypertext/"
                "hyperlink"
                'all))
    (help (#:interface:goto
                "/u/croap/vercous/rapport/hypertext/"
                "hyperhelp"
                '((3 (1 . all)))))
    (notes (#:interface:goto
                "/u/croap/vercous/rapport/hypertext/"
                "abstract"
                'all)))
```

In this example, there are three links to external documents, which are implemented by an annotation in the "hyperlink" decor with the sub-types "source", "notes" and "help". The Lisp function (:goto) is associated to each of these links. Activating a link will jump to the position in the document concerned (after having loaded it and displayed it in a new window if this document has not yet been opened).

"all" and ((3 (1 . all))) are two examples of paths. The "all" path designates the root of the tree, while the "(3 (1 . all))" path designates the particular sub-tree corresponding to "the third child of the root, then the first element of the list node (implemented as binary tree)".

The names of links give the user some information on what kind of document is connected here.

Unlike HyperCard, we do not use a ad-hoc language such as Hypertalk to implement links. Any Lisp code may be put into the links and activated by buttons. However tailor-made functions (such as :goto function) have been implemented for this application and function calls to those functions are generated interactively.

5.2 Interface

The HyperCard-like user interface allows the user:
- To create a specific link (i.e of a given name) from the current object to another object (tree or subtree) designated by its name or its location pointed out with the mouse. As in HyperCard, the interactive creation of a link generates code, Lisp in this case taking the place of Hypertalk.
- to create a new type of link; the user is prompted for the name of this new link. The link is then created at the current place but as yet without referencing anything. Predefined links (like link on bibliography or help link) may be automatically loaded and connected to predefined documents.
- to display a link marker: The display is object-oriented. By default, the link is displayed by its name, but it is possible to define another method. In particular, the user can display all or part of the object referred to by the link.
- to delete a link.
- to edit a link as a Lisp tree using Centaur-Lisp environment.
- to activate a link using a button that is created dynamically and displays the name of the link.

Example of displayed links:

```
[notes]
[help]
[CEN87]
```

The links "notes" and "help" are displayed by name (display by default) whereas the bibliographic reference link (whose name is "bib") is displayed by the bibliographic reference it refers to.

5.3 Dynamic links

As the updating and management mechanisms for the paths have not yet been fully implemented, we tried in parallel another quite different approach by introducing some semantic aspect.

For example, the reference to section 3 of a document simply means that the selected section is the third section at the moment when it is read on paper (the linear reference being the most appropriate to a written medium). What in fact interests us is the section entitled "Structured Editing", even if it may be found in section 2 or section 4 in another version of the document.

The solution adopted is to create an executable link in the form of a call to a search function (:find). This carries out the search by pattern matching on an incomplete tree structure that represents a section titled "Structured Editing".

In this case the link will be implemented in the following form:

```
(selectq arg1
    (ref (#:interface:find
              "/u/croap/vercous/rapport/hypertext/"
              "mydocument"
              (#:interface:section "Structured Editing"))))
```

This kind of link is called "implicit link", by Brown [BRO88b], by opposition to "explicit link" between two specified documents. The command "find" dynamically establishes a link on an object satisfying a certain criterion (such as a certain pattern in a text or tree structure). In the case where the find command is interpreted as "search the following occurrence" a link will even be established on a set of objects.

We used here the model of the document to improve the information retrieval mechanisms. Both the structure (search in depth- or breadth-first order) and the abstract syntax may be combined in the search mechanism. By taking advantage of the formal description of the objects handled (including syntax and semantics) and by introducing more sophisticated semantic criteria, we will have the means to implement hypertext systems whose consistency may be verified and maintained.

6 Conclusions

We have argued the benefits in combining the structured editing and the hypertext approaches for managing documents. First we replace a great number of small text units, linked both with structured and un-structured links, with large structured documents connected by some (instead of very many) unstructured links.

The Hypercentaur prototype validated the use of a generic structured editor as support for implementing an hypertext network. Formal document models provide the system with a sound basis for managing hierarchical links, both for updating links and for building structured views of the information. On the other side, the user is given a clear model of documents, which lets him navigate from one high level structure to another without being disoriented.

Executable non-hierarchical links have been implemented either as goto functions using path access in a large document, or as search functions using tree pattern matching. Even if these approaches are not new by themselves (compare to the Goto and Find functions in Hypertalk), their implementations take full advantage of structured documents.

Going further in that direction and based on the formal approach, these links should be semantically defined so that they may be **interpreted** by the system when activated. Semantic links via an appropriate logic will improve the control and consistency of hypertext systems. These links could be alternatively implemented using a query language in place of Lisp, which would increase the search power in the database, under the condition that the formal semantics of the document have been defined [Rijsbergen8686].

On the other hand, the notion of structured views of hyperdocuments should be extended by increasing the power of decompilation languages used in the structured editors [Borras *et al.* 1987], or by generalizing the notion of conceptual documents [Nanard 1987], which allow the definition of a (a posteriori) mapping between (part of) a hypertext document and the structured document that is displayed or printed.

Still under development, Centaur and Hypercentaur are even now good platforms for experimenting with the use of generic mechanisms for hypertext environments. We intend in particular to study further the "runtime layer", which we have not yet investigated thoroughly.

7 Acknowledgements

The author wishes to thank F. Rouaix for many fruitful discussions and for having implemented most of the hypercentaur features.

Thanks are also extended to A. Bisseret who inspired much of this work through his enthusiastic initiation into HyperCard.

References

[Apple87] Apple Computer Inc., *Macintosh HyperCard user's guide*, 1987.

[Bisseret87] A. Bisseret, *Towards computer-aided text production*, Rapport de Recherche, INRIA No.665, May 1987.

[Brown88 b] P.J. Brown, Linking and searching within hypertext, *Electronic publishing*, vol.1(1),45-53, April 1988.

[Brown88 c] P.J. Brown, Hypertext: The Way Forward CACM, vol.31(7),183-191, 1988.

[Borras87] P. Borras, D. Clément, Th. Despeyroux, J. Incerpi, G. Kahn, B. Lang, V. Pascual, *"CENTAUR: The system"*, Research Report, INRIA 777, December 1987.

[Clément88] D. Clément, *Designating subtrees in Centaur*, GIPE, Esprit project N0.348, January 88.

[Conklin87] J. Conklin, Hypertext: An Introduction and Survey, *IEEE Computer*, Vol.20, No.19, Sept.1987.

[Donzeau80] V. Donzeau-Gouge et al., *Programming environments based on structured editors, The Mentor experience*, Rapport de Recherche INRIA, n.26, 1986.

[Donzeau84] V. Donzeau-Gouge, G. Kahn, B. Lang, B. Mélèse, Document structure and modularity in Mentor, *Proc. of the ACM Software engineering Symposium on Practical software development environments*, Software Engineering notes, 1984, Vol. 9 - no 3.

[Engelbart68] D.C. Engelbart, W.K. English, A Research Center for Augmenting Human Intellect, *AFIPS Conf. Proc.*, Vol.33, Part 1, he Thomson Book Company, 1968.

[Feiner88] S. Feiner, Seeing the Forest for the trees: Hierarchical Display of Hypertext Structure, it ACM Conference on Office Information System, Palo Alto, 23-25 March 1988, *SIGOIS Bull.*, Vol.9(2-3), p.205-12, April-July 1988.

[Fiderio88] Janet Fiderio, A Grand Vision, *Byte*, October 1988.

[Frisse88] Mark Frisse, From Text to Hypertext, *Byte*, October 1988.

[Frilley89] F. Frilley, *Differenciation d'ensembles structurés*, Thèse de Doctorat, Université Paris VII, Février 1989.

[Furuta88] R. Furuta, V.Quint, J.André, Interactively editing structured documents, *Electronic Publishing*, vol.1(1),19-44, April 1988.

[Garg88] Pankaj K.Garg, Abstraction mechanisms in hypertext In *Communications of ACM*, Vol.31, No.7, July 1988.

[Halasz90] F. Halasz, M.Schwartz, The Dexter Hypertext Reference Model, *Proc. of Hypertext Standardisation Workshop*, January 16-18, 1990, NISTSP 500-178, pp. 95-131.

[Joloboff87] V. Joloboff, Représentation des documents: Etat de l'art, recherche, *Actes des Journées "Structure de/for Documents"*, p 81-103, Aussois, Janvier 1987.

[Jordan89] D.S. Jordan, D.M. Russel, A.M.S Jensen, R.A. Rogers, Facilitating the Development of Representations in Hypertext with IDE, In *Proc. of Hypertext'89*, Pittsburgh, Pennsylvania, 5-8 November, 1989.

[Lang85] B. Lang, *Mentor. Design and implementation of the kernel of a program manipulation system*, Conference on integrated project support environment, J.A.McDermid Ed,York, 1985.

[Lucarelli88] D. Lucarelli, A search strategy for large document bases, *Electronic Publishing*, Vol.1(2), p.105-116, Sept.1988.

[Medina82] R. Medina-Mora, *Syntax directed editing: toward intergrated programming environments*, CMU-CS-82-113, Carnegie-Mellon University, 1982.

[Mélèse84] B. Mélèse, Structured editing - Unstructured editing, Coopération and complémentarity, *Actes de 2ième Colloque de génie logiciel*, Nice Juin 1984.

[Morris87] R.A. Morris, The Interleaf User Interface, in PROTEXT III: *Proceedings of the Third International Conference on Text Processing System*, J.J.H.Miller ed.,p.20-29, Boole Press,1987.

[Nanard85] M. Nanard, L. Nanard, J. Falgueirettes, *Top down or Bottom up Approach for Document Structuration*, In PROTEXT I, Dublin, October 1985.

[Nanard87] M. Nanard, L. Nanard, Interactive Manipulation of Structured Documents, In PROTEXT IV, Boston, October 1987.

[Nanard88] M. Nanard, H. Richy, L. Nanard, Conceptual documents - Mechanisms for specifying active views, *ACM Conference on Document Processing Systems*, Santa Fe, Dec. 1988.

[Quint86] V. Quint, I. Vatton, Grif:An Interactive System for Structured Document manipulation, In *Proceeding of EP'86 Conférence*, Univ. of Nottingham,14-16 April 1986.

[Quint89] V. Quint, I. Vatton, Modularity in Structured Documents, In *Proc. of WOODMAN'89*, Rennes (France), May 29-31, 1989.

[Reiss84] S.P. Reiss, Graphical Program development with PECAN Program Development System, In *ACM Sigplan Notices*, Vol 19(5), 1984.

[Rijsbergen86] C.J. Rijsbergen, A non-classical logic for information retrieval, *The Computer Journal*, Vol.29(6), p.29-33, 1986.

[Teitelbaum81] T. Teitelbaum, T. Reps, The Cornell program Synthesizer: a syntax directed programming environment, *Communication of the ACM*, Vol 24(9), pp. 563-573, 1981.

[Walker88] J.H. Walker, Supporting Document development with Concordia, *IEEE Computer*, p.48-59, January 1988.

[Yankelovitch87] N. Yankelovitch, G.P. Landow, D. Cody, Creating Hypermedia Materials for English Literature Students, SIGCUE, spring/summer 1987.

[Zellweger88] P. Zellweger, Active Paths through multimedia documents, In J.C van Vliet (editor), *Document Manipulation and Typography*, Proc. of EP'88, Nice (France), April 20-22, 1988.

An ODA Page Planner for Professional Publishing

Giovanni Guardalben and Mose' Giacomello

Hi.T Srl
Ingegneria per la Microinformatica,
Via Carlo Steeb 7, 37122 Verona,
Italy.

ABSTRACT: By its own nature, *Professional Publishing* requires that document processing be completed in many steps. This is in stark contrast to *Desktop Publishing*, where all actions leading to the printed page are performed by a single application and usually by the same person. Nowadays, a typical *Professional Publishing* environment comprises a large database and processing server, usually on mainframe, and many external processors performing integrated functions, usually on independent workstations. We believe that the front-end function of layout page planning can be served by local applications running on relatively inexpensive graphics workstations. *PcPage* is a personal computer application that tries to ease and make more efficient the work of layout page planning. Since page planning is a transitional step in document processing, it interacts with other tools and applications. To do so, it has to be built on rich data structures and standard data exchange mechanisms. With these goals in mind, we based *PcPage* on the *ODA/ODIF ISO* standards and we chose *Microsoft Windows* as its graphics interface environment. This paper describes *PcPage* implementation of the *ODA* hierarchical data structure and the sophisticated user interface built upon it.

1 Introduction

In this paper, we describe a software prototype for improving *page planning* (also called page layout dummying) in *Professional Publishing* environments, such as newspapers and magazines. The software product, called *PcPage*, is a *Microsoft Windows* [Ms-Windows88] application and it runs on personal computers equipped with high resolution graphical displays. It allows an excellent view of page details for fine sizing of small elements of the page.

PcPage internal and exchange data structures are based on the *Office Document Architecture (ODA)* [Oda88] standard in order to have a truly expandable data system and to achieve high portability.

Unlike most pc-based publishing products, *PcPage* is not a Desktop Publishing (DTP) product. In fact, as stated previously, this *page planner* is aimed at the *Professional Publishing* market, and hence, the functions it is meant to support are fewer and more specialized than those performed by any commercial DTP product [Chen88].

1.1 The Professional Publishing Market

In a small publishing environment, a single person, or a small group performs all the steps leading to the printed page. For these people, it is preferable to use a full-featured DTP product and try to fit the creativity of graphics professionals to the capabilities of a software tool. Basically, a small printing shop requires a *multi-function* publishing tool even to the extent of producing lower quality printouts.

On the contrary, a large volume, *Professional Publishing* environment has very different requirements. The different activities required to produce the final printed material are generally performed by scores of different people, with varied degrees of technical skills. Usually, the department organization sets the constraints for the tools to be used. Especially now, with the so-called *fourth-wave* in full swing (whereby off-the-shelf hardware is packaged with customized publishing software), more and more companies pretend that the publishing software be adjusted to their needs, rather than the contrary.

Since it is hard to produce huge, all-encompassing software products that respond to the needs of diverse organizations, we think that the *Professional Publishing* market should be proposed *sets of integrated tools*, each performing a very specific and unique function. In this way, the same tool could be re-used in many different environments, provided that its functional interface to others tools (or functions) and its user interface be flexible enough for different people.

Furthermore, a tool should not require frequent feed-back to other *adjacent* tools, because this may result in overall productivity losses. For instance, a typical *page planner* usually provides the composition engine (i.e., the composer) with areas where the text has to *flow*. A dumb *page planner* does not know how much text may *flow* in its areas, and does not even know how much text is actually available to fill its areas. With such a crude tool, just to remove text overflows, or empty spaces in the page, the interactions with the composer are continuous for the processing of every single page element.

It is therefore mandatory to have *smart* tools that require limited feedback with adjacent tools in the production line. In the case of a *page planner*, being smart may be associated with the ability to estimate area occupation by text, without having to perform text composition. Or, it may be derived from the graphical capabilities of the tool, whereby the visual *weight* of page elements may be inferred from the resulting page model, without requiring WYSIWIG display of the hyphenated and justified text.

1.2 What is Page Planning ?

We may define *page planning* as the act of establishing the appearance of a printed page, by *designing* all areas that contain page elements such as text, tables and images. By *area design,* we intend area filling, dimension specification, relations to neighbouring areas and presentation feature attribution [Luniewski88].

An area may be filled by many different page elements. There is a choice among *text, tables and images.* This choice sets the criteria for dimension specification, relations to neighbours and presentation features. For instance, an area filled with text, may require different margins from those of an area containing an image.

Furthermore, a text area (for instance, an article) may have lower overlapping priority than an image area and as a consequence it will always be hidden under an image. Finally, a text area may need different presentation features (which include also typographical aspects of an area) from those of an image area. All these features represent the final product of a *page planner.*

Since *page planning* is one of the many functions of the publishing process, it interacts with adjacent tools performing different activities. It does so, by exchanging data and process information. A *page planner* stands between the content producer (i.e., the text writer and the image producers) and the composition engine (or composer). A *page planner* establishes the *relations* between the content elements and the areas where the content is shown. These pieces of information, together with the contents, are fed to the composer.

There are many aspects of a *page planner* that may improve productivity. A realistic model of printed page may aid the graphics professionals to decide the size and the typographical features of an area. Approximate calculations of the amount of text that may fit an area, may reduce the need for frequent text recompositions. Furthermore, it may be useful to have libraries of single or groups of pre-formatted areas with relative attribute data [Johnson88].

1.3 PcPage

We feel that *PcPage* provides an answer to many of the requisites of an efficient *page planner.*

It is fully configurable: the user may decide the units for the grid, the rulers and the movements. Besides, it may specify unique units for specific objects, or for a special display called the *indicators* display, which shows the current cursor position, the current object size and position (plus the most recent size and position changes).

It may calculate approximate *text occupation* even for very fragmented text areas or for linked text areas (such as an article spread over many areas) by means of empirical functions.

It introduces (configurable) very powerful *overlapping* rules for the different types of page elements. Although page elements may ultimately be reduced to text, tables, or images, they are further subdivided into more specialized types such as titles, articles, etc.

Further, we believe that the following features add an extra level of sophistication to the product:

- it is a PC-based product using a powerful and yet economic graphics interface platform: Microsoft Windows;
- it may work both as a network station and in terminal emulation;
- its internal data structure and interchange format are taken from the *ODA* standard [De la Beaujardeire88];
- its programming structure is built according to the *object-oriented* paradigm, although the actual coding is done in C language [Alagic88; Cox87].

In the next sections, we are going to describe in more details the technical aspects of the *ODA* data structure implementation (Section 2), and the functionality of the product, with special emphasis on *page planning* (Section 3). Then, we draw final conclusions (Section 4).

2 The Oda Data Structure in PcPage

2.1 Introduction

ODA is a standard of structured documents. The *ODA* standard defines its notion of a document, of a document class, and of the basic processes of editing, formatting, and imaging [Oda88; Murata89; Peterlongo89; Muscate89].

Within a document, two different *hierarchical structures* can be distinguished. The *logical* structure shows the composition of a document from *logical* components such as sections and paragraphs. The *layout* structure shows the composition of a document from *layout* elements such as pages, frames and blocks.

Besides *ODA*, *ODIF* (Office Document Interchange Format) is a standard developed by ISO to facilitate the interchange of documents. While *ODA* describes the concepts embodied in the standard in English, *ODIF* describes the bit and bytes of the actual encoding format.

An ODA Page Planner for Professional Publishing

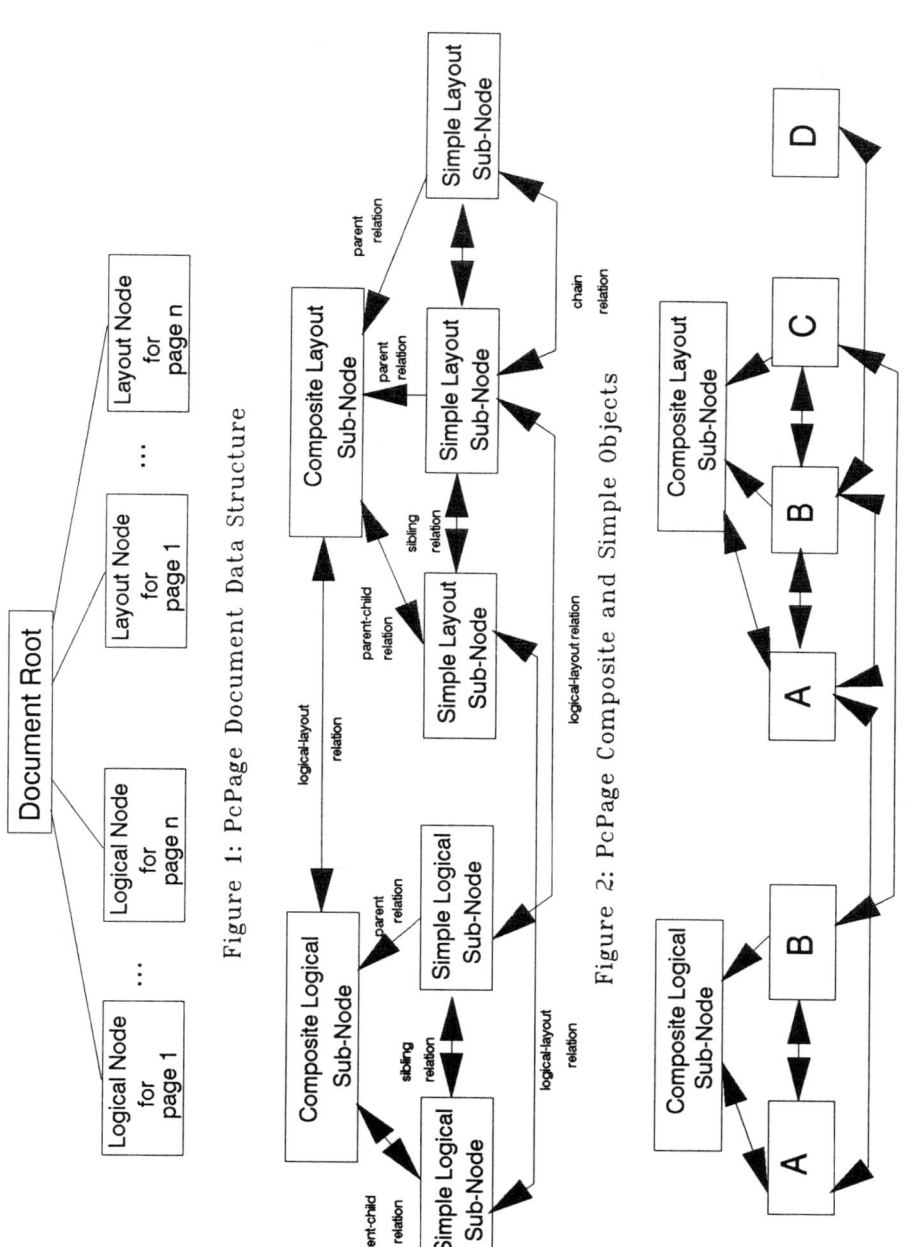

Figure 1: PcPage Document Data Structure

Figure 2: PcPage Composite and Simple Objects

Figure 3: Document Chain and Composite Object Interaction

We have chosen the *ODA* standard as the underlying data structure for *PcPage* for many reasons. The most important one is the *adaptability* of the *ODA* data model. The *ODA* standard can be applied to a variety of publishing environments.

Different publishing environment may privilege the usage of either of the two hierarchical structure mentioned above. For instance, the common *word processor* uses almost exclusively the *logical* structure of a document, since all *layout* information is within the text and very little *layout* structure is available. At the opposite side, in a newspaper environment the *layout* of a document is strongly emphasized, since almost every *layout* element has also a *logical* significance. Thus the *logical* hierarchy is almost redundant.

Furthermore, thanks to the *ODIF* standard, data exchange with other publishing tools and products is greatly eased. In most cases, we find that using a rich data model facilitates data exchange, since it is easier to build data converters when all data elements are defined within our model. And, *ODA* is surely a rich and flexible data model [Behrman88].

Finally, we like *ODA object-oriented* document architecture. Documents are represented with hierarchies of objects, which are instances of object classes. With this model, the actual programme implementation is greatly facilitated, provided that *object-oriented* programming techniques are utilized.

2.2 PcPage Data Structures

Following the *ODA* data model, *PcPage* data structure is made of two hierarchical structures: the *logical* structure and the *layout* structure. In our data model, for ease of development, we define a common ancestor root to all higher level nodes of both the *logical* and the *layout* trees. We call this root node the *document root*.

Underneath the *document root*, we find *logical* and *layout* page nodes, as shown in Figure 1. According to our *page planner* requirement specifications, there is no need to group pages into page sets and refer to them as a single entity (node). In the *page planning* process, the page is the ultimate criteria for selection.

Although both the *logical* and the *layout* page nodes may refer to the same document page, their semantic is quite different. The *layout* page node is the root node of all the *layout* sub-nodes whose top-left corner is in that page (in this way, *PcPage* can handle areas straddled over two pages). The *logical* page node is the root node of all the *logical* sub-nodes that are related to a *layout* sub-node whose top-left corner is contained in that page.

An ODA Page Planner for Professional Publishing

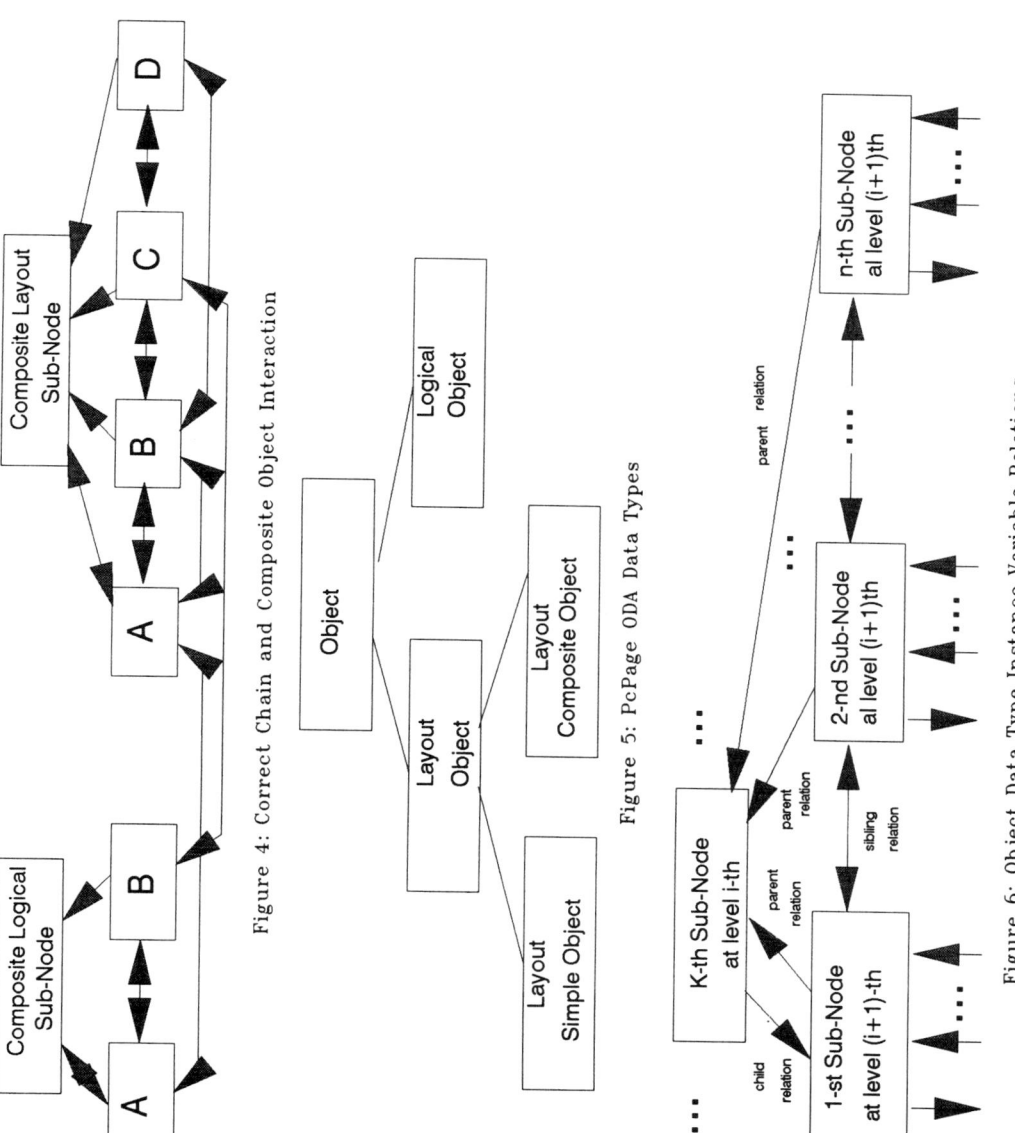

Figure 4: Correct Chain and Composite Object Interaction

Figure 5: PcPage ODA Data Types

Figure 6: Object Data Type Instance Variable Relations

Since a *logical* sub-node may be related to more than one *layout* sub-node, it belongs to the same page of the first related *layout* sub-node. A *logical* node is always related to one or more *layout* nodes. For instance, an article (a *logical* sub-node) may fill one or more areas (*layout* sub-nodes) on one or more pages. The article *logical* sub-node belongs the *logical* page node corresponding to the *layout* page containing the first article area.

A *logical* and a *layout* sub-nodes may be the roots to lower level *logical* and *layout* sub-trees, as in Figure 2. We call these sub-nodes, *composite* nodes. At the lowest level, a sub-node is just a leaf of the *logical* or the *layout* structure. We call this sub-node, a *simple* node. In *PcPage* data structure, we assume that a *composite logical* sub-node is always related to a single *composite layout* sub-node, whereby a *simple logical* sub-node may be related to more than one *simple layout* sub-nodes. This may seem an unnecessary restriction in our data model. However, we find that it does not produce any unwanted side-effects on the user interface functionality and it improves data access speed and simplicity.

The relationship between a *logical* and a *layout* sub-node is implemented in *PcPage* as follows. Since a single *logical* sub-node may be related to more than one *layout* sub-node, a logical sub-node is linked to a list of *layout* sub-nodes.

To improve efficiency, instead of including a list of pointers to *layout* sub-nodes in the *logical* sub-node, each *layout* node contains a forward and backward dedicated pointer to the following and the preceding *layout* sub-node. The backward pointer of the first *layout* sub-node of the list points to the related *logical* sub-node. We call the *layout* sub-node list, a *chain* (Figure 2). There are intriguing interactions between a *chain* and a *composite* object.

Let us consider the case of Figure 3 and Figure 4. Figure 3 shows an example of incorrect interaction between a *chain* and a *composite object* (or *group*). In Figure 3 example, we find a *composite logical* sub-node related to a *composite layout* sub-node. The *composite logical* sub-node contains two *logical* sub-nodes, A and B respectively. There is a *composite layout* sub-node and four *simple layout* sub-nodes. Of these four, three (A, B and C) belong to the *composite layout* sub-node, and one, D, does not. We also find that the *logical simple* sub-node A is related to *layout simple* nodes A, B and D, and that the *logical simple* sub-node B is related to the *layout simple* sub-node C. Since any node of the two hierarchies can be manipulated by editing operations such as *cut*, *copy* and *paste*, it results that by cutting the two related composite objects, the *layout simple* sub-node D is left with an incorrect dangling pointer to thenon-existent *layout* sub-node, B. Figure 4 shows a possible correction of above example.

2.3 Object Oriented Implementation

As mentioned before, *ODA* is an *object-oriented* document architecture. Documents are represented with hierarchies of objects, which are instances of object classes. In *PcPage*, we have given an *object-oriented* interpretation of some aspects of *ODA*. We have introduced the following object data types, as shown in Figure 5: **Object, LayoutObject, LogicalObject, LayoutSimpleObject, LayoutCompositeObject.**

The *Object* data type takes care of establishing the tree structure of the *logical* and *layout* hierarchical structures. Each *Object* is a node of a tree. Each node has the same data structure, which is given by the following instance variables: a pointer to the parent, a pointer to a preceding sibling, a pointer to a next sibling and a pointer to the first child (see Figure 6). The model is very simple (a linked list structure), but it allows fast prototyping and development, thanks to the fixed size of each node data structure. The methods implemented by the *Object* data type are those of node creation, update, deletion and those of forward and backward tree traversal.

The *LayoutObject* data type is a specialization of the *Object* data type. Besides inheriting all *Object* methods, it has additional instance variables and methods. Each *layout* node has a pointer to a *logical* node, a forward and backward pointer to other *layout* objects belonging to a *chain*. Besides, each *LayoutObject* carries scalar data such as dimensions, object type, units. The methods introduced by the *LayoutObject* data type refer especially to *chain* management and layout property attribution.

The *LogicalObject* data type is a specialization of the *Object* data type. Each *logical* node points to a *layout* node by means of pointer to *layout Object*. *Logical* objects carry information about the content and the type of page element (i.e., article, title, summary, etc.).

The LayoutSimpleObject and LayoutCompositeObject are a refinement of the LayoutObject data type. Their main purpose is to handle object appearance, relations (especially overlapping properties) and display sequences (to handle properly transparency and opacity). The LayoutCompositeObject methods refine the management of Object composite objects.

The actual programming of the *object-oriented* structure has been done in C. It is well-kwown that C allows *object-oriented* programming (by means of pointers and structures), but does not support it. It is well underway the conversion of the *ODA* data structure manager to C++.

3 PcPage User Interface

3.1 General Functions

PcPage is a *Microsoft Windows* application that allows the user to update and display document pages by graphical means only. When specific events occur, the user may be prompted for an answer through *dialog boxes* or application dependent interaction tools [Furuta82]. To facilitate user actions, the functionality of all available tools follows closely *Microsoft Application Style Guide* [Ms-Windows88].

The application is based on a main graphical program and a set of corollary utility programs. These programs permit total *configuration* of page parameters.

It is possible to define page units, ruler units, page object units and size and movement indicators units, as shown in Figure 7. The user may define complex grids with regular or user-specified sticky positions. Furthermore, the user can establish its own object overlapping rules and transpareny and opacity relations among objects.

All above configuration parameters are grouped into *layout styles*. These styles may be page specific or whole publication specific. During page loading, the user is prompted for a choice of page style and publication style.

Some parameter configuration choices can be made also while working interactively on a page. For instance, the user may specify one of three *zoom* levels: a whole page zoom, a half page zoom and a quarter page zoom. Each page in its own zoom level is displayed in a *child* window and its dimensions are always scaled to maintain fixed x:y ratio. A page can always be worked on, whatever the size of the encapsulating window.

The user can also choose dynamically from three (out of eight) default *grid* configurations for both x and y axes. Each *grid* contains marked positions both at regular positions and at user defined spots.

There are many ways of *displaying* a page. Page elements may be shown with or without borders and with or without grid. It is also possible to show those page elements that overlap others. Finally, pictures may be displayed in full details or only with a default background pattern to improve page redisplay time.

The user is given prompt feedback from whatever action he performs. For instance, the system cursor changes its shape to suggest possible actions. When the cursor is moving idle it is represented by an arrow. When it meets a selected page element (usually a rectangle) it may change into a double-arrow

An ODA Page Planner for Professional Publishing

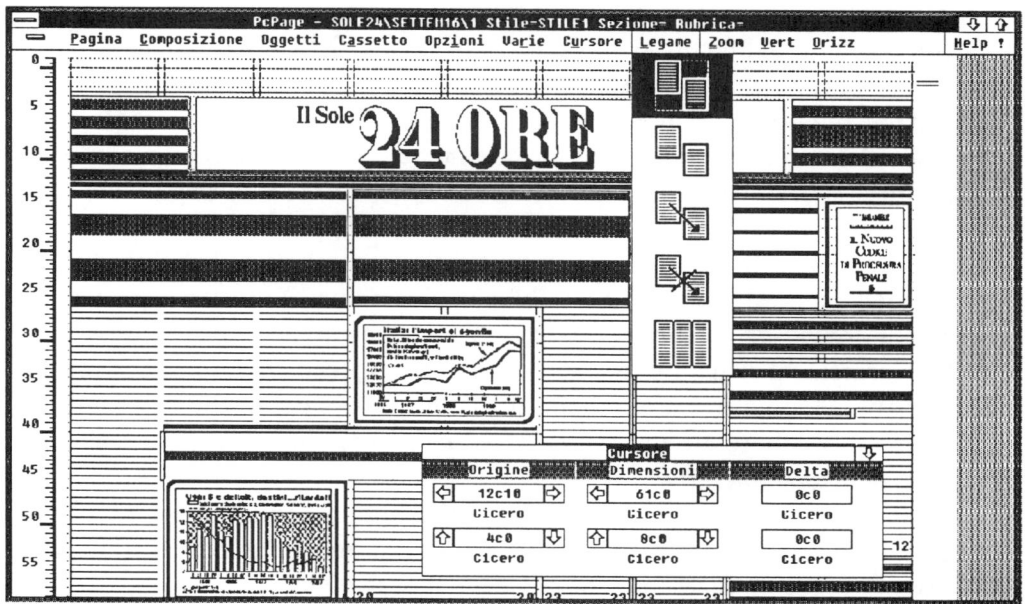

Figure 7: PcPage Indicators and Working Modes

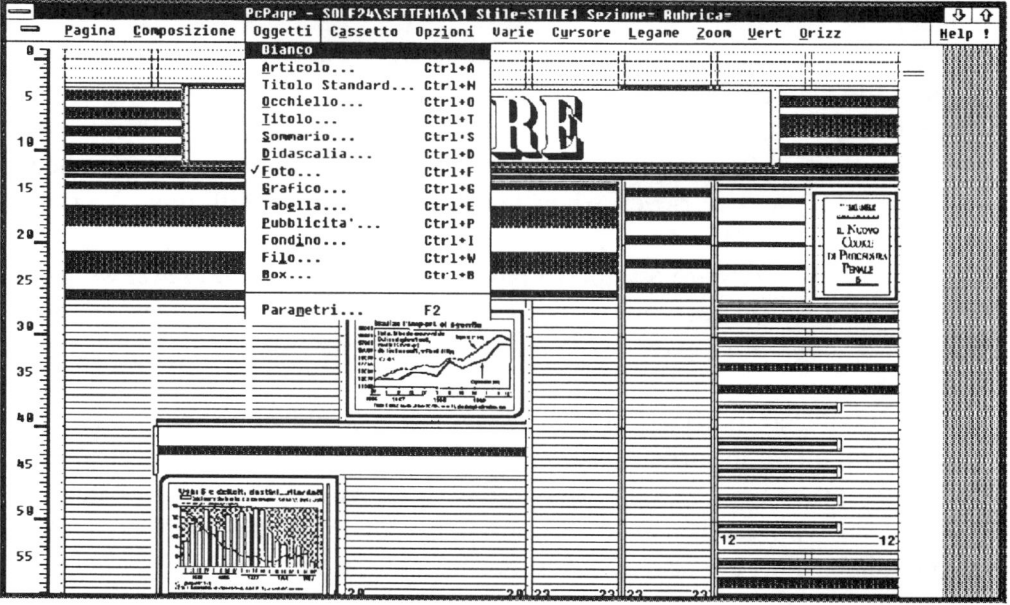

Figure 8: PcPage Predefined Page Elements

segment whose inclination indicates possible direction movements. To provide accurate visual feedback of cursor movement, the cursor may become a cross-hair of the size of the page.

Finally, the user may choose among a set of special working *modes* (Figure 7). The selection is made by pressing icon menu items on the main menu bar. When in a special working *mode*, the actions performed on page elements assume different semantic. For instance, when the application is in the *group mode*, every time the user clicks on an area, the same area is included in a predefined or newly formed *group* of page elements. As a consequence, a *simple* or *composite layout* sub-node is given a new parent sub-node on the *ODA* hierarchical structure. Similarly, when the special *chain mode* is recalled, every click on a text area, chains it to other text areas in the *ODA layout* structure. Also, there are inverse *working modes*: i.e., there is a remove *group mode* and an *unchain mode*.

So far we have described general tools that support and make it easier to create the *layout* of a page and to define its attributes. In the next section, we discuss about creation, update and deletion of page elements.

3.2 Creation, Update and Deletion of Page Elements

All page elements have rectangular shape. By overlapping *rectangular page* elements of different types and sizes, we may obtain areas of almost any shape.

Objects (or *page elements*) are created graphically by the usual *rubberbanding* technique. An object may be created, updated and deleted at any time during a page editing session. A single object or a group of objects (see previous Section 2.2) may be copied to a temporary storage buffer (namely, the *clipboard*) and retrieved when necessary even by a different Windows application [Foley84]..

All *page elements* are assigned a type at creation time. In *PcPage*, we have chosen a set of fourteen predefined object types. Among them we find: *articles, titles, summaries, pictures, boxes, classifieds, etc.* (for a complete list see Figure 8)

By default, an object is of type *blank*. A *blank* object has always the highest overlapping priority of all object types. That is, a *blank* object always hides any other types of objects underneath it. When parts of an object are hidden, all typographical and presentation properties that are tied to the object dimensions are also affected. For instance, when a *title* covers parts of an *article*, the amount of text that may be contained in the *article* is obviuosly reduced. Since *PcPage* is a *page planner*, it is paramount to be able to estimate property changes as a result of *layout* modifications. *PcPage* offers many tools and features to aid a page designer in its endeavor. For every *article page element*, it is possible to obtain an approximated estimate of the amount of text that may fit into the *article* area. To do so, every object area is decomposed into minimal rectangles and heuristic formulas are applied to them, with very accurate text estimate results. The design of *title page elements* is also eased by providing default *title* configurations based on the *title* current area size.

Finally, a page designer is helped by visual display of the page he is working on. *Page elements* that contain text are shown very realistically by lines whose *number* and *interline leading* are equal to those of the final composed text. *Title* areas are shown with lines whose thickness is proportional to the *title* character point size. Special elements such as *classifieds*, *graphics* and *tables* are displayed with special background patterns to distinguish them easily. Boxes surrounding text may be built with rounded or straight line corners having variable curvature radiuses.

4 Conclusion

PcPage is a *Professional Publishing* application that performs the front-end work of *layout page planning*. It is built upon a graphical interface toolkit (Microsoft Windows) and runs on any personal computer.

To perform effective and efficient *page planning*, *PcPage* can address and update typographical and presentation properties for almost every object on a page. It interactively provides the user with immediate feedback for every action it performs. This is achieved by keeping on-line reference to every *page element*. This requires a comprehensive data model and efficient retrieval methods. For this reason, the data structure and related access procedures are modelled upon the *ODA* standard hierarchies.

One of the important advantages of having chosen *ODA* as *PcPage* data model, is *ODA* data exchange format *ODIF*. Since *PcPage* is a supplier of document properties to other processors, it needs to supply them frequently and possibly with extremely different formats. Having chosen *ODA* rich data model, it is easier to convert the data to transfer.

Currently, *PcPage* is employed by the Italian financial newspaper **Il Sole 24 Ore** in its page layout department. *PcPage* is not a final product, but rather a continuously improving software prototype. Future developments include the integration of *PcPage ODA* data structure with an *object-oriented* database server running on a dedicated machine.

Acknowledgements
This work was supported by **Unisys Italia.**

References

[**Alagic88**] SuadAlagic', *Object-Oriented Database Programming*, Springer-Verlag New York Inc, 1988.

[**Behrman88**] J.Behrman-Poitiers A.Keil & H.Loebl, "Hard copy rendition of ODA-documents," in Hans van Vliet (ed.), *Document Manipulation and Typography*, Proceedings of the EP88 Conference, Cambridge University Press, 1988.

[**Chen88**] Pehong Chen and Michael A.Harrison, "Multiple representation document development," *Computer*, Vol.21, No. 1, Jan. 1988.

[**Cox87**] J.Cox, *Object-Oriented Programming*, Addison-Wesley, Reading, Mass, 1989.

[**De la Beaujarderie88**] J.-M. de la Beaujarderie, "Well-established document interchange formats," in Hans van Vliet (ed.), *Document Manipulation and Typography*, Proceedings of the EP88 Conference, Cambridge University Press, 1988.

[**Foley84**] J.D.Foley and A.Van Dam, *Fundamentals of Interactive Computer Graphics,* Addison-Wesley, The Systems Programming Series, 1984.

[**Furuta82**] Richard Furuta, "Document formatting systems: survey, concepts and issues". *Computing Surveys*, Vol.14, 1982.

[**Johnson88**] Jeff Johnson and Richard J.Beach, "Styles in document editing systems," *Computer*, Vol. 21, No. 1, Jan. 1988.

[**Luniewski88**] A.W.Luniewski, "Intent-based page modelling using blocks in the Quill document editor," in Hans van Vliet (ed.), *Document Manipulation and Typography*, Proceedings of the EP88 Conference, Cambridge Univ. Press, 1988.

[**Murata89**] M.Murata, "An object-oriented interpretation of ODA," in *WOODMAN 89* - Workshop on Object-Oriented Document Manipulation, ed.J.Andre, May 29-31 1989, Rennes (France).

[**Muscate89**] H.A.Muscate, "ODA document editing in the office systems," in *WOODMAN 89* - Workshop on Object-Oriented Document Manipulation, ed.J.Andre, May 29-31 1989, Rennes (France).

[**Ms-Windows SDK88**] *Software development kit version 2.1*, Microsoft Corporation, 16011 NE 36th Way, Box 97017, Redmond, Washington 98073-9717.

[**ODA88**]. ISO/DIS 8613, *Information processing - Text and office systems -* Office Document Architecture (ODA) and interchange format.

[**Peterlongo89**] M.Peterlongo, "Object-oriented environment of ODA editing," in *WOODMAN 89* - Workshop on Object-Oriented Document Manipulation, ed.J.Andre, May 29-31 1989, Rennes (France).

flo—A Language for Typesetting Flowcharts

Anthony P. WOLFMAN and Daniel M. BERRY
Faculty of Computer Science
Technion
Haifa 32000
ISRAEL

ABSTRACT : flo is a language for including *flowcharts* into documents typeset using the UNIX™ ditroff. A basic flowchart can be created with minimal effort by inputting only the basic algorithm written in a Pascal-like notation. The example below illustrates the general capability of flo. The flowchart to the left is obtained from the input to the right.

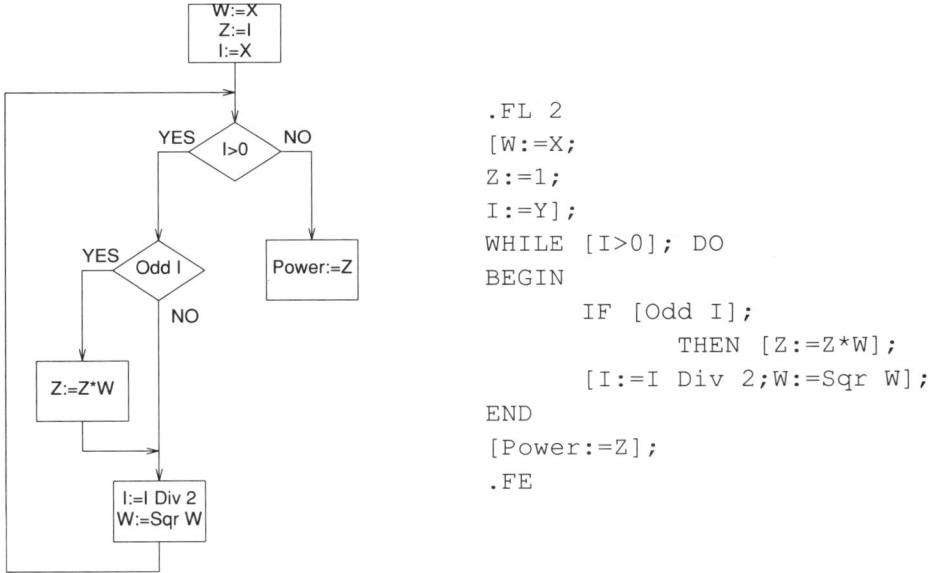

```
.FL 2
[W:=X;
Z:=1;
I:=Y];
WHILE [I>0]; DO
BEGIN
        IF [Odd I];
             THEN [Z:=Z*W];
        [I:=I Div 2;W:=Sqr W];
END
[Power:=Z];
.FE
```

This input uses default settings except for a sizing parameter in the .FL command. flo is a pic preprocessor, which in turn is a ditroff preprocessor. flo lets most of its input pass through untouched; it translates flo commands lying between .FL and .FE into pic commands that draw the flowcharts.

This paper was typeset camera-ready using flo, pic, ditroff, and other ditroff preprocessors.

KEY WORDS : Flowcharting, Typesetting, Ditroff, Pic.

1. Introduction

Many papers written in computer science deal with algorithms. In many but not all cases, a flowchart, either by itself or accompanied by a program in some programming language, is a convenient representation of the algorithm. Indeed, as a result of recent experiments showing the superiority of flowcharts over pseudocode for helping programmers understand algorithms [Scanlon 1989], flowcharts may be coming back into fashion!

In addition, today, almost all papers in computer science are prepared with the aid of some formatting system capable of preparing output for printing on devices, such as laser printers and phototypesetters, that are capable of drawing arbitrary figures. These formating systems include batch-oriented systems such as **troff** [Ossana 1976], **ditroff** [Kernighan 1982], T_EX™ [Knuth 1984], L^AT_EX [Lamport 1984], and **scribe** [Reid 1980], as well as a host of WYSIWYG programs running on systems with high-resolution screens.

Many of these formating systems include facilities by which non-textual material may be included and formated along with the text. These include bibliographical citations, line-oriented pictures possibly with some limited filling, graphs (charts), directed graphs, tables, formulae, source program code, arbitrary POSTSCRIPT™ documents, and back-of-document indices. Space limitations preclude giving more detailed citations.

There exists no suitable tools integrated into the **ditroff** family for producing and including into **ditroff** documents flowcharts such that the description of the flowchart is its algorithm rather than its physical layout or topology.

The project described herein was to develop a **pic** [Kernighan 1984] preprocessor, called **flo**, that prepares a flowchart given a linear representation of an algorithm. Since there exists a version of **pic**, called **tpic**, that can be used with L^AT_EX, **flo** can be used to prepare flowcharts for inclusion in documents typeset with either **ditroff** and L^AT_EX. Thus, **flo** is useful for those situations in which it is felt that a flowchart will help; in other situations, it is obviously of no use.

This paper describes the design and implementation of **flo**. A complete description of the use of the language is found in [Wolfman 1989]. As is common with papers describing a new formating tool, this paper was typeset using **flo**, **pic**, **ditroff**, and other **ditroff** preprocessors, preparing output for a POSTSCRIPT printing device. The command lines to print this paper were

```
refer -l -e -n -p refsidx -sADT paper | \
      fix.bibliography.labels > paper.ref
flo paper.ref | pic | tbl | eqn | psroff -mcup
```

All the diagrams in this paper were prepared as flo inputs.

The following example demonstrates the capabilities of flo. Besides the algorithm in a Pascal-like notation, this example has additional commands and attribute settings that adjust the sizes of nodes, spaces between adjacent nodes, and arc placement. This fine-tuned example differs from the purely algorithmic example of the abstract, in which all of the layout is by flo supplied defaults. Given the input[1],

```
.ps 7
.FL
@pic {scale = 1.4} ;
defshape ends shape is oval:
        {ellipse ht $1 wid $2} shapew is 0.6;
stmtshapeh is 0.25 ;
queryshapeh is 0.3 ;
spaceh is 0.25;
spacew is 0.2;
[START] with ends;
[($y_1,y_2,y_3,y_4$)←($x_1,x_2$,1,0)] shapew is 1.7;
WHILE [$y_1$>$y_2$];
        DO [($y_2,y_3$)←(2$y_2$,2$y_3$)] shapew is 1.2;
LOOP
        IF [$y_1$≥$y_2$] ;
                THEN [($y_1,y_4$)←($y_1-y_2,y_4+y_3$)] shapew is 1.5;
        EXITIF [$y_3$=1] config is RIGHT;
        [($y_2,y_3$←(div($y_2$,2), div($y_3$,2))] shapew is 1.9;
        @up ;
END
[($z_1,z_2$)←($y_1,y_4$)] shapew is 1.1;
[HALT] with ends;
.FE
.ps
```

flo produces the flowchart in Figure 1.

2. Previous Solutions

From the need to provide better documentation for computer programs, a host of

---

[1] For clarity, the input is shown after processing by eqn. The text that has been processed by eqn is shown in the Helvetica sanserif font to make it standout against the Courier typewriter font normally used to show input. The same holds for all other examples involving eqn text. The full input for this first example appears in [Wolfman 1989].

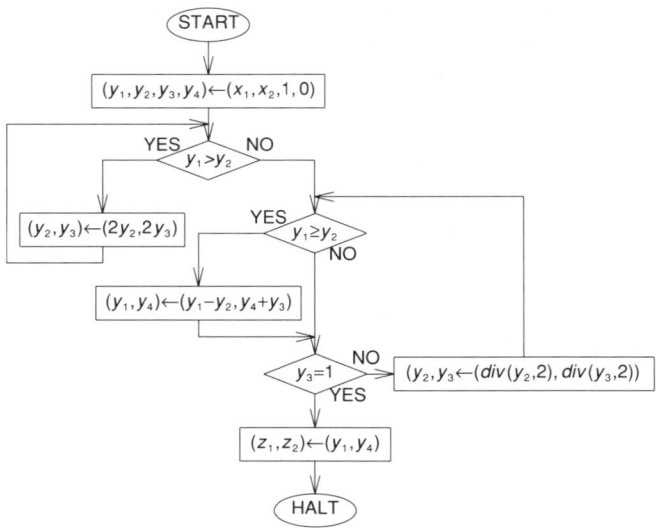

Figure 1: Flowchart with eqn text

programs to generate flowcharts have been written. For a full summary of these programs see [Wolfman 1989]. There are five basic kinds of programs that have been used for drawing flowcharts. The first kind, the batch general flowchart drawing program, e.g., that reported in [Knuth 1963], attempts to be general enough to handle any flowchart, but in fact, handles none very well. Flowcharts are spread over several pages with the use of a common label appearing at the nodes in place of a cluttering, possibly inter-page, arc drawn between the nodes. The other kinds all require the user to work directly with the topology of the flowchart rather than just the algorithm it represents. These include the WYSIWYG flowcharting drawing program, e.g., flo draw 1.10 [Freund 1987], the batch general directed graph drawing program, e.g., dag [Ganser 1988] or drag [Trickey 1988], the batch general figure drawing program, e.g., pic, and the WYSIWYG general figure drawing program, e.g., fig [Sutanthavibul 1988].

3. Goal and Requirements

The goal of this project was to enable the user to input an algorithm in some sort of psuedo-Pascal notation and get as output a flowchart of that algorithm. The program, called flo, should behave as follows. The input to flo should be embeddable in ditroff input surrounded by .FL and .FE. The flo program should let most of the input pass through untouched. It should transform the flowchart description lying between the .FL and .FE into a pic specification of the requested flowchart, laid out nicely according to the user's needs.

It should be that by inputting only the algorithm, provided that the resulting flowchart is not too big, some flowchart is produced. Moreover, it should be possible to adjust the layout of the flowchart by merely adding to the basic algorithm additional layout information. When the effect of this information is to be global, it should be possible to give it once. When the effect should be local to a particular node or arc, it should be possible to give it as part of the node's or arc's specification. This layout information should look almost like comments added, as an afterthought, to the algorithm, and not like part of the algorithm.

As flo produces pic code, and ditroff forces all pic pictures to fit within a page, flo flowcharts are constrained to fit on one page. To get a multi-page picture, the user must divide the picture explicitly into one page pictures. Since nodes have a certain minimum readable size, this one page limitation limits the complexity of the flowcharts that can be specified. Moreover, nowadays, most programs are built using structured programming techniques, which yield well-nested, goto-less programs.

In building the flo language and program, advantage can be taken of the nature of one-page flowcharts to build a program that draws small, structured flowcharts well, possibly at the expense of slightly less smooth performance for the more complicated flowcharts. For the cases in which the program would yield a layout not what the user had in mind, the language should provide commands by which the user may direct the construction of the layout. The program may also allow the user to fall back to pic and to ditroff if necessary, just as pic allows the user to fall back to ditroff

Equally important is to exclude from flo's requirements the ability to handle other software-related diagrams, such as module diagrams and data-flow diagrams. Certainly, these can be faked using flowcharts elements with nonstandard shapes and inverse translation to a nonsense pseudo-Pascal algorithm. However, it is better to use pic, dag, or drag for a more direct representation.

4. The Development Method

There were two main parts to this project. The first was to design the flo language. The second was to design of the flo program. Which should be designed first, the language or the program? At first, there might seem to be no problem. After all, the language is designed first and then its processor is written.

It is necessary to know the language in order to be able to write the processor. However, it is all too easy to pile feature after possibly unimplementable feature into a language. On the other hand, it is necessary to know what is implementable in order to know what language features are reasonable.

This cycle was broken, by first writing a draft of the language's user's manual, which contained example-laden explanations of all the desired features. As the program was not written yet, the first author hand-translated each flo input example into the pic input that he expected flo would create. After that, he attempted to write a program that would process the language described by the manual, that would translate each flo example into something equivalent to the hand-generated pic input for the example. Whenever this attempt got bogged down in syntactic, semantic, or synergistic problems, missing or unimplementable features, inconsistencies, or just plain messiness, work on the program stopped and another iteration was begun. These discoveries led to changes in the manual and corresponding changes in the program. This process was repeated until a manual and a program were created such that the manual described the entire language handled by the program and the program translated all flo input examples into suitable pic input. Typesetting a manual so related to a program is a also good test of the program.

In this interative process, the second author played an extremely critical, picky customer and user who was particularly grouchy at the slightest sign of inconsistency, nonuniformity, and nonorthogonality.

The manuals for pic and grap [Bentley 1984] exhibit the same relation to their languages. Thus, we suspect that the same method was followed by Kernighan and Bentley in the development of pic and grap.

5. Details of Implementation

5.1. Major Semantic Problems

The program has to be designed in such a way to enable an easy automatic layout in most cases. At the same time, it has to supply a handle to enable the user to control the layout directly if need be. This handle has to enable the user a multitude of alternate layout types depending on flow direction, condition configuration, node size, space between nodes and general flowchart structure The program must also be designed to avoid intersecting loops and arrows. The following subsections discuss the more interesting elements of the solution.

5.2. Bubbles

After examining a great deal of flowcharts, it was noticed that flowcharts took on different dimensions not only depending on their internal structure and node size, but also on the spacing between the nodes. For example, the same flowchart could seem short and fat and long and thin depending only on the spacing between the nodes. Therefore, it was decided to add to flo the ability to control these dimensions. At first, the first author thought only to let the user specify the type of flowchart, i.e., "fat", "thin", etc. Such a general description is too fuzzy to be the basis of an algorithm. On the other hand, to have to specify all the exact dimension is too burdensome on the user. Finally, the first author got the idea of bubbles.

A node's *bubble* is defined as a bounding box around that node. No other node, other node's bubble, or return loop may encroach on a given node's bubble. The only entity that may cross a bubble boundary is an arrow connecting two nodes, and the arrow must be going to or from the node contained inside the bubble. The entire flowchart is therefore a mosaic of bubbles, not unlike the way a TeX-formatted document is a mosaic of boxes, each containing a unit of text [Knuth 1984].

5.3. Chewing Gum

The presence of query (conditional) nodes causes layout problems. After each query there are two sub-flowcharts one for the *Yes* answer and one for the *No* answer. Figure 2 shows a flowchart with two sub-flowcharts marked. The sub-flowcharts themselves may contain query nodes and therefore nested sub-flowcharts. A sub-flowchart is a series of nodes beginning with the first node following a query on one of its answer arcs end ending with the last node under control of that answer of the query or with the last node before looping back to before the query. The special series of nodes beginning with the very first node and ending with the last node or the first query node is called the root sub-flowchart. The dimensions of each sub-flowchart is known only after it has been drawn completely. Each sub-flowchart's position in relation to its sibling sub-flowchart can be known only after the dimensions of both sub-flowcharts have been calculated. As a first approximation, each sub-flowchart is drawn immediately below its query node. When the dimensions of both sub-flowcharts of a query node are finally calculated the sub-flowcharts are pulled as close together as their bubbles allow, as if held together by an elastic chewing gum. This chewing gum has certain similarities to TeX's *glue* [Knuth 1984].

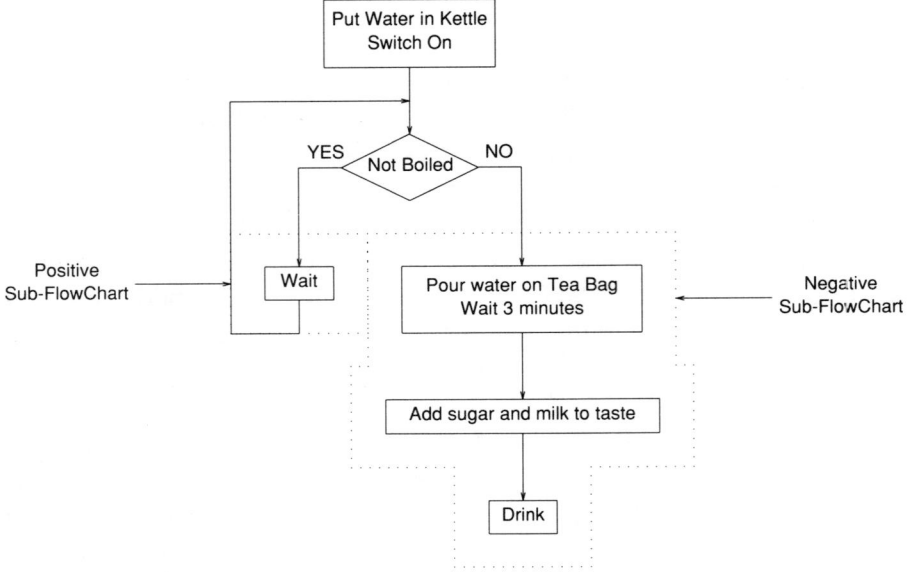

Figure 2: Flowchart with two sub-flowcharts marked

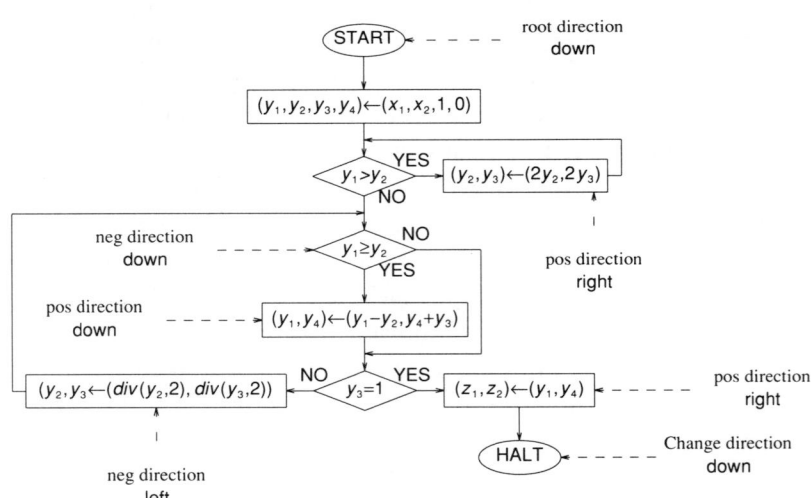

Figure 3: Flowchart with changes of direction marked

5.4. Configurations

After examining numerous flowcharts, it was noticed that the layout of any flowchart is determined by the position of the sub-flowcharts of its query nodes. *Query configurations* were introduced to specify these positions. There are twelve configurations in all, six basic ones and and six variations of these, which reverse the positions of the *Yes* and *No* arcs.

After settling on this method of controlling layout, the major design problem was naming the configurations. They were originally named C1, C2, C3, etc. Reacting to his own difficulty remembering which one is which, the second author suggested using names mnemonic of their layout, such as O, P, Q, DASH, LEFT, RIGHT, and the ...N variations thereof.

5.5. Direction & Movement

In order to be able to control layout, it is necessary also to be able control direction of flow. Normally, the direction of flow is determined by the configuration of the last query. For example, the direction of both sub-flowcharts of an O configuration query is down. The user may want, however, to change the direction of the flow within a sub-flowchart.

The *direction* of the flow is the direction from the last node to the current one. The default direction of the root sub-flowchart is down. After a query node, the direction of each sub-flowchart is defined by the query's configuration. A direction may be changed by using the appropriate command. flo does not allow changing the flow direction at the beginning of a sub-flowchart because doing so may cause a conflict with the configuration. Figure 3 shows a flow chart in which every change of direction and initial direction of a sub-flowchart is marked. Only when the desired direction differs from the default or configuration-defined direction, must a direction command be given. The direction commands must be used carefully, because they can conflict with the configuration system.

A node may also be moved in relation to its default position. The parameterless @move command moves the subsequent node in the current direction a distance equal to the size of the node's bubble. An optional argument provides a multiplier to the movement. The unit of movement was chosen to be the size of the bubble of the next node, because this distance is the most obvious unit to a user who is looking at a version of the flowchart. Figure 4 shows a flowchart in which one, marked, node has been moved a single unit. The figure also exhibits the portion of the input containing the @move command.

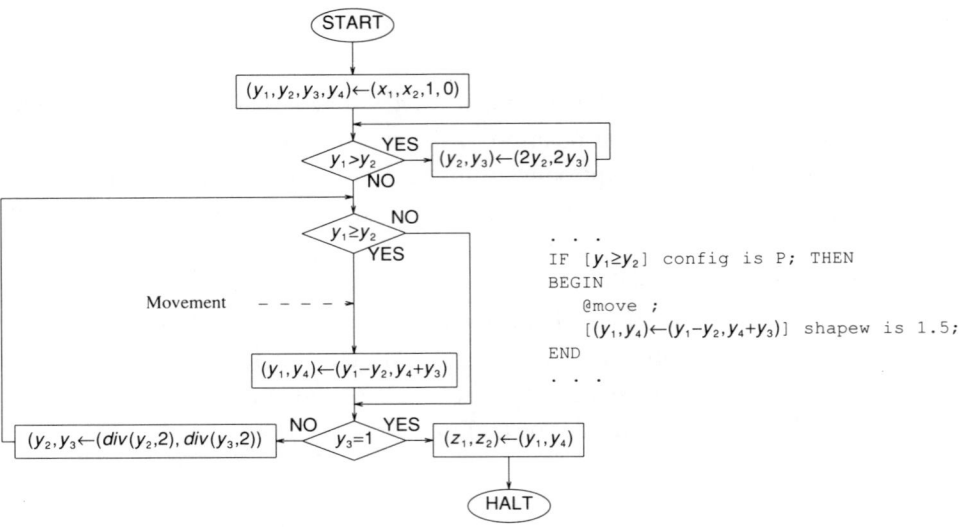

Figure 4: Flowchart with movement marked

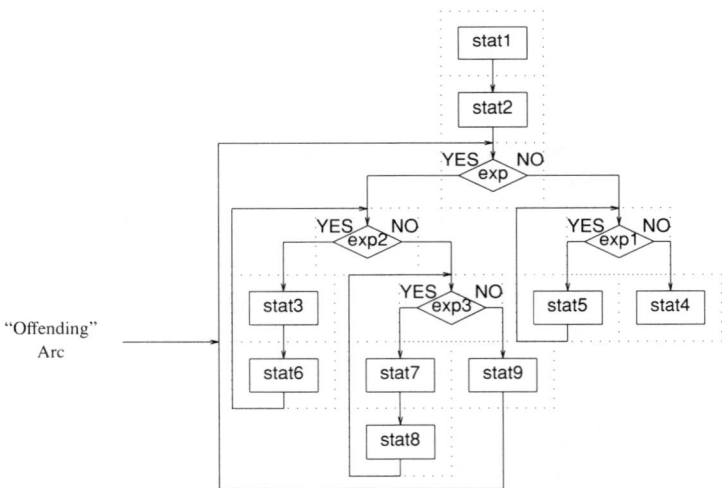

Figure 5: Flowchart with nested loop and offending arc marked

5.6. Routing

As might be expected, the most troublesome arcs to draw are the *loopback* arcs. Fortunately, the language is made up of only the so-called structured control-flow commands, conditionals, while loops, repeat loops, etc., with *no* gotos allowed. This constraint completely eliminates intersecting loops, because all loops are nested one inside the other. It also completely eliminates arcs from one sub-flowchart to another. With **flo** providing all of these control structures, a goto is hardly ever needed. Ultimately, the user can program goto arcs using embedded **pic** commands. The extra complexity that a goto command would add to **flo**'s routing algorithm makes having it too expensive.

In computing the layout of the nodes, any non-nested loop can be drawn immediately, because its loopback arc has only to go round its own local sub-flowchart, whose dimensions are known. A nested loop is trickier. Its loopback arc may have to go round a sub-flowchart that has not yet been drawn. Call this sub-flowchart the *offending sub-flowchart* and the arc the *offending arc*. Then, the exact layout of the offending arc can be determined only when the offending sub-flowchart has been drawn. The chewing gum pulls the arc to hug the bubble of the offending sub-flowchart. Figure 5 contains an example of a nested loop. The bubbles are shown to show how the offending arc's path is determined.

5.7. pic *Macros*

In order to facilitate debugging of **flo** and to make it easy to add new constructs in the future, all of the basic building blocks and routing patterns are implemented as **pic** macros in two files, **db.pic** and **route.pic**, includable from **pic** input. The **pic** input that **flo** creates is but a series of invocations of these macros. **db.pic** contains the shape macros, and **route.pic** contains the routing macros. Both of these files are `copyd` at the beginning of each flowchart definition.

This approach greatly reduced the development time of **flo**. For a great deal of the bugs found during the development, it sufficed to change the macro definitions, and it was not necessary to recompile the **flo** program.

5.8. Data Structure

Each flowchart drawn by **flo** is represented as a directed tree graph in which each vertex represents a sub-flowchart and the edges represent the parent-to-child relation among the sub-flowcharts. The vertices are implemented as data records and the edges are implemented as pointers to these data records. Each vertex's data record contains a pointer to the list of the individual nodes in the vertex's

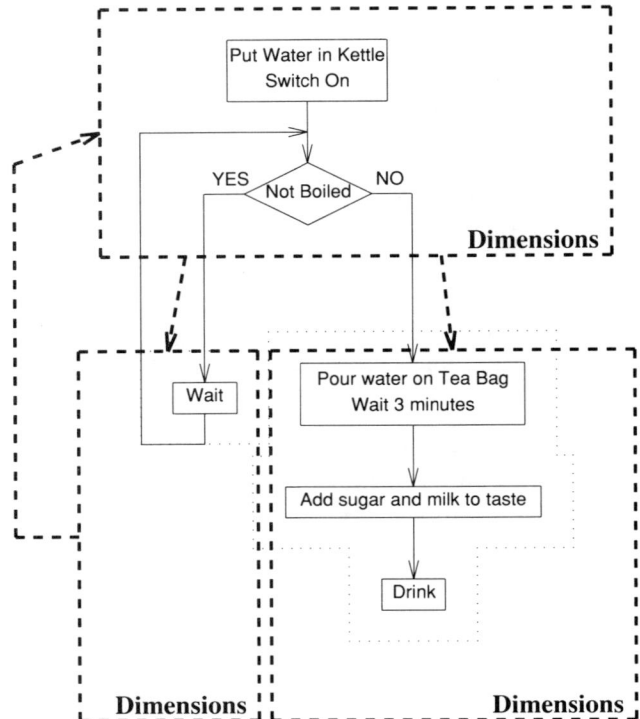

Figure 6: Flowchart superimposed on its data structure

sub-flowchart, and the calculated dimensions of the vertex's children. The list elements contain the text and attributes of the nodes. If a vertex has no children, and its sub-flowchart's nodes are in a loopback path, then the vertex's record contains a pointer to the node to which the loopback arc is directed. Figure 6 shows the data structure of the flowchart of Figure 2.

6. Conclusions

In most cases, from just the algorithm, flo produces a correct and aesthetically pleasing flowchart, as required by the goals of this project. The global and local attribute specifications allow the user to customize the appearance of the flowchart.

The main advantage of flo over some of the programs mentioned in Section 2 is that usually all that is needed is the basic algorithm. The user hardly ever needs to be concerned about the layout, as determining the layout is flo's job. If any changes are required in the algorithm, flo automatically rearranges the layout. On a WYSIWYG system, the user has to rearrange the layout, and with dag and drag, the user has to input the new topology of the flowchart.

A big drawback of flo is one inherited from pic. Like pic, flo cannot draw a node to fit round any text. The user may either specify the size of each node locally to fit exactly round its own text or specify a single global size large enough to fit round the largest text item.

There are certain algorithm constructs that flo does not support. For example, flo cannot handle certain types of nested *Repeat* loops. To handle them, the user has to fall back on pic commands. This problem never occurred in real life; it occurred only during testing during which all sorts of anomalous algorithms were presented to flo. In fact, the authors have yet to encounter a real live algorithm that flo cannot handle.

On the whole, the authors have found flo a useful and easy-to-use tool, that seems to work even under fire. The authors found that the flowcharts flo produces are more symmetric and better aligned than flowcharts laid out by hand in the early versions of the user's manual!

flo has withstood the ultimate test! A member of the first author's master's thesis examining committee, hell-bent on tripping up flo, gave to the first author an algorithm to flowchart. flo worked the first time and produced a flowchart that was pleasing *even* to that committee member!

Among the suggestions for future work are (1) an include file facility, enabling the user to keep a file of commonly used macros and global changes and include them in any flo input, (2) to be able define shape by pic macros, (3) to be able to define construct macros, e.g,. a *for* construct macro, and (4) to be able to specify arcs as splines. All these enhancements can be added with relative ease. All that is needed is to add the appropriate definition to the lexical analyzer and to write the handling procedure. In some cases, the handling procedure can be borrowed from the pic program.

Acknowledgements

POSTSCRIPT is a trademark of Adobe Computer Systems. TeX is a trademark of the American Mathematical Society. UNIX is a trademark of AT&T Bell Laboratories.

REFERENCES

[Bentley84] J.L. Bentley and B.W. Kernighan, 'GRAP — A Language for Typesetting Graphs, Tutorial and User Manual', Computing Science Technical Report No. 114,

AT&T Bell Laboratories, Murray Hill, NJ 07974 (December, 1984).

[Freund87] G. Freund, 'flo draw 1.0', Program for IBM PC-Compatibles (1987).

[Ganser88] E.R. Ganser, S.C. North, and K.P. Vo, 'DAG—A Program that Draws Directed Graphs', *Software—Practice and Experience*, **18** (11), 1047-1062 (November, 1988).

[Kernighan82] B.W. Kernighan, 'A Typesetter-independent TROFF', Computing Science Technical Report No. 97, Bell Laboratories (March, 1982).

[Kernighan84] B.W. Kernighan, 'PIC — A Graphics Language for Typesetting, Revised User Manual', Computing Science Technical Report No. 116, Bell Laboratories (December, 1984).

[Knuth63] D.E. Knuth, 'Computer-Drawn Flowcharts', *Communications of the ACM*, **6** (9), 555-563 (September, 1963).

[Knuth84] D.E. Knuth, *The TeXbook*, Addison-Wesley, Reading, MA, 1984.

[Lamport84] L. Lamport, L^{A}T$_E$X: *A Document Preparation System*, Addison-Wesley, Reading, MA, 1984.

[Ossana76] J.F. Ossana, 'NROFF/TROFF User's Manual', Technical Report, Bell Laboratories (October 11, 1976).

[Reid80] B. Reid, 'Scribe: A Document Specification Language and its Compiler', Ph.D. Dissertation, Carnegie Mellon University, Pittsburgh, PA (October, 1980).

[Scanlon89] D.A. Scanlon, 'Structured Flowcharts Outperform Pseudocode: An Experimental Comparison', *IEEE Software*, **6** (5), 28-36 (September, 1989).

[Sutanthavibul88] S. Sutanthavibul, 'fig', Program implemented at the Computer Science Dept.,, University of California, Berkeley (1988).

[Trickey88] H. Trickey, 'DRAG — A Graph Drawing System', in *Electronic Publishing '88*, ed. J. André and H. van Vliet, Cambridge University Press, Cambridge, UK, pp. 171-182, (1988).

[Wolfman89] A.P. Wolfman and D.M. Berry, 'flo—A Language for Typesetting Flowcharts', Technical Report, Computer Science, Technion, Haifa, Israel (December, 1989).

Design of Hypermedia Publications: Issues and Solutions

Paul Kahn†, Julie Launhardt†, Krzysztof Lenk††, Ronnie Peters††

† Institute for Research in Information and Scholarship, Brown University
†† Department of Graphic Design, Rhode Island School of Design

ABSTRACT: For a hypermedia collection to function properly, an author must successfully combine the verbal language of the document content with an equally persuasive visual language of hypermedia design. This visual language should help define a sense of hierarchy in the presentation of information, create a sense of order, structure and clarity, and allow the user to focus on what is alike and what is different. This paper discusses some of the issues that face the designer of hypermedia documents being considered by a joint research team of software engineers, software designers, content specialists and graphic designers. We discuss specific implementation issues that informed the creation of *Exploring the Moon* and *The Dickens Web*, the first two hypermedia publications created with IRIS Intermedia version 3.0. In analyzing these two works as well as ideas for future hypermedia publications, we have identified a new set of issues which we list at the end of the paper.

KEYWORDS: hypermedia, graphic design, Intermedia

1. Hypermedia Document Design Issues

Hypermedia is the term used to describe software systems which support navigational linking between documents of several types (i.e. text, graphics, animation, etc.). Intermedia, the research hypermedia system developed at Brown University's Institute for Research in Information and Scholarship (IRIS), supports the editing, display, and linking of text, structured graphics, bitmap graphics, animations, and video documents in a single integrated system [Yankelovich 1988]. This software offers the designer a number of features with which to work. Some, like the shape and position of the link marker, are relatively inflexible artifacts of the system design. Others, like the formatting of text and graphics within a document frame, are more open-ended features that must be shaped to serve a particular purpose.

1.1 Presentation on the Screen
The hypermedia system presents information solely on the computer screen. This is an important difference between hypermedia and most software designed to edit and format text and graphic data. Word processing, page layout, or two-dimensional graphics software use the computer screen as an intermediate step. The "soft copy" presented on the computer screen is a convenient and malleable surrogate for the final "hard copy" to be delivered on paper or film. As a result, how information is presented on the screen is not as important as how it will appear on the printed page. This is not true in the case of hypermedia documents. For hypermedia, the luminescent surface of the computer screen *is* the page.

1.2 The Perception of Order

In *Entropy and Art: an essay on disorder and order,* Rudolf Arnheim points out the importance of order and hierarchy to human perception.

> Order is a necessary condition for anything the human mind is to understand. Arrangement such as the layout of a city or building, a set of tools, a display of merchandise, the verbal expression of facts or ideas, or a painting or a piece of music are called orderly when an observer or listener can grasp their overall structure and ramification of the structure in some detail. Order makes it possible to focus on what is alike and what is different, what belongs together and what is segregated. When nothing superfluous is included and nothing indispensable is left out, one can understand the interrelation of the whole to its parts, as well as the hierarchic scale of importance and power by which some structural features are dominant, others subordinate. [Arnheim 1971]

Hypermedia offers a new challenge to our sense of order and hierarchy. On the highest level, our design efforts must address this challenge. The use we made of typography, negative space, consistency in formatting, and other design strategies described below are subordinate to this larger principal. Hypermedia design must establish a sense of order on the surface of the computer screen.

1.3 Experiences with Real Systems and Real Materials

A great deal of thought and effort has gone into the design of the Intermedia user interface. Starting with the visual language of the Macintosh Toolbox, IRIS researchers have developed a group of editors and a set of general system functions. We have followed principles of visual consistency and simplicity throughout the development cycle. The result is a system which is innovative and powerful yet simple to learn and to use.

Intermedia has been used to support courses in an experimental classroom at Brown from January 1986 up to the present. During the first three years, materials were created with a series of development versions of the software. There was no opportunity to employ consistent rules of graphic design in a rigorous fashion to the materials as they were being developed. The software features, the hardware platform, and even the monitor size changed drastically during this period. In April 1989, a version of Intermedia, called *IRIS Intermedia version 3.0*, was released as a generally available software product. As part of the software release, we created our first hypermedia publication, a collection of linked documents that would stand as an example of educational materials for others to emulate and learn from.

This first collection, titled *Exploring the Moon*, is a set of materials on the Apollo lunar missions that had been developed by Katie Livingston, Jane Aubele, and Professor James Head for use in a Brown University course on Planetary Geology [Livingston 1989]. This material was chosen for publication for several reasons. Most of the material already existed in electronic form, having been prepared for a HyperCard stack. After adding and rescanning some materials, the collection was still relatively small (a little over 100 individual documents, about 1.2 megabytes of data) but at the same time provided deep coverage of its subject domain. It contained a rich mixture of text and graphic materials. Copyright of the graphic materials was not a problem, since the entire collection was either extracted from or based upon NASA and other U.S. Government publications.

In the fall of the same year, we began the more ambitious project of creating the second Intermedia publication by extracting materials about Charles Dickens from *Context32*, the Intermedia materials used to support Professor George Landow's survey course on British Literature [Landow 1989]. The larger collection is a continual "work in progress" containing materials on dozens of authors and related social and historical topics, which is added to each semester by Professor Landow and his students. We sought to create a coherent example of the work, suitable for distribution, titled *The Dickens Web* [Landow 1990]. Dickens was chosen as the subject because the materials about him and *Great Expectations* (the novel taught in the course) are of the highest quality and exemplify the kind of intricate connections between literary, historical, and social forces the collection is intended to support. The collection consists of approximately 250 documents including original essays, brief quotations from secondary sources, concept diagrams, and timelines plus scanned reproductions of out-of-copyright book illustrations and portraits.

It was clear from the beginning that a critical element was lacking in both these collections: *graphic design*. The authors, content specialists in their respective fields, had selected images and texts that fit their pedagogical purpose, but, as is often the case with textbook authors, they did not have an overall image of how to graphically present this material to their readers. The Intermedia system was intended to provide a flexible environment for authors to create their own materials, rather than provide design templates or a set of design constraints. To address this problem, IRIS requested assistance from members of the graphic design department of the Rhode Island School of Design (RISD). An editorial and design team consisting of the present authors identified several areas that needed attention.

2. Hypermedia and Print Media

The team sought to define what it means to design hypermedia document collections. The first problem is to determine what is *not* unique. That is, what aspects of hypermedia documents require the same application of graphic design principles as printed documents. The remaining problems arise when hypermedia is used to convey information in new ways.

We have identified three graphic design principles used in print media (newspapers, posters, magazines, books) that are appropriate for the design of hypermedia collections:

The Rules of Type: The relationship of type, leading, and line length to legibility are as important on the computer screen as they are on the printed page. The output device for Intermedia is the Apple Macintosh screen, which supports a resolution of 72 dots per inch. This compares unfavorably with the 1250 lines per inch of output devices used to create the image of type on a printed page. To maintain legibility of type, adjustments must be made to account for the low resolution of the output device.

Consistent Formatting: The importance of consistent formatting rules for individual documents and collections of documents are largely unchanged. When designing a single publication or series of publications, the repetition of consistent formatting rules is an important factor for supporting reader orientation. The same is true for hypermedia, though, as noted below, hypermedia presents additional orientation problems.

Clear Information Graphics: Most characteristics that determine whether a black and white information graphic is clear or confusing do not change simply because that graphic is on soft rather than hard copy. Some adjustments must be made for the relatively low resolution of the computer screen, the focal distance from which the reader approaches the image on the screen, and the effects that reflected light from a print media versus transmitted light from hypermedia have on contrast and shading.

2.1 The Intermedia Publication and the Book

The presentation of information on the computer screen has some similarities to one of the book's earliest forms, the scroll. In Mediterranean antiquity, before the technology of binding leaves of papyrus or parchment between boards was developed, the method for creating portable collections of written material was to roll and tie continuous pieces of papyrus into a scroll [Roberts 1983]. The way in which a scroll stores and presents information to the reader is interesting in the context of our present work on the computer screen. In a scroll, information is stored on either side or above and below the area being read. This is similar to the operation of the scrolling bars of the document window on the computer, and the present practice of revealed information only within the document window. In either case, the reader does not know what information is just out of view. Unlike the pages of a book, which are of a fixed size, the viewing area of a scroll can be broadened or narrowed. As a result, the demarcation between visible and hidden information on the surface of a scroll is not as clear as the edges of a book page.

Even in the case of the scroll, the reader is oriented to the magnitude of the collection by being able to hold the entire collection in her hands. In contrast, a visual examination of the surface of the computer screen does not give the reader the same kind of access to the hypermedia publication as a whole. The hypermedia documents are 'hidden' within the memory of the computer and the visual appearance of the icons that represent each document does not express the same information as spines of bound volumes on a shelf or stacks of papers on a desk.

There are other interesting comparisons to be made between hypermedia and the printed book. Yankelovich, Meyrowitz, and van Dam [Yankelovich 1985] point out a fundamental difference between the two: that information in a book is static. Once committed to ink on paper, the information cannot be changed without reprinting the book. Their table of comparison emphasized the greater potential for reader interaction found in electronic media. While print media offers advantages in areas such as portability, established standards of typography and graphic design, and general aesthetic appeal, the reader of a book cannot alter the content or customize the arrangement of a printed page to suit individual needs. Intermedia, designed in large part by Yankelovich and Meyrowitz, challenges this relationship between the author and the reader. The Intermedia reader must actively create the sequence in which information is presented. Within the limit of permissions established by the author, the reader is also invited to add to and alter the information being presented.

While this area of comparison is entirely valid, there are other issues of orientation and meta-information that should not be overlooked. These include a consideration of the non-verbal information found in the book as a physical object, the differing relationship between verbal and visual language in the two mediums, and a comparison of the sensory channels through which the book and the computer screen present information to the reader.

The physical presence of a book, i.e. its weight, size, method of binding, its cover (hard or soft), can tell the reader something about the publication before it is read. Flipping quickly through the pages will tell the reader about the type of publication, the amount of copy, the size of type, the number of illustrations (if any). Our visual sense is the primary channel through which we receive information from a book.

However, a person reading a book uses more than just the sense of sight. A book can be picked up and oriented to the viewer's requirements. The "hard" nature of the book brings in such sensory information as the physical feel of the pages, the weight of the book, the smell of the ink, evidence of past ownership, and so forth.

By convention, books have bound pages that are expected to be read with a directional orientation. While this directionality varies from culture to culture (Greek and Latin reading horizontally left to right, Hebrew and Arabic reading horizontally from right to left, Classical Chinese reading vertically right to left), the page of a book in the European tradition is, by convention, read from top left to bottom right. The contents of pages within a book are most commonly organized in a linear, sequential fashion.

2.2 Combining Verbal and Visual Language Systems

Intermedia already contains parts of the visual language of hypermedia. In addition to the visual elements inherited from the Macintosh toolbox, such as pull-down menus, document icons, etc., these include unique features such as the link marker, the highlighting of the anchor extent, and the web view.

However, Intermedia, like most computer software, has been designed largely from the perspective of a verbal language system. Each document is surrounded by a frame. Within that frame the conventions of the book page and the linear order of our verbal language are maintained. Intermedia also supports webs of navigational links, connections between selections in multiple documents. These connections are non-sequential and bi-directional. The hypermedia author has the tools to create a collection of information both vast and complex. The same author has the potential to create complete visual and intellectual chaos and confusion.

This power to connect elements in separate documents and go beyond the conventions of our verbal language system begets the need to create a clear and persuasive visual language of hypermedia presentation. For a hypermedia collection to function properly, an author must successfully combine the verbal language of the document content (what Landow has elsewhere called "the rhetoric of hypertext" [Landow 1989]) with an equally persuasive visual language of hypermedia design. This visual language should help define a sense of hierarchy in the presentation of information, create a sense of order, structure and clarity, and allow the user to focus on what is alike and what is different.

Strictly from the point of view of visual language, the computer screen offers a limited palette. The simplicity of the means of representation on the computer screen does not accommodate all the solutions open for investigation in two- and three-dimensional modes of operation. A comparison of Intermedia with the two-dimensional and three-dimensional design reveals the relative narrowness of this new medium [see Table 1]. However, by investigating and applying theory from two-dimensional work on paper and three-dimensional design to the challenges presented by Intermedia, it is possible to look at new aspects of graphic representation and find new solutions.

	Three-dimensional	Two-dimensional	Intermedia
Sight	length, breadth, depth	length, breadth	length, breadth
	absorbed light	absorbed light	transmitted light
	reflected light	reflected light	—
	transmitted light	—	—
	visual elements	visual elements	visual elements
	constructional elements	—	—
	relational elements	relational elements	relational elements
	animation	—	animation
Sound	X	X	—
Touch	visual elements	—	—
	constructional elements	X	—
Smell	X	X	—
Illusionary elements	conceptual elements	conceptual elements	conceptual elements
	relational elements	relational elements	relational elements

Table 1: Comparison of the three modes of operation

3. Creating Intermedia Publications

3.1 Document Organization

Creating handout materials for a particular class requires less forethought and design than creating a general-purpose textbook. Until April 1989, Intermedia had been used solely to develop materials for courses, and not to produce a formal publication. To create a complete publication, we had to take a new look at how information was presented.

In Intermedia, users create *documents, folders, anchors, links,* and *webs*. Documents are an abstract representation of individual files in the Unix file system, and may be collected into a hierarchy of folders. Anchors are selections within documents, and they may be joined to form bi-directional links. Webs are special documents that represent collections of anchors in documents and the links between these anchors. While the links and anchors in a web are stored in a database, not in the documents themselves, they appear as an overlay on the documents when the web is opened.

Intermedia does not have a separate facility for managing a group of folders or documents as a single "hypermedia document." The system allows links to be made between any selection in any document anywhere in the file system.

To establish a clear, logical, and visual relationship between the folder hierarchy and an Intermedia web, the convention was established that all documents in a hypermedia publication would be in one "parent" folder. Further, we used the hierarchical file system to organize documents into logical groups within that folder according to subject. The documents in *Exploring the Moon* were sub-divided into folders according to six Apollo missions. The documents in *The Dickens Web* were sub-divided into folders for topics such as history and literary relations. Documents that correspond to the front matter and index of a book publication were placed in the "parent" folder so that they would be immediately apparent to the reader.

3.2 Graphic Formats for Document Types

Intermedia supports many windows open on the screen at a time. Following a link adds information to the screen display, rather than dismissing the current display and replacing it with another one. The entire system encourages users to maintain simultaneous visual contact with several different documents.

The opening of multiple documents creates a structure of overlapping windows within the overall frame of the computer screen that has no fixed and predictable order. This order is not random, however. The author can determine the initial size and position of each window, but cannot determine the sequence in which windows will appear or the number of windows open at any particular time. The reader's choice can be visually confusing, as many windows pile on top of each other and the reader is confronted with a diversity of intersecting rectangles and visual styles. We sought methods to create an underlying structure that would bring order to this diversity by maximizing visual familiarity and minimizing visual distraction.

To accomplish this we established a basic visual style and screen placement for each document type. By document type here, we mean the conceptual type of the document within a particular collection. By using the same typography, margins, screen placement, and other visual cues for each document type, we made it easier for the reader to recognize the kind of document that had been opened and see the differences between types of documents.

Intermedia 3.0 supports two typefaces: Times and Helvetica. For *Exploring the Moon* we mixed the two, using Times 12/14 for body text and Helvetica 14/16 for titles and picture captions. For *The Dickens Web,* which contains a great deal more text, we abandoned Times altogether. Helvetica 12/14 was chosen as the base type because of its legibility on the screen. Being a sans serif design, its simplicity and open forms adapts well to low screen resolution. The relatively large point size and leading for body text (9/10 to 10/12 is commonly used in books) proved absolutely necessary to support screen legibility. We reduced to 4.5 inches the usual 6 inch text column used for standard 8.5 by 11 inch cut-sheet pages. The narrower column for text on the screen was used for much the same reason as it is in newspaper layouts: to increase legibility of multiple blocks of text.

The white space within a document frame was treated as an important design element in both text and graphics documents. In particular, the left edge of text documents can affect basic legibility by supporting or detracting from the reader's ability to pick up the next line in a column. This left edge white space is all the more important when stacks of several document windows interact on the same screen layout. With this in mind, we became increasingly generous with the left margin in text, broadening it to a full inch when designing documents to appear on the 22-inch Apple monitor for *The Dickens Web*. We maintained balanced white space around all graphic images. In the case of many photographic images in *Exploring the Moon* that depended on a black background, this value was reversed. In these cases, the black edge was needed to support the illusion of a black background and a white image in the foreground.

3.3 Screen Position for Document Types

Printed page design traditionally uses an underlying grid to maintain visual balance between elements in a layout. The layout divides the page into one or more columns separated by "gutters" of white space. Text and graphics elements are generally constrained within this grid, which acts much like a frame for a picture. Balanced use of white space helps the reader detect edges and repeating the position of elements on sequential pages helps the reader to maintain the continuity of a text.

We experimented with an underlying grid for both publications. *Exploring the Moon* is visually simpler than *The Dickens Web*. This first publication consisted of four basic document types: prose summaries, maps, photographs with captions, and prose transcripts associated with photographs. A single visual style was established for each type and then a general zone on the 12-inch Apple monitor was assigned to each, corresponding roughly to a page layout grid. Thus, photographs were designed to always open on the upper left of the screen, with the associated prose transcript opening on the lower left. The document window for these transcripts was made rather narrow, since we assumed the reader would rather scroll through the prose of the transcript while maintaining visual contact with the associated photograph than obscure the image with a larger window. Examples of this are shown in Figures 1-3.

The Dickens Web presented more complex problems. The information repre-

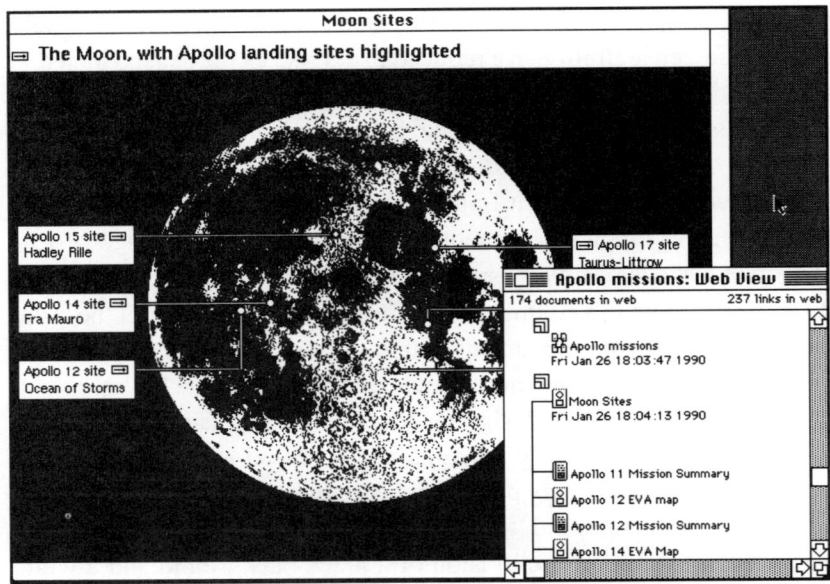

Figures 1: This first of three figures showing a sequence of documents being opened in *Exploring the Moon*, illustrating the placement of document types. This figure shows the lunar map overview with the web view in the foreground.

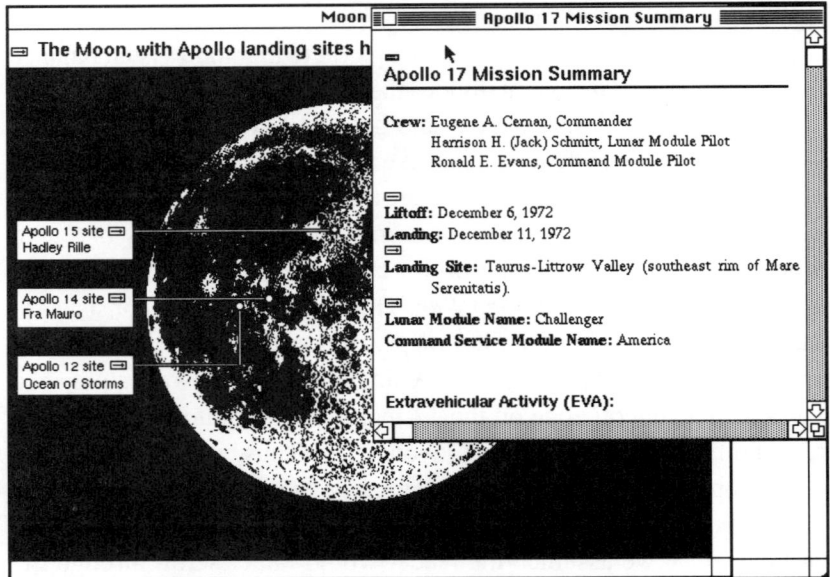

Figures 2: Following a link from the site of the Apollo 17 landing in Figure 2 brings the mission summary essay to the foreground on the upper right. Scrolling through this essay and following a link from the mention of Nansen Crater places a photo of the site on the upper right.

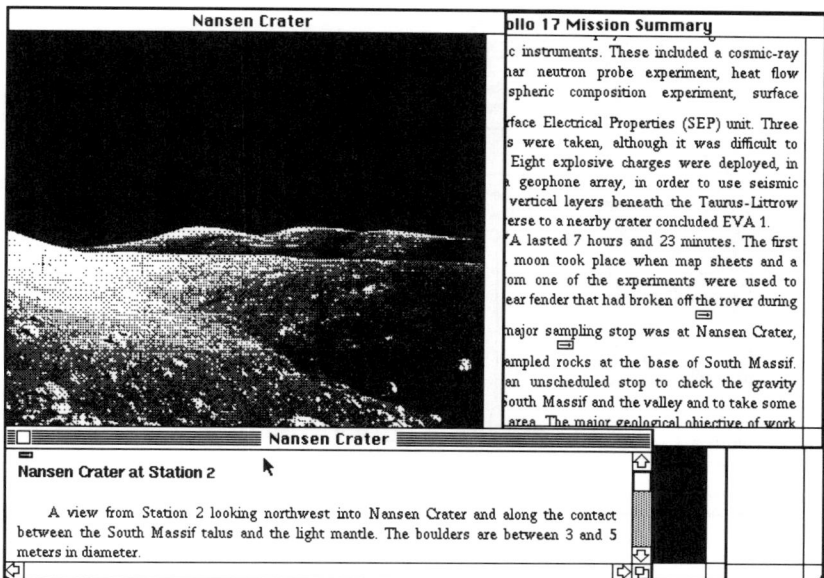

Figures 3: Following another link from this photo brings a caption document to the foreground, covering the lower part of the photo.

sented in *Exploring the Moon* is of a concrete nature. The overviews, which serve as indices and navigational tools for the collection, are photographic maps with links from text labels on these maps to information about places and things. The more abstract information in *The Dickens Web* relies on abstract overviews to show the reader what kinds of information are included and the inter-relationship among the various elements. These overviews take the form of information diagrams.

The original diagrams, developed by Professor George Landow over several years of using Intermedia for teaching, were re-interpreted. An underlying grid was used within the document frame to balance the white space between elements and to organize lines used to show relationships. A visual language of rectangles, rounded rectangles, and lines was developed, making use of four line weights and two colors (black and gray). Only horizontal and vertical lines were used, since any degree of skew caused distracting jagged effects. To reduce visual interference, no lines were allowed to cross (see Figures 4 and 5). Wherever possible, strong visual images (scans of photographs, engravings, or line drawings) were used as the central focus for these diagrams. This use of illustration worked particularly well in the case of author and novel overviews.

Just as the overviews in *The Dickens Web* were more complex than the overviews in *Exploring the Moon,* designing a screen grid for *The Dickens Web* and determining its document types were likewise a more difficult task. There are three major

Design of Hypermedia Publications

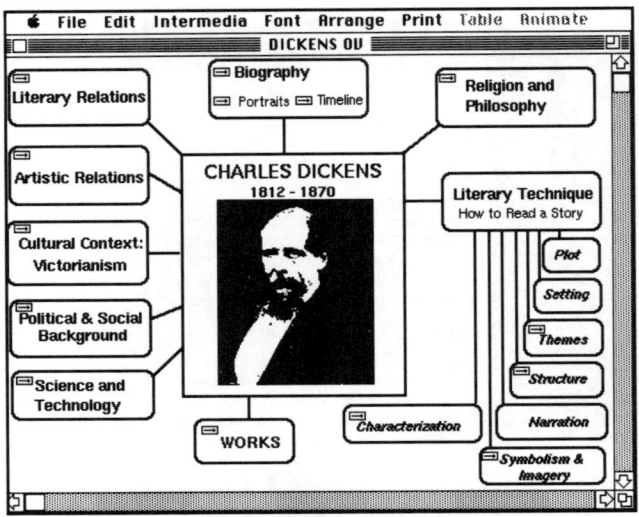

Figure 4: This shows a comparison of an author overview used in the Intermedia classroom collection and the same overview redesigned for *The Dickens Web*. A stronger visual image was selected and the rectangles were organized according to a 10-pixel grid.

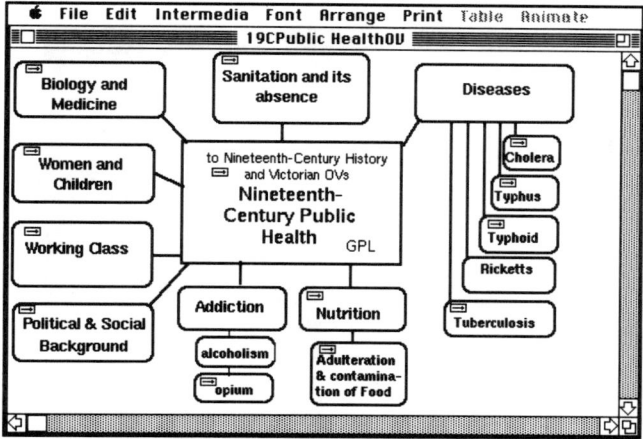

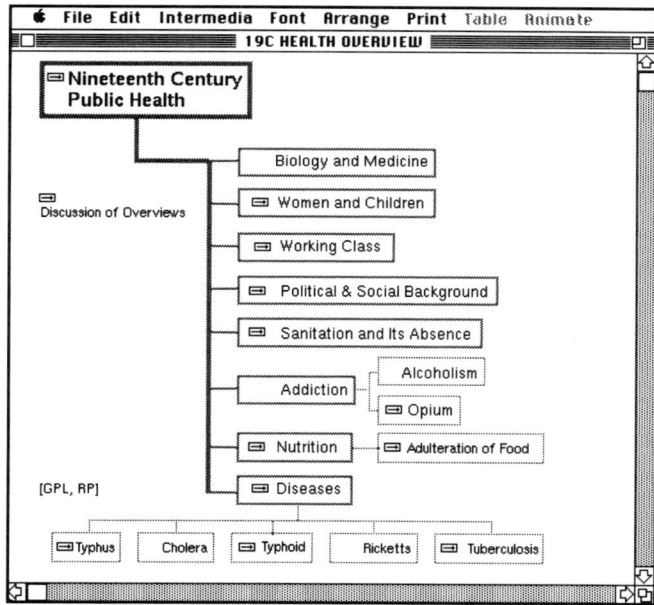

Figure 5: This shows a similar comparison for the more abstract overview of public health issues. Three levels of hierarchy are clearly expressed with minimum variation in type size by using variations in line weight and black/gray color.

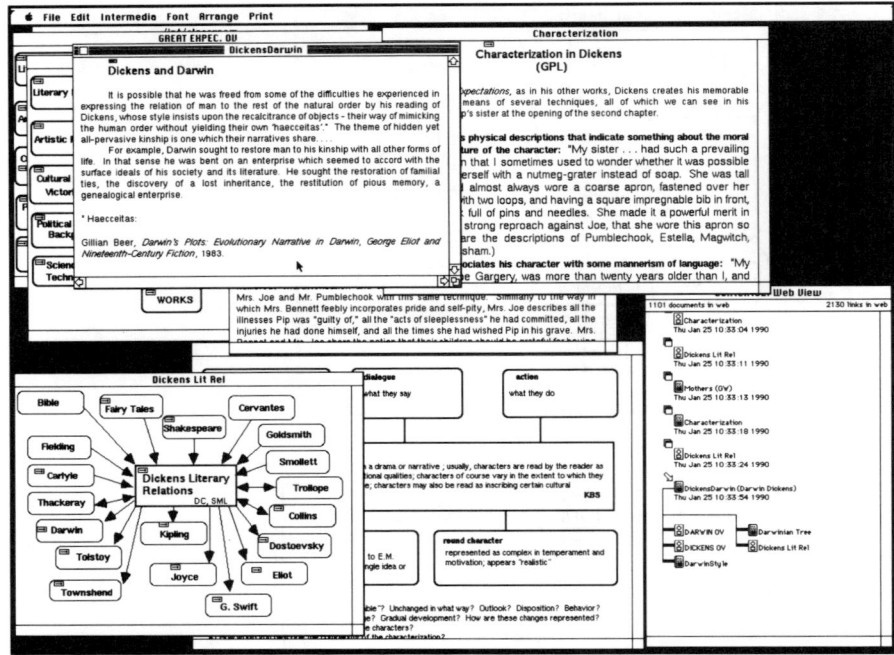

Figure 6

Figure 7

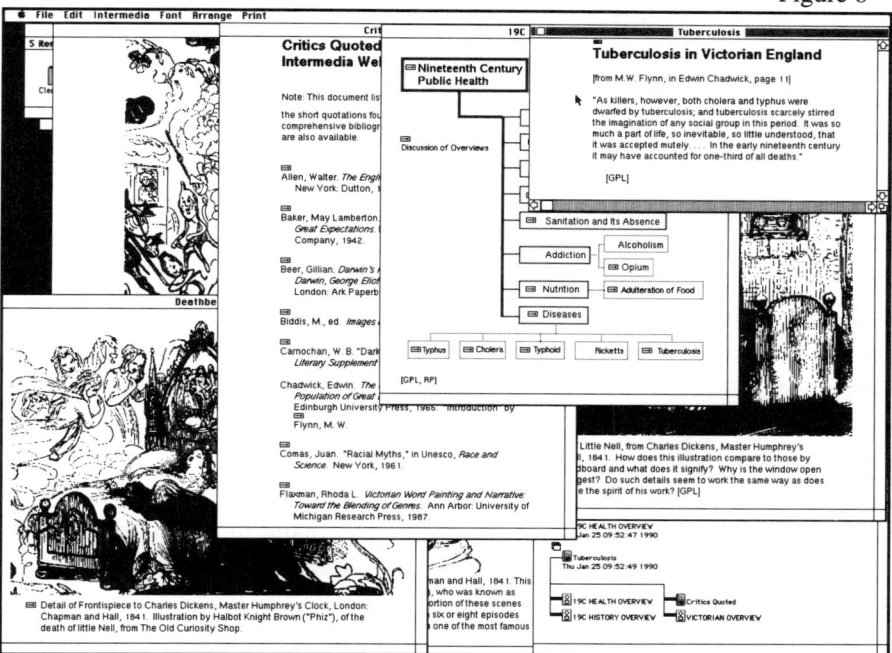

Figure 8

Figure 6 shows a screen with seven documents open from the Intermedia classroom collection. Notice the variations in type size among similar document types and the minimal use of white space within the frame of both text and graphic documents. Figure 7 and 8 shows a similar arrangement of redesigned documents open in *The Dickens Web*. The wider margins, narrower columns of text, and window alignment with the edges of the screen help establish an underlying sense of visual order.

---

types of text documents: student essays, two- or three-paragraph quotations from literary or historical critics, and original essays of a page or more written by a number of contributing authors. Also included in the collection are numerous timelines, and book illustrations, several types of overviews of varying size and complexity, and bibliographies. Some of the timelines are intended to be viewed side-by-side, and therefore should not overlap on the screen when opened, and many of the illustrations are quite large (see Figures 6-8). Because of this complexity, the overall grid design for this collection had to be less rigid than the one developed for *Exploring the Moon*, while still providing enough order to lessen the confusion once a number of documents had been opened on the screen.

3.3 Closure and Open-Ended Design

It is our intention that an Intermedia publication express a lack of closure on the subjects it covers. As previously stated, a feature of Intermedia is the lack of distinction between the author and the reader, and the ease with which information can be added and modified. In both publications we wanted the reader to see that the information being presented could be extended.

For *Exploring the Moon*, we added a folder of documents on the history of lunar astronomy. Anyone examining these documents would see that they are clearly related to each other. However, these essays and illustrations were not linked to each other or to documents on the Apollo missions. It was our intention to draw the reader into the process of extending the web by adding links to these documents in any way they saw fit. By example, we hoped that this would suggest the many kinds of information that could be added to the existing web.

The Dickens Web is a more obviously incomplete collection. We began by selecting only those parts of *Context32* that were linked to the documents about Dickens, but the relationships were not so simple. We chose to leave some "unlinked" topics in the overview diagrams, as well as to include a very sparsely linked overview of Jane Austen's *Pride and Prejudice*. Despite the fact that its relationship to Dickens was not crucial, we included a collection of about forty documents on the various religious traditions in England. It is our hope that the reader will see by these examples that the collection represents part of a much larger whole, and that the directions in which the collection could be expanded are many and various.

4. Future Work

This initial work has led us to propose several more topics of future research in this area.

4.1 Integration of motion

The research version of Intermedia supports video and animated graphic documents. In future publications which use these new document types, the graphic design of static text and graphics documents must account for their visual relationship to these dynamic elements in the collection. We are exploring various strategies for displaying link markers in dynamic media that will not interfere with the playback of an animation or video sequence.

4.2 Wayfinding

Hypermedia collections must convey to the user how things are interconnected. It must also be clear to the user how to navigate among the different parts of a collection. This is as much a design problem as it is a computational one. The Intermedia Web View helps the user answer important orientation questions such as "where have I been" and "where can I go" [Utting 1989]; however, the problems of seeing relationships that go beyond nearest-neighbor graphs and individual history lists remains. Much is to be learned from navigation aids in traditional book design: sidebar notes, page tabs, running line numbers, header/footer text, etc.

4.3 Document Types

Intermedia, like many other hypermedia systems, supports different *representational* document types such as text, graphics, and timelines. However, the software itself does not have any facility for identifying different *conceptual* document types such as overview diagram, photograph, map, or transcript [Halasz 1989]. To support these conceptual document types, we made use of graphic design cues and screen position. It is clear that a great deal more support could be built into the hypermedia system itself. Differences in document icons, document frames, and collection of text and graphic styles would all be interesting areas for experimentation.

4.4 Color and Transparency

The research version of Intermedia supports the use of color and transparency. These two new features open up important areas for further graphic design work. In addition to its obvious use in diagrams, color and related lighting effects could be used to distinguish stacks of windows. The use of transparent overlapping documents to support group annotation is already being explored. The general use of transparent stacks of related documents is also a promising area of study.

4.5 Redesign the Visual Desktop

We have worked thus far within the visual language provided by the Macintosh toolbox. All Intermedia documents are presented within the system-wide frame of the Apple menu bar, pull-down menus, dialog boxes, window controls, and representations of document names. A recent paper from Fitch RichardsonSmith

[Evenson 1989] correctly suggests that we should develop a more appropriate visual language for hypermedia cues. We believe that a coordinated redesign of both the exterior frame of the operating environment and the symbols used within the document frame to support hypermedia movement are needed to better support an appropriate sense of order for complex hypermedia.

References

[**Arnheim 1971**] Rudolf Arnheim, *Entropy and Art: an essay on disorder and order,* Berkeley: University of California Press, 1971.

[**Evenson 1989**] Shelly Evenson, John Rheinfrank, and Wendy Wulff. "Towards a Design Language for Representing Hypermedia Cues." *Hypertext '89 Proceedings.* November 5-7, 1989, Pittsburgh, PA. New York: ACM, 1989. 83-92.

[**Halasz 1989**] The authors are indebted to Frank Halasz's discussion of representational vs. conceptual document types during the "What's Wrong With Our Systems?" panel at Hypertext '89.

[**Landow 1989**] George Landow. "Hypertext in Literary Education, Criticism, and Scholarship." *Computers in the Humanities,* Vol. 23, No. 2 (June 1989): 173-198.

[**Landow 1990**] George Landow, et al. *The Dickens Web.* IRIS Intermedia collection. Providence, RI: Institute for Research in Information and Scholarship, Brown University, 1990.

[**Livingston 1989**] Katie Livingston, Jane Aubele, and James Head. *Exploring the Moon.* IRIS Intermedia collection. Providence, RI: Institute for Research in Information and Scholarship, Brown University, 1989.

[**Roberts 1983**] Colin H. Roberts and T. C. Skeat, *The Birth of the Codex,* London: Oxford University Press, 1983.

[**Utting 1989**] Kenneth Utting and Nicole Yankelovich. "Context and Orientation in Hypermedia Networks." *ACM Transactions on Information Systems,* Vol. 7, No. 1 (January, 1989): 58-84.

[**Yankelovich 1985**] Nicole Yankelovich, Norman Meyrowitz and Andries van Dam. "Reading and Writing the Electronic Book." *IEEE Computer,* Vol. 18, No. 10 (October 1985): 16-30.

[**Yankelovich 1988**] Nicole Yankelovich, Bernard J. Haan, Norman Meyrowitz and Steven M. Drucker. "Intermedia: The Concept and the Construction of a Seamless Information Environment." *IEEE Computer,* Vol. 21, No. 1 (January 1988): 81-96.

Strengths and Weaknesses of Database Models for Textual Documents

B.N. Rossiter† and M.A. Heather‡

† *Computing Laboratory, Newcastle University,*
Newcastle upon Tyne, England NE1 7RU
‡ *Sutherland Building, Newcastle Polytechnic,*
Newcastle upon Tyne, England NE1 8ST

ABSTRACT: User requirements in large and complex textbases are discussed in the light of current models. Examples applying relational and semantic models suggest criteria for a more fundamental approach involving the merger of object-oriented programming techniques with database methods in future complex object textbases.

KEYWORDS: document modelling, databases, complex objects.

1 Introduction

Little attention has been paid to text as structured data. Much of administrative data is in the form of textual strings but these tend to be treated as atomic entities independent of any relationship between words. Text retrieval and hypertext systems are based on physical divisions in documents and physical positions of words and rely on features like inversion, position operators and physical connections. By exploiting fully current technology such as multi-windowing and the emerging object-oriented programming, there have been significant advances in document manipulation in the provision of natural user interfaces [Pasquier-Boltuck et al 1988] and browsing systems [Brown 1988; Furuta and Stotts 1989]. There has been little regard for the very fine logical structure that lies beneath the physical form, even in recent data models for hypertext [Tompa 1989]. To handle large amounts of data of complex structure, more advanced file handling techniques will be required in the areas of full text information systems, electronic publishing, email, office automation, bulletin boards and conferencing.

Database technology needs to be extended from its present emphasis on simple objects to deal with complex objects such as text [Stonebraker et al 1987; Heather and Rossiter (in press)], CAD/CAM, CASE, knowledge bases and complex business information. In this paper, the work reported at WOODMAN'89 [Heather and Rossiter 1989] is refined with particular attention being paid to the semantics of class structures and symbolic keys. The aim is to show the potential of the developing object-oriented database technology for modelling textual documents.

2 Demands of Textual Applications on Filing Systems

As a first step in formulating a model, the demands made by textual applications on the technology of filing systems have been analyzed by drawing on applications at both Newcastle and elsewhere. The first two columns of figure 1 summarize the results which have been reported more fully elsewhere [Rossiter and Heather 1990]. This paper considers the implications of the requirements for database systems. Besides the obvious structural properties listed in section 1 of figure 1, many of the other needs also place demands on textual filing systems: context and proximity matching require fine index structures; thesauri introduce further types of data; referential transparency, to provide navigational facilities as in hypertext, requires links from one text to another ideally using symbolic identifiers; trails made while navigating text structures need to be recorded as fully-fledged data [Zellweger 1989; Sillitoe et al 1990]; and updating involves the major problems of version management and the modelling of dynamic behaviour such as the life cycle of a document.

Three inherent requirements for modelling text structures need to be satisfied for a successful database initiative: dynamic selection of unit size; representation of non-hierarchical text structures; and description of data in generalized and specialized forms.

Unlike informal systems which might store text as a continuous stream of characters, formal systems need an object unit. Traditionally a choice has been made governed by the storage capability of the system, by the human capacity for searching, retrieving and comprehending the information, and by the character of the document which will often be determined by traditional printing techniques. Thus, for example, the size of a legal statute is controlled by parliamentary business and other political factors. However, one unit alone is insufficient for all purposes. With text objects, it should be possible to retain the ability of natural language to keep the choice of unit dynamic and with the option of lazy evaluation to postpone any decision until the full circumstances and context of use are known.

	Free Text	Relational stand.	Relational extend.	Semantic E-R extend.	Semantic Taxis	Object-oriented
1. Design of STRUCTURE for holding text						
• unlimited size of fields and records	yes	not yet	not yet	-	-	-
• symbolic identification of records	limited	yes	yes	yes	yes	yes
• data models						
. hierarchical	yes	yes	yes	yes	yes	yes
. non-hierarchical (shared sub-obj.)	no	no	diff.	yes	yes	yes
. ability to retain un-normalized data	yes	no	no	-	yes	yes
• dynamic control of unit size (aggreg)	no	diff.	diff.	no	yes	diff.
• generalization and specialization (inher.)	no	no	no	yes	yes	yes
2. VIEWS						
• derived structures	no	yes	yes	yes	yes	yes
• parallel texts	no	no	poss.	-	poss.	poss.
3. RETRIEVAL						
• fast	yes	no	yes	-	-	-
• non-procedural interactive languages	yes	yes	yes	no	no	no
• closure	no	yes	yes	no	no	no
• words + phrases in text						
. context	yes	no	yes	-	-	yes
. proximity matching	yes	no	yes	-	-	yes
• keywords						
. free vocabulary	yes	yes	yes	-	yes	yes
. controlled vocabulary (thesauri, stop)	yes	yes	yes	-	yes	yes
. 'formatted' data	limited	yes	yes	-	yes	yes
• identifiers of text (symbolic key)	limited	yes	yes	-	yes	yes
4. Various formats for DISPLAY						
• human	yes	yes	yes	-	-	-
• machine-machine (wp, mark-up)	yes	yes	yes	-	-	-
5. TEMPORAL management with consistent updating						
• in-place modification, addition of data	yes	yes	yes	no	yes	yes
• dynamic behaviour - control of doc. life	no	no	no	no	yes	yes
• version management	yes	no	no	-	-	diff.
• concurrent access	yes	no	no	yes	-	yes
• value inheritance for natural data loading	no	no	no	yes	-	yes
6. INTEGRITY						
• protection against hardware failures	yes	yes	yes	-	-	-
• referential	no	yes	yes	no	yes	yes
• value	yes	yes	yes	-	yes	yes
7. SECURITY						
• whole file	yes	yes	yes	-	-	yes
• designated fields, data driven	yes	yes	yes	-	yes	yes
8. NAVIGATION through texts following conceptual paths						
• referential transparency (hypertext)	no	yes	yes	-	yes	yes
• trail maintenance	no	yes	yes	-	yes	yes
9. Textual ANALYSIS						
• function integrated with data	no	no	no	no	yes	yes
• word frequency lists, distribut. freq.	yes	yes	yes	no	yes	yes
• statistical tests e.g. sentence length	yes	yes	yes	no	yes	yes
• word co-occurrences	yes	no	no	no	yes	yes
10. SEMANTIC aids						
• parsing	no	no	poss.	-	poss.	poss.
• predicate logic, machine translation	no	no	poss.	-	poss.	poss.
• cognitive textual types	no	no	poss.	-	poss.	poss.
11. MULTI-MEDIA						
• integration of text and other data	no	poss.	poss.	poss.	poss.	poss.

Figure 1: User Requirements for Textbases and their Satisfaction by Database Techniques.

There are texts for which hierarchical structures are inadequate. Shakespeare and legal texts are good examples. Their essential characteristic is that units may need to be linked to multiple units at higher levels of the tree structure rather than the single unit allowed in hierarchical structures. Such structures suggest the need to examine models described later where words are considered as atoms of data to be built dynamically into a variety of complex molecular objects.

Linked particularly with the navigation requirements described earlier is the need to generalise when describing text structures. For example, in a hierarchical text structure, any one part of the tree may usually cite any other part. The textbase can be viewed at two levels: generalisation for an abstract overview in which any type of text object cites any other type; and specialization for a more detailed representation in which a specific type of text object cites another specific type.

3 Semantic Models and Text Structures

Database models can be categorized into two main types: basic and semantic. A range of semantic models has been proposed in order to incorporate more features, constraints and abstractions than are found in the basic ones in an attempt to represent more closely the real world. These include the Entity-Relationship (E-R) Model [Chen 1976] and Taxis [Mylopoulos et al 1980]. Text because of its complex nature usually requires full semantic models to capture completely its structure and examples of Chen, Taxis and others have been developed at Newcastle.

3.1 Models for Expressing Static Aspects

The viewpoint of Chen is that database design is concerned primarily with the occurrence of entities and the relationship between them. An E-R diagram of a UK statute could be represented in the form of figure 2(a) using rectangles to denote entity-types and diamond-shapes to denote relationships. A relationship flagged '*' is mandatory, otherwise it is optional. All relationships are one-to-many (1:N) bar one. The idea of generalisation is employed with the scope of a generic entity-type being delineated by the enclosure of its associated specializations within a thickly-lined rectangle. The generic structures defined are *node* to represent all possible text units from an act through parts and schedules to subsections and subparagraphs and *text* to represent the units holding the main part of the text - section,

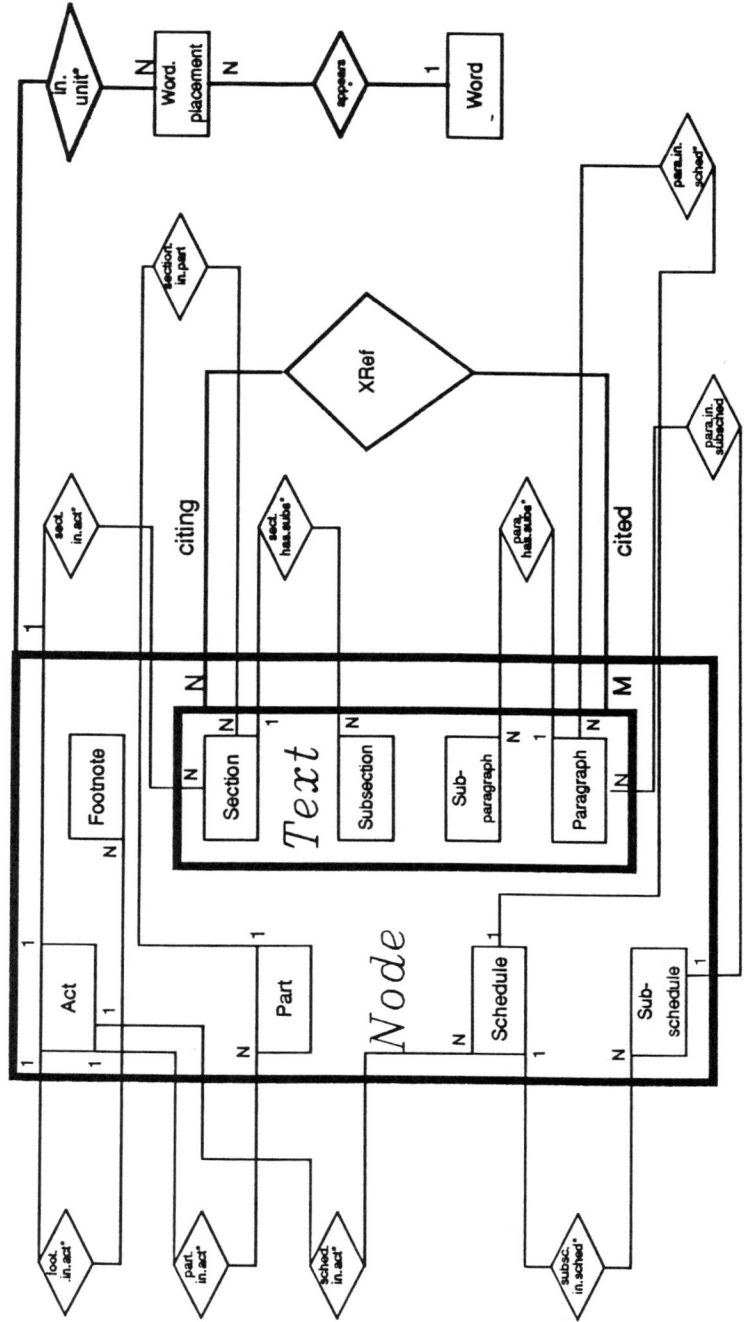

Figure 2: The Chen Entity-Relationship Model of Statutes: (a) Diagram

subsection, paragraph and subparagraph.

The idea behind *text* has already been introduced: its creation enables the involuted many-to-many (N:M) *XRef* relationship to be simplified into an entity of type *text* may cite another entity of type *text*. In the absence of generalization, sixteen different relationships would be required to handle all the possible cross references: an entity of type *section, subsection, paragraph* or *subparagraph* may cite any other entity of type *section, subsection, paragraph* or *subparagraph*. The idea behind *node* is that a generic identifier can greatly simplify addressing and aggregation operations by removing the need for end-users to know the specific structures involved. The base object in the E-R diagram is *word.placement* whose identifier contains two attributes *all.unit.id*, the symbolic identifier for the generalization *node*, and *word#* the physical position of the word in the unit addressed by *all.unit.id*. The entity-type *word*, representing in effect a word list, is in a one-to-many relationship with *word.placement*. The nature of *all.unit.id* is described later.

3.2 Class Structures

The structure of the statutes of figure 2(a) can be viewed as the complex object shown in figure 3. Two types of hierarchy are embedded within the class structure:

- An aggregation hierarchy represented by solid lines to indicate potential groupings of data. A common aggregation will be of *word.placement* to create dynamically any specialization of the generic object *node*. To Sakkinen [1989], this hierarchy represents incidental inheritance.

- An inheritance hierarchy represented by dotted lines to indicate the automatic inheritance of properties (attributes) by lower level objects from higher ones through 'isA' relationships. Thus *text* is a generic object from which the subobjects *section, subsection, paragraph* and *subparagraph* inherit properties such as text formatting attributes. Other forms of inheritance are for identifiers: textual objects can inherit their identifiers from *node* as described later. To Sakkinen, this hierarchy represents essential inheritance.

Similar rich structures are encountered in other texts such as Shakespeare's plays where the terminology of overlapping fields is used in the humanities to describe the structures. Fields are neither contiguous to each other nor contained completely within one another: lines, stage directions and speeches overlap each other with no clear structure other than that they

```
Act(year, chapter, title, date, preamble, arrangements,
    crossnotes, + 14 formatting attributes)
Part(part#, year, chapter, part.headings, part.subheadings,
    crossnotes, footnotes.old.statutes, + 5 formatting.attributes)
Section(section#, year, chapter)
Section.in.Part(section#, part#, year, chapter)
Subsection(ss#, section#, year, chapter)
Schedule(schedule#, year, chapter, schedule.headings, crossnotes,
    omissions, footnotes.old.statutes, + 29 formatting attributes)
Subschedule(subschedule#, schedule#, year, chapter,
    subschedule.headings, crossnotes, omissions,
    footnotes.old.statutes, + 29 formatting attributes)
Paragraph(para#, schedule#, year, chapter)
Para.in.Subsched(para#, subschedule#, schedule#, year, chapter)
Subparagraph(subp#, para#, schedule#, year, chapter)
Footnote(footnote#, year, chapter, footnote.text)
Word(word, word.description attributes)
Word.placement(all.unit.id, word#, word)
Node(all.unit.id)
Text(text.id, marginal.note.other, crossnotes, omissions,
    footnotes.to.old.statutes, + 20 formatting attributes)
XRef(citing.text.id, cited.text.id)

Notes: 1) The italicised attributes comprise the identifier.
       2) all.unit.id, text.id, citing.text.id and cited.text.id are
          defined in figure 4.
```

Figure 2: The Chen Entity-Relationship Model of Statutes:
(b) Partially-normalized Table-types

each contain one or more words of text.

3.3 Identifiers

For a complete E-R model, the diagram of figure 2(a) has been augmented with information on attributes and identifiers. Figure 2(b) shows this information for the statute law. Many of the tables are not fully normalised: some text formatting attributes have multiple values for each identifier value. Further normalisation to remove such dependencies would require the creation of more entity-types which would complicate the model considerably and produce an unnatural structure.

Figure 4 defines the generic identifiers in Taxis-like class structures. The

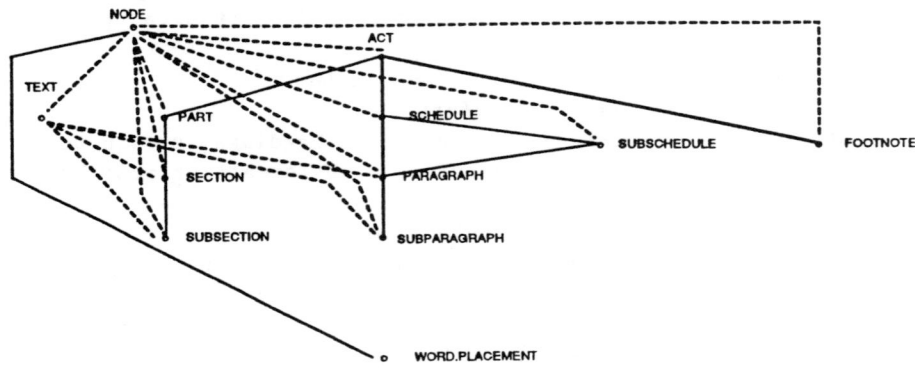

Figure 3: Class Structure for Objects Occurring in Legal Text

```
define AnyDataClass Node              define AnyDataClass Text isA Node
  ss#:{|ssmin:ssmax|}                   changeable
  section#:{|sectmin:sectmax|}          marginal.note.other:string
  part#:{|partmin:partmax|}             crossnotes:string
  subp#:{|subpmin:subpmax|}             omissions:string
  para#:{|paramin:paramax|}             footnotes.old.statutes:string
  subschedule#:{|subsmin:subsmax|}      formatting.attribute1:string
  schedule#:{|schmin:schmax|}           formatting.attribute2:string..
  footnote#:{|footmin:footmax|}       unique
  year:{|yearmin:yearmax|}              text.id:(year,chapter,section#,
  chapter:{|chapmin:chapmax|}             ss#,schedule#,para#,subp#)
unique
  all.unit.id:(year,chapter,part#,    define AnyDataClass XRef
    section#,ss#,schedule#,             citing.text.id:set of Text
    subschedule#,para#,subp#,           cited.text.id:set of Text
    footnote#)                        unique
                                        XRef:(citing.text.id,
                                              cited.text.id)
```

Figure 4: Taxis-like Specification of Symbolic Key for Statutes

identifier *all.unit.id* of the class *node* is a polynomial comprising the hierarchical sequence of an object in the statute law structure. In this study, the polynomial components are integers within the ranges shown, thus *ss#* takes values between *ssmin* and *ssmax*. The identifier of the other generic entity-type *text* is defined as *text.id* with a subset of the attributes of *all.unit.id* inherited in the 'isA' relationship between *node* and *text*. The attributes of the entity *XRef* are the keys of the citing and cited text units *citing.text.id* and *cited.text.id* respectively. These attributes draw their values from the domain *text.id*. Generic symbolic keys have been used throughout our work to provide a powerful mechanism for flexibly manipulating the complex object structure of figure 3 [Rossiter and Heather 1988].

3.4 Models for Expressing Dynamic Aspects

Major deficiencies of the E-R and Borkin models are that they have no defined operations and thus cannot handle dynamic control of the life-cycle of entities. Semantic models which enable such dynamic structures to be expressed as well as static ones have therefore also been examined such as Taxis, the Event Model and SHM+. The model Taxis illustrates the potential of this approach and its use is being explored at Newcastle for control of the legal drafting process [Rossiter and Heather 1990].

4 Basic Models and Text Structures

4.1 The Relational Model

None of the basic models is rich enough in capability to satisfy all requirements in manipulating complex textual structures. Hierarchical and network models can be quickly discounted but a more detailed discussion is necessary to illustrate weaknesses in a relational approach 'flattening' the data. The relational model offers the power of the network model but with a simple and elegant method of data manipulation. The E-R model given earlier for law can be implemented directly by mapping the table-types in figure 2(b) on to conventional relations: one table-type per relation. There is a major difficulty in this transformation for text structures: the unnormalized data for figure 2(b) cannot be retained in the relational model. Also, the semantics of the E-R diagram are now represented implicitly; for instance, the structure of the objects:

   act -> schedule -> paragraph -> subparagraph -> word.placement

is represented by a series of relations whose attributes carry the inter-object relationships so that the basic hierarchical structure is not explicitly conveyed to the user as in the E-R diagram. For users with detailed knowledge of the relational model, a clear advantage is the ease with which keys as formatted data can be manipulated giving flexibility in unit size for display and symbolic addressing for navigation. Standard set operators can provide aggregation of data, dynamic variation of the unit of retrieval as users' needs change, cross-referencing and closure. Users with little knowledge of the relational model, however, are dependent on views predefined by the database administrator to achieve abstractions such as aggregation.

There is also the problem of indexing text in a versatile manner. There is no concept of a global index: a single index cannot readily be constructed for a series of attributes in different relations across the textbase to facilitate searching on a particular generalized abstraction. It is not easy to build a single word index on the abstraction *text* defined earlier.

4.2 Extended Relational Approach

The logical approach for improving the flexibility of relational systems in manipulating text is to flatten the data so that it is completely normalized to the word level. The existence of the base relations shown in figure 2(b) and of relations holding word positions in the text should provide data structures which can satisfy most user requirements. However, some features of figure 2(b) are not easy to represent. The keys *text.id*, *citing.text.id* and *cited.text.id* essential for generalization cannot strictly be defined as in figure 4 for that conflicts with the entity integrity rule: no component of a primary key can be null. This can be overcome by recording null values as zeroes. For the purists, though, three logical word indexes are needed in the form of the relations shown below to represent the three distinct paths to *word.placement* via *footnote*, *subsection* or *subparagraph*. Also shown is the relation *request* which contains the words in the user's search request.

Word.H2 (*word#, footnote#, year, chapter*, word)
Word.H3 (*word#, ss#, section#, year, chapter*, word)
Word.H4 (*word#, subp#, para#, schedule#, year, chapter*, word)
Request (*word*)

The word index relations can be quickly searched by dividing them by the relation *request*. The unit searched can be varied dynamically by taking appropriate views of the index using the projection operator. Thus if relation *request* contains the search terms A and B, a search for A and B in the same subsection can be achieved by:

```
Word.H3 [year, chapter, section#, ss#, word] divideby Request[word]
```

and in the same schedule by:

`Word.H4 [year, chapter, schedule#, word] divideby Request[word]`

A clear disadvantage of the approach of flattening the data is that no standard set operators exist for constructing the word indexes and it is not realistic to expect users to input such structures manually. Operators to perform the flattening of normal text could be user-written but this would involve additional effort and would be likely to result in inefficient code.

The manipulation of biblical text in relational databases has also been considered in detail [Heather and Rossiter (in press)]. It was found feasible to normalize this data to the word level and employ SQL or relational algebra for searching the data against different unit sizes and for aggregating the data as necessary. The biblical data are represented by a complex object with the single path:

> testament -> book -> chapter -> verse -> word.placement

Although this path is much simpler to manage than the multiple paths of law shown above, the approach of 'flattening' the data was found to be cumbersome for data manipulation, to hide the natural structure of the data from the user and to have adverse performance implications when reconstituting aggregations for documents in large textbases. Only with extensive mediation, between the system and the user, is a natural interface provided with a high level of data abstraction.

5 Object Oriented Systems

In advanced languages such as Ada, C++ and Simula, the concept of class structure and variable unit size is well established through the extensible type system with the ability to declare abstract data types. Some of these languages allow subobjects to inherit properties from higher-level objects and inter-object communication. These object-oriented systems readily allow iterative searching of complex objects, multiple levels of abstraction and a natural ability to handle dynamic aspects with function fully integrated with data [Bloom and Zdonik 1987], all important issues for textbases.

The use of object-oriented programs for database management is in its early stages. Advances depend on programming systems being developed to handle persistent data such as in the early work by Atkinson with PS-Algol [Atkinson et al 1981]. One of the first developments was GemStone

[Copeland and Maier 1984] which is related to SmallTalk and uses the Opal language for data definition and manipulation. Abstract data types can be defined, object identity is preserved and objects participate in one or more collections to provide a shared subobject facility. Behavioural aspects are handled by messaging.

The strengths of the object-oriented approach lie in the ability to import advanced programming techniques into areas of data modelling in which database technology has been traditionally weak. However, in the management of persistent data, object-oriented systems have a number of significant weaknesses. These include many of the standard functions which are an essential part of any database system. Thus security, concurrency, transaction control, archiving and some aspects of integrity are achieved by primitive methods, if at all. Optimisation of data storage and indexing are at an early stage perhaps analagous to that of the first relational systems.

Of greatest significance, perhaps, is that owing to their procedural nature, many object-oriented systems do not provide the non-procedural interactive languages that end-users require for data manipulation. Procedural interfaces requiring some knowledge of high-level programming languages may be acceptable in engineering applications where the clientale usually has a relatively sophisticated programming background. However, in areas such as text and office automation, it is considered that procedural interfaces are not appropriate to the environment. Clearly, ad hoc query languages could be designed for applications by writing an interface program in a host language. However, the more durable non-procedural languages have been based on mathematical methods, such as relational calculus and algebra, applied to a conceptual model of the data. There is thus, owing to a lack of emphasis on conceptual modelling techniques, a layer of control missing from current object-oriented systems to provide the necessary user environment. There are also difficulties with closure: if the result of a query is presented as a table, that is not a viable structure for further work.

6 Discussion

The last six columns of figure 1 show the extent to which our critical requirements for textbases are met by the techniques of free text retrieval, ISO-standard relational database, extended relational database with facilities to flatten textual data, semantic models oriented towards static and dynamic aspects such as E-R and Taxis respectively, and object-oriented systems. A hyphen indicates incomplete information is available.

Free text retrieval systems suffer from limited data structuring ability, lack of navigational aids and an inability to model dynamic behaviour. Standard relational systems provide better data structuring and navigational facilities but their performance in context searching, other than on base units, is questionable and proximity searching is not available. Extended relational systems with flattened textual data can achieve a better performance and, through some ability to model complex objects, provide the basis of a unified model for multi-media data and of initiatives in advanced text processing such as semantic parsing. However, aggregation is a cumbersome task for a user and dynamic behaviour is not addressed. The E-R model has not been directly implemented so the information in the figure is incomplete but, with the lack of defined operations, it cannot be a complete solution.

Whether in the guise of semantic models like Taxis or databases such as GemStone, object oriented approaches appear to offer the most promise. Such systems handle quite naturally variable unit size, shared subobjects, dynamic behaviour and integration of function and data, and have considerable promise in multi-media modelling. The semantic models, in particular, also handle aggregation well through subtyping declarations. However, so far, object-oriented systems have presented relatively procedural interfaces to users, do not readily provide closure, are rather limited in standard database functions such as concurrent access and have not proved themselves in terms of performance. The optimum solution for users of textbases would therefore appear to be a merger of advanced database technology as in semantically-enriched relational systems with advanced object-oriented programming to create object-oriented textbases. Such textbases should be thought of as object-bases rather than pure database or object-oriented systems. It should not be pretended that such a merger will be easy. The cultural differences between the two approaches present many difficulties [Tsichritzis and Nierstrasz 1988] and much research of a fundamental nature is still required to attain a single complete multi-media model.

References

[Atkinson81] M P Atkinson, K J Chisholm, and W P Cockshott (July 1981), PS-Algol: an Algol with a persistent heap, *ACM SIGPLAN Notices* **17**(7).

[Bloom87] T Bloom and S B Zdonik (1987), Issues in the Design of Object-oriented Database Languages, OOPSLA'87 Conf. Proc., *ACM SIGPLAN Notices* **22**(12) 441-451.

[Brown88] P J Brown (1988), Hypertext: the way forward, in: *Document Manipulation and Typography*, ed. J C van Vliet, Cambridge 183-191.

[Chen76] P P-S Chen (1976), The Entity-Relationship Model – towards a unified view of data, *ACM TODS* 1(1) 9-36.

[Copeland84] G Copeland and D Maier (1984), Making SmallTalk a Database System, *Proc ACM/ SIGMOD Int. Conf. Management of Data*.

[Furuta89] R Furuta and P D Stotts (1989), Programmable Browsing Semantics in Trellis, in: *Hypertext'89 Proc.*, Special Issue - SIGCHI Bulletin 27-42.

[Heather (in press)] M A Heather and B N Rossiter (in press), Syntactical Relations in Parallel Text, in: *Proc. 15th Int. ALLC Conf.*, ed. Y Choueka, Jerusalem 1988.

[Heather89] M A Heather and B N Rossiter (1989), Theoretical Structures for Object-based Text, in: *WOODMAN'89*, edd. J André and J Bézivin, BIGRE **63-64** 178-192.

[Mylopoulos80] J Mylopoulos, P A Bernstein, and H K T Wong (1980), A Language Facility for Designing Database-Intensive Facilities, *ACM TODS* **5** 185-207.

[Pasquier-Boltuck88] J Pasquier-Boltuck, E Grossman and G Collaud (1988), Prototyping an Interactive Electronic Book System using an Object-Oriented Approach, in: *Lecture Notes Comp. Sci.*, Springer-Verlag **322** 177-190.

[Rossiter88] B N Rossiter and M A Heather (1988), Data Models and Legal Text, *CC-AI* **5**(1) 39-55.

[Rossiter90] B N Rossiter and M A Heather (1990), *Towards the Object Oriented Text Base*, Computing Laboratory, University of Newcastle upon Tyne, Technical Report, no. 297.

[Sakkinen89] M Sakkinen (1989), Disciplined Inheritance, *ECOOP'89 Proceedings*, (ed.) Cook, S, Cambridge 39-56.

[Sillitoe90] T J Sillitoe, B N Rossiter and M A Heather (1990), Trail Management in Hypertext: in: *BNCOD-8 Proc.*, ed. A Brown, Pitman.

[Stonebraker87] M Stonebraker, J Anton, and E Hanson (1987), Extending a Database System with Procedures, *ACM TODS* **12**(3) 350-376.

[Tompa89] F W Tompa (1989), A Data Model for Flexible Hypertext Database Systems, *ACM Trans Information Systems* **7**(1) 85-106.

[Tsichritzis88] D C Tsichritzis and O M Nierstrasz (1988), Fitting Round Objects into Square Databases, ECOOP'88 Proceedings, in: *Lecture Notes Comp. Sci.*, Springer-Verlag **322** 283-299.

[Zellweger89] P T Zellweger (1989), Scripted Documents: A Hypermedia Path Mechanism, in: *Hypertext'89 Proc.*, Special Issue - SIGCHI Bulletin 1-14.

A structured document database system*

Pekka Kilpeläinen, Greger Lindén, Heikki Mannila, Erja Nikunen

Department of Computer Science
University of Helsinki
Teollisuuskatu 23
SF-00510 Helsinki
Finland

ABSTRACT: We describe a database system for writing, editing, and querying structured documents. The structure of the text is described using a context-free grammar, and the operations are implemented using a powerful query language. The system supports the use of user-defined multiple views of the documents: one view can contain all the structure explicitly, while another can contain only part of the document and have only part of the structure visible. This makes the system flexible for different editing tasks. The system is implemented in C using a relational database system.

1 Introduction

Text with a structure is quite common: dictionaries, reference manuals, annual reports etc. are typical examples. In recent years, research on systems for writing structured documents has flourished: see, e.g., [André et al. 1989 a,b; Furuta 1989; Quint 1989] for recent surveys of the field. The SGML and ODA standards (see [Joloboff 1989; Barron 1989; Brown 1989]) have further increased the interest in the area.

The Helsinki Structured Text Database System (HST) is an environment for writing, editing, and querying structured documents. The system uses context-free grammars for modelling the structure of documents. The HST system differs from previous work in several respects.

Firstly, HST is a *database system*, with a powerful query language. The user interface translates the user's commands into this language, and they are then executed. We feel that the manipulation and storage of structured documents can benefit from the research done in the database area. The use of a query language makes it possible to apply, e.g., the ideas from query optimization.

---

*This work was supported by the Academy of Finland and by the Technology Development Center (TEKES).

Secondly, the HST system user interface is based on the idea of *multiple views*.[1] Some editing tasks are easiest to do in a structured view, while other tasks can best be done when the structure of the document is not as explicitly represented. The HST system allows the user to keep several views of the same document. Whenever the text in one view is edited, the system automatically modifies all the other views correspondingly. The views are defined by giving an annotated version of the grammar describing the structure of the document. The views and their updates are implemented using the query language and an automatic technique for inverting simple queries.

The system does not do any natural language processing: the parts of text in the leaves of the tree are just uninterpreted strings for the system. Another part of document processing not addressed is text formatting. The HST system is able to do some primitive formatting, but mostly we just use the views to generate input for some specialized formatting program (e.g., LaTeX).

The HST system is developed in cooperation with three industrial partners: a computer manufacturer, a publisher, and a government agency whose task is to produce dictionaries for Finnish and Swedish and their dialects.

The HST system is implemented in C using X Window System and a relational database system. The current version (January 1990) is a working prototype, but there is not much experience yet on the use of the system by novice users.

In this paper we give an overview of the HST system. The rest of the paper is organized as follows. Section 2 gives an example of the use of the system. Section 3 discusses the data model used for describing the structure of documents, while Section 4 shows how multiple views of one document are defined and updated. Section 5 outlines the query language used, and Section 6 gives an overview of the architecture of the system. Section 7 is a short conclusion.

2 An example of the use of HST

Suppose a user wants to establish a large collection of bibliographic references. Assume the structure of such a document has been defined using a context-free grammar, as follows.

1. list → publications
2. publications → publication*

---

[1] See Section 4 for references to related work on multiple views.

3. publication → authors title journal volume year pages
4. authors → author*
5. author → initials name
6. initials → text
7. name → text
8. title → text
9. journal → text
10. volume → text
11. year → number
12. pages → start end
13. start → number
14. end → number.

Note that the grammar defines only the logical structure, not any details of formatting.

For a user who just wants to read the list of references, assume a representation of the form

```
N. Yankelovich, N. Meyrowitz, A. van Dam: Reading
and writing the electronic book. IEEE Computer 18
(1985), 15-29.
```

has been defined. For another user interested in editing the list of references and adding new references, a representation like

```
authors:
   author: N. Yankelovich
   author: N. Meyrowitz
   author: A. van Dam
title: Reading and writing the electronic book
journal: IEEE Computer
volume: 18
year: 1985
pages: 15-29
```

can be more useful.

Still another user might only want to see how long articles certain authors produce, and thus the appropriate view could contain only part of the document:

```
authors:
   author: N. Yankelovich
```

```
author: N. Meyrowitz
author: A. van Dam
pages: 15-29
```

Suppose now the user has edited the list of references and wants to produce input for LaTeX from the result. That is, he/she would like to have a represention like

```
\item
N. Yankelovich, N. Meyrowitz, A. van Dam:
Reading and writing the electronic book.
{\em IEEE Computer} : {\bf 18} (1985), 15-29.
```

In HST, a view is defined by giving an *annotated grammar*. Such a grammar contains a modified production for some of the productions of the original grammar. The modified production can omit some of the nonterminals of the original production, reorder the remaining ones, and insert terminals.[2]

For example, the publication list grammar could be annotated as follows to produce output suitable for LaTeX.

1. list → publications

    ```
    list    -> '\documentstyle{article} '
               '\begin{document} '
               '\begin{enumerate} '
               publications
               '\end{enumerate} '
               '\end{document} '
    ```

2. publications → publication*
3. publication → authors title journal volume year pages

    ```
    publication -> '\item '
                   authors ': ' title
                   ' {\em ' journal '}'
                   ' {\bf ' volume '}, '
                   year ', ' pages '.'
    ```

4. authors → author*[3]

---

[2] An annotated grammar is actually a syntax-directed translation, in the sense this term was used in the 1970's [Aho & Ullman 1972].

[3] Here we use a convenient shorthand for describing how regular expressions are handled in view definitions. A simple alternative would be to write the production without using iteration, and in that case no extension to the formalism would be needed.

```
authors -> author*
*.separator = ', '
```

5. author → initials name

```
author -> initials ' ' name
```

6. initials → text
7. name → text
8. title → text
9. journal → text
10. volume → text
11. year → number
12. pages → start end

```
pages -> start '-' end
```

13. start → number
14. end → number.

An example of the screen of the current version of HST is shown in Figure 1. The user has opened two views of one document.

Suppose now the view definition has been given, but the user wants to produce a LaTeX list for only those references where the publication year is after 1980. This is done choosing from the menu the entry for search with the condition

```
year in publication > 1980.
```

The result is a document, and the LaTeX view of it can be fed to the formatting program to produce output.

3 Data model

The data model used in a database system is very important: it determines how data can be organized and manipulated. As in, e.g., [Gonnet & Tompa 1987 a; Bancilhon & Richard 1984; Coray et al. 1986; Furuta et al. 1988; Quint & Vatton 1986] the structure of documents is described in HST using context-free grammars. Thus, in database terminology, grammars correspond to schemas, and parse trees correspond to instances. Hence the data in HST is in the form of parse trees.

Besides grammars, the data model of HST contains *attributes*, which are values stored at the nodes of the parse tree. Thus the grammars are actually attribute grammars (see, e.g., [Aho *et al.* 1986]). Attributes are used to implement hypertext links: an attribute of a node can contain a pointer to another node.[4] The query language makes it possible to form links between different nodes automatically, for example, to link a citation to the corresponding entry in a bibliography. Attributes can also be used to represent other auxiliary information, for example for formatting purposes. They also have an important task in the implementation of incremental processing of text queries.

In HST grammars are considered to be structured text. Hence they can be edited in the same way as other documents; no separate mechanisms are necessary.

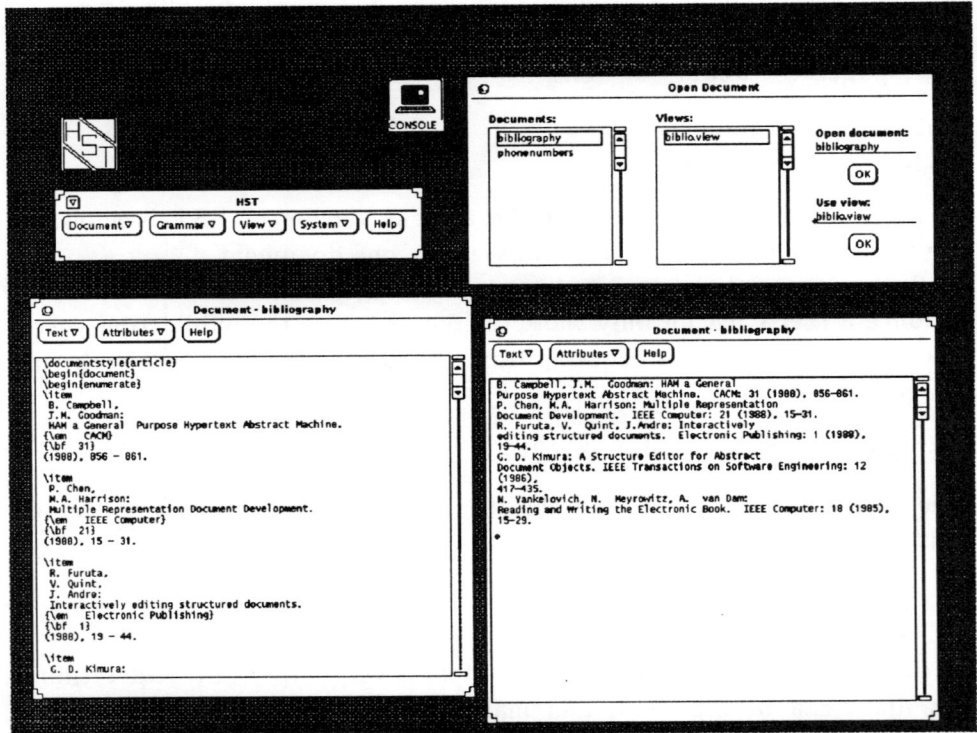

Figure 1: An example screen.

---

[4]Hence the target of a link can be an entity of any size.

4 Multiple views

Multiple views are an integral part of the HST system. Next we describe in more detail the reasons for adopting them, their definition, and their implementation.

Structured editors have been studied extensively in the field of programming environments (see, e.g., [Reps & Teitelbaum 1989]). The experience seems to be that structure is sometimes useful and sometimes harmful. A recent survey on the advantages and disadvantages of structure-oriented editors for programming languages can be found in [Minör 1990]. We aim at a flexible system, where the structure can be used only when it is useful. The user should be able to use whatever view is most convenient. This approach makes it possible to input and output documents in, e.g., SGML format to HST.[5] We want to be able to define views in a simple way, so that even a non-expert user can provide his/her own definitions, if needed.

Our starting point is that a textual view of a structured document is a representation of (part of) the document as a string. The user can edit a textual view using an ordinary text editor or a specialized one, perhaps offering some support for certain operations.

The view generated from a node in the parse tree corresponding to a production is computed by generating the views of the subtrees mentioned in the annotated production and by inserting appropriate strings.

Let G be the grammar defining the structure of a document d, and let R_1 and R_2 be two annotated versions of G. Denote the textual views of d corresponding to R_1 and R_2 by r_1 and r_2, respectively. Suppose the user modifies view r_1, yielding r_1'.

Then the system parses r_1' using R_1. The result is a parse tree t_1'. From the grammars G, R_1, and R_2 the system automatically generates queries that transform t_1' to d' (a parse tree over G) and further to t_2' (a parse tree over R_2) and to r_2' (an updated view corresponding to R_2). If the view is partial, then d' must be merged with d. (See Figure 2.)

This process is described in more detail in [Nikunen & Mannila 1989].

Changes in an arbitrary view cannot be transformed back to the original document. For example, consider the case where both the original grammar and the annotated grammar are

$A \rightarrow BC$
$B \rightarrow \text{text}$
$C \rightarrow \text{text}$

---

[5]Provided that some of the peculiarities allowed by SGML are not used.

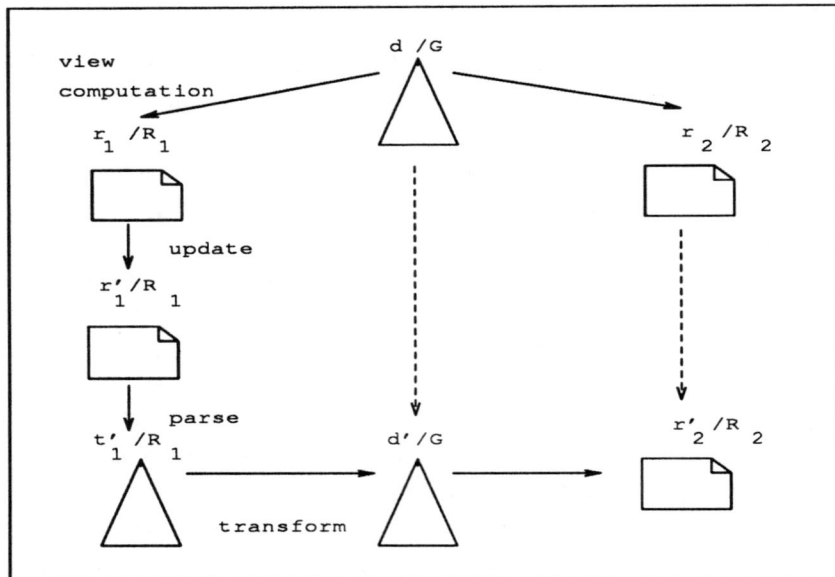

Figure 2: Manipulation of views. Triangles denote parse trees, and the rectangles denote textual views. The notation d/G means document d corresponding to a grammar G.

Then the resulting view contains no information about what part of the text was produced by B and what part was produced by C. Thus there is no unique way of mapping the changes in the view back to the original document.

One important aspect in implementing multiple views is *incrementality*. If several views of one document are shown at the same time, the system maintains them in a consistent state. When the user changes part of one view, we do not want to compute all the other views from scratch. Rather, we want to compute only those parts of the other views that were affected by the change. Luckily, this is fairly easy to solve reasonably well. One just keeps markers describing the boundaries of the modified part of the document. By looking at these, the transformations can be redone only partly. For example in the publication list example the two views of it are such that if we change one reference in one view, modifications needed to make the other view consistent affect only to the part showing the same reference.

Next we briefly describe other work related to the use of multiple views. An early paper describing this idea is [Chamberlin *et al.* 1981]. For a highly specialized case of view updating, see the description of the VorTeX system [Chen & Harrison 1988]. Also Lilac [Brooks 1988] supports two views. The **pedtnt** system described in [Furuta *et al.* 1988] allows users to edit the formatted text representation of the document, and heuristics modify the structure accordingly. Grif [Quint & Vatton 1986; Furuta *et al.* 1988] allows definition of both full and partial views. Partial views are defined by describing which logical objects are visible in different views.

Work on view updates with similar goals as ours has been reported by Yellin and Mueckstein [1986; 1988], who discuss a method to invert attribute grammars. Several programming language environments have multiple representations.

5   Query language

The query language of HST is called PQL (parse tree query language). It is loosely based on the language presented in [Gonnet & Tompa 1987 a,b], but includes some extensions (e.g., attributes). The language is a procedural language with assignments and control structures (loops, procedures, functions). Additionally, it includes specific operations for manipulating parse trees. The language is described fully in [Kilpeläinen *et al.* 1989].

One design decision in HST is that the query language is not meant to be used by the end user. PQL is used mainly for writing the functions that are called by the user interface. For example, the query for the references published after 1980 would be translated to approximately

> `every publication in d where (year in this) > 1980.`

Here d is the document containing the list of references. Similarly, the transformation from one view into another is translated to a PQL program containing a few lines.[6]

The end users can use existing views of documents or define new ones by annotating grammars. The queries for locating parts of documents are specified by giving conditions on the structure and the actual text of the document, as in the above example. Preliminary experience suggests that this combination is fairly common. The end users give the queries by selecting appropriate components from the menus.

An interesting research question is the design of a simple nonprocedural query language for structured documents. Something combining the elegance of Query-by-Example and the expressive power of Prolog could be useful.

---

[6]Of course, these lines call some functions generated from the definition of the views.

6 Structure of the system

The HST system consists of four main components: the user interface, the compiler, the parse tree machine, and the database component.

The user interface is a standard windowing interface with pull-down (or pop-up) menus. It is implemented using the X Window System and the XView toolkit. The user interface generates small expressions in the PQL language and sends them for evaluation. It receives from the parse tree machine uninterpreted strings (i.e., current values of views) and shows them in its editor windows. The compiler, written using Yacc and Lex, transforms PQL to the parse tree machine language.

The parse tree machine (PTM) is a simple virtual stack machine. The PTM contains about 60 different instructions. It receives code from the compiler and returns strings to the user interface. The PTM does not know how the parse trees are actually stored in the database; it accesses the parse trees using some simple routines. This makes it possible to change the underlying data structures easily.

One important part of the parse tree machine is the generic parser, which is able to parse an input string using a given grammar. We currently assume that the grammars describing views are in LL(1) form. This does not seem to be an overly restrictive assumption.

The documents are stored using a relational database system. We use a fixed number of schemas to represent all documents.[7] Basically, each node and leaf in the parse tree corresponds to one row in a relation. The implementation is straightforward. The use of a relational database is a potential source of inefficiency: retrieving large texts in small pieces can be slow. However, if the structure is not too detailed, the trees are shallow, and contain few nodes. Using a relational database gives efficient buffer management, recovery, integrity constraints, concurrency control, etc., in addition to easy implementation.

A database system for structured documents needs to keep several types of information: grammars, view definitions, names of documents, etc. In HST this information is stored as parse trees. Actually the whole database is structured as one large parse tree, whose subtrees are user's documents, grammars, and the like.

---

[7]An alternative would be to use a schema for each nonterminal; for documents with large and changing structure this might be slow.

7 Concluding remarks

We have given an overview of HST, a structured document database system. It is based on using context-free grammars for describing the structure of documents. The system includes a powerful query language following the lines of Gonnet and Tompa. The user interface supports multiple representations of one text; these views are defined by annotating the grammars defining the structure of the document. HST is implemented using a relational database system.

The HST system combines ideas from database research and compilers to a reasonably simple implementation. Several interesting practical issues remain to be verified. One is the usefulness of multiple views for large editing tasks, e.g., in editing a dictionary. Another is the suitability of the query interface for end users.

References

[André et al.89a] J. André, R. Furuta, and V. Quint, "By Way of an Introduction. Structured Documents: What and Why?", in J. André, R. Furuta, and V. Quint (eds.), *Structured Documents*, Cambridge University Press, The Cambridge Series on Electronic Publishing, 1989, 1–6.

[André et al.89b] J. André, R. Furuta and V. Quint (eds.), *Structured Documents*, Cambridge University Press, The Cambridge Series on Electronic Publishing, 1989.

[Aho et al.86] A. V. Aho, R. Sethi, and J. D. Ullman, *Compilers - Principles, Techniques, and Tools*, Addison-Wesley, 1986.

[Aho & Ullman72] A. V. Aho and J.D. Ullman, *The Theory of Parsing, Translation, and Compiling*, vol. I and II, Prentice-Hall, 1972.

[Barron89] David Barron, "Why use SGML?", *Electronic Publishing*, vol. 2, no. 1, 1989, pp. 3–24.

[Bancilhon & Richard84] F. Bancilhon and P. Richard, "Managing Texts and Facts in a Mixed Data Base Environment", in G. Gardarin and E. Gelenbe (eds.), *New Applications of Data Bases*, Academic Press, 1984,

[Brooks88] K. P. Brooks, "A Two-view Document Editor with User-definable Document Structure", Research Report 33, Digital Systems Research Center, Palo Alto, 1988.

[Brown89] Heather Brown, "Standards for Structured Documents", *The Computer Journal*, vol. 32, no. 6, December 1989, pp. 505–514.

[Chamberlin et al.81] D. D. Chamberlin, J. C. King, D. R. Slutz, S. J. P. Todd, and B. W. Wade, "Janus: An interactive system for document composition", Sigplan Notices 16(6), 1981, pp. 82–91.

[Chen88] Pehong Chen, "A Multiple-Representation Paradigm for Document Development", Report UCB/CSD 88/436, Ph.D. Thesis, 1988, Computer Science Division (EECS), University of California, Berkeley.

[Chen & Harrison88] P. Chen and M. A. Harrison, "Multiple Representation Document Development", *IEEE Computer*, vol. 21, no. 1, January 1988, pp. 15–31.

[Coray et al.86] G. Coray, R. Ingold, and C. Vanoirbeek, "Formatting Structured Documents: Batch versus Interactive", in van Vliet, J.C. (ed.) *Proceedings of the International Conference on Text Processing and Document Manipulation*, Cambridge University Press, 1986.

[Furuta89] R. Furuta, "Concepts and Models for Structured Documents", in J. André, R. Furuta and V. Quint (eds.), *Structured Documents*, Cambridge University Press, The Cambridge Series on Electronic Publishing, 1989, 7–38.

[Furuta et al.88] R. Furuta, V. Quint, and J. André, "Interactively editing structured documents", *Electronic Publishing*, vol. 1, no. 1, 1988, pp. 19–44.

[Gonnet & Tompa87b] G. H. Gonnet and F. Wm. Tompa, "Mind Your Grammar: A New Approach to Modelling Text", CS-87-13, University of Waterloo, 1987.

[Gonnet & Tompa87a] G. H. Gonnet and F. Wm. Tompa, "Mind Your Grammar: A New Approach to Modelling Text", in *Proceedings of the Thirteenth International Conference on Very Large Data Bases*, 1987, 339–346.

[Joloboff89] Vania Joloboff, "Document Representation: Concepts and standards", in J. André, R. Furuta and V. Quint (eds.), *Structured Documents*, Cambridge University Press, The Cambridge Series on Electronic Publishing, 1989, 75–105.

[Kilpeläinen et al.89] Pekka Kilpeläinen, Greger Lindén, Heikki Mannila, Erja Nikunen, and Kari-Jouko Räihä, "Data model of the Helsinki Structured Text Database System HST", Technical Report, University of Helsinki, Department of Computer Science, 1989.

[Minör90] Sten Minör, *On Structure-Oriented Editing*, Department of Computer Science, Lund University, 1990.

[Nikunen & Mannila89] Erja Nikunen and Heikki Mannila, "Views of structured documents", University of Helsinki, Department of Computer Science, 1989.

[Quint89] Vincent Quint, "Systems for the Manipulation of Structured Documents", in J. André, R. Furuta and V. Quint (eds.), *Structured Documents*, Cambridge University Press, The Cambridge Series on Electronic Publishing, 1989, 39–74.

[Quint & Vatton86] V. Quint and I. Vatton, "GRIF: An Interactive System for Structured Document Manipulation", in J. C. van Vliet (ed.), *Proceedings of the International Conference on Text Processing and Document Manipulation*, Cambridge University Press, 1986.

[Reps & Teitelbaum89] T. W. Reps and T. Teitelbaum, *The Synthesizer Generator*, Springer-Verlag, 1989.

[Yellin88] D. M. Yellin, *Attribute Grammar Inversion and Source-to-source Translation*, Lecture Notes in Computer Science 302, Springer-Verlag, 1988.

[Yellin & Mueckstein86] D. M. Yellin and E.-M. M. Mueckstein, "The Automatic Inversion of Attribute Grammars, *IEEE Transactions on Software Engineering*, vol. 12, no. 5, May 1986, pp. 590–599.

The Integration of Structured Documents into DBMS

José Valdeni DE LIMA[†] and Henri GALY[‡]

[†] *Universidade Federal do Rio Grande do Sul*
Caixa postal 1501—90210 Porto Alegre—RS, Brazil
vdelima@sbu.ufrgs.anrs.br
[‡] *Laboratoire de Génie Informatique (URA CNRS 398)*
IMAG-Campus BP 53 X 38041 Grenoble Cédex, France
galy@imag.imag.fr

ABSTRACT: The modeling of structured documents creates enormous problems for database designers. Those problems are related to the requirements to consider the logical structure and the exchange of documents in an open system. We want to be able to handle documents, both as atomic objects and as objects composed of other objects. We first try to classify different possible approaches according to the typical database concepts. After describing an integration of the ODA Standard to a functional type model, the "Fact Model", we describe the implementation of a functional interface built on the top of a relational DBMS, ORACLE.

KEY WORDS: structured documents, databases, logical structures, complex objects, ODA, ODIF, functional models, ORACLE, DOEOIS.

This work has been initiated as part of the ESPRIT Project 231: *Design and Operational Evaluation of Office Information Servers* (DOEOIS), in conjunction with the Bull Research Center.

1 Introduction

Many computer-based applications in the office environment require the ability to handle the logical structures of documents. In the case of letters, composed of a heading made of the sender's name and address, a main part and a conclusion, we want to be able to answer requests such as: "What are the names of the senders for letters that deal with the price of computers?". Similarly, intelligent document retrieval systems can take advantage of the logical structure in order to perform refined indexing and access.

This paper discusses the problem of handling structured documents in a DBMS from two main points of view, namely Modeling and Implementation. Both aspects are presented within the concrete framework of the DOEOIS Project [DOEOIS 1986 a; 1987 a, b]. From the modeling point of view, the approach taken is to integrate the ODA Model with the functional model used in the project, the Fact Model (FM), in a such way that documents appear as a predefined class of entities with a particular semantic and behavior. This integration concerns the profile and the logical structure of ODA documents, introduced in FM as structural properties of the class of documents.

From the implementation point of view, the strategy has been to concentrate the document storage and retrieval functions in a specialized module in order to take advantage of particular and well suited methods. In addition, this has allowed to isolate a structured documents management facility that can be coupled to a relational system to extend its applicability in the office environment.

A prototype Office Information Server (OIS) has been developed using the above described approach. The ODA/ODIF encoding has been retained not only as an exchange format but also as a basic storage format in order to simplify and accelerate document "internalization" (storing a document generated by an application) and document "externalization" (putting the document into a representation understood by the application).

The logical structure of the ODA Model can be used to help the creation, storage and retrieving of those documents as shown by De Lima [1988]. ODA is the most convenient standard to describe the whole logical structure of the structured documents [Horak1985; ECMA1985].

We begin this article by summarizing, in section 2, relevant concepts and notions from many different areas such as Informations Systems, DBMS and Modeling of Complex Objects as multimedia documents. Our intention, in section 3, is not to describe specifically this or that multimedia document model, but rather to present a survey of the constructors of those models and their constraints. Section 4 shows an integration of the ODA Model to the Fact Model (FM), and section 5 presents the present state of the OIS prototype, and its extensions. The appendix gives the functional interface of our prototype of a Structured Documents Manager.

2 Concepts and notions

The diversity of concepts and notions in the field of object modeling is often a source of misunderstanding. For instance, Pascot *et al.* [1988] use the words "Information" and "Data" as synonyms whereas in reality they are different. As H. Von Foester, quoted by C. Collet [1987], put it: "Information is the most vicious of conceptual chameleons".

We found it interesting to define the concept of "information" in this work: notions used for this definition may facilitate the understanding of the usual concepts (such as schema, type, class, etc.), and the DBMS evolution can be seen thanks to the introduction of those notions.

2.1   Original Concepts and Notions

We can define "information" according to this formula:

$$\text{Information} = \text{Value} + \text{Context} + \text{Representation}$$

The representation notion includes two sub-notions: the form and the system of representation. To explain this formula, let's suppose the existence of the value 11—which according to the context can mean the number of chairs in a house, the age of a child, etc.; for instance, as used in the two statements below:

a) There are 11 chairs in Diogo's house

b) Diogo is 11 years old.

The information in these statements is still incomplete because neither the form nor the system of representation of the value has been defined. It is true that the implicit form of representation of our use of numbers is generally made through the arabic numerals, using the decimal numbering system as a system of representation. But, in Diogo's case, whom we know well, the system of representation of the information in statement b) is the binary numbering system. For us, it is obvious: Diogo is really three years old.

We must notice that this last value three uses, as a form of representation, a series of letters, and, as a system of representation, the English language. The standardization of the form of representation, as for instance the fact of always using letters, is a good way of abstracting the representation. The main interest of this approach is to render the search through the content independent of the real representation. So, the request "Which are the sentences that inform us about Diogo's age?" can give us, as a result:

>   Diogo is 3 years old
>   Diogo is 11 years old
>   Diogo is three years old
>   Diogo is III years old.

The representation notion is very much linked with the problems of storage, of access and of information presentation. The binary numbering system and the coding such as ASCII or EBCDIC have made possible data storage in a computer. Now, we will define a few usual concepts in DBMS.

2.2 Concepts and Notions associated with DBMS

If we use the previous notions, we can say that a schema is defined by means of this formula: Schema = Context + Representation

As a matter of fact, a schema describes the structures (context), and the possible values (representation) of all the objects of a class. As we insert the semantics of an application into a DBMS, the context becomes more complete. As to the description of the context, which varies according to one model and another, we identify several methods: by constructors such as choice, aggregate, list, etc. [Collet 1987; Velez 1984]; by notions of generalization, specialization, aggregation (semantics models); and by notions of fact, function, entity (functional models), etc. [Gibbs 1985].

The concepts of type and class are perfectly understandable with the help of the notion of representation. For instance, the indication of the "integer" type for an object determines the shape (numerals), and the system of representation (binary, decimal, octal, etc.). An occurrence is a specific schema associated with the set of values of this schema: an occurrence is completely-specified information.

2.3 Concepts and notions associated with documents' modeling

The concepts and notions vary, and sometimes the same concept has several references which are different (because of different technical terms), according to various models. The Multimedia Documents Model (MDM) of Rabitti [1985] is very close to the ODA Model, by which it has been inspired to a great extent. Essentially, we can find out three fundamental concepts in MDM: the conceptual structure corresponding to the generic logical structure, the logical structure corresponding to the specific logical structure, and the formatted structure, which includes generic and specific structures.

As a matter of fact, the concept of conceptual structure of MDM, as well as the concept of generic logical structure in ODA, corresponds to the concept of the schema of a class of documents. The construction of a schema is made by the means of the constructors offered by the model. The constructors are based on notions such as link, direction, order, level, unique identification, null values, etc. We will proceed to a classification of those models, later in this article.

The link notion exists practically in all models. For instance, in FM, the declaration of fact [A, B] is automatically followed by the creation of two links: the functions A⟶B and B⟶A [DOEOIS 1986 b].

There are applications for which the concept of level is very useful. For instance, when someone uses documents, it is very interesting to know that the body of those documents is made of chapters. This hierarchical notion is possible only if the level notion exists. The example quoted before in FM doesn't allow anyone to know whether A and B are at the same level, whether A is the superior level compared to B, or the opposite.

The operator "Group By" of the SQL language and the operator "Order By" of the HDBL language, proposed at IBM-Heidelberg [Pistor and Anderson 1986; Linnemann *et al.* 1988], exist because the order notion is fundamental for handling documents, as shown by Güting [1988]. We distinguish the order of repetitive elements (homogeneous objects) at one level, and the order among non-repetitive elements (heterogeneous objects) linked with an element belonging to a superior level. The order of a chapter in a book is an example of an ordering of repetitive elements, and the order of the components of a book (title, introduction, chapters, conclusion), is an example of an order between heterogeneous objects. The concept of order is necessary to answer questions such as "What is the order of the chapter which deals with the handling of the logical structure of documents?", or "Which is the name of the first author of the article whose title is 'Databases and Structured Objects'?". The order of the logical heterogeneous elements is also needed for reading and editing.

The very important question of the constraints is fully developed by De Lima [1988; 1989]. Now, we will compare models according to their constructors.

3 Models, objects' constructors, and restrictions

Models can be characterized by their constructors, and by their restrictions on how these constructors can be combined.

Figure 1 shows that in the Relational Model, the set constructor can only be combined with the tuple constructor. The set constructor is linked neither with another set constructor, nor directly with atomic values. In this same figure, one sees that the N1FN Model presents a quite arbitrary restriction of link alternation between its set constructor and tuple constructor. This restriction, which doesn't limit the expression power of the model, can simplify the formalism.

The Abiteboul and Grumbach Model for Complex Objects [1987], and the NST Model ("Nested Sequences of Tuples") of Güting [1987, 1988], have no restrictions of link between their constructors because the notion of order is not present. As a matter of fact, the difference between the Complex Object Model and the NST Model is the introduction of the order notion in the set constructor, which becomes thus the sequence constructor.

The restrictions on links between the constructors of MDM, FM [DOEOIS 1986b; DOEOIS 1987c], HDBL [Linnemann *et al.* 1988] and ODA, are also shown in figure 1. You should notice that the links between the FM constructors don't reveal the meaning of their compounds as it is the case of the other models.

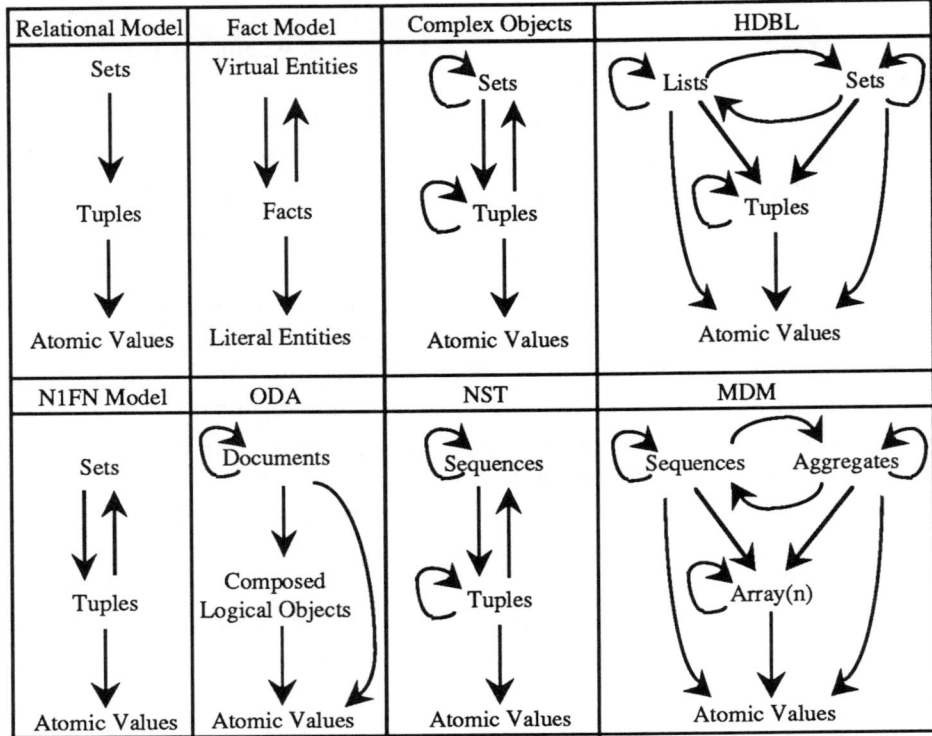

Figure 1: Possibilities of links between constructors

The fact constructor of FM is the very link with the constructors of virtual or literal entities. It doesn't possess the notion of order, or of hierarchy, which prevents from the interpretation of the components. As for the document constructor of ODA Model, it cannot be linked with any other document constructor: a document cannot be composed of other documents. As to the sequence constructor of MDM Model, it can only be used with the same components. Consequently, modeling of the same situations, with the help of MDM, requires a higher level in the case one uses for instance the HDBL Model.

A constructor can also be distinguished from another by the use or the non-use of some notions already studied before. For instance, the set constructors present in the Relational Model, N1FN [Abiteboul and Grumbach 1987], V-Relation [Bancilhon 1982] and Structured Objects [Abiteboul and Grumbach 1987; Linnemann 1988], are different from the sequence constructor of the NST Model because the notion of order is not present in the former. All the type constructors of the object models presented on the figure 1—apart from the constructors of FM entities—possess the notion of hierarchy.

As a result, we can distinguish three important types of links:

- Non-hierarchical links. The fact constructor of FM doesn't have the notion of hierarchy. The entity constructors of FM can't be be directly linked. In this model, all the links must be explicitly declared like facts.

- Hierarchical links without order, which can be found in the constructor of sets (HDBL, Relational, N1FN, etc.), tuples (HDBL, Relational, Complex Objects, etc.), and aggregates (MDM, TIGRE [Velez 1986], Formulaire [Collet 1987]).

- Ordered hierarchical links. Ordered links can be found in constructor of sequences (MDM, NST, etc.), of lists (HDBL) and of arrays (TIGRE, etc.).

Now, we will show how we have integrated the ODA Model to FM.

4 Integrating the ODA Model

The Fact Model doesn't allow a complete treatment of structured documents because: (i) FM doesn't have the notion of order; (ii) FM doesn't have the notion of hierarchy; (iii) FM doesn't permit the declaration of a fact as a result of the composition of intermediate functions (locally defined); and (iv) in the FM framework it is impossible to reach directly the totality of a compound element as if it were an atomic one. As a consequence, we must expand this model in order to integrate the ODA Model. This integration allows the manipulation of the profile and the elements of the logical structures of documents.

4.1 ODA Content

The integration of the ODA content is made by the predefined fact

$$[Document(0,*), content(0,1):ODA]; \qquad (1)$$

It defines the function: content(Document)$\rightarrow$ODA, which identifies the ODA value associated with the document entity. We call "ODA value" an instance of the ODA entity class, the external representation of which is an ODIF encoded document.

An important restriction is that the ODA type is available only in the predefined fact (1): no other ODA entity can be used with the Schema. Whereas a document entity is not mandatorily related to an ODA value, an ODA value must necessarily be associated with one or several document entities.

4.2 Profile's attributes

In order to integrate the profile notion to FM, in the first version of the OIS, the six following facts are predefined:

[Document(0,*), authors(0,1):String]; (2)
[Document(0,*), title(0,1):String]; (3)
[Document(0,*), subject(0,1):String]; (4)
[Document(0,*), abstract(0,1):Text]; (5)
[Document(0,*), docdate(0,1):Date]; (6)
[Document(0,*), credate(0,1):Date]; (7)

Those facts (the list of which can grow according to the needs), define functions that allow the manipulation of the profile attributes. When an ODA value is entered as the content of a document, the profile's attribute values are extracted and given as values to the corresponding functions defined by the above facts. It is impossible to modify these attributes which are inherent to the ODA value: the only way to modify them is to change the ODA value itself.

4.3 Documents' logical structure

We introduce the special Doc_Elem entity, which provides special semantics for defined functions:

- Hierarchization of the fields and joint-fields: the declaration of the fact [A,B] entails the declaration of only one function: A⟶B.

- The Doc_Elem entity is a compound, or an atomic entity: one can refer either to the entity as a whole (Book.chapter) or to one of its parts (Book.chapter.section).

- Implicit order of multivalued elements. The system automatically keeps the order of those elements. One designates this order by the means of an entire function called order, for instance: order(chapter), or more simply by using an index: chapter[i].

To specify a function on Doc_Elem, some restrictions on the ODA original logical structure are defined:

[A (a1, a2) : B, C (c1, c2) : Doc_Elem (<list of constraints>)]

In order to understand this manipulation, we give some examples of functions to describe the class of letters:

[Letter, sender:Doc_Elem]; (8)
[Letter.sender, name:Doc_Elem]; (9)
[Letter, Doc_Elem(addressee(name, address))]; (10)
Sender : Doc_Elem; (11)

The Integration of Structured Documents into DBMS 161

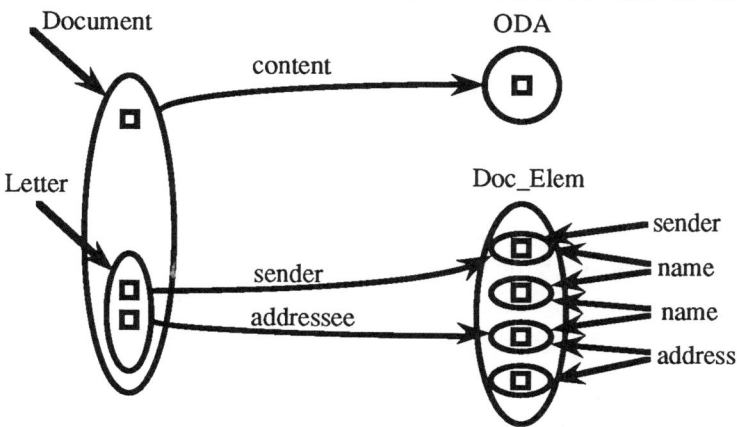

Figure 2: FM's logical structure of documents

The FM Schema resulting from the declarations (6), (1) and (8 to 11) is represented in figure 2.

- (8) creates the local function: sender(Letter)⟶sender

- (9) creates the local function: name(Letter.sender)⟶Doc_Elem

  A local function requires first, for its designation, the composition of the original global function with other local functions. For instance, to designate the function name of the sender, we write: "Letter.sender.name".

- The (10) declaration is a shorter way of expressing several functions from a global function. This declaration creates those following functions:

    addressee(Letter)⟶addressee
    name(addressee)⟶name
    address(addressee)⟶address

Then, we can designate the properties:

- Letter.addressee (addressee of the letter, seen as an atomic object)

- Letter.addressee.name (letter's addressee name)

- Letter.addressee.addressee (letter's addressees address)

5 Implementation
5.1 The DOEOIS Project

The DOEOIS Project has produced two prototypes, the most important of which is the "Office Information Server" (OIS). The OIS prototype was designed to integrate the management of: (i) alphanumeric data, (ii) multimedia structured documents, (iii) activities and office procedures, (iv) time and histories [OIS 1988]. This prototype has an architecture that allows the distribution of the Server in a distributed environment. It works on a Bull SPS 7 computer as a front-end for the ORACLE DBMS, with a transaction manager and an interface for programming.

Concerning the management of multimedia structured documents, several functions compatible with the ODA/ODIF standard have been implemented, and a whole library of encoding/decoding functions for ANSI (X-409) has been written. In order to create an instance of a document, we use the ODIF compatible operation:

>*Intern_Doc (Sdoc, <file_name>, Base_Code)*
>Sdoc:　　　　surrogate of the instance of the document
><file>:　　　　file containing the document coded in ODIF
>Base_Code:　code of the OIS database

Note that it is always possible to create instances by the use of another operator compatible with another standard, for example SGML [ISO 1986], Grif [Quint 1986], Troff, etc. The only thing required is to write the decoding procedures for those standards, and to recognize the logical elements that must be manipulated. The OIS manages the ODA content and the profile elements. The ODA content allows the application of the operator "Talks About", using the signature method [Jimenez 1989]:

>Select　Guide.title
>Where　Guide.content Talks About "La Joconde";

5.2　Extensions of the OIS Prototype

Extensions, which will deal with logical structures in a more complete manner by considering the levels, order, and renaming of the logical elements, are being developed. The search of a logical element during the internalization of a document will be made by the following function:

>*Search_Int_Cont_Log (Sdoc, Sf, List_Offset, <constraint>, Base_Code)*
>Sf:　　　　　　surrogate of a fact linked with Sdoc document
>List_Offset:　　array of portions of content answering the question
><constraint>:　constraint giving the hierarchy of the logical
>　　　　　　　element that must be stored, for instance:
>　　　　　　　<Guide.picture.figure.legend>,
>　　　　　　　<Guide...figure>, etc.

Consequently, we will be able to answer this kind of SQL-like request:

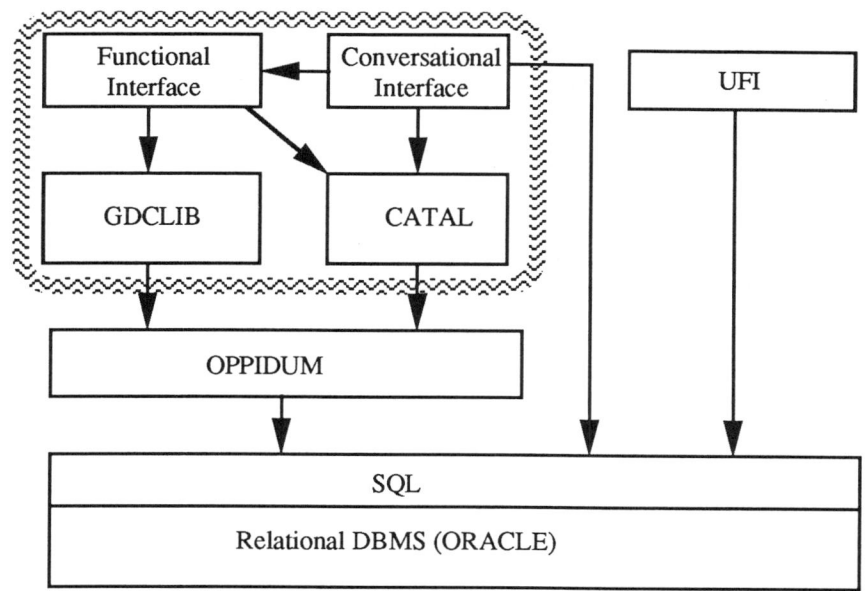

Figure 3: Architecture of the Autonomous Documents Manager GESDOC

    Select   Guide.title
    Where   Guide.picture.figure.legend Talks About "La Joconde";

and this other one:

    Select   Guide ... figure.title
    Where   Guide... figure.legend Talks About "La Joconde";

The notation ... means that we can make a search without knowing about all of the logical structure (we only know the structure of the figure). We think that this case occurs very often.

Those extensions are not implemented on OIS, but on an autonomous relational documents manager (actually called GESDOC), that we present here.

5.3 The autonomous Document Manager GESDOC

GESDOC is a prototype of a document manager, intended to handle classes of ODA/ODIF structured documents. It is built as a front-end of the ORACLE relational DBMS. It is independent of OIS, and could be considered as a support for extending SQL.

OPIDUM (Oracle Procedural Interface for Distributed Unix Machines), a by-product of the DOEOIS Project, provides a high-level Oracle programming interface for the language C, as it has both the advantages of the precompiler (queries simply expressed in SQL) and HLI (no precompilation phase). Access to Oracle is done by function calls where SQL statements are given as a parameter. SQL statements themselves can contain variables allowing parametrized queries. OPIDUM make possible an application running on one machine on a network to access and manipulate data in an Oracle database that resides in another machine anywhere on that network.

GDCLIB (low-level Documents Manager) and CATAL (Catalog Manager) are librairies, part of the OIS prototype, with the extensions seen before. The documents are shown as tuples of relations. The conversational interface is generally used for tests, and functional interface by applications. The appendix describes this interface.

GESDOC provides a controlled extension of Relational DBMS by supporting the introduction of a new type "Document" that is a composed one. The next step would be to extend the SQL compiler to accept, for example, this kind of statement:

Create Table Museum (name char (20) . . . guide document)

The first invocation of an object document (here "guide") entails a call of the function Init (see the Appendix).

6 Conclusion

After having reviewed different concepts and notions related to complex object modeling, we have presented a survey of the constructors and the restrictions inherent to these models. The need for the notions of order and hierarchy concerning the models that aim at modeling structured multimedia documents is fundamental. We have shown how to integrate the ODA Model into a functional model that was not adapted to handle structured documents.

The DOEOIS Project has developed the OIS Prototype, which supports access by contents on documents (operator "Talks About"). Though we have all the tools to reach the level of the content portion, this prototype doesn't permit us to describe the logical structure of documents, or their manipulation as objects made of other objects. This deficiency comes from the semantic difficulties—mainly the problems of hierarchy, specialization and inheritance. We have tried to cope with those problems by introducing the notion of compound entity and the notion of non-reciprocal facts.

Finally, our present work is oriented towards three goals:

- First of all, in the complex objects models for multimedia documents, a more formal study is needed to grasp the introduction of concepts and notions such as hierarchy, order, null values, unique identifier, etc.

- Secondly, we must give precise definitions of the inheritance aspects linked with the generalization/specialization concepts.

- And finally, a more ambitious task must be undertaken to determine new storage and access methods better adapted to the complex objects (for more details, see [DeLima 1990].

The autonomous relational Document Manager GESDOC provides a low-level prototype support for extending a DBMS according to those goals.

Acknowledgements

We want to thank Mauricio Lopez from the Centre de Recherche BULL; as well as Jean-Pierre Martin, Paul Berard and Claudia Jimenez, with whom we have directly worked about ODA documents and their integration into FM.

References

[Abiteboul87] Serge Abiteboul and Stéphane Grumbach, "Bases de Données et Objets Structurés", Technique et Science Informatiques, Vol 6 No 5, 1987.

[Bancilhon82] F. Bancilhon et al., "Verso: A Relational Back End Database Machine", Proceedings of the International Workshop on Database Machine, San Diego, 1982.

[Collet87] Christine Collet, Les Formulaires Complexes dans les Bases de Données Multimédia, Thesis of Doctor UJF, Grenoble, November 1987.

[DeLima88] José Valdeni De Lima, "Un Estudo Sôbre o Tratamento da Estrutura Lógica de Documentos", Proceedings of the XIV Conferencia Latino Americana de Informática, Buenos Aires, September 1988, 402–416.

[DeLima89] José Valdeni De Lima, "Traitement de la Structure Logique de Documents Multimédia", Proceedings of the VII Convocatoria Bianual de la Convención Informática Latina, Barcelona, March 1989, 580–598.

[DeLima90] José Valdeni De Lima, Gestion d'Objets Composés dans un SGBD: cas particular des Documents Structurés, Thesis of Doctor UJF, Grenoble, March 1990.

[DOEOIS86a] DOEOIS, "Bibliographical Annex, Bibliographical Informations and Standards" in OIS Overview, 1B1 Deliverable, January 1986.

[DOEOIS86b] DOEOIS, "A Semantic Data Model for Complex Databases", Proceedings of ETW Conference, September 1986.

[DOEOIS87a] DOEOIS, Document Representation in an Office Information Server, 2B3 Deliverable, January 1987.

[DOEOIS87b] DOEOIS, Model and Future Office Information Server Functionality, 3A3/3A5 Deliverable, March 1987.

[DOEOIS87c] DOEOIS, Data Definition and Data Manipulation Services, OIS-DH-01.01, April 1987.

[DOEOIS88] DOEOIS, "Project Achievements," December 1988.

[ECMA85] European Computers Manufacturers Association, TC29 group, Standard ECMA-101 Office Document Architecture, ECMA/TC29/85, September 1985.

[Gibbs85] S. J. Gibbs, "Conceptual Modeling and Office Information Systems", in: D. Tsichristzis (ed.), Office Automation, Springer 1985, 193–225.

[Güting87] Ralf Hartmut Güting et al., An Algebra for Structured Office Documents, IBM Almaden Research Center, San Jose, California, Report RJ 5559, March 1987.

[Güting88] Ralf Hartmut Güting, "Modeling Non-Standard Database Systems by Many-Sorted Algebras", Lehrstuhl Informatik VI, University of Dortmund, West Germany, March 1988.

[Horak85] W. Horak, "Formats: Current Status of International Standardization", Office Document Architecture and Office Document Interchange IEEE Computer, October 1985, 50–60.

[ISO86] I.S.O., Information Processing—Text and Office Systems—Standard Generalized Markup Language, Vol ISO 8879, October 1986.

[Jimenez89] Claudia L. Jimenez Guarin, Opérations d'Accès par le Contenu à une Base de Documents Textuels. Application à un Environnement de Bureau, Thesis of Doctor INPG, Grenoble, July 1989.

[Linnemann88] V. Linnemann et al., "Design and Implementation of an Extensible Database Management System Supporting User Defined Data Types and Functions", Proceedings of the 14th VLDB Conference, Los Angeles, California, 1988, 294–305.

[Pascot88] Daniel Pascot, et al., "Express-MLD: Une Approche de Développement Rapide Centré sur le Modèle Logique de Données", Modèles et Bases de Données, No 10, juillet 1988, 17–35.

[Pistor86] P. Pistor, and F. Andersen, Principles for Designing a Generalized NF2 Data Model with an SQL-type Language Interface, IBM Heidelberg, 1986.

[Quint86] V. Quint and I. Vatton, "Grif: an Interactive System for structured Document Manipulation", in: J. C. Van Vliet (ed.), Text Processing and Document Manipulation, Cambridge University Press, 1986, 200–213.

[Rabitti85] F. Rabitti, "A Model for Multimedia Documents", in: D. Tsichristzis (ed.), Office Automation, Springer, 1985, 226–249.

[Velez84] Fernando Velez, Un Modèle et un Langage pour les Bases de Données Généralisées, Thesis of Engineer-Doctor, INPG Grenoble, 1984.

Appendix: Functional Interface

To use the autonomous documents manager, one must first create the necessary environment: four interface relations (DOCUMENT, AUX1, AUX2, AUX3), and some invisible relations (storage of original content of document and indexes, and catalog). DOCUMENT is the main storage relation of all the documents. AUX1, AUX2 and AUX3 are temporary single-attribute relations to store surrogates of documents (Sdoc). By using this system, one can define subsets of documents with the concept of one-level specialization (LETTER, BOOK, etc.).

The function *Init* creates this minimal environment, with a standard profile (Authors, Subject, Abstract, Title, Creation_Date, Doc_Date), and Catalog Relations. Profile attributes are implemented like attributes of DOCUMENT. The most significant functions of this prototype are:

Alter_Add_Profile (Standard, Attribute, Type,T_Value) to add a new profile attribute.

> Standard: code in which the document is coded (presently, only ODA/ODIF)
>
> Attribute: name of the profile attribute to be added
>
> Type: Integer, String, Text, etc.
>
> T_Value: to specify single/multivaluated, optional or not, and null values.

Index_Doc_Elem (Relation, Attribute, Element) to index documents according to some generic logical element, independently of their complete structure.

> Relation: set of documents (= a class), default is DOCUMENT
>
> Attribute: attribute of the relation that contains surrogates Sdoc
>
> Element: name of one generic logical element.
>
> This function uses the low-level function of GDCLIB Search_Int_Cont_Log, that we have seen before in section 5.2.

Index_Doc (Relation, Attribute) to index documents according to a predefined generic structure that is defined in the Catalog Manager.

Selec_Doc_Elem (Relation_In, Attribute_In, Path, <expression>, Relation_out, Attribute_Out) to select classes of documents.

> Relation_In: class of documents that must be filtered, default is DOCUMENT
>
> Attribute_In: attribute of Relation_In that contains surrogates Sdoc
>
> Path: name of one generic logical path:
>
> > Content: all the document
> >
> > Abstract: profile attribute
> >
> > Title, Subject, etc: other profile attributes

<Element>: name of logical element

<Path>: path of logical element (using generic description)

<expression>: filtering expression

Relation_Out: set of selected documents, default is AUX1 relation

Attribute_Out: attribute of Relation_Out that contains surrogates Sdoc.

Create_Doc (Standard, <file>) to internalize one document (actually one expressed in the ODA/ODIF standard). It returns the surrogate of the new document. This function uses the low-level function of GDCLIB Intern_Doc, that we have seen before in section 5.1.

Delete_Doc (Sdoc)

Extern_Doc (Sdoc, <file>) to export the Sdoc document.

Index_Doc_Elem (Sdoc, Path) to index a logical path of one document Sdoc.

Index_Doc (Sdoc)

Select_Doc (Sdoc, Element, <expression>) to know if an element of one document contains an expression.

Show_Struct_Doc (Sdoc) to show the specific logical structure of Sdoc.

Electronic Publishing — Practice and Experience

David F. Brailsford[†], David R. Evans[†], and Geeti Granger[‡]

[†] *Electronic Publishing Research Group*
Department of Computer Science
University of Nottingham
Nottingham, NG7 2RD
England

[‡] *John Wiley & Sons Limited*
Baffins Lane
Chichester, PO19 1UD
England

ABSTRACT: *Electronic Publishing—Origination, Dissemination and Design* ('*EP-odd*') is an academic journal which publishes refereed papers in the subject area of electronic publishing. The authors of the present paper are, respectively, editor-in-chief, system software consultant and senior production manager for the journal. *EP-odd*'s policy is that editors, authors, referees and production staff will work closely together using electronic mail. Authors are also encouraged to originate their papers using one of the approved text-processing packages together with the appropriate set of macros which enforce the layout style for the journal. This same software will then be used by the publisher in the production phase. Our experiences with these strategies are presented, and two recently developed suites of software are described: one of these makes the macro sets available over electronic mail and the other automates the flow of papers through the refereeing process. The decision to produce *EP-odd* in this way means that the publisher has to adopt production procedures which differ markedly from those employed for a conventional journal.

KEYWORDS: journal production, computer aided refereeing system, remote file access.

1 Introduction

Over the last ten years electronic publishing (EP) has emerged as a research area in its own right and in the last five of these it has become one of the most active areas of applied computer science. This increased activity led to the notion that the EP community should have a regular publication of its own, featuring refereed papers on all aspects of EP research. In late 1987 one of us (DFB) founded just such a new journal and became its editor-in-chief. The title *Electronic Publishing— Origination, Dissemination and Design* ('*EP-odd*' for short) was chosen and John Wiley Ltd. agreed to be the publishers. An initial 'pilot issue' was produced in January 1988 and the journal now appears four times per year. The decision to cover EP in its full generality is reflected in the statement on 'Aims and Scope' which reads as follows:

"*EP-odd* is an International journal which publishes refereed papers on all aspects of electronic publishing. A broad interpretation of the topic is taken and we wish to encourage articles in such areas as structured editors, authoring tools, hypermedia, document bases, production of concordances and indexes, document displays on workstations, electronic documents over networks, integration of text and illustrations, typeface design, imaging hardware relevant to electronic publishing etc. (although this list is far from exhaustive)."

The editor-in-chief of *EP-odd* also acts as the UK/Europe editor and he is assisted by a US co-editor—this latter post being occupied, for the first two years of the journal's existence, by Richard Beach of Xerox PARC. More recently, pressure of work has caused him to resign and to hand over to a new US editor who, nothing daunted by his workload as Programme Chairman and Local Organiser of this present EP90 conference, brings to *EP-odd* his many years of experience in the EP field. It has been noted elsewhere [Brailsford89a] that this new editor combines continuity, by having the same first name as his predecessor, with subliminal typographical allusions, by having a surname which is an anagram of "the archetypal German (geometric) sans, and perhaps the least ungainly of this rather austere species" [Sutton68]. Richard Furuta takes over as *EP-odd* co-editor starting with Issue 1 of Volume 3.

The sub-title of the present paper tries to combine descriptive accuracy with a gentle nod in the direction of John Wiley's existing journal, *Software—Practice and Experience*. Later sections of the paper will reveal that the decision to allow authors to participate in the production cycle of their accepted papers has not been without its ups and downs. An alternative sub-title could well have been 'Tales from the War Zone'.

In a previous paper on the production of *EP-odd* [Brailsford89b] there is some extra background on laser-printer and electronic mail technologies together with some notes on two other experiments in 'electronic publishing'. In the present paper we focus, in Section 2, on the strategic decisions about the production of *EP-odd*. Section 3 gives more details of our experiences, so far, with the macros and document styles for *troff*, TeX and LaTeX, all of which can now be acquired over the computer networks using electronic mail (e-mail). The problems of tracking papers through the refereeing process are recounted in Section 4 and some initial software to address these problems is described. Finally, Section 5 describes the production process for *EP-odd* at the Chichester (UK) office of John Wiley Ltd., and the ways in which this process differs from that used in other journals.

2 Some strategic decisions

From the start it was realised that a new journal about EP might be expected to employ 'leading edge' EP technology for its own creation and production.

Equally, the editors and production staff were aware that beyond every leading edge lies a bottomless abyss and so the idea of a 'truly electronic' journal, with optional video and voice inserts, disseminating full-colour browsable hypertext over the computer networks, was dismissed at the outset for all the boringly predictable technical reasons. Instead, we decided to stay with a traditional hard-copy published form but to use as many computerised aids as we could in the pre-publication stages.

The three text-processing systems initially supported for the authoring of *EP-odd* papers were *troff* [Ossanna77], $T_{E}X$ [Knuth79] and Ventura Publisher®. Bearing in mind that many of our potential authors would be computer scientists, the ready availability of the first two systems made them an almost automatic choice. At the same time we did not want to seem indifferent to the rise of Desktop Publishing programs and, of these, Ventura Publisher seemed to offer facilities for longer and more structured documents by virtue of its tag sets.

All three systems were potentially capable of being processed into the PostScript® page-description language, which combines comprehensive facilities for imaging characters, line diagrams and half-tones with the very potent advantage that its imaging model is independent of device resolution. This enables papers to be proofed on laser-printers during copy editing, before being sent to a typesetting bureau for final output, on bromide, from a PostScript typesetter. In retrospect the decision to standardise on PostScript as the common final form has been every bit as significant as the choice of authoring software.

From the very beginning we were prepared to distribute to our authors, on request, the same set of macros and tags, for each of the authoring systems, that would be used in the final production of the journal. This approach has also been used, quite recently, for various EP conference proceedings including those that you are now reading, The advantages are very clear because, in short, one cannot divorce form and content in the world of electronic publishing. Authors need to become involved in the production cycle of their paper, knowing from the outset whether they have abided by its page limits, and with all the advantages of seeing line diagrams, equations, photographs and tables at the right size and in the right positions.

The main problem with this approach is that macros and document styles cannot automate every last context-sensitive detail of page design. Ideally, authors need to learn, very rapidly, the aesthetic considerations which underlie good page layout. In a 'one-off' set of conference proceedings the occasional badly-placed diagram or awkward 'widow' can be tolerated and laser-printed camera-ready copy is usually acceptable. For a journal it is important that the layout standards and attention to detail should not fall below what could have been achieved by the conventional production mechanisms. In asking John Wiley Ltd. to publish our journal we were very aware that text processing schemes such as TeX and *troff*, having been written by computer scientists, would probably not be the systems of choice if the publishers were given a free hand. On the other hand our plans depended on the publisher being prepared to produce the papers using the same text processor that the author had already chosen. Fortunately, one of us (GG) is a senior production manager at Chichester and had already used TeX extensively; the other two of us have had several years of experience with *troff* and its macro sets.

3 Macro sets for *EP-odd*

The difficulties of using either *troff* or TeX in their raw state are well known. The bewildering number of typesetting commands, and their very low-level nature, leads very quickly to an urgent need for macro packages so that the appalling machinations of the basic commands can remain mercifully obscure. Jonathan Seybold once said that 'TeX is not for the faint-hearted' and, even more tellingly, a humorous item was received over the mail networks some time ago, which, in defining UNIX[†] expertise, gave hallowed pride of place to the ability to write *troff* macros. The eight levels of expertise were divided into *beginner*, *novice*, *user*, *knowledgeable user*, *expert*, *hacker*, *guru* and *wizard*. The required achievements for the last-named category were:

```
wizard     Writes device drivers with 'cat >'
           Fixes bugs by patching the binaries
           Can answer questions before you ask them
           Is on first-name terms with Ken, Dennis and Bill
           Writes his own troff macro packages
```

We were lucky to acquire a starting set of *troff* macros, initially written by Brian Kernighan and Mike Lesk for the journal style of *Software—Practice and Experience*, which have now been extensively adapted to form the *ep* macro set for *EP-odd*. An equivalent set of TeX macros was developed at Chichester and have been used to produce 7 of the papers published so far.

Although the *ep* macros for *troff* have been used by various authors the TeX macros have not been so much in demand. The reason for this seems to be the rising popularity of a more heavily configured version of TeX known as LaTeX [Lamport86]. In response to author demand we have developed a LaTeX document style for *EP-odd* which is an adaptation of a style originally written by Richard Furuta for the book on 'Structured Documents' [André89] (this same style being the forerunner of the one used for these conference proceedings).

[†] UNIX is a trademark of Bell Laboratories.

To date we have published 7 regular issues of the journal comprising some 26 papers. Of these 13 have been produced using *troff* (11 were supplied by the authors in that form; 2 were converted from other word processors, into *troff*, by the editor-in-chief), 7 have been produced in TEX (6 were submitted in that form; 1 was converted from LATEX to TEX), 5 have been produced using LATEX and 1 using PostScript. So far no paper has been submitted simply as a typescript, and there has been very little interest in Ventura Publisher.

The Author Guidelines for *EP-odd* allow for camera-ready copy to be accepted though the conditions laid down are very stringent; page layout details have to be followed exactly and the final submission must take the form of a typesetter bromide. Although we have not yet had copy in this form, a recent paper from Zeev Becker and Dan Berry [Becker89] was submitted as typesetter-ready PostScript—which in some ways can be thought of as a form of electronic camera-ready copy. This paper describes the typesetting of Hebrew, Japanese and Chinese using *triroff*, which is an adapted version of the UNIX typesetter-independent *troff* program. The paper needed to be typeset using *triroff* itself but time constraints did not allow this extra software to be installed at Nottingham. Instead, the authors were given the page range to be used and spent many hours in adapting the *ep* macros for use with *triroff*. Copy-editing corrections were sent to the authors, who were also left in charge of page layout. The final version of the paper was submitted as a PostScript file to the editor-in-chief by electronic mail. The large number of Chinese, Japanese and Hebrew characters in this paper classified it, beyond doubt, as 'difficult copy' but the policy of adopting PostScript as the common final form allowed us to publish it with relative ease.

3.1. Incorporating Diagrams

There are facilities in TEX, LATEX and *troff*, either built-in or made available by preprocessors, for setting out mathematics, diagrams and tables. However, these simple descriptive schemes cannot cope with illustrations such as photographs, screen dumps and complex line-diagrams. Fortunately all of this material can be represented as PostScript and it can be generated from software such as CricketDraw®, or Adobe Illustrator®, or it may take the form of bitmaps in PostScript 'image' format. An increasing number of authors are choosing to send at least some of their illustrations in this form.

Whatever the source of the PostScript it still has to be incorporated into a document whose final output form may also be PostScript, but whose source format uses a very different text-processing model. If one can define start and end markers at the source level, which denote where the PostScript is to be inserted, together with some means of telling the text processing software what the overall size of the diagram will be, then the PostScript insert can be passed on, unaltered, to the back-end device-driver module. This merges the insert into the PostScript already produced from the surrounding material. These facilities are provided by *psfig*[Batchelder88] which allows PostScript inserts to be included in TEX and *troff* source code. The *troff* markers used by *psfig* are .F+ and .F- and between these a small set of commands is allowed for indicating such things as the height and width of the diagram. To reinforce this information there must be a BoundingBox comment at the head of the PostScript file, which must also conform to Adobe's standards for Encapsulated PostScript [Adobe87].

3.2. Remote Acquisition of Macros via Electronic Mail

In the early days of *EP-odd*, macros were sent to intending authors by the editor, or a colleague, using either electronic mail or a floppy disc.

In addition to the macros themselves there is a variety of further information available about the journal, such as the instructions for authors on the use of the macros, order forms, lists of past papers and so forth. However, distributing these extra files would be very time consuming if every intending author, or interested party, had to be mailed personally. Since many of the authors for the journal have easy access to the academic computer networks, it was decided to provide automatic remote access to these files.

Remote access to information over a wide area network[1] is possible by several different procedures. Files may be transferred using a file transfer protocol (FTP) from one host computer to another [Gien78]. FTP is a protocol in the presentation layer (layer six) of the International Standards Organisation (ISO) reference model for open systems interconnection (OSI). Many computer systems now support this protocol, which allows remote user logging in and authorisation, remote directory listings (to see what is available), and transfer of human-readable or binary files. By the use of *anonymous* FTP, where the user does not need a username on the remote host, it is possible to allow controlled access to a restricted part of the machine, thus enabling files to be transferred to interested parties. At present we can only provide the full facilities for access to the *EP-odd* files, via anonymous FTP, over our *local* campus Ethernet.

To allow wider access to the *EP-odd* files it was necessary to implement a mail server, since many potential authors can send e-mail to our host machine. The mail server is a program which is activated on receipt of a message, and is able to parse a simple language contained within the message body. The language keywords are described in table 1 and they denote operations which the sender of the message wants the mail server to perform.

---

[1] For a good description of computer networks see [Tanenbaum81].

Keyword	Mail server response
`help`	Send the help file, and ignore any other requests.
`index [category]`	Send the index for the category, if specified, or else the top-level index. Ignore any other requests to send files.
`send category file`	Send the requested file or files. If the filename ends in '.zba' then `compress` the file and run it through `btoa`, to reduce the size of the returned message.
`path <e-mail address>`	Specify a return mail path to the author for machines which prove difficult to get to.

Table 1: Language syntax and responses for the mail server

The mail server actually contains several different categories of information for retrieval, and stores each of these in a sub-directory. The top-level directory and the sub-directories each have their own indexes, which may be retrieved to see what is available for transfer. Normally the help file would be obtained by the user with his first message, then an index, or indexes, in the next, and then any files that were of interest. As an example, to obtain a set of *EP-odd* macros, one sends the following message:

```
To: ep-server@uk.ac.nott.cs
Subject:

send EPodd epodd.shar
```

It is possible to specify a complete return address with the *path* command for those mail addresses where the mail server cannot reply successfully by using the received mail header information.

The mail server is implemented as a set of ten UNIX shell scripts [Bourne78], with the message parsing being done by an AWK program [Aho85]. This allowed the server to be written fairly easily using the existing software tools available under UNIX.

To automate the maintenance and running of the server there are several shell scripts that can be run automatically or manually. There is a daemon which is run automatically at various times throughout the day to check the server's queue of pending messages, and to send out the replies (this is normally executed outside working hours). Statistics of how much it has been used are produced weekly from the log file, and show that approximately 400 files (approximately 5.3Mbytes) have been transferred over the last year.

Each category is easily updated with new information by the use of a *makefile*[Feldman78] which will rebuild the indexes by running a *makeindex* shell script, and update any other files using the rules in the *makefile*. This makes the general maintenance of the server very simple, and in fact is left to run on its own for weeks without human intervention.

At present the server contains about 300K of information in the *EP-odd* category, ranging from the macros and style files, to the instructions for authors, and the lists of past papers.

4 The Refereeing Process

4.1. Present Procedures

The refereeing process is one of the most time-consuming aspects of an editor's work for any journal. The administrative work load for this process is quite considerable even when the paper flow is low. For *EP-odd*, the rules are that papers must be submitted initially as conventional hard-copy. They will then be sent to two suitable referees, with a request for a report within a fixed period of time. If the paper is accepted it may need to go back to the author for the referees' comments to be taken into account. Only after such revision can the paper be re-submitted by electronic mail, preferably as marked-up source for one of the allowed authoring systems. The editor performs some final tidying up before the paper goes to Chichester for final copy-editing and pagination. At every stage of this process a record is needed of the progress of each paper so that the editors can plan future issues of the journal and track the progress of papers through the system.

The passage of a paper through the refereeing process has, until now, been conducted entirely by paper-based records, but the advantages of a computerised scheme are self-evident:

- The records will be easier to maintain and the current status of any paper will be easier to determine.

- It will be easy to obtain a list of papers which are at a particular stage of the refereeing process.

- It will be possible to automate the sending of reminders, both to referees and authors, for the return of reports or revised papers.

- The more mundane tasks, such as producing status reports and standard form letters, could also be automated.

4.2. The Computerised Refereeing System

As an undergraduate Computer Science team project, four undergraduates chose to implement a system for aiding the editor in the refereeing process. The main aims of the system were to store all necessary details of each paper, and its referees, in a database of some description. This could then be used to automate some of the processes listed in the previous section.

One restriction imposed on the project group was that the system should run on the UNIX system so that the editor-in-chief would be able to access it easily, and to make it easy to interface the system to electronic mail. It also needed to be terminal independent, and written in a modular fashion, in order to allow enhancements to be made in the future.

The design of the refereeing system, called '*Wizepp*' (Wizard Electronic Publishing Project!), was based on the use of a 'database' (actually a UNIX file with a fixed-record structure imposed on it), and a set of programs that could modify it. Figure 1 shows how the different programs interact with the database in

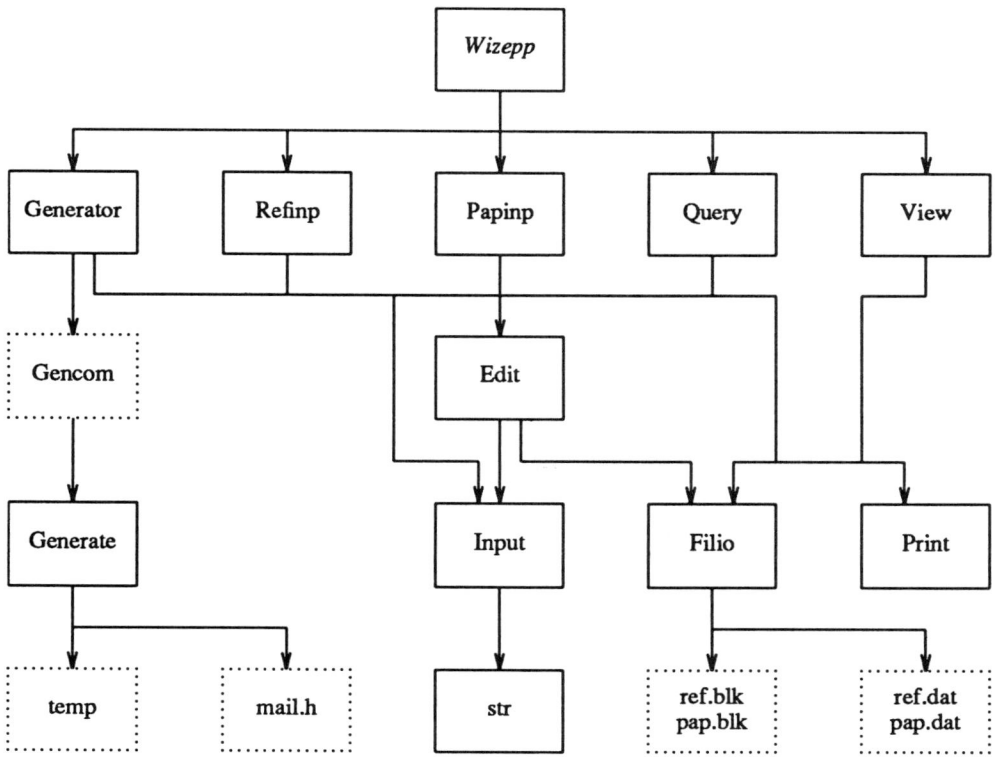

Figure 1: Program and database interaction for *Wizepp*

Wizepp. Each of these programs import standard modules that provide useful routines to access the database. The dotted boxes in figure 1 indicate data files, with the pap.dat and ref.dat files being the paper and referees databases respectively. The files pap.blk and ref.blk are blank records used as templates during the editing of some other record. This helps to maintain the integrity of the database by updating a record only when it is complete.

Wizepp was designed so that the user entering data could either use *Wizepp* itself to be presented with menus of commands to be carried out (edit or update paper information, add new paper, edit referees database etc), or the commands could be called directly from the command line (see the second row of figure 1).

The whole system is menu driven using the *curses* terminal-independent library routines which makes it accessible from a wide variety of dumb terminals.

At each stage where the user is asked to enter data he is presented with the present value for that field (which may be empty) and a series of dots indicating how much information may be held in the field. For example, an author's name may be up to 28 characters long and so the field might appear as:

```
    Mr F J Bloggs...............
```

It is then possible to move backwards and forwards within the field using the cursor keys, and to insert text in the middle as well as appending to the end. Some elementary checks are carried out to ensure, for example, that digits are not allowed in names and alphabetics are not allowed in numbers.

Once the paper details have been input for the first time the referees' names will be prompted for, and these checked for in the separate referees database. If the referee is not already known to the system he or she can be added as a new entry at this point. The system will also ask for a date by which the referees' reports are due back so that automatic reminders can be generated.

So far *Wizepp* allows the paper details to be input into its database, permits easier modification of the paper details than the old paper-based records, and can display the status of the papers in the system. The following are planned as enhancements in the near future:

- Improve the letter generator to align form letters correctly on the *EP-odd* stationery.

- Provide another interface for automatically sending status reports to the editor on a weekly basis.

- Automatically remind the referees and authors when reports and amended papers are due back.

5 Final production stages

The main job carried out at Chichester is the final copy-editing and pagination. Each paper is processed using the same text processing system that was used for authoring. The computer used at Chichester is a SUN 386i system, which makes UNIX and MS-DOS available on the same workstation; this system is connected via a LocalTalk network to other Macintosh and IBM PC computers. The connection of the SUN machine to the wide-area computer network, and thus to the UK and US editors, is via dial-up line and modem. This permits short e-mail messages to be exchanged with editors and authors but the communications software, and the modem itself, both need upgrading before it will be possible to transfer papers from Nottingham to Chichester over the network. For this reason the source text of the papers is usually sent down from Nottingham on either floppy discs or on SUN magnetic tape cartridges.

Once the material is available for a particular issue it is processed through the appropriate text formatting system to produce laser-printed proofs, which are sent to authors and editors for approval. When the final amendments have been made the altered source documents are processed again and the PostScript output thus obtained is stored as MS-DOS files on an IBM PC machine. These files are sent off, on IBM 5¼ inch floppy discs, to a typesetting bureau, which produces the bromide. The bromides are then returned to the production department at Chichester and final pasting-up is carried out for any illustrations that were not included in the original source file. The completed camera-ready copy is then sent to the printers.

5.1. Practice and Experience to date

The authoring schemes we support—*troff*, TEX and LATEX—all have some sort of default style for items such as tables, lists and footnotes and some kind of control over where these appear on a page. However, these crude mechanisms easily break down and it is not uncommon to find figure 6 appearing before figure 5, or table 2 before table 1. Much of the effort in Chichester centres around the fine-tuning of these details and this requires a carefully planned production schedule. The detailed adjustments to spacing and positioning were easy to effect in TEX because of the accumulated expertise with that system at Chichester. The same process in *troff* can be much more frustrating on those occasions where the requested changes do not seem to work, but most problems can be solved by requesting help from Nottingham.

Without doubt the most noticeable change in *EP-odd* papers over recent months has been the desire to use LATEX. This system is very 'author friendly' because its highly structured nature makes it very easy to generate section numbers, cross references, new sections, itemised lists and so on. However, the commands to do all this are more concerned with the *logical* structure of the document than with its *physical* appearance. Provided one is happy with the default layouts produced by LATEX everything is easy, but if any layout detail needs to be changed it can be appallingly difficult to make this happen—not the least because it is hard to apportion the problems that occur between LATEX itself and the underlying TEX codes that it produces. We have not made any great use, as yet, of the BIBTEX pre-processor for LATEX but we hope that this can be tailored, along the same lines as the *refer* pre-processor for *troff*, to enforce a uniform 'house style' for references.

It has already been noted that several authors have submitted diagrams in the form of PostScript inserts. The *psfig* package can usually handle these with no problem, provided that the supplied PostScript truly conforms to Adobe's rules for Encapsulated PostScript. Unfortunately on the occasions where these rules are not followed it can be very time-consuming to analyse the PostScript code to determine the correct `translate` and `BoundingBox` commands to align and resize the diagram correctly. Another problem concerns the sheer size of the PostScript files for those illustrations which are dumps of workstation screens. Although *EP-odd* illustrations are normally produced in black and white only, a screen dump from a colour workstation can amount to more than 2 Mbytes of uncompressed PostScript. Fortunately, there is a facility in *psfig* which allows a diagram to be placed as a blank box, at the proofing stage, to cut down on the computer processing overheads. One memorable paper, recently, had no less than **seven** such screen dumps, each of which took 30 minutes to image on an Apple LaserWriter II. In principle, these same screen dumps should have been sent off for imaging, on bromide, at the PostScript typesetting service (with each dump occupying two high-density floppy discs) but the costs of 3½ hours of typesetter time would have been prohibitive. In this particular case the laser-printed screen-dumps were pasted into the final copy.

5.2. Production problems

The novel factors with *EP-odd* from the viewpoint of the production staff are:

- The production of the journal is 'in-house' at Chichester. Copy for other journals would normally be sent to outside agencies for keyboarding.

- The papers arrive on disc rather than as typescript. Their appearance is much closer to the 'final form' than would normally be the case.

- The editors and many authors use e-mail daily and expect the production staff to be equally assiduous in checking e-mail and responding to it.

The last point is an important one. It takes quite some time to acquaint production staff with new technologies and, though we would not want to read any significance into this, *EP-odd* has now had three Production Editors, each of whom has had to be initiated into the delights and mysteries of e-mail. This training and administrative overhead was certainly not taken into account when the journal was first mooted. The benefit of having the staff at Chichester on e-mail is that day-to-day problems with *EP-odd* can be put right very quickly. The main drawback is the tendency to rely too heavily on this high-speed communication for informing the production staff of last-minute alterations, or in the editors assuming that a deadline is met if the required copy is sent out by e-mail at the stroke of midnight on the day in question.

5.3. *Other benefits*

There is no doubt that experience with *EP-odd* has given John Wiley Ltd. an invaluable introduction to a future where authors, editors, referees and production staff may be drawn together, ever more tightly, in the origination, dissemination and design of a journal. Indeed, since *EP-odd* was started a new Wiley journal called *Concurrency—Practice and Experience* has been founded and it has the stated policy of encouraging all authors to use LaTeX. The experiences with *EP-odd* have greatly facilitated the setting up of a LaTeX style for this journal and in forewarning the production staff of what they were letting themselves in for!

ACKNOWLEDGEMENTS

We would like to thank SUN Microsystems for providing us with a SUN 3/160 for the support of *EP-odd*, and also Rupert Weare, Geoff Dennis, Simon Gooch, and Wendy Chui for their work on the *Wizepp* refereeing system.

References

[Adobe87] Adobe Systems Inc, *Encapsulated PostScript File Format*, (EPSF Version 1.2) March 1987.

[Aho85] Alfred V. Aho, Brian W. Kernighan, and Peter J. Weinberger, "Awk—A Pattern Scanning and Processing Language, Programmer's Manual", Computing Science Technical Report No. 118, AT&T Bell Laboratories, Murray Hill, New Jersey 07974 (June 1985).

[André89] J. André, R. Furuta, and V. Quint (eds.), *Structured Documents*, Cambridge University Press, 1989.

[Batchelder88] Ned Batchelder and Trevor Darrell, *Psfig—A Ditroff Preprocessor for PostScript files*, Computer and Information Science Dept., University of Pennsylvania. Internal Report 1988.

[Becker89] Zeev Becker and Daniel Berry, "triroff, an adaptation of the device-independent troff for formatting tri-directional text", *Electronic Publishing—Origination, Dissemination and Design*, vol. 2, no. 3, October 1989, pp. 119–142.

[Bourne78] S. R. Bourne, "An Introduction to the UNIX Shell", Computing Science Technical Report, Bell Laboratories (12th November, 1978).

[Brailsford89a] David F. Brailsford, *Electronic Publishing—Origination, Dissemination and Design*, Editorial, vol. 2, no. 4, December 1989,

[Brailsford89b] D. F. Brailsford and R. J. Beach, "*Electronic Publishing*—a Journal and its Production", *Computer Journal*, vol. 32, no. 6, 1989, pp. 482–493.

[Feldman78] S. I. Feldman, "Make—A Program for Maintaining Computer Programs", Computing Science Technical Report, AT&T Bell Laboratories, Murray Hill, New Jersey 07974 (August 1978).

[Gien78] M. Gien, "A File Transfer Protocol (FTP)", *Computer Networks*, vol. 2, September 1978, pp. 312-319.

[Knuth79] D. E. Knuth, *TEX and METAFONT: New Directions in Typesetting*, Digital Press and the American Mathematical Society, Bedford Mass. and Providence R.I., 1979.

[Lamport86] Leslie Lamport, *LATEX: A Document Preparation System*, Addison-Wesley, Reading, Mass., 1986.

[Ossanna77] J. F. Ossanna, "NROFF/TROFF User's Manual", Bell Laboratories: Computing Science Technical Report No. 54 (April 1977).

[Sutton68] James Sutton and Alan Bartram, *An Atlas of Typeforms*, Lund Humphries, 1968.

[Tanenbaum81] Andrew S. Tanenbaum, *Computer Networks*, Prentice-Hall International, Englewood Cliffs, New Jersey, 1981.

ADAPT: Automated Document Analysis Processing and Tagging

John Handley and Stuart Weibel

OCLC Online Computer Library Center
Office of Research
6565 Frantz Road
Dublin, OH 43017-0702, USA

ABSTRACT: ADAPT is a document processing system that automatically builds full-text databases from document images. The major components of the process are scanning, image segmentation, optical character recognition (OCR), layout object identification, and database building. A retrieval system and user interface completes the functionality. The system features a general document representation that includes the document image and an SGML tagged version. Standards are adhered to where applicable.

KEYWORDS: document processing, full-text retrieval, document structure analysis, abstract syntax notation one.

1 Introduction

The variety of electronic document representations can be viewed as a continuum from the physical to the logical. At one extreme a simple document image serves as a surrogate for the paper version. At the other extreme is an electronic document consisting of descriptive tags and content. This latter form allows many kinds of interaction including editing, full-text retrieval, and reformatting, i.e., electronic publishing. The goal of document structure analysis (DSA) systems is to turn document images into complete electronic documents without incurring the costs of human intervention.

There are several experimental systems under development that address the document capture and representation issues (see, for example, [Zidar 1988; Bender 1988; Thoma *et al.* 1985]). Such systems typically involve scanning, image segmentation, object classification and optical character recognition. Among the problems that plague automated systems is the imperfect nature of the available technology (OCR scanning in particular). Corruption in the data must be corrected by humans (a costly and often impractical solution) or accepted as is. The ADAPT system design accommodates this reality by providing a document representation that provides access to the document image (at the lowest level of functionality) as well and as a fully tagged (albeit somewhat less than perfect) ASCII record. The user will determine what is acceptable based upon the information need and available resources. This approach also allows reprocessing records as DSA techniques improve.

The document representation consists of three parts: the document image, a tagged version based upon document structure analysis, and auxiliary data. The tagged OCR ASCII version of the document might well serve the majority of a user's needs. Many errors in scanned text are obvious and innocuous to a user. For cases where this is not so, the image would be available for corroboration of text accuracy. In a production system, images, being more costly in time and computing resources to retrieve and handle, might well be available on a central server. The auxiliary data are a by-product of the DSA processing and contribute a geometric description of the objects found on the pages. These data are useful for screen composition and subsequent DSA processing.

At one end of the continuum, a document record can simply be a document image with a rudimentary tagged version. The other extreme of the representation is a fully tagged document, relying on the image only for scanned graphics. A typical document will be somewhere in between: the document analysis produces some simple tagging (eg., author, abstract, remainder of the text, and references). The text could have many errors from the OCR processing, but nonetheless be suitable for indexing.

2 System Overview

Figure 1 represents the overall system design for the document processing system. The document image is captured by scanning (either paper or microfilm). The page images are segmented and a list of features for each page objects is produced. The page objects are classified as, for example, noise, graphics, or text. Those objects classified as text are processed with an OCR system and tagged. A database containing the images, tagged text and auxiliary data is built. The full-text database system we use (Newton) was developed for OCLC's full-text products and retrieval systems. After indexing, the database is mounted on our database server. Many databases can be mounted simultaneously on the server, which can be accessed by multiple clients in a Unix environment. A retrieval and display interface was constructed to demonstrate the system and to collect retrieval data. The details of user interfaces and formatting of output are important production system considerations, but are of only minor concern to our research activities. The ADAPT system allows access both to the image and to the

Figure 1: ADAPT system overview

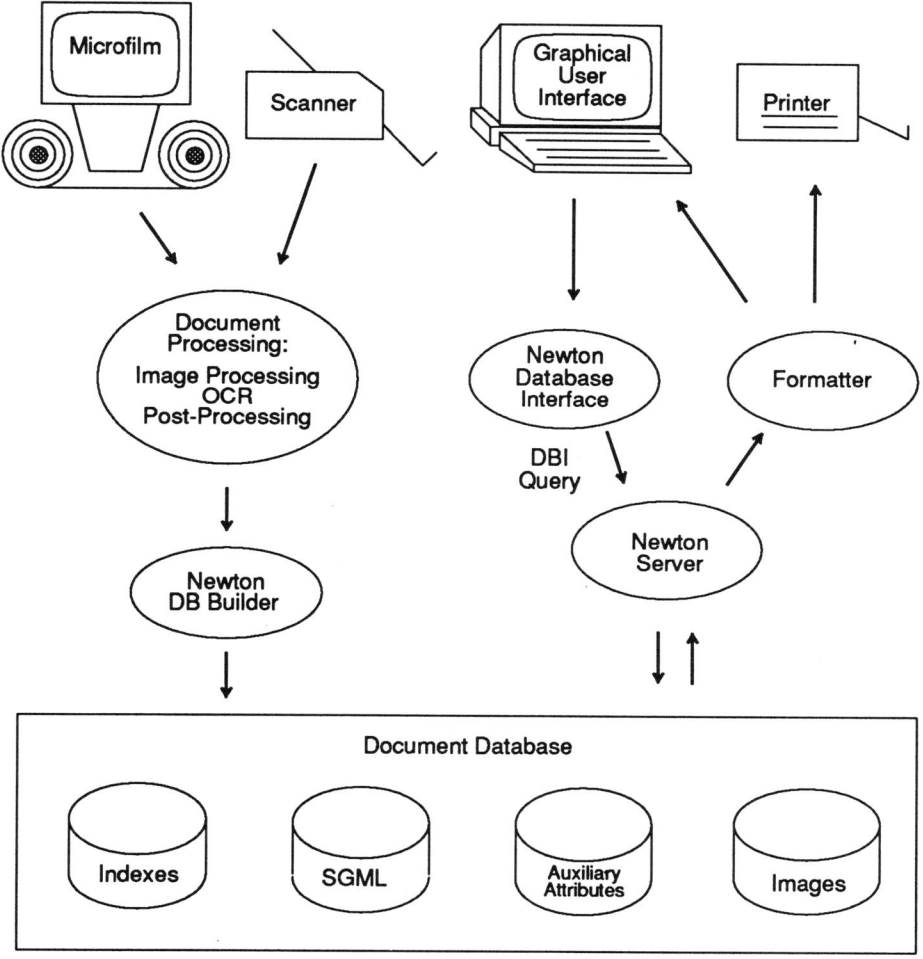

tagged text. However, no manual post-editing is done for error correction. Our philosphy is to make the process as automatic as possible, even at the expense of quality, with the expectation that due to our modular design we will be able to take advantage of better commercial and research subsystems as they become available. The databases we build will not become obsolete.

Indeed, they can be improved by reprocessing as more effective techniques become available.

3 Image Capture

The ADAPT system does not specify the source of the document images. The input images simply must be in Tagged Image File Format (TIFF) [Aldus Corporpation 1989]. TIFF provides for a directory of images (i.e., all the page images of a document) and information about the image as well. The image description includes information about the resolution, size, whether it is gray level, color or bi-level, whether dithering was performed, and what compression scheme was used. The TIFF format is used by many scanner manufacturers and VAR's. It is also a useful storage format within the document record.

4 Document Structure Analysis

After the document page images are scanned, they are segmented. Document segmentation and analysis is an active research area (see [Wilcox & Spitz 1988; Nagy et al. 1988; Ingold et al. 1988] for recent work and [Nadler 1984] for a survey). We modified one which performed well and could be extended to many object types on the page (line drawings, text, dithered contones, etc.).

The first stage in segmenting a document image is to separate objects from the background. This is done using the run-length smoothing algorithm of Wong, Casey, and Wahl [Wong et al. 1982]. This is a pixel classification scheme where black pixels stay black, white pixels (at 300 dpi) that are simultaneously members of a horizontal run-length less than or equal to 375 and vertical run-length less than or equal to 625 are painted black, and white pixels in a horizontal run-length less than or equal to 38 are painted black. The black pixels constitute the foreground. The contiguous black components are identified by building a line adjacency graph [Pavlidis 1982]. The coordinates of a bounding rectangle of each component are stored. For each rectangle, measurements are taken on the original image. Among the measurements taken are the mean and variance of the horizontal and vertical black run-lengths, respectively.

Given that each rectangle encloses some document object and a list of features, the next task is to use the features to classify the objects. Typical classes are text, graphics, and noise. A tree based classifier, Classification and Regression Trees (CART) [Breiman et al. 1984], is used to identify the objects. This method makes minimal assumptions about the data, can mix nominal and ordinal data, and performs well on other classification tasks.

To build the classification tree, we process document images using the segmentation procedure above and use a training interface to display the images with the rectangles overlaid. Using a mouse, a trainer points to the object and keys in an object type. The result, a list of objects with their features and proper class, is stored in a file which is used to build the classifier. The CART program reads the file and builds a classification tree. This tree is implemented as a procedure within the processing code.

Following the segmentation and classification steps, rectangles classified as containing text are used to build a zone list. The image plus the zone list are sent to the OCR system (Calera CDP 9000) for recognition. The output is a list of text objects.

Automated markup analysis is based on the notion that page layout reflects the document designer's understanding of the structure of a document and therefore provides clues that are useful in assigning roles to a document object. For example, titles are typically prominent and occur very early in the document; graphics, whether line drawings or halftones, typically have legends or captions which occur in predictable places. References are characterized by their location and conformance to one of a variety of formats.

In addition, semantic information provides obvious information about certain document objects. The words "Abstract", "Introduction", and "Summary," to name but a few, all are associated with standard document structural elements. Personal or corporate names can be identified by comparisons with name authority files.

Such information can be applied to the identification of document components through the use of a rule-based system. Previous work in the Office of Research demonstrated the effectiveness of this approach in identifying title page components [Weibel *et al.* 1989]. A similar approach is being applied to identify document components in Project ADAPT. The text objects are written to a file with the appropriate SGML tags. At present we use a simple document type definition based upon the best recognition we hope to achieve.

Further processing of the image is done for display. There are three versions of the page images. The full 300 dpi image suitable for printing, a scaled version for reading on a monitor, and an icon version. Since we have color monitors capable of displaying 256 colors, the scaled and icon versions are gray scale. To get a gray scale image from a 300 dpi bitmap, we filter the image with a 5×5 Bartlet filter and scale it down to 75 dpi for screen display. A 19×19 Bartlet filter is used for the icon versions [Crow 1981].

5 Indexing and Retrieval

The Newton retrieval system is a generalized text retrieval engine used in a variety of OCLC's production and experimental systems. Its generality stems from the fact that it can index and retrieve any datatype represented in ISO Abstract Syntax Notation One (ASN.1) [ISO 1986]. Representing document records in ASN.1 format facilitates data exchange with other systems as well. The indexing is done by building an inverted file containing tokens and a postings list. To build an index one must supply a data description and a list of fields with corresponding extraction functions. For example, some fields are indexed using a word extraction function while others, such as the abstract field, are indexed using a function that extracts phrases.

To build a database, the SGML-tagged documents are converted to ASN.1 form using a series of Unix *lex* and *yacc* utilities.

The retrieval system consists of the ASN.1 database, index, database server, and client(s). The link between the database and client is a general database interface enabling support of the ANSI/NISO Z39.50 Information Retrieval Service and Protocol [ANSI/NISO 1988]. This protocol allows a database application on one computer to query a database system on another. While the protocol is not implemented in this version, we are poised to take advantage of it.

The Project ADAPT client is a graphical user interface for searching and document display. It incorporates a variety of options for query, browsing, and display.

5.1 Query Options

The database can be queried using a Boolean combination of terms searched across the entire database or restricted to specific fields (author, title, abstract). When Newton services a client it returns a database-specific map of fields that can be searched selectively; the client application has the option of restricting retrieval by field or simply viewing the database as a unified inverted file.

5.2 Browsing Options

Browsing options include the ability to browse the OCR index of terms. Although there are many corrupted terms in this index, it will nonetheless be useful for search term selection; users can easily identify related corrupted terms and include them in their search. The user also has the option to browse citations to articles in the database. These bibliographic entries are the only record components that are actually entered manually. Eventually automated entry of this information (extraction from actual document) will be attempted.

A third form of browsing that has been implemented is that of page icons. These are miniature versions of pages that can be loaded rapidly and scanned when the user is looking for some specific graphic image or when a sought-after piece of information is known to be on a page with a particular look. Thus, the overhead of loading and scanning many full size pages can sometimes be obviated by taking advantage of this visual recall aspect of memory.

Figure 2: ADAPT prototype graphical user interface

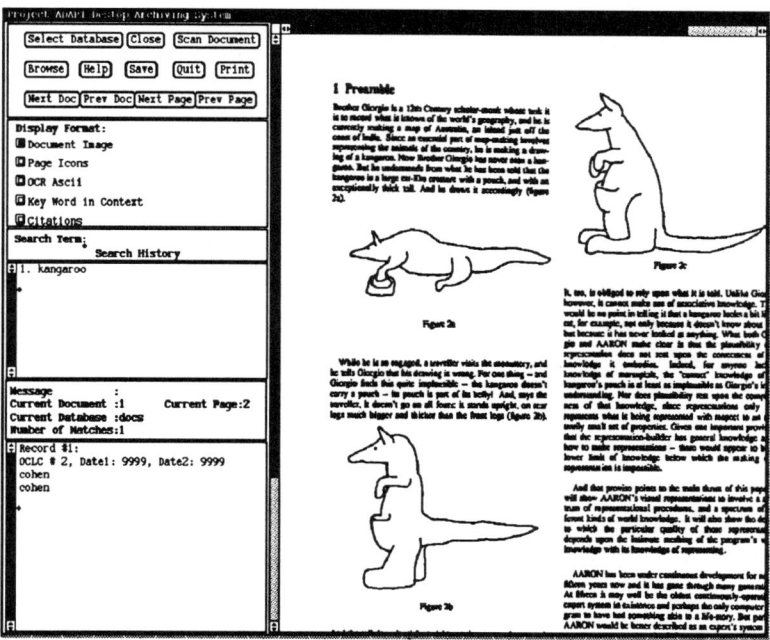

5.3 Display Options

Figure 2 illustrates the graphical user interface currently in use in the prototype. The interface provides an array of display options. When a suitable key word is searched, the user can display results in any of the following ways:

- *Full page image:* the bitmapped image is always available for display, however this is also the most time consuming to retrieve, hence the system provides means to judge the relevance of a document or page prior to retrieval of the image.

- *Keyword in context:* the OCR output line in which the word appears, bracketed by the previous line and next line. Selecting a retrieved line initiates loading the full page image or a citation to the document.

- *Page icons:* As indicated above, page icons can be displayed when the user is searching for an item by visual recall. Selecting an icon subsequently loads the full image.

- *OCR text:* A complete page of OCR text can be displayed. This is faster than the bit image and may suffice for many fact retrieval purposes even in its corrupt form.

- *Bibliographic Citation:* displaying the citations retrieved offers a quick alternative to viewing pages. Selection of a citation allows retrieval of the document in one of the other formats.

- *Unwrapped Galley Images:* The pages can be unwrapped to present the paragraphs and associated graphics in their logical galley order. This may be advantageous in cases where screen resolution requires larger type sizes to permit reading. This may also have advantages where it is not necessary to retain page breaks or layout from the original document.

6 Summary

The problem of providing better access to paper or microform collections will persist for the foreseeable future. Project ADAPT represents one approach to mapping physical documents into successively richer electronic representations. The strategy embodied in this work is based on three guiding principles:

- Support for important standards that will facilitate data interchange and interoperability, including SGML, ASN.1, Z39.50, and TIFF,

- Functional extensibility that allows improved or additional technology to be integrated into the system as it becomes available,

- Dynamic updating of the document database: New documents can be added and processed automatically with minimal human intervention,

- A distributed model of retrieval, display, and processing based on the client-server model.

7 Acknowledgements

Other members of the Project ADAPT research team are Martin Dillon, Craig Henderson, Charlie Huff, Mustafa Thamer, and Dan Weibe. We are grateful for the assistance of Thom Hickey, Bob Haschart, Mei-Chin Chung, and Mike Oskins for assistance with the database system and interface.

References

[**Aldus89**] Aldus Coporation, "Tag Image File Format Specification Revision 5.0," Seattle, WA 98104, June 1989.

[**ANSI/NISO88**] ANSI/NISO, "American National Standard for Information Retrieval Service Definition and Protocol for Library Applications (Z39.50-1988)," Transaction Publishers, New Brunswick, NJ, January 1988.

[**Bender88**] Avi Bender, "An Optical Disk-Based Information Retrieval System," *Library Hi Tech*, vol. 6, no. 3, 1988, pp. 81–85.

[**Breiman84**] Leo Breiman, Jerome H. Friedman, Richard A. Olshen and Charles J. Stone, *Classification and Regression Trees*, Wadsworth International Group, Belmont, California, 1984, 358 pages.

[**Crow81**] Franklin C. Crow, "A Comparison of Antialiasing Techniques," *IEEE Computer Graphics and Applications*, January 1981, pp. 40-48.

[**Ingold88**] Rolf Ingold, Rene-Pierre Bonvin and Giovanni Coray, "Structure Recognition of Printed Documents," *Document Manipulation and Typography*, Proceedings of the EP88 Conference, Cambridge University Press, 1988, pp. 59–70.

[**ISO86**] "Information Processing – Open Systems Interconnection: Specification of Abstract Syntax Notation One (ASN.1)," International Organization for Standardization (ISO), Switzerland, 1986.

[**Nadler84**] Morton Nadler, "Document Segmentation and Coding Techniques," *Computer Vision, Graphics and Image Processing*, vol. 28, no. 2, 1984, pp. 240-262.

[**Nagy88**] George Nagy, Junichi Kanai, Mukkai Krishnamoorthy, Mathews Thomas and Mahesh Viswanathan, "Two Complementary Techniques For Digitized Document Analysis," Proceedings of the ACM Conference on Document Processing Systems, December 1988, pp. 169–176.

[**Pavlidis82**] Theo Pavlidis, *Algorithms for Graphics and Image Processing*, Computer Science Press, Rockville, MD, 1982, 416 pages.

[**Thoma85**] G. R. Thoma, S. Suthasinekul, F. L. Walker, J. Cookson and M. Rashidian, "A Prototype System for the Electronic Storage and Retrieval of Document Images," *ACM Transactions on Office Information Systems*, vol. 3, no. 2, July 1985, pp. 279–291.

[**Weibel89**] Stuart L. Weibel, Michael Oskins and Diane Vizine-Goetz, "Automated title page cataloging: a feasibility study," *Information Processing and Management*, vol. 25, no. 2, 1989, pp. 187–203.

[**Wilcox88**] Lynn D. Wilcox and A. Lawrence Spitz, "Automatic Recognition and Representation of Documents," *Document Manipulation and Typography*, Proceedings of the EP88 Conference, Cambridge University Press, 1988, pp. 47–57.

[**Wong82**] K. Y. Wong, R. G. Casey and F. M. Wahl, "Document analysis system," *IBM Journal of Research and Development*, vol. 26, 1982, pp. 647–656.

[**Zidar88**] Judith A. Zidar, "National Agricultural Text Digitizing Project: System Startup and Operation," National Online Meeting Proceedings-1988, Learned Information, Inc., Medford, NJ, pp. 443-448.

Recognition Processing for Multilingual Documents

A. Lawrence Spitz

Xerox Palo Alto Research Center
3333 Coyote Hill Road
Palo Alto, CA 94304 USA

ABSTRACT: We have extended earlier work on document recognition systems to include multilingual documents, specifically those containing both English and Japanese. The segmentation process divides the page into areas of homogeneous content and produces a hierarchical representation of page layout called the segment map. There is an initial halftone segmentation pass, followed by text/graphics segmentation. Text segments are subjected to analysis to determine whether they are English (roman) or Japanese, before routing the output to the appropriate character recognition process. Graphics segments are routed to a raster-to-vector converter. Having identified text and graphics segments, we then attempt to recognize their individual internal structures and merge all of this information into an intermediate representation from which output transformations are performed. We have implemented three output filters, two for commercial document formatting systems, and one into an international standard document architecture.

KEYWORDS: document recognition, segmentation, character recognition, vectorization, multilingual.

1 Introduction

Document recognition systems which perform analysis of scanned images of documents and generate structured representations have been described by Wong *et al.* [1982], Ciardiello *et al.* [1988] and Tsuji [1988]. Wilcox & Spitz [1988] described an analysis system with an output representation compatible with an electronic publishing system. All of these systems were limited to the processing of documents written in a single language. This system provided an analysis of scanned document images, built a hierarchical structure describing the text and non-text portions of the page, and performed character recognition on the text. It preserved bitmaps of graphical and pictorial (halftone) structures and analyzed layout to generate a document representation compatible with a single commercial electronic publishing system. This paper describes extensions to this set of capabilities.

The original system did not provide any transformations of line art and its segmentation algorithm was not robust in the presence of skew, noise and some relatively simple layouts. It presumed the text to be comprised of only roman characters and to be restricted to the English language.

Because of the difficulty of keystroking large character sets, in Japan there is an even greater cultural, and presumably commercial, imperative for document recognition than in countries which use the Roman alphabet. However many Japanese documents contain significant numbers of roman characters, in the form of either a romaji representation of Japanese or, more commonly, non-Japanese text. Japanese documents also exhibit multiple text orientations. Japanese text may flow left to right, top to bottom as in English documents, or top to bottom, right to left. We have extended the original system to accommodate the structures found in this example of multi-lingual documents.

In addition to adapting our system to multi-lingual documents, we extended its capabilities to provide for halftone and graphics representation. The system currently supports a number of different output formats and has been designed to make customizing output for new formats simple. A schematic representation of the recognition process is outlined in Figure 1.

2 Input

We started with scanned images of paper documents. It was our original intent to use 400 spi digitizations of the document because of the high spatial frequency content of Japanese characters, particularly kanji. In practice we found that high quality 300 spi digitizations were adequate for both segmentation and recognition.

A lossless transformation is performed on the page image which yields a linked-list representation of each connected component or "mark". This linked-list data structure permits rapid, ordered manipulation of the graphical structures on the page. In the case of roman characters there is nearly a one to one correspondence between marks and characters, the exceptions being 'i' and 'j' and punctuation marks where it takes more than one mark to represent the character, and ligatures such as "fl" where a single mark represents more than one character, for example. Serious degradations in image quality also lead to tenuous associations between marks and characters. For example, low contrast image acquisition may lead to broken characters, and high contrast to touching characters: accidental ligatures. Each mark is characterized by the position and dimensions of its bounding box, as well as by other information not directly used by the segmentation process.

Skew in the document image is detected by a modified Baird [1987] technique. This technique involves determining the positions of fiducial points relative to each mark in the page frame and testing over a range of angles looking for the best alignment. Skew is compensated for by translation of the mark origin coordinates into the proper coordinate system. Because skew increases the area

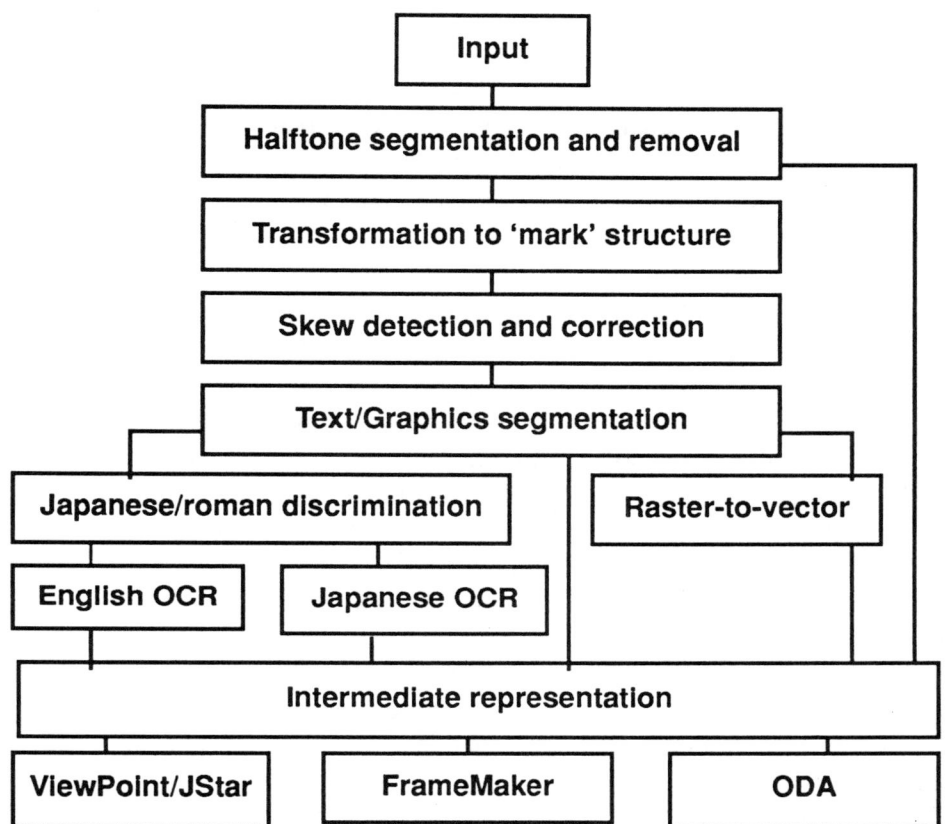

Figure 1: Information flow in the recognition process

bounded by a structure in an unskewed rectangular coordinate system, this effect is compensated for at the time of character recognition.

3 Segmentation

The internal representation of the document during the segmentation process is of the form of a linked list of the coordinates and dimensions of the homogeneous rectangular areas of the document: a "segment map". Each segment carries with it a classification. The classification may be representative of the layout meaning of the segment: page frame, margin, river or column, or of the content of the segment: text, graphics or halftone, or combinations of the layout and content attributes: text line, text block or text column. Qualification can be made to the classification of segments. Text segments can be classified as being roman or

Japanese, and Japanese segments can be classified as having horizontal or vertical text orientation.

All segments are rectangular, aligned with the page coordinate system and the minimal bounding boxes about the marks that they contain. The segments in the lists are moved into a hierarchical data structure, yielding a representation of the document which captures the salient features about the layout and content.

3.1 Page Layout

The segmentation process starts out by traversing the linked list of marks looking for "rivers" of white space within the page frame. Horizontal rivers delineate headers or footers, if present. The remainder of the page is processed by looking for vertical rivers which separate the page into columns. Failure to find a simple multiple column arrangement leads to search to find horizontal rivers which might divide the page into differing numbers of columns, or different alignments of columns, at the top and bottom of the page.

The set of rivers thus found define the boundaries of the islands of print material in the image. The islands are considered to be proto-columns and are processed independently. Measurements of character width, spacing, leading, etc. are made on an island by island basis allowing for widely varying styles between islands, but leaving style variations within islands unaccounted for. Each island is "shrink wrapped" around the marks contained within it resulting in a text or graphics frame.

Because of their relatively wide horizontal spacing, lines of Japanese text with vertical orientation are represented as individual columns.

3.2 Halftone Removal

The halftone segmentation process is executed before the text/graphics segmentation. The areas of the page which contain halftone information are blanked out before the text/graphics segmentation process. The early removal of halftones results in increased processing efficiency because of the large number of small connected components for which no further processing is necessary. A notation is made of the location and dimensions of each halftone segment removed. This information is entered directly into the segment map.

3.3 Text/Graphics Segmentation

Within each island, on the basis of their distribution of size and complexity, marks are first classified as being text, graphics, or "small". Text marks are aggregated into words on the basis of vertical overlap and horizontal proximity. Words are aggregated into text lines in the same manner, but with relaxed criteria for horizontal proximity. In each case, word and line, the minimum bounding rectangle is maintained so that words that contain characters having ascenders and descenders as well as x-height characters include enough vertical space to contain these features.

Note that Japanese text is usually set without word spaces. In this case, there is no spatial distinction drawn between the word and line data structures.

Some of the marks previously classified as small, 'i' dots and punctuation for example, will be within the line bounding box, These marks are re-classified as text. Small marks which touch but are not completely included in the text bounding boxes, are later re-classified as text. The remaining small marks are re-classified as graphics.

Graphics marks are aggregated into graphics segments. No graphics mark will be included in the growing graphics segment if its inclusion would result in the graphics bounding box touching a text bounding box not already included. Text which is partially included in the bounding box of a graphics segment causes the boundaries of the graphics segment to be expanded to include the entire textline segment. Thus text within graphics is an allowable construct, but the graphics segment cannot be grown to include text which starts out spatially isolated. Figure 2 shows some of the possible relationships between text and graphics In Figure 2(a) two separate graphics segments are kept separated since their aggregation into a single segment would necessarily also include text not already within graphics. In 2(b) there is no intervening text so the two graphics segments are merged into a single segment. Figure 2(c) shows the expansion of the minimal enclosing rectangle to include all of a line of text which would only be partially included in the minimlly enclosing rectangle.,

3.4 Evaluation of Segmenter Performance

We employed a test set of 27 "office" documents consisting of patents, journal articles, business letters, forms and a facsimile standard test chart. This set comprises Japanese-only, English-only and bi-lingual documents. The subjective scale for grading of segmentation performance is detailed below:

    A perfect segmentation.
    B segmentation which is less than perfect but which is acceptable given character position information. It often reflects that segment boundaries have been incorrectly, but benignly expanded due to noise.

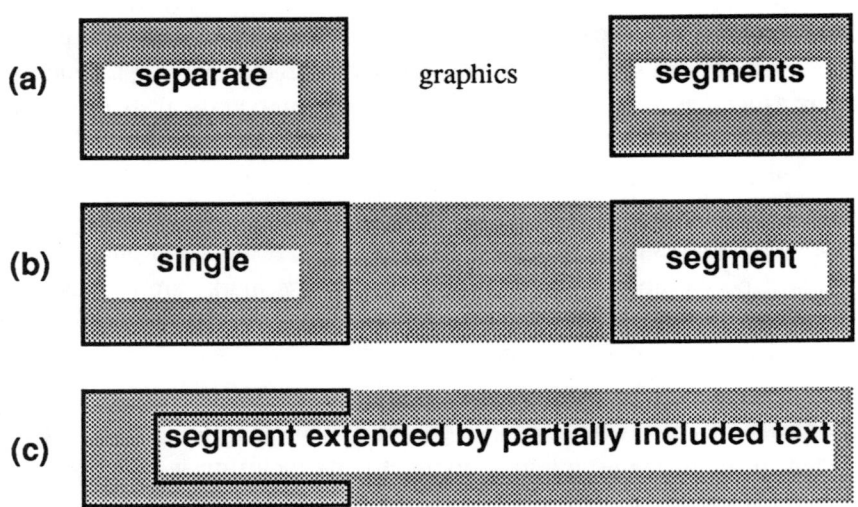

Figure 2: Text/graphics relationships. (a) graphics segments separated by text. (b) merged segment. (c) graphic segment extended by text.

    C   segmentation errors are understandable in light of the anomalous layout of the page.

    D   document contains structures which are not accounted for in the segmentation algorithms. Examples are inter-column line numbers and ruling separated segments, vertical roman text and diagonal text.

    F   complete failure of the segmenter to produce useful output

The 27 documents were graded as shown in Table 1. A grade of A or B implies that no layout editing would be required for an accurate representation of the page. A grade of C implies that the editable representation can be easily made to conform to the ideal. Documents graded D or F cannot be expeditiously corrected by editing. A single document can have more than one grade if the segmenter is deemed to have performed significantly differently on different portions of the page.

One of the test documents is shown in Figure 3. In Figure 3(a) the document itself is shown. Figure 3(b) shows the result of the segmentation process. The header and footer have been separated from the balance of the page. The footer contains only the page number. Text columns and blocks are outlined by rectangles. The Japanese and English portions of the abstract are delineated into separate text blocks. Graphics segments are indicated by crossed diagonals though that is difficult to see in the case of the horizontal ruling near the bottom of the left column. Text lines associated with the line art at the bottom of the right column have caused the expansion of the boundaries of the graphics segment to include them. Text lines, both roman and Japanese are shown with cross-hatchng..

#	Description	Grade	Comments
1	Japanese patent (title page)	B	A few fragments of text missing, for unknown reasons
2	Japanese patent (title page	A	
3	Japanese patent (body page)	B	Unnecessary split into 4 columns (2x2). Completely benign.
4	Japanese patent (body page	A	
5	Japanese patent (flowchart)	CD	Improvement will rely on dealing with graphics text interaction
6	Japanese patent	D	Inter-column line numbers
7	Journal article (first page)	A	
8	Journal article (first page)	A	Segmentation correct even in presence of considerable noise
9	Journal article (body page)	A	
10	Journal article	A	Dashed lines disappeared for unknown reason.
11	Journal article	A	
12	US patent (first page)	A	
13	US patent (body page)	D	Inter-column line numbers.
14	US patent (body page)	AB	Has vertical Roman and dotted lines.
15	US patent (body page)	D	Inter-column line numbers.
16	Journal article	A	
17	Journal article	A	
18	Journal article	AB	Correct handling of tables will rely on character position information.
19	Journal article	AB	Correct handling of tables will rely on character position information.
20	Journal article	B	Unnecessary spilt into 4 columns (2x2). Completely benign.
21	book	A	
22	business letter	AB	One segment extended by noise
23	magazine (title page)	C	Unaligned columns
24	magazine (title page)	A	Some large text detected as graphics
25	standards chart	AC	Inset graphics capability not yet implemented
26	business letter	A	
27	invoice	A	No obvious mistakes, but very complex. Hard to evaluate

Table 1: Results of segmentation evaluation.

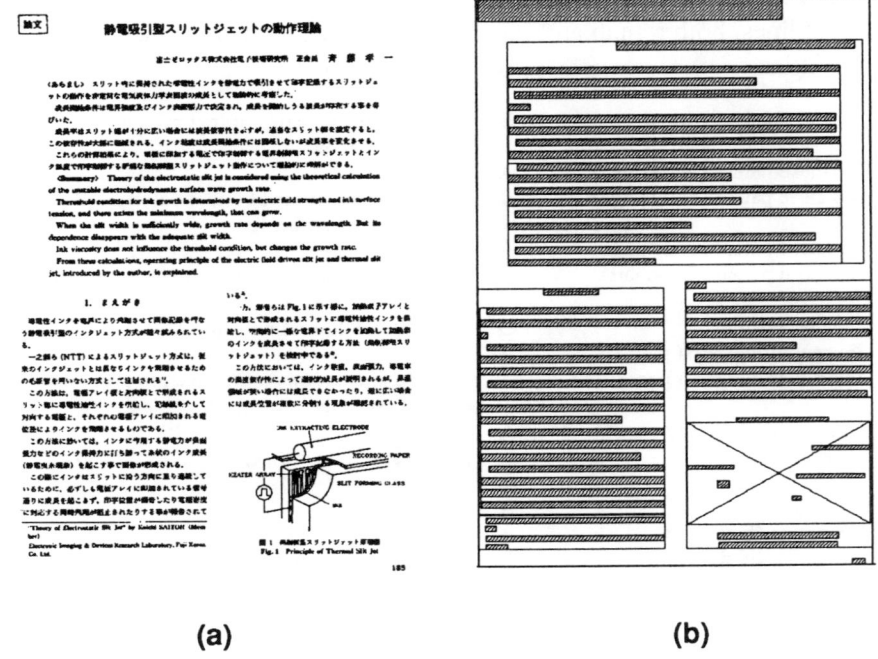

(a)   (b)

Figure 3: Document number 7 from the test set. Note the the document contains both a Japanese and an English abstract.

4 Text Processing

4.1 English/Japanese Discrimination

In invoking the recognition process, it is possible to specify explicitly that the document to be recognized is Japanese or English. In the event that neither of these is specified, it is necessary to determine the character content of the document. We have chosen to make this determination on a line-by-line basis for horizontal text and on a column-by-column basis for narrow columns consistent with containing single Japanese vertical lines of text.

Japanese text has several attributes which are possible starting points for discrimination function which can reliably determine which character recognition process should be used on the text segment. Japanese text is set mono-spaced while mono-spaced roman text is becoming less common as typewriters give way to word processing and laser printers. However, mono-spaced output is still available on laser printers and other computer printers so relying on the spacing to rule out the possibility of text being roman is futile. Also, Japanese text can and often does include proportionally spaced roman characters and numerals, thus discrimination based on spacing will not work.

Roman characters may have ascenders and descenders while Japanese characters do not. While not all Japanese characters have bounding boxes which fill the character cell, the large majority fill the cell from left to right. Fukuda *et al.* [1989] have taken advantage of this aspect of the difference between English and Japanese text in developing a discriminant function for the identification of the two types of text. Also many Japanese characters, both kanji and kana, have more than one connected component, a relatively rare situation in roman text. Again, because Japanese text can contain roman characters, the generalization about bounding boxes relative to character cells is weakened, particularly in the presence of roman capital strings.

In general kanji characters are optically quite dense and contain high spatial frequencies while the kana characters are quite light. Japanese text contains a mixture of kanji and kana resulting in a blotchy "color" for the printed representation. Roman text tends to have a much more homogeneous "color".

Each textline is processed to determine its language attribute. The discrimination function is described in detail in Spitz [1990]. It relies on the presence of a statistically significant difference in the distribution of a measure of local optical density between Japanese and roman text. The distribution is unimodal above a low optical density threshold associated with inter-character spaces for roman text, and is more complex for Japanese. See Figure 4. This

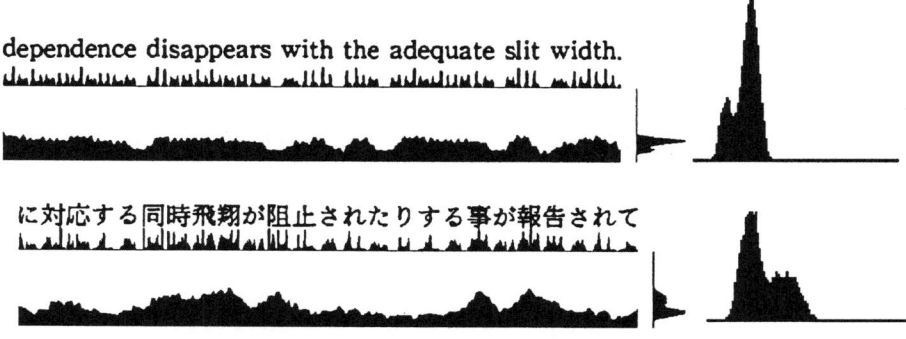

Figure 4: Shows an English (roman) text line, a Japanese text line, their vertical projection profiles, optical density functions and distributions of optical density.

statistical measure suffers on short lines where there is insufficient data on which to make significant statistical measures. In these cases, usually found in "widows", the classification of the line above is taken. In the cases of ambiguous classification due to mixtures of Japanese and roman text, the language attribute is set to Japanese.

4.2 Character Recognition

We used different character recognition processes for Japanese and English text. While commercially available Japanese OCR is capable of recognizing romaji characters, it performs poorly on proportionally spaced text. Also the Japanese processors do not use dictionaries for disambiguation, even for the English portions of their input. Therefore, for English text, we continued to use the Kurzweil character recognition process as described in our earlier paper. The Kurzweil character recognition is more accurate and much faster than the Japanese processors. For Japanese we used a commercially available processor from Fuji Denki.

5 Hierarchy

Lines of the same orientation and language attribute and similar type size and leading and which exhibit horizontal overlap are aggregated into text blocks which also carry a language attribute. Aggregation of text lines and blocks into text columns is permitted if no graphics or halftone segments would be included.

Starting with lists of segments classified as words, lines, blocks, halftones, graphics, columns and text columns, a spatial hierarchy is built. Lines and blocks completely contained in graphics segments are subsumed by them. The remaining lines and blocks are placed hierarchically below text columns. The still remaining lines, blocks, text columns, graphics and halftone segments are placed below columns. The page frame overlays, and therefore includes, the set of columns.

The resulting tree describes the layout structure and content of the page. For some applications it might be desirable to traverse the entire tree. Since only text can exist below text in our trees, and since it is advantageous from both performance and functional aspects to process the largest possible amounts of text at one time, we only traverse a particular branch of the tree until a node containing only text is encountered. Note that Japanese and roman text lines will never be found in the same node.

6 Intermediate Representation

The segment map and content information, both graphical and textual, are encoded in an intermediate representation [de La Beaujardiere 1990] which is rich enough to support translation into a wide variety of editable document formats.

At this stage only layout structure is represented. Within each frame the graphical and textual information is presented, but no logical information such as paragraph identity or text flow is encoded at this level. The graphical structures are transliterations of the vector lists produced by the raster-to-vector processor which include endpoint locations and line thickness. The textual information includes 16 bit representations for each Japanese character as called for in the Xerox Character Code Standard [1987].

7 Output Formats

In each of the examples described below, a WYSIWYG editor can manipulate both the textual and line art content as well as change the basic layout of the page.

The original implementation transformed directly into Maker Interchange Format (MIF). In the interest of providing more generally usable capability we used our intermediate representation as a basis for several editing systems. We have implemented three output filters to transform from the intermediate representation to two commercial electronic publishing systems, FrameMaker [1989] (using MIF) and ViewPoint/JStar [1984]. The Japanese version of FrameMaker provides considerable capability for editing complex compound documents, including specifying multiple paths of text flow necessary for multi-lingual documents. In its current version FrameMaker does not have the capability of handling vertical Japanese text, so we represent this property by a series of individual vertical columns of text, each one character wide. ViewPoint and its Japanese companion product, JStar, also have considerable capabilities in the editing of multi-lingual documents. In JStar, vertical text orientation is handled properly, hence we are able to cast Japanese vertical text directly.

Office Document Architecture (ODA) is an international standard for the interchange of documents [Horak 1985, ISO 1989]. It was not designed as an editable form, however several editors for the ODA representation have been developed. Hayashi *et al.* have produced one of these editors. Most ODA documents are rich in logical structure, while the recognized documents we produce do not contain values for logical attributes. Nevertheless we have found it convenient to use the ODA editor for manipulating recognized documents.

8 Summary

We have developed a system which is useful for the analysis of a restricted range of multi-lingual office documents, specifically those containing English and Japanese text along with halftones and line art. We have tested this system against a variety of office documents and found acceptable performance. In 14 out of the 27 documents (52%) the segmentation performance was graded A or perfect, and in 21 cases (78%) the lowest grade on a document was A or B indicating that no further editing of the layout structure was necessary.

We expect to extend this work to include information about the logical structure of the document. We will rely on the layout information, content and stylistic models to provide the basis on which to draw inferences about logical structure.

This work was performed at Fuji Xerox Systems Technology Research Laboratory in Ebina, Kanagawa, Japan with the assistance of others in Yoyogi, Japan and Palo Alto, California. Many people played a role in making this project successful. The principal participants were Katsuhiko Itonori, Yutaka Nakamura, Noboru Shimizu and myself. However, considerable contributions were made by Jean-Marie de La Beaujardiere, Yusuke Ishida, Hidetaka Miyake, Junichi Ohsumi and Masaharu Ozaki.

References

[Baird87] H.S. Baird., 'The Skew Angle of Printed Documents", *Proceedings of the SPSE Symposium on Hybrid Imaging Systems*, Rochester, N.Y. 1987, pp. 21-24

[Becker84] Joseph D. Becker, "Multilingual Word Processing", *Scientific American*, July 1984 vol. 251, no. 1.

[Ciardello88] C. Ciardiello, G. Scafuro, M. T. Degrandi, M. R. Spada and M. P. Roccotelli, "An Experimental System for Office Document Handling and Text Recognition", *Proceedings of the 9th International Conference on Pattern Recognition*, Rome, Italy 1988.

[de La Beaujardiere90] Jean-Marie de La Beaujardiere, "A Language for the Description of the Results of Document Recognition Processes", (in preparation)

[Frame89] FrameMaker Reference, (1989). Frame Technology Corporation, San Jose, California.

[Fukuda89] K. Fukuda, M. Hino and T. Machida, "Method of Distinguishing English and Japanese Text in a Document by Employing Rectangles Circumscribed around Continuous Components of Black Picture Elements", Information Processing Society of Japan, 1989 (in Japanese)

[Hayashi89] N. Hayashi, S. Kazuo, H. Nakatsuyama,Y. Suzuki and M. Murata, "Some ODA Layout Control Problems Revealed by a Prototype Editor", *Woodman '89*, Rennes, France, 1989

[**Horak85**] W. Horak, "Office Document Architecture and Office Document Interchange Formats: Current Status of International Standardization". *IEEE Computer*, 18(10)50-62, October 1985

[**ISO89**] "Office Document Architecture", International Standards Organization, *International Standard 8613*, 1989

[**Spitz90**] A. Lawrence Spitz, "A Discriminant Function for Roman and Japanese Text Images" (in press)

[**Tsuji88**] Y. Tsuji "Document Image Analysis for Generating Syntactic Structure Description", *Proceedings of the 9th International Conference on Pattern Recognition*, Rome, Italy 1988.

[**Wilcox88**] Lynn D. Wilcox and A. Lawrence Spitz "Automatic Recognition and Representation of Documents" in *Document Manipulation and Typography*, J.C. van Vliet (ed.), Cambridge University Press, 1988.

[**Wong82**] K. Y. Wong, R. G. Casey and F. H. Whal, "Document Analysis System" *IBM J. Res. Develop.*, 26(6), 1982 647-656

[**Xerox87**] Xerox Character Code Standard, *XNSS 058708*, Xerox Systems Institute, Sunnyvale, California 1987

Editing Images of Text

Gary E. Kopec and Steven C. Bagley

Xerox Palo Alto Research Center
3333 Coyote Hill Road
Palo Alto, CA 94304, USA

ABSTRACT: Most document recognition systems are based on the paradigm of *format conversion*, in which scanned document images are converted into a structured symbolic description which can be manipulated by a conventional document processing system. While this approach is attractive in many respects, there are situations in which complete recognition and format conversion is either unnecessary or very difficult to achieve with sufficient accuracy. This paper describes Image EMACS, a text editor for binary document images which illustrates an alternative to the format conversion paradigm. The inputs and outputs of Image EMACS are scanned images of text and the primary document representation within Image EMACS is the image itself, rather than a symbolic description of it. The goal of Image EMACS is to allow images of text to be created and manipulated as if they were conventional text files. The central insight behind Image EMACS is that many text editing operations may be implemented directly in terms of geometrical operations on image blobs, without explicit knowledge of the symbolic character labels (i.e. without character recognition).

KEYWORDS: document recognition, text editing, bitmap editing

1 Introduction

Recent advances in image scanning, storage and retrieval have stimulated interest in incorporating scanned documents within electronic document systems. Most approaches to this problem are based on the paradigm of *format conversion*, in which document recognition procedures such as page segmentation, character recognition, and raster-to-vector conversion are applied to a scanned document image to produce a structured document description which completely captures the content and format of the original document. [Wilcox & Spitz 1988; Wong *et al.* 1982]. The resulting symbolic description is intended to be used in lieu of the original scanned image for all subsequent document processing.

Format conversion is an appropriate approach when significant use will be made of the resulting symbolic document representation. Examples of such applications include reformatting (e.g. converting between single- and multi-column layout), language translation, transfering a large amount of material from one document to another, and full-text database entry. There are, however, other scenarios which involve performing relatively small amounts of editing on documents which originate in image form (either printed or electronic) and are to be retained in image form after modification. Examples include last-minute correction of spelling mistakes before xerographic reproduction, modifying viewgraphs at conferences, fax-based exchange of document drafts, and recreational forgery[1]. In such situations, creating a structured electronic representation for the document is not the main objective, but is at most an intermediate step taken to facilitate an image-to-image transformation. An editing strategy based on format conversion followed by editing and re-rendering faces at least two problems in such situations.

First, the accuracy and robustness of current recognition algorithms are too low for totally autonomous operation. As a result, format conversion typically involves a significant amount of manual proofreading to correct recognition errors. The effort required to proofread a long or complex document may be excessive if the ultimate goal is to perform a small amount of simple editing. Second, while format conversion may successfully capture the content and logical structure of a document, it is less likely to preserve typographic details such as hyphenation, line breaks, leading, and fonts. A desirable property for an editor of image-based material is that it function as an identity system unless the user explicits carries out editing operations. The state of the art in document recognition is unlikely to satisfy this criterion for the forseeable future.

This paper presents Image EMACS, a text editor for scanned document images which illustrates an alternative to the format conversion paradigm. The inputs and outputs of Image EMACS are binary text images and the primary document representation within Image EMACS is the image itself, rather than a symbolic description of it. The goal of Image EMACS is to allow images of text to be created and manipulated as if they were conventional text files. Image EMACS attempts to avoid the format conversion problems noted above by adhering to a principle of *demand-driven analysis*. Image EMACS performs image analysis only to the extent necessary to carry out operations explictly requested by the user.

Image EMACS may be viewed as an extreme form of WYSIWYG (what you see is what you get) page composition system. As such, it provides two distinct, but related, classes of editing operations. The first class is based on viewing text as a linear sequence of characters. The linear sequence model forms the basis for common text editing operations such as character insertion and deletion, string

---

[1] Recreational forgery is the construction of obvious parodies for humorous purposes.

search and linear cursor movement. The second class of operations is based on viewing text as a two-dimensional arrangement of glyphs on an image plane. Operations of the second class are concerned with aspects of typography such as character and line spacing, and line justification.

The linear text editing operations of Image EMACS are patterned after those of the text editor EMACS [Stallman 1986]. In terms of linear text editing, the user of Image EMACS should succumb to the illusion that he or she is using EMACS to edit an ordinary text file, displayed as lines of characters, although Image EMACS will really be manipulating image components extracted from a bitmap.

The typographic facilities of Image EMACS are currently not patterned after any particular system and are relatively primitive. Many aspects of typographic structure take the form of global constraints on the spatial arrangement of text elements. Detecting and enforcing such constraints is computationally expensive and the development of appropriate algorithms to do so is a topic of current research [Tsuji 1988]. For this reason, the typographic facilities of Image EMACS are only those necessary to support linear text editing and to imitate certain simple capabilities found in EMACS.

The remainder of this paper is organized as follows. Section 2 describes the Image EMACS linear text editing model and its implementation in terms of sequences of connected image components. Section 3 discusses typography in Image EMACS and the facilities for character positioning and line justification. Section 4 briefly illustrates the use of Image EMACS for editing foreign language and handprinted text. Section 5 discusses several other systems which are similar, in various respects, to Image EMACS. Section 6 identifies directions for future work. Finally, section 7 contains a brief summary.

2 Linear Text Editing in Image EMACS

Text editing in Image EMACS is based on the observation that an individual character in an English "book" style typeface is usually realized as a single connected region of black pixels (a connected component [Horn 1986] or "blob"). This suggests that text editing operations on a binary image of text may be implemented in terms of the manipulation of image blobs. The correspondence between characters and connected components is well-known and is exploited in many character recognition systems [Kahan *et al.* 1987]. The central insight behind Image EMACS is that *many text editing operations may be implemented directly in terms of geometrical operations on image blobs, without explicit knowledge of the symbolic character labels* (i.e. without character recognition).

In (ordinary) EMACS, editing operations are performed on a *buffer*, a conceptual one-dimensional array which contains the linear character sequence representing a text document. Image EMACS constructs a similar sequence from an image of text by first segmenting the image into a sequence of lines and then performing connected component analysis on each line. Line segmentation is based on the assumption that lines are separated by at least one complete row of blank (i.e. '0'-valued) pixels. Fig. 1 shows a sample text image with a bounding rectangle drawn around each character[2].

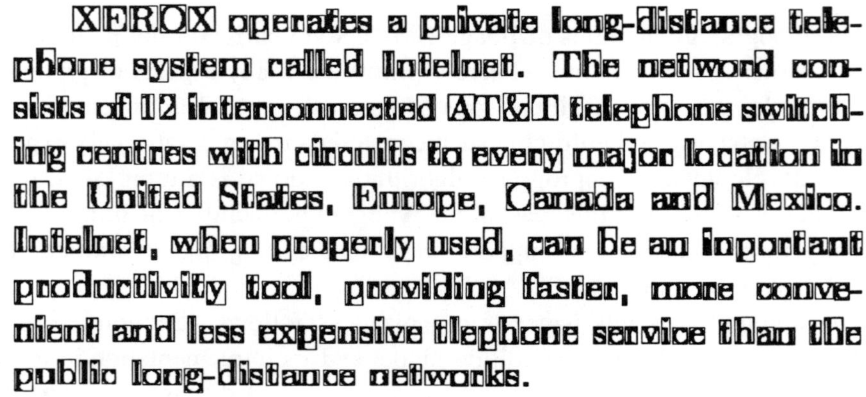

XEROX operates a private long-distance telephone system called Intelnet. The network consists of 12 interconnected AT&T telephone switching centres with circuits to every major location in the United States, Europe, Canada and Mexico. Intelnet, when properly used, can be an important productivity tool, providing faster, more convenient and less expensive tlephone service than the public long-distance networks.

Figure 1: Connected component analysis of a sample text image. A bounding rectangle is shown around each set of connected components which have been grouped into a character-like unit.

There are several important situations in which the correspondence between characters and connected components is more complicated than a simple 1-to-1 mapping. For example, a single blob in an image may be the image of several characters if the characters are blurred together or form ligatures (e.g. 'fi' and 'ffi'). Fig. 1 contains an example of merged characters, the 'as' in 'faster' on the seventh line. Conversely, several blobs may belong to the same character if parts of the character have dropped out or the character intrinsically includes several parts (e.g. 'i', ';'). Finally, formatting "characters" such as `Space` and `CR` are usually not manifested as printed glyphs at all.

Image EMACS handles multi-part characters with simple connected compo-

---

[2]The terms "character" and "connected component" will frequently be used interchangably, and in place of the more precise description "a group of connected components that probably looks like a character".

nent grouping rules based on vertical alignment[3] of component bounding boxes. These rules seem to correctly handle 'i', 'j', and all punctuation symbols except for double quotes (' " ' and ' " '). Fig. 1 contains several examples of 'i' and 'j'. The current implementation does nothing special about ligatures; they are treated as single characters.

White space (`Tab` and `Space`) is not explicitly represented in Image EMACS but is simply the absence of a component. If the horizontal distance between two consecutive components on a line is larger than a settable threshold, the intercomponent space is considered to correspond to a real `Space` character and thus to indicate a word boundary. For simplicity, each interword space is treated as a single `Space` character, independent of its size. Finally, each line is assumed to be terminated by an implicit CR. Although `Space` and CR are not represented explicitly, they behave like ordinary printing characters during text editing operations such as cursor movement, insertion/deletion, and search.

Note that the principle of demand-driven analysis implies that the correspondence between characters and blobs needs to be established only for portions of the text which are actually manipulated by the user. Regions which are viewed but not edited are not necessarily analyzed by the editor.

Table 1 identifies a small subset of the Image EMACS linear text editing commands[4]. Most editing operations take place in the vicinity of a distinguished buffer position which is marked by a *cursor*. The cursor movement commands identified in table 1 adjust the position of the cursor.

The insertion and deletion commands provide various forms of "cut and paste" editing. For example, the command `kill-region` removes the characters between the cursor and a second buffer position called the *mark*. Killed text is stored on a *kill ring* from which it can be *yanked* back, either at the same position (to undo the kill) or at a different position (to move the killed text). The command `copy-select-char` inserts at the cursor a copy of the character located under the mouse. Fig. 2 illustrates a simple use of `copy-select-char` to correct a spelling mistake in the text of fig. 1.

Inserting characters by normal typing requires establishing associations between the keyboard keys and the character images (i.e. key bindings). The key binding commands in table 1 create and manipulate key bindings for printing characters. The command `key-bindings-from-font` binds keys to char-

---

[3] Vertical alignment means similarity of horizontal position.

[4] EMACS commands are issued by clicking one of the mouse buttons (e.g. `Mouse-Left`), by pressing one or two keyboard keys plus an optional modifier key (`Control`, `Meta`, `Super`, or `Shift`, abbreviated C-, M-, S-, Sh-, respectively) or by typing M-X followed by the complete name of the command. The associations between commands and sequences of keyboard strokes are called *key bindings*.

Key Binding	Command Name
Cursor Movement Commands	
C-E	end-of-line
C-F	forward-char
C-N	down-line
M-F	forward-word
M->	end-of-buffer
Mouse-Left	move-cursor-to-mouse
Insertion and Deletion Commands	
C-D	delete-char
C-K	kill-line
C-W	kill-region
C-Y	yank
M-D	kill-word
C-Mouse-Left	copy-select-char
Key Binding Commands	
printing chars	insert-self
C-S	incremental-search
(M-X)	teach-chars
(M-X)	key-bindings-from-font
(M-X)	key-bindings-to-buffer
(M-X)	key-bindings-from-buffer

Table 1: Examples of Image EMACS linear text editing commands.

acter images taken from a stored font. When key bindings are set from a font, documents produced using Image EMACS look very much like those from a conventional word processor, except that they are represented as bitmaps rather than as sequences of character codes.

The command `teach-chars` puts Image EMACS into a special "teach-emacs" mode for binding keys to character images drawn from an existing text document. When the user types a key in teach mode Image EMACS binds a copy of the character under the cursor to the key and advances the cursor. After exiting teach mode, any of the "taught" character images can be inserted by typing the corresponding key.

The command `key-bindings-to-buffer` creates a buffer containing an iconic representation of the current key bindings which can be edited and saved just like any other image. The command `key-bindings-from-buffer`

expensive tlephone

(a)

expensive telephone

(b)

Figure 2: Example use of `copy-select-char` to correct a spelling mistake. A copy of the first 'e' in 'expensive' is inserted after the 't' in 'tlephone'. (a) Before. (b) After.

causes the current buffer to be interpreted as such a representation and establishes the indicated key bindings.

Image EMACS has no facility for automatically wrapping text from one line to the next as characters are inserted. Instead, as discussed in section 3 below, lines may extend indefinitely to the right.

Image EMACS implements character search by comparing the character image bound to a specified key with successive character images in the buffer until the match score exceeds a preset threshold. Matching is performed by binary cross-correlation [Duda & Hart 1973]. The `incremental-search` command for string search begins matching and moving the cursor as soon as the first character of the search string is typed; successive characters extend the search string and move to the next match.

The setting of the match score threshold affects the relative numbers of incorrect positive and negative match decisions. Experience with Image EMACS suggests that false matches are preferred to missed matches, because false hits simply increase the number of times the search for a particular string must be repeated to reach the desired instance, whereas missing a match might cause the overall search to fail. For any given setting of the threshold, match performance increases with the length of the search string. Correlation-based matching is particularly effective for character images drawn from a stored font, since the absence of scanner noise means that the match threshold may be raised (which reduces false hits) without increasing the number of misses.

3   Typography in Image EMACS

Image EMACS assumes that all text occurs in a single column of horizontally oriented lines, without any embedded multi-line figures, underlining, or vertical rules. Text is assumed to be set in an ordinary "book" face without decorative features such as "drop caps". As noted previously, consecutive lines must be separated by at least one row of blank pixels.

The text column is assumed to occupy a single page defined by Cartesian pixel coordinates in which X increases to the right and Y increases downward. When an image file is read into a buffer the top and left edges of the file image are taken to fall on the X and Y axes of the page image plane, respectively. The image plane is conceptually infinite in all directions, although there are no commands which can cause text to move to the left of the Y axis and no way to begin a line above the X axis. However, it is possible for a character to extend above the X axis, e.g. as the result of adjusting its baseline (see below).

The most basic typographic facilities in Image EMACS are concerned with the horizontal and vertical positioning of characters within a line of text. When a character x is inserted between two characters c_1 and c_2, Image EMACS must determine appropriate values to use for the horizontal distances from c_1 to x and from x to c_2. A simple case, which illustrates the basic strategy, occurs when (1) c_1, c_2 and x are all printing characters; (2) the original distance between c_1 and c_2 was less than the interword space threshold; and (3) x was originally followed by a printing character c_3 which was separated from it by less than the interword space threshold. In that case, the distance from c_1 to x is set equal to the original distance between c_1 and c_2 and the distance from x to c_2 is set to the original distance between x and c_3. In short, the spaces after c_1 and x are preserved.

The horizontal positioning strategy is illustrated in fig. 3, which adds character bounding boxes to the example of fig. 2 to show the intercharacter spacing. The space between the 't' and 'e' in 'telephone' in fig. 3(b) is equal to the space between the 't' and 'l' in 'tlephone' in fig. 3(a). Similarly, the space between the 'e' and 'l' in 'telephone is equal to the space between the 'e' and 'x' in 'expensive.

Variations of the above rule handle situations in which c_1, c_2, or x originally occur at the beginning or end of a word, so that the original space after c_1 or x exceeds the interword space threshold. For example, if x originally was the last, but not the only, character of a word, then the new space between x and c_2 is set equal to the original space *before* x. If x was originally an isolated character, then the space between x and c_2 is set to a fixed intercharacter distance. Similar rules apply when x is a Space character and when characters are deleted.

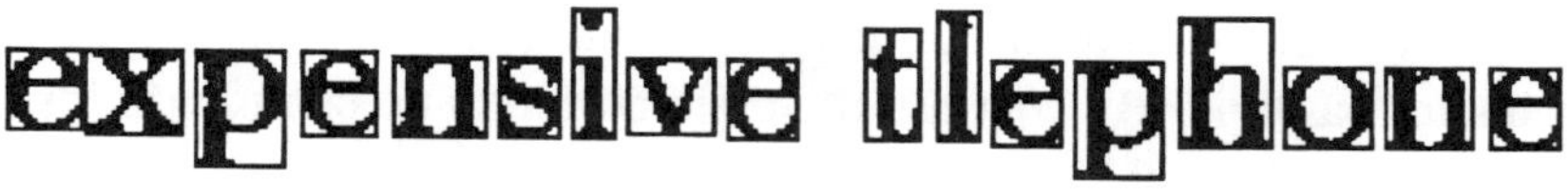

expensive tlephone
(a)

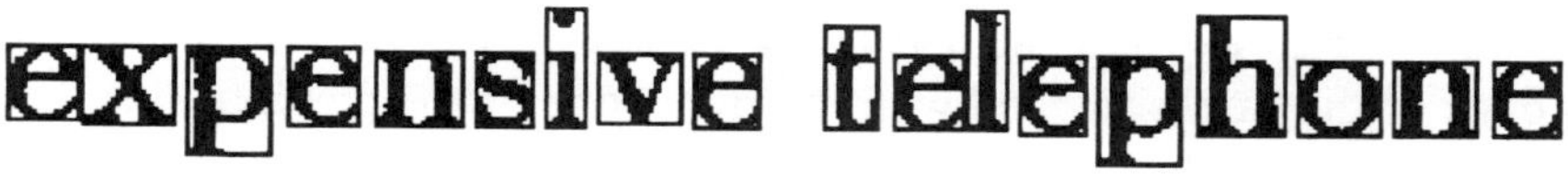

expensive telephone
(b)

Figure 3: Horizontal character positioning. A copy of the first 'e' in 'expensive' is inserted after the 't' in 'tlephone', using `copy-select-char`. (a) Before. (b) After. The spaces after the 't' and 'e' are preserved in 'telephone'.

The strategy of horizontal positioning allows the amount of space which preceeds or follows a character to depend (implicitly) on the identity, style and size of the character. As a result, it tends to produce more satisfactory results than simply using uniform spacing. However, as described above, spacing is determined from the context from which a character originated, rather than from its context after being moved or copied. Thus, incorrect spacing can occur with characters, such as 'j', for which the amount of kerning varies significantly as a function of context.

Vertical positioning of an inserted character is accomplished by aligning the baseline of the character with the baseline of the surrounding text. The baseline at the point of insertion is estimated by taking the median of the bottom Y coordinates for a set of 5 characters consisting of the character at the insertion point plus its 2 immediate neighbors to each side. This estimate provides satisfactory results as long as the neighbor set does not contain too many lower case descenders ('g', 'j', 'p', 'q', 'y') or punctuation marks which lie above the nominal baseline (e.g. '^', '-', ' " ', ' " ').

The baseline of an inserted character is estimated by applying the above procedure to the place where the character originated, if that location is known. Otherwise, the bottom of the character is assumed to be its baseline.

Experience with Image EMACS suggests that errors in baseline estimation are much more objectionable than errors in horizontal spacing. The importance of vertical positioning motivates the inclusion of several commands which can be used to explicitly adjust the vertical alignment of a character. For example, the command `adjust-baseline` is used to manually set the baseline position for a character. The user is presented with the 5 candidate positions which are used by the internal median-based estimation procedure and selects one of them as the character baseline. By contrast, there are currently no commands for manual adjustment of horizontal character position.

A number of commands are provided for adjusting the interword spacing in a line and the alignment of a line relative to the line above it. For example, the command `fill-line` adjusts all of the interword spaces in a line until the right edge of the line is aligned with the right edge of the previous line, holding the left edge of the line fixed. This command is typically used to reestablish right-justification for a line of text that has changed in length. Similarly, the command `indent-line` slides a line left or right to align its left edge with the left edge of the previous line and the command `center-line` centers the line relative to the previous line. These two commands move the line rigidly, i.e. without changing the interword spacing.

4 Foreign Language Text Editing

Image EMACS is based on a principle of demand-driven analysis in which a text image is interpreted only to the extent necessary to support a specific set of text editing operations. As discussed above, Image EMACS analyzes a text image into a vertical sequence of "lines", where each line is a horizontal sequence of "characters". A line is a horizontal strip of image which is bounded above and below by blank rows. A character is a collection of image blobs assembled according to simple grouping rules. Thus, the terms "line" and "character", while suggestive of rich semantics, actually correspond to relatively weak assertions about the geometric structure of typeset English text. In particular, similar assertions may be made about the written forms of many languages besides English, as well as by notational systems other than typeset text.

The above observation suggests that creating text image editors for (selected) foreign languages might be relatively simple, given Image EMACS as a base. Moreover, the generality of the image analysis used in Image EMACS suggests that even the current version, developed for editing images of typeset English, might be useful for editing other types of graphical material as well. While these possibilities have not been explored systematically, fig. 4 illustrates results typical of those observed in informal experiments using the current system.

Fig. 4(a) shows the connected component analysis of a small sample of horizontally lined Chinese text. The text lines are correctly identified, as are most of the characters within each line. However, several characters are split horizontally into multiple components. This reflects the fact that the current grouping rules

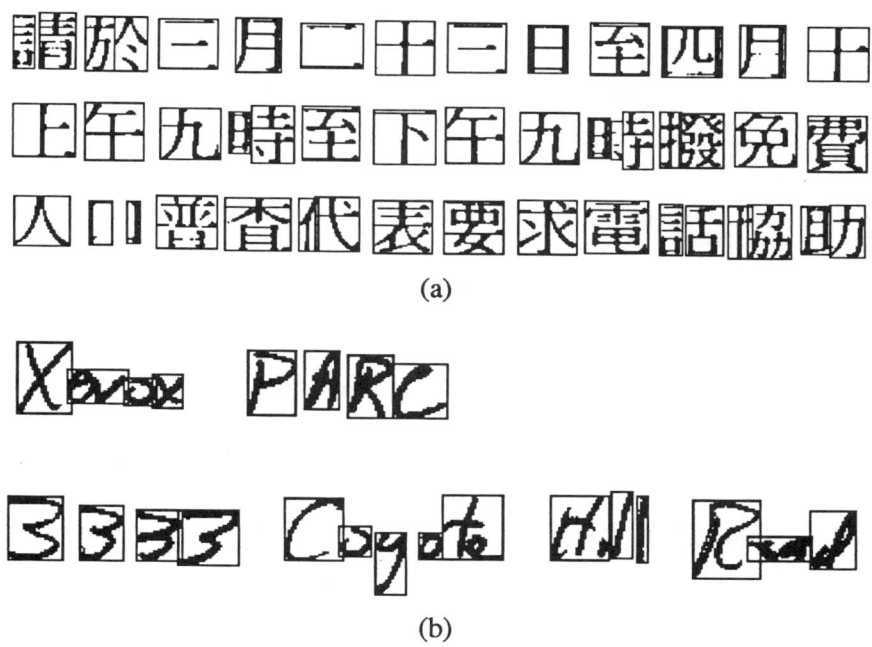

Figure 4: Connected component analysis of text which is not typeset English. A bounding rectangle is shown drawn around each set of connected components which have been grouped into a character-like unit, *using grouping rules developed for typeset English text*. (a) Typeset Chinese. (b) Handprinted English.

are based exclusively on vertical alignment of bounding boxes. More satisfactory grouping rules would exploit the typical uniform spacing of Chinese text. Of course, a satisfactory Chinese editor would also have to accommodate both vertically and horizontally lined text.

Fig. 4(b) illustrates connected component analysis of handprinted English text. As this example suggests, the gross typographies of handprinted and typeset text are similar. However, handprinted text typically manifests significant context-dependent fluctuation in character baseline. As a result, the appearance of handprinted text is often unnatural after cut-and-paste editing.

5 Related Work

Image EMACS appears to be the first system explicitly designed to support interactive text editing of scanned document images. However, there are several systems for bitmap manipulation which embody some of the features of Image

EMACS.

The system closest to Image EMACS in design philosophy is Scott Kim's Viewpoint [Kim 1987], a bitmap editor for text and graphics which was the subject of Kim's PhD thesis. Viewpoint was conceived as an exploration of the interplay between computers and graphic arts and the way in which computers might support visual thinking. A basic feature of Viewpoint, shared with Image EMACS, is that the fundamental data structures are images rather than structured symbolic descriptions. Viewpoint applies this principle more broadly than Image EMACS; in Viewpoint, every aspect of the editor's state is represented explicitly in the screen image and can be manipulated by editing the screen bitmap. For example, an image of the keyboard appears at the bottom of the screen; by editing the image inside the picture of a key, the user changes the appearance of the character that appears when that key is pressed.

The Viewpoint screen is organized as a fixed array of 10 pixel × 10 pixel cells. This constraint greatly simplifies image parsing and allows straightforward implementation of some interesting behaviors. For example, Viewpoint embodies a novel context sensitive definition of the beginning of a line. When a CR is typed, the cursor moves down to the next row of cells and then to the left until it encounters a cell that contains an image which is not currently in any of the keyboard cells (and therefore, by hypothesis, is not a "character"). However, the cell array screen model effectively limits text to fixed pitch fonts and restricts the class of images for which Viewpoint is useful. In particular, Viewpoint is only intended to edit images which have been created using Viewpoint and and is not designed to handle scanned documents.

System Zero [Levy 1987] combines typical bitmap editing functions with facilities for imposing simple typographical constraints, such as linear figure alignment and figure spacing adjustment when a figure is inserted or deleted from a line. System Zero was conceived primarily to illustrate broad theoretical issues in figural theory. Compared with Image EMACS, its support for specific text editing operations is undeveloped.

The Fontrix editor [Kleper 1987] allows complex images containing both text and graphics to be constructed using a glyph-based paradigm in which small images are bound to keyboard keys. These images can be positioned anywhere on the screen and combined in various ways with the existing screen image. However, like Viewpoint, Fontrix performs little or no image analysis and is not intended for editing scanned images.

Finally, Suenaga and Nagura [Suenaga & Nagura 1980] describe a non-interactive editor that uses handwritten marks, similar to proofreader's marks, to perform cut-and-paste rearrangement of blocks of texts and graphics on a scanned page.

6 Future Directions

There are several directions in which the development of Image EMACS could continue. The most obvious limitation of the current system is its limited typographic functionality. As noted previously, Image EMACS supports only a simple page model, elementary rules for character positioning, and primitive facilities for manual format manipulation. One overall approach to developing improved typographic functionality might be to explicitly imitate the capabilities of an existing publishing system to produce something like an Image FrameMaker or Image Ventura.

A second possibility for future work based on Image EMACS is the creation of image editors for graphical material other than text, such as block diagrams, graphs and other forms of line art. The result might be a system resembling an Image Macdraw or an Image Adobe Illustrator.

A third possibility is to seriously pursue the development of foreign language text image editors. It might be feasible to a construct a modular multi-lingual editor by coupling a collection of general image parsing and user interface facilities with a set of more specialized functions to create an integrated set of language-specific editing modes.

7 Summary

Experience with Image EMACS suggests that a surprising range of text editing operations may be implemented without character recognition or sophisticated image analysis. However, this observation should not be construed as an argument against creating and editing structured symbolic descriptions of document images. Rather, the purpose of this paper is to point out and begin investigating research territory that has not previously received very much attention.

Conventional bitmap editors are applicable to a relatively unconstrained class of images but typically have no recognition capability. As a result, they provide no support, and are tedious to use, for complex, but highly structured, graphical operations such as text editing. Conversely, systems based on the format conversion paradigm create symbolic descriptions which greatly facilitate structured document processing tasks. However, they are typically limited in the range of document images which they will handle reliably.

Bitmap editors and conventional document recognition systems thus fall at opposite ends of a spectrum parameterized by increasing operation complexity and decreasing image generality. This suggests the existence of interesting intermediate points, characterized by partial analysis appropriate for a wide (but not universal) class of images and the ability to perform a useful (but incomplete) set of document processing operations. Image EMACS is an attempt to identify one such intermediate point.

Acknowledgements

David Levy and Jim Mahoney provided support, encouragement and good ideas throughout this project. Portions of the work were supported by DARPA under NRCC research contract N00140-86-C-8996.

References

[Duda73] R. Duda and P. Hart, *Pattern Classification and Scene Analysis*, 1973, New York: John Wiley.

[Horn86] B. Horn, *Robot Vision*, 1986, Cambridge: The MIT Press.

[Kahan87] S. Kahan, T. Pavlidis, and H. Baird, "On the recognition of printed characters of any font and size", *IEEE Trans. on Pat. Anal. and Mach. Intel.*, vol. PAMI-9, no. 2, Mar. 1987.

[Kim87] S. Kim, *Viewpoint: Towards a Computer for Visual Thinkers*, Ph.D. dissertation, Computers and Graphic Design, Stanford University, 1987.

[Kleper87] M. Kleper, *The Illustrated Handbook of Desktop Publishing and Typesetting*, TAB Books, 1987.

[Levy87] D. Levy, *On the design of tailorable, figural editors*, SSL Report P89–00018, Xerox PARC, Palo Alto, CA, January 1987.

[Stallman86] R. Stallman, *GNU Emacs Manual*, Free Software Foundation, Cambridge, MA, 1986.

[Suenaga80] Y. Suenaga and N. Nagura, "A facsimile based manuscript layout and editing system by auxiliary mark recognition", *Proc. IEEE 5th Int. Conf. on Pattern Recognition*, 1980.

[Tsuji88] Y. Tsuji, "Document image analysis for generating syntactic structure description", *Proc. IEEE 9th Int. Conf. on Pattern Recognition*, Rome, Italy, 1988.

[Wilcox88] L. Wilcox and L. Spitz, "Automatic recognition and representation of documents", in J. C. van Vliet (ed.), *Document Manipulation and Typography*, Cambridge University Press, 1988; also in *Electronic Documents Laboratory Research at EP'88*, EDL Report EDL-89-1 [P89–00049], Xerox PARC, Palo Alto, CA, January 1989.

[Wong82] K. Wong, R. Casey, and F. Wahl, "Document analysis system", *IBM J. Res. Develop.*, vol. 6, pp. 642–656, Nov. 1982.

Automatic Generation of Gridfitting Hints for Rasterization of Outline Fonts or Graphics

Sten F. Andler

IBM Almaden Research Center
650 Harry Road
San Jose, California 95120-6099

ABSTRACT: The advent of bitmapped displays and printers, high-function page description languages, and outline fonts, have dramatically changed the ability of computers to produce typeset documents. Using outline fonts and rasterizing them into bitmaps on demand eliminates costly storage of raster bitmaps for all combinations of device resolution and type size. The problem, however, with these resolution-independent fonts are that aesthetic quality is hard to achieve at low device resolution and/or small font sizes. This paper presents a method for achieving aesthetic quality without manual intervention.

1 Introduction

With the coming of bitmapped displays and printers, high-function page description languages, and outline fonts, the ability of computers to produce typeset documents has dramatically changed. Such documents may be produced for electronic distribution (to be viewed on a display or printed remotely), WYSIWYG editing and draft printing (to be edited and printed locally), or final quality camera-ready output (e.g. from a photocomposer). Using mathematical descriptions (i.e. spline outlines) of the fonts and rasterizing them into bitmaps on demand eliminates the costly storage of raster bitmaps for all combinations of device resolution and type size, and makes it practical to provide a large number of compatible fonts (with compatible metrics) for most of the possible output devices.

The problem, however, with these resolution-independent fonts are that aesthetic quality is hard to achieve at low device resolution and/or small font sizes. Manually created bitmaps for characters can be hand-tuned to yield the best possible legibility and "look" of the characters, whereas a naive rasterization of outline fonts can yield very unpredictable and hard-to-read characters depending on how the outlines match up with the relatively coarse rasterization grid. In this paper we will present a method for overcoming these problems without manual intervention, by automatically finding gridfitting hints for the character outlines.

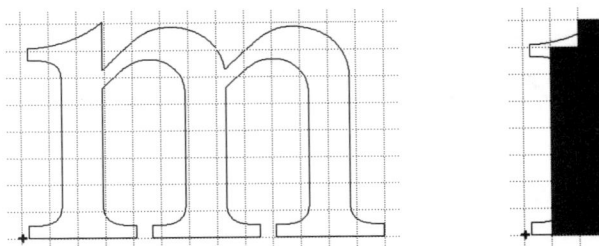 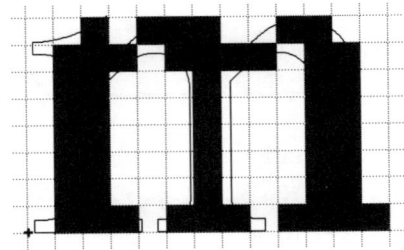

Figure 1: Naive rasterization of lower case m

2 Gridfitting Hints

In Figure 1, you can see how the outline of a lower-case "m" could be placed on a coarse rasterization grid with the reference point lining up with the grid pattern. The stem width of 1.45 pixels may overlap more than 50% of two pixel columns as with the first stem (0.55, 0.9), or may fully cover one pixel column and less then 50% of the surrounding pixel columns as with the second stem (0.1, 1.0, 0.35). Depending on the particular rasterization algorithm in use, this could result in stems that are either two and one pixels wide, respectively, or two and three pixels wide. In either case, the regularity of the character has been destroyed, and the corresponding change to the rhythm of the text will make it harder to read. You may also notice that the serifs rasterize asymmetrically and that the supposedly identical arches between the stems are rasterized differently. To counteract these problems, the outline has to be fitted to the rasterization grid. This can be done by adding rasterization constraints to the description of the character. We will call such constraints "gridfitting hints". Several such schemes have been described in the literature [Apley 88][Hersch 87][Karow 87] and several others have been developed as proprietary algorithms, e.g. by Adobe Systems [Adobe 90], Compugraphic, Imagen, and Folio [Folio 87].

We have adopted a variant of the grid constraints described in [Hersch 87]. Each hint is represented as a horizontal or vertical reference line and an optional width. For stem hints the reference line is the center of the stem, and the width represents the width of the feature. For curve hints the reference line represents the position of the extremum, and the width is set to zero. For serif hints the reference line is the center of the serif, and the width represents the width of the serif.

Automatic Generation of Gridfitting Hints

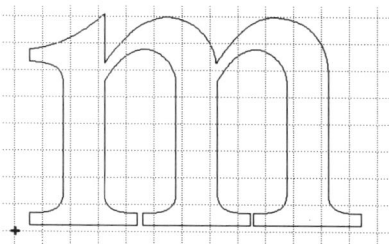 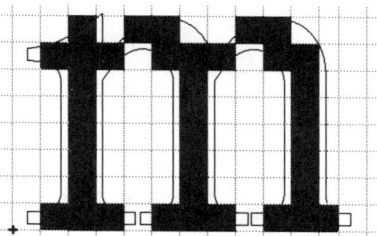

Figure 2: Gridfitted rasterization of lower case m

The effect of these hints are to center the stems and serifs on the grid and adjust the positions of curve extrema, as can be seen in Figure 2. This rearrangement of the character produces uniform stem widths, visible and identical serifs, and identical rasterization of other identical parts of the character, such as the arches between the stems. Furthermore, curves are positioned so that flat spots and isolated pixels are avoided.

Figure 3 shows the difference that using these three kinds of hints makes. The text in the figure has been rasterized for a 240 pel per inch raster. The left column shows rasterization without hints and the right column was rasterized with hints enabled. The font used is a Press font to which hints were added manually. The top block is 10 point text and each block is successively one point smaller so the last block shows 6 point text.

At 10 points, there are only minor observable differences between the columns. You may notice that several curve extrema have been rasterized better on the right. In the bottom and upper left parts of the "g", the isolated pixels have disappeared, and in the bottom part of the "e", the flat spot has disappeared. At 9 points, however, uneven stem widths start to show up in the left sample, while the text on the right has uniform stem widths. This difference is even more striking at 8 points - see for example the word "human". Another problem showing up at 8 points is the disappearance of thin stems - see the horizontal stem of "f" and "t", and at 7 points the horizontal stem of "e". At 7 points we can also see the disappearance of some lower-case serifs ("h", "l") and at 6 points some upper-case serifs as well. All these defects have been corrected on the right by the three simple gridfitting hints we have defined.

However, the egg only got larger and larger, and more and more human: when she had	However, the egg only got larger and larger, and more and more human: when she had
However, the egg only got larger and larger, and more and more human: when she had come	However, the egg only got larger and larger, and more and more human: when she had come
However, the egg only got larger and larger, and more and more human: when she had come within a few yards	However, the egg only got larger and larger, and more and more human: when she had come within a few yards
However, the egg only got larger and larger, and more and more human: when she had come within a few yards of it, she saw	However, the egg only got larger and larger, and more and more human: when she had come within a few yards of it, she saw
However, the egg only got larger and larger, and more and more human: when she had come within a few yards of it, she saw clearly that it was	However, the egg only got larger and larger, and more and more human: when she had come within a few yards of it, she saw clearly that it was

Figure 3: Non-gridfitted vs. gridfitted text (240 pels/inch)

Other types of hints which we plan to explore include reference line and symmetry hints. Reference line hints are discussed in [Betrisey & Hersch 89], and preserve x-height, cap-height, and descender line. Symmetry hints would preserve intra-character symmetries, in such characters as asterisk (*) or quote ("), as well as inter-character symmetries between pairs of characters such as curly brackets ({,}).

3   Automatic Hint Generation

Although the addition of gridfitting hints to outline fonts has (to a degree) overcome the manual steps of hand-tuning involved in converting the mathematical description of character outlines into device dependent bitmap representations, there still remains the (until recently) manual task of inserting the gridfitting hints in the outline description. The problem of fully automating outline fonts, i.e. automatically adding gridfitting hints to the outlines of all the characters in any outline font, has been the subject of proprietary research for some time [Folio 87]. But even after the announcement of Sun's OpenFonts [Sun 87], which makes the technology available for licensing by type foundries and others, the details of the process remains proprietary. We present here an alternative method for automatically analyzing the characters of a font (or any piece of graphics that satisfies the basic assumptions) to generate the type of gridfitting hints we have described earlier.

The procedure for automatically inserting gridfitting hints on our outlines consists of six steps, which will be explained in more detail later:

1. Analyze curve angles: In this step we find the tangents of each curve segment at each end point, and determine the angles between curves at the end points and the total exterior angle swept by each curve. We use this information to compute the winding direction of each outline and also in a later step to detect serifs.
2. Determine parts: If the character or graphics consists of several disconnected parts, each one will be handled separately by the gridfitting mechanism. In this step we analyze the outlines to determine the relationship of contours. We use this information to find major parts and determine which contours form outside or inside boundaries.
3. Find stems (for each part): In this step we determine the location of vertical and horizontal stems by finding all near-vertical and near-horizontal lines. Collinear lines are joined to account for broken stems. The lines are then paired to form a stem for which the center-line and width are computed. Then we determine which knots should be affected by each stem hint.
4. Find extrema (for each part): Next we find all extrema on smooth (continuous first derivative) parts of the outline, and determine which knots should be affected by the extremum hints. We then attempt to pair "outside" and "inside" extrema wherever possible, to preserve the thickness of curved parts.
5. Find serifs (for each part): We use information on the location of stems from item 3 to direct our search for serifs that terminate such features. The changes in direction of the contour associated with serifs are analyzed based on the knot and curve angles computed in item 1. The serif hints affect points that are part of the serif.
6. Insert hints in outline: Now we are ready to insert into the outline description all the hints generated in item 3 through item 5. We do this by applying the hints to sets of knots on the outline, and determine that the hints are properly nested.

3.1 Assumptions

In order to properly process the outlines according to the steps above we need to assume some basic properties of the outlines we are processing. If these properties are not satisfied by a source font or a piece of graphics, some preprocessing is necessary.

1. An outline defines one or more disjoint parts. Parts may touch each other at isolated points, but do not overlap.
2. Each part is described by an outside contour and zero or more inside contours. Contours may touch each other at isolated points, but do not cross.
3. Each contour is a closed non-intersecting curve and consists of curve segments which may be lines, conics, or Bezier cubics.
4. All global or local extrema and inflection points occur at knots connecting two curve segments. This implies that each curve segment spans at most one quadrant (i.e, the curve angle never exceeds 90°.)
5. The font has been "regularized" so that stems that are intended to be equal width are mathematically equal in width.

The above assumptions are satisfied by most outline font descriptions, and generally hold true for fonts delivered in the URW formats CN (lines and conics) and BE (lines and Bezier cubics).

3.2 Analysis of curve angles

Contours consist of curve segments that may be straight lines, conics, or Bezier cubics. Straight lines are described by end points (S, E). Conics are described by end points (S, E), midpoint (M), and a roundness factor (rf) [Saito 85]. Cubics are described by the end points (S, E) and two additional Bezier control points (A, B) [Boehm et al. 84]. For each of the curves, the points S and E are end points of the curve. We wish to compute the angle contribution of each curve segment (curve angle) and the angle contribution of each end point (knot angle).

Since there are no self-intersections in any curve segment, the curvature of a segment can be characterized by the changes in the tangents between the end points (S, E). The curve angle never exceeds 90°. For Bezier curves, the two other control points (A, B) define the tangent vectors: $\overline{SA}$ is tangent at S and $\overline{BE}$ is tangent at E (see Figure 4.) For straight line segments, defining $A = E$ and $B = S$ means $\overline{SA}$ and $\overline{BE}$ define the tangents at the end points of the straight line.

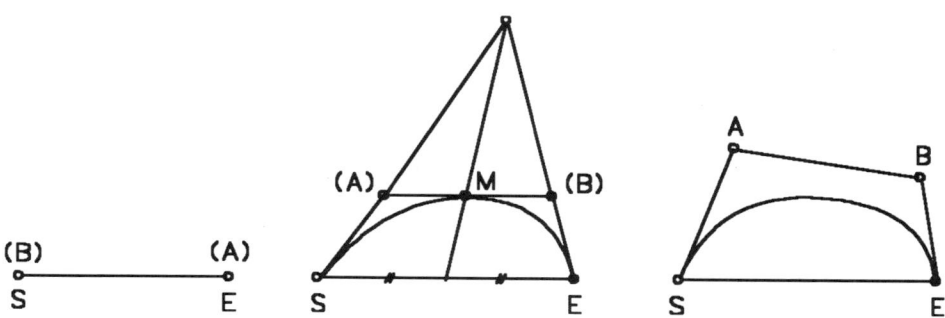

Figure 4: Control points for lines, conics, and cubics

As shown in Figure 4, points A and B can also be defined for conics so that $\overline{SA}$ and $\overline{BE}$ are tangent at S and E, respectively (see the Appendix.) From the appendix, the formulas for computing the points A and B are $A = M + rf(S - E)/2$ and $B = M - rf(S - E)/2$.

For each curve segment in the contour, we are interested in the curve angle, the angle between the end point tangents, and the knot angle, the angle between the tangents at the end of the previous segment and the start of the current segment. For the whole contour we are interested in the winding direction, i.e. whether the inside is to the right or left of the contour.

The curve angles and knot angles are easily computed. Let $\bar{v}_1 = (a_1, b_1)$ and $\bar{v}_2 = (a_2, b_2)$ be unit vectors parallel to the tangents in question. Then using a formula for the vector cross product we have $|\bar{v}_1 \times \bar{v}_2| = |\bar{v}_1| |\bar{v}_2| \sin \phi$, where ϕ is the desired angle between the two vectors. Using another formula for the vector cross product we have $\bar{v}_1 \times \bar{v}_2 = (a_1 b_2 - a_2 b_1)\bar{k}$, where $\bar{k}$ is a unit vector perpendicular to the plane of $\bar{v}_1$ and $\bar{v}_2$. Since $\bar{v}_1$ and $\bar{v}_2$ are also unit vectors, we have $|\phi| = arcsin|cp|$, where $cp = a_1 b_2 - a_2 b_1$. The actual direction of ϕ is given by the sign of the scalar component cp of the cross product; if $cp > 0$ we have a left turn ($\phi > 0$), and if $cp < 0$ we have a right turn ($\phi < 0$).

The winding direction is computed by adding up all angles (knot and curve) in the contour. If the result is $+360°$ then the winding direction is left and the inside is to the left of the contour. If the sum is $-360°$ then the winding direction is right and the inside is to the right.

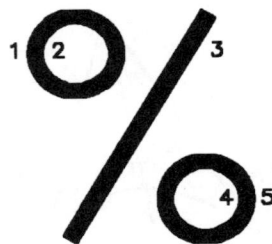

Figure 5: The contours of a percent sign

3.3 Determination of Parts

Character outlines, or other graphic objects satisfying our assumptions, consist of one or more disjoint parts, each consisting of an outside and zero or more inside contours. In this section we shall describe how we determine the various parts and the relations between their contours. As an example, consider the percent sign in Figure 5. It has three parts consisting of contours (1, 2), (3), and (4,5). Of these, contour 2 is inside contour 1, and 4 is inside 5. Contours 1, 3, and 5 are outside boundaries, whereas 2 and 4 are inside boundaries.

We start by comparing each pair of contours to determine the relation *IsInside*(i,j), which is *true* if contour i is inside contour j, and *false* otherwise. We do this by picking a point on contour i and determining if it is inside contour j. If it is inside, then the entire contour is inside according to the assumption that contours do not cross. We determine whether the sample point is inside by considering a horizontal scanline through the sample point and finding the number of vertical crossings made to the left of the sample point by curve segments in contour j. If the number of crossings is odd, then the sample point is inside contour j, otherwise it is outside.

To resolve cases where one or more knots actually lie on the scanline, we use a modification of Pavlidis' rules for filling of polygons[Pavlidis 85]. To compute the number of crossings, we need to determine for each curve segment if we should *count* or *ignore* it, or whether the crossing is *ambiguous*. If the number of crossings is *ambiguous*, then another point on contour i is picked and the procedure repeated.

We consider the algorithm first for the case where the segment of the contour is a straight line segment starting at S and ending at E:

1. If S and E are both above or both below the scanline, or both to the right of the sample point, then return *ignore*.
2. If S and E are both on the scanline then return *ignore* if both points are to the left of the sample point, otherwise return *ambiguous*.
3. If either S or E is on the scanline then return *count* if the endpoint is to the left of the sample point and the other endpoint is above the scanline, otherwise return *ignore*, unless the endpoint touches the sample point, in which case return *ambiguous*.
4. Finally, the endpoints must be on either side of the scanline. Compute the intersection point of the line SE with the scanline. If it is to the left of the sample point then return *count*, otherwise return *ignore* unless the intersection is at the sample point, in which case return *ambiguous*.

The result of this process is that cases a, b, and c in Figure 6 will count as a single crossing (odd), cases d and e will count as two crossings (even) and f and g will count as zero crossings (also even).

For conic segments and Bezier cubic segments the process is similar. We note that in each case the curve segment is contained within a convex hull made up of the points (S, A, B, E) (Figure 7). The number of crossings cannot be determined if the sample point falls within the convex hull. Since each curve segment spans at most one quadrant, the hull is usually quite tight. To further increase the chances that the sample point falls outside of the hulls, we start by subdividing the curves once. The conic section subdivides trivially into the two triangles SAM and MBE (see the Appendix), and for the cubics we use one step of the method usually known as Bezier subdivision. Now determine again if the sample point is contained in either polygon. If so, return *ambiguous*. If not, the influence of each curve segment is equivalent, with respect to polarity of the number of crossings, to a straight line from the starting point to the ending point. Again, we can use the algorithm above to determine this number.

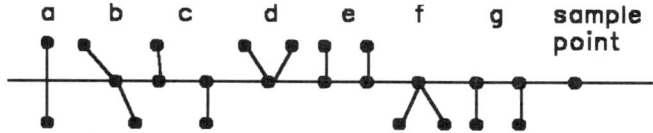

Figure 6: Scanline crossings

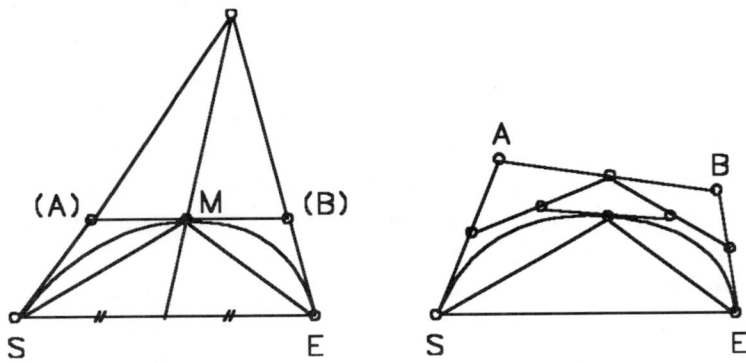

Figure 7: Convex hulls for conics and Bezier cubics

In most cases, the single subdivision of the curve segments and the occasional choice of another sample point will suffice to determine the relation *IsInside(i,j)*. In rare instances not likely to be encountered in actual fonts, further subdivision may be necessary.

3.4 Finding Stems

To determine the major stems in each part of the character or graphics, we start by finding all near-vertical and near-horizontal lines. A vertical line is defined as one whose x-coordinates differ by less than a constant *epsLine* and whose y-coordinates differ by at least *minLine*, and similarly for a horizontal line. The lines that we find in this manner are classified as left or right boundaries (bottom or top) using the previously determined information about winding directions and inside/outside boundaries. Collinear boundaries of the same class are combined. An attempt is then made to pair left and right boundaries if they overlap vertically, and bottom and top boundaries if they overlap horizontally. Those left-right or bottom-top pairs that are within a reasonable distance, *maxStem*, of each other get combined into a stem hint. If there is an overlap of stems within a part, then only the thinner stem is kept.

Once individual stems have been identified, we determine what set of control points on the part should be affected by each hint. For vertical stems the leftmost one is allowed to affect all the control points on the contours of the part, in effect moving the entire part while centering the stem on the grid. The next leftmost stem is allowed to affect all points from halfway to the first stem to everything on the right, in effect holding the first stem in place while moving the rest of the part to center the second stem. And so on, for the third leftmost stem, etc. This gradual positioning of the stems while moving large portions of the character can affect the width of the character by $(n-1)/2$ pixels, where n is the number of stems. However, the advantage of preserving equal distances between stems usually outweighs the disadvantage of width errors. For horizontal stems, each one is allowed to affect only its immediate neighborhood, to prevent distortion of horizontal reference lines, which would be much more apparent than the error in character width. All horizontal stems are allowed to affect those control points which are located between halfway to the next lower stem and halfway to the next higher stem, except for the lowest stem, which is allowed to affect points within a distance, *epsBar*, of the bottom of the stem, and the highest stem, which is allowed to affect points within a distance, *epsBar*, of the top of the stem.

3.5 Finding Curve Extrema

Since our assumptions about the outlines require that all extrema be located at end points, the task of finding them is straightforward. The type of extrema we are looking for are on continuous parts of the curve, so we need only search knots where the curve is smooth. We allow each extremum to affect all points within a small distance, *epsDist*, of the extremum knot. To preserve the width of curved parts we need to pair up extrema on the inside and outside and let the outside extremum determine the positioning of both. In order to do this we sort the vertical (horizontal) extrema by x (y), and classify the extrema as inside or outside based on the previously determined information about winding direction and inside/outside boundaries. When extrema are combined in this manner, the sets of affected points are merged. If after the pairing, one or more of the vertical (horizontal) extrema are at the same x (y) value, then they can be combined and their set of affected points merged.

3.6 Finding Serifs

We detect the location of serifs by using information about the location of stems together with information about the angles of the contour. Serifs are characterized by an outward turn close to 90° followed by an inward turn of over 180°, and are located at the end of stems. The set of control points affected by the serif hint includes all the points on the serif itself.

3.7   Inserting the Hints in the Outline Description

The hints are now represented as reference lines, optional widths, type of hint, and a set of affected points. The set of affected points may consist of several subsets of contiguous control points on the outline. Since within the outline the position of a control point is specified relative to the previous control point, a hint can be applied by adding a relative offset immediately before the first affected control point (an "apply" instruction), and adding a reversal of that offset (a "reverse" instruction) after the last affected control point. For each set of contiguous points, the hint is applied to the first point in the set, and reversed after the last point in the set. At run time, the effect of a hint is computed only once, at the first encounter of an "apply" instruction, and the value is then applied uniformly at each subsequent "reverse" or "apply" instruction. For this scheme to work correctly, the hints must be properly nested.

3.8   Proper Nesting of Hints

When affected point sets of different hints overlap, it is necessary that hints get applied in a well-defined order. We note that vertical hints are completely independent from horizontal hints, since a vertical adjustment cannot change the value computed for a horizontal adjustment, and vice versa. We therefore need only introduce a priority ordering within the group of vertical hints and within the group of horizontal hints, respectively. To ensure proper evaluation and application of hints of the same orientation, the hint value of higher priority must be evaluated and applied to all affected points before a lower priority hint is evaluated (if the affected point sets are not disjoint.) Since stem hints typically affect large portions of a character, we give them the highest priority; then follow serifs and curve extrema, in that order. Within a class of hints, such as stems, we assign priority in the order left-to-right and bottom-to-top, with respect to the location of the reference line.

Since, in our implementation, hint values are computed when we encounter the first point of the affected set on the contour, it is important that these first points are encountered in order of priority of the respective hints (if there is an overlap between the affected points). A sufficient condition for this is the following: If the affected point sets $a(h_1)$ and $a(h_2)$ of two hints h_1 and h_2 have a non-empty intersection, where the priority of h_1 is higher than the priority of h_2, then $a(h_2)$ must be a subset of $a(h_1)$.

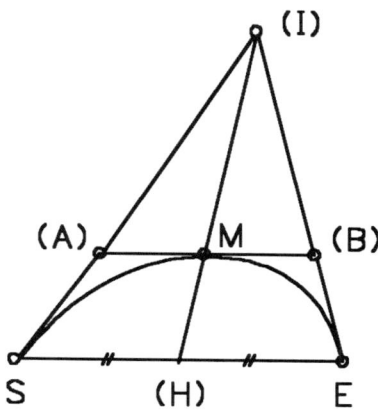

Figure 8: Various control points for conics

Appendix: Representations of Conic Sections

The form of conics we use is the midpoint form described by Saito [Saito 85]. In the midpoint form, a conic is described by the three points S, M, and E, and a roundness factor $rf = IM/IH$ (see Figure 8). The point H is the midpoint of the line $\overline{SE}$ and the point I is the extension of the line $\overline{HM}$ so that $I = H + \overline{HM}/(1-rf)$. One can also show that I is the intersection of the tangents to the conic at S and E.

In Pratt's intersection form [Pratt 85], a conic is described by the three points S, I, and E, and a sharpness factor $sf = MH/IM$. The two forms can be freely interchanged, and the conversion formulas are simple. To get from the intersection form to the midpoint form compute $M = rf * H + (1 - rf) * I$, where $rf = 1/(1 + sf)$, and $H = (S + E)/2$. To get from the midpoint form to the intersection form compute $I = H + (M - H)/(1 - rf)$ and $sf = (1 - rf)/rf$.

An advantage of the midpoint form over the intersection form is that the midpoint lies on the curve, while the intersection point can be arbitrarily far removed. This allows control over the precision needed to represent the numbers. A similar advantage is that the roundness value lies in the range $[0, 1]$, whereas the sharpness value can be arbitrarily large. A disadvantage of the midpoint form may be that it gives only indirect control of the tangents at the endpoints, which makes it less suited for interactive use. A good interactive editor should hide this problem and allow the tangents to be modified independently from the roundness. To store either form requires 7 numbers (three control points and a scalar value), or 5 numbers if the starting point is defined by the notion of a "current point".

The points S, I, and E define a triangle that fully encloses the conic. It is very easy to construct a tighter convex hull for the conic by computing the points A and B in the figure. The conic is entirely contained in the two triangles SAM and MBE. From Figure 8, it is easy to see that the triangles SIE and AIB are similar. Since rf is the ratio of IM to IH it is clear that $\overline{MA}$ is $rf \times \overline{ES}/2$ and therefore $A = M + rf \times \overline{ES}/2$ and similarly $B = M - rf \times \overline{ES}/2$.

References

[Adobe 90] "Adobe Type 1 Font Format" Adobe Systems, Inc., Mar 1990

[Apley 88] Apley, P.G. "Automatic Generation of Digital Typographic Images From Outline Masters" "SIGGRAPH'88 Course on Digital Typography" 1988.

[Betrisey & Hersch 89] Betrisey C, and Hersch, R.D. "Flexible Application of Outline Grid Constraints" in "Raster Imaging and Digital Typography" Cambridge University Press, Oct 1989, pp 242-252.

[Boehm et al. 84] Boehm, W., G. Farin, and J. Kahmann "A Survey of Curve and Surface Methods in CAGD" Computer Aided Geometric Design vol 1, 1, 1984, pp 1-60

[Folio 87] "Folio. An Introduction to its Technology, Products & Founders" Folio Inc., MountainView CA, 1987.

[Hersch 87] Hersch, R.D. "Character Generation under Grid Constraints" ACM Computer Graphics vol 21, 4, 1987, pp 243-252

[Karow 87] Karow, P. "Digital Formats for Typefaces" URW Verlag, Hamburg, W. Germany, 1987

[Pavlidis 85] Pavlidis, T. "Scan Conversion of Regions Bounded by Parabolic Splines" IEEE Computer Graphics and Applications June 1985, pp 47-53

[Pratt 85] Pratt, V. "Techniques for Conic Splines" ACM Computer Graphics vol 19, 3, 1985, pp 151-159

[Saito 85] Saito, T. "Character Generation Using Conic Splines" IBM Thomas J. Watson Research Center, Research Report RC 11193, Jun 1985

[Sun 87] "OpenFonts announcement" Sun Microsystems, MountainView, CA, Mar 1987

Chinese Fonts and their Digitization

Y.S. Moon and T.Y. Shin

Department of Computer Science
The Chinese University of Hong Kong
Shatin, New Territories, Hong Kong

ABSTRACT : This paper presents the state-of-the-art in digital Chinese font design. Both academic and industrial achievements are covered. We first highlight the difficulties in Chinese typography which are not encountered in English typesetting. Existing techniques for designing digital Chinese fonts are then examined, with their limitations identified. Finally, we propose future research directions, taking into account the recent trend in outline font technology.

1 Background

While electronic publishing has become a vital office automation tool in North America and Europe in the last few years, it is still not widely utilized in the wealthy Asian countries including Japan and the Asian "Four Little Dragons" (Hong Kong, Korea, Singapore and Taiwan). The obvious obstacle is the general lack of digital fonts for their ideographical characters.

The objective of this paper is to survey the state-of-the-art in digital font technology for the Chinese language, covering both academic and industrial experiences. Since the majority of Japanese and Korean characters (Kanji and Hanja) are similar or even identical to the Chinese characters used in China, Taiwan, Hong Kong and Singapore, it suffices for us to concentrate our discussion on the Chinese characters only. In the first instance, we survey those characteristics of Chinese fonts which make their digitization so difficult. This is followed by an overview of the design and manufacturing processes for the fonts. Lastly, future directions of research are identified.

2 Characteristics of Chinese Fonts

In China, the first movable types, based on adhesive clay, were invented around 1040 A.D., four hundred years before Gutenberg's invention in Europe. In the long course of Oriental printing history, many analog typefaces have been developed. Nevertheless, digital Chinese typefaces are rare. The difficulties of the digitization process are, at least, partially due to the deficiencies intrinsic to the Chinese characters themselves.

2.1 Extensive Character Set

Unlike English, the Chinese character set changes with time. It is estimated that at least 50,000 to 60,000 characters have ever been used since their invention a few thousand years ago [Dong 81]. In mainland China, efforts have been made to simplify the characters by combining similar ones during the last 35 years. Hence, the number of their commonly used characters is slightly less than those used in Hong Kong, Singapore or Taiwan.

To encode the characters as internal 16-bit computer codes, two standards are in use. One is the GB code used in China [PRC-NS 81] covering about 7,000 commonly used characters, while the other is the BIG-5 code used in Taiwan [CNS 86] covering about 5,400 commonly used and 7,600 less commonly used characters. If we merge these two standards without duplication, about 18,000 characters remain.

However, most typesetters have only about 8,000 analog fonts for each Chinese typeface, since enormous human efforts would be needed to create fonts for all the 18,000 characters. Whenever a font is missing during composition, an editor simply creates an ad hoc replacement or even leaves a blank for it. Such lack of a complete analog font set, as to be explained later, puts a severe obstacle for digitizing the Chinese fonts.

The huge number of characters brings also a severe storage problem. Many laser printers and typesetters, such as the Apple LaserWriter NTX (Asian version), require special hard disks just to store the fonts. The following table summarizes the storage requirements of some commonly needed bitmap font sizes for 18,000 characters.

size :	16 x 16	24 x 24	32 x 32	48 x 48	64 x 64
storage :	576 KB	1.3 MB	2.3 MB	5.2 MB	9.2 MB

To reduce the time spent on rasterization, font caching has been applied in typesetting and laser printing of English characters [Fuchs & Knuth 85] [Adobe 88]. The need for a similar technique is evidently more urgent in Chinese typesetting, because of the huge character set involved. The approaches adopted for English, unfortunately, are not suitable for the Chinese language, since the average Chinese character repetition rate is far less than that of English characters. However, as demonstrated in figure 1, the usage frequencies of the Chinese characters are not evenly distributed. Consequently, when formulating a caching scheme for them, one could exploit the usage statistics of Chinese characters, see for example [Bei et al 88] and [Lin 76].

2.2 Spatial Complexity and Hierarchical Structure

Chinese characters can be viewed as hierarchical composition of distinct components, called *radicals*, which are further decomposed into basic elements called *strokes* (see figure 2). Yet, radicals of a character may be physically connected in practice. This is true not only with ancient writings, but with most modern typefaces too. For instance, some of the logical components of the characters in figure 3 have formed a single island of ink.

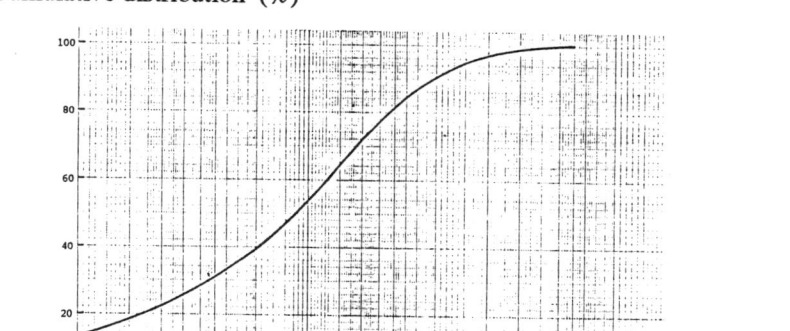

Figure 1. Cumulative usage distribution of 6000 Chinese characters

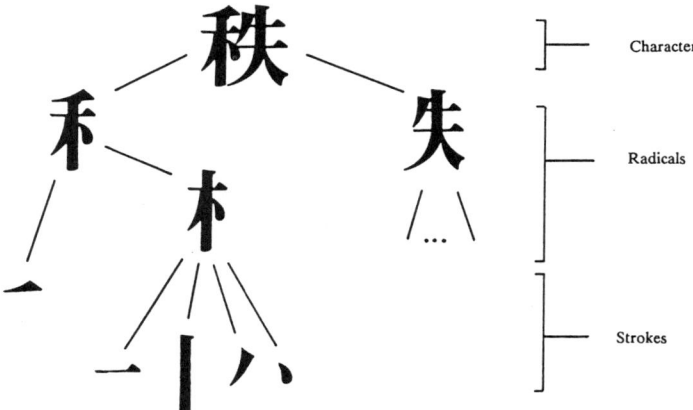

Figure 2. Hierarchical composition of a Chinese character

High stroke count is another feature of Chinese characters. Characters with as many as 30 strokes are not uncommon, as illustrated in figure 3. Thus, the Chinese fonts are obviously more densely packed than the English fonts. This property makes the rasterization of outline fonts very difficult, especially if small bitmaps for visual display purposes are required. The traditional manual fine-tuning for individual bitmaps [Bigelow 85] is totally impractical for Chinese, considering the number of characters involved. One solution is, therefore, to seek general purpose hinting for rasterizing the Chinese fonts. On the other hand, antialiased, gray-level screen fonts have been used for English characters [Warnock 80]. This holds some potentials for the Chinese language, and should be investigated further.

Chinese printing uses mono-spacing, which implies that the character bounding boxes are of fixed dimension. However, as in English, visual adjustment of individual characters relative to their boundary boxes is sometimes necessary in order to compensate for optical delusions. Figure 4 illustrates some examples. Concepts like serifs, ascenders, x-heights are never used, if not yet developed, in designing Chinese fonts. Because of this lack of design rules, the styles of Chinese fonts are sometimes less consistent than English fonts.

Figure 3. Examples of simple and complex Chinese characters

Figure 4. Relationship between characters and their bounding boxes

Chinese Fonts and their Digitization

2.3 Method of Construction

Like their English counterparts, the outline of many Chinese typefaces such as the Song, Imitation-Song, Ming, Hak (bold), and Yuan (circular) can be described by simple geometric forms, such as lines, arcs, Bezier or spline segments. Figure 5 demonstrates some popular fonts. However, some traditional Chinese typefaces like the Kai and the Chio are essentially made up of wrinkled edges produced by soft brushes. These edges are difficult, if not impossible, to be generated by conventional font design tools.

Figure 5. Some popular Chinese typefaces

3 Manufacturing Digital Chinese Fonts

Existing techniques fall into two streams. The first approach, which works on a character basis, is in principle consistent with practices in English type design. The second approach, which composes characters from structural components, is foreign to English typography.

3.1 Character-oriented Methods

The letterform of each character is here viewed as an indivisible pattern. Preparation of one character is therefore totally independent of another. Methods in this class, therefore, all rely on existing analog masters. According to their end products, nevertheless, we can classify these methods into two different categories.

3.1.1 Bitmap Fonts

A simple approach involving minimal efforts is to directly digitize existing analog font masters, although the scanned patterns often contain noisy edges, requiring manual touch-ups. Another disadvantage is that the digitization process must be repeated many times when creating bitmap fonts of different sizes.

To avoid repeated digitization, a bitmap can be scaled up or down to generate bitmaps of arbitrary sizes. Yet, simple scaling up of bitmaps produces staircasing effects due to undersampling, and necessitates interpolation. Scaling down is no better, and causes deformed or even missing features [Moon & Cheang 89]. Special algorithms for scaling Chinese bitmap fonts, in particular, can be found in various literatures [Casey et al 82], [Yeung & Cham 87], and [p.157-163, Zhao & Xu 87].

At present, most popular bitmaps adopted by most computer manufacturers in Hong Kong and Taiwan were developed by the Taipei Computer Industry Association [Taipei 89]. Four point sizes for five typefaces are available, each covering 5401 primary and 7650 secondary characters. Basically, these fonts have two weaknesses. The four sizes (namely, 24 x 24, 32 x 32, 48 x 48 and 64 x 64) are designed for screen and dot-matrix printer resolutions. These fonts are, therefore, inadequate for use on laser printers and typesetters. Worst of all, the quality of some fonts, especially those less common ones, are poor. In some manufacturers' implementation, they are even occasionally missing or wrongly inserted in the font libraries.

3.1.2 Outline Approach

Synchronizing with modern digital font development which emphasizes on describing the outline of characters using geometrical primitives like lines, arcs and curves, digital outline fonts are evolving in Japan, Hong Kong, Korea, Singapore and Taiwan.

3.1.2.1 Manual Outline Tracing

Most outline font developers in the Orient are original analog font designers. A natural way for them to migrate from the human-oriented approach to the computer-oriented technology is to trace the outline of a font manually [pp.134-140, Rubinstein 88]. In fact, Altsys's Fontographer [Altsys 89], a commercially available manual outline tracing system, is widely used in these countries.

With this approach, a designer specifies corner and tangent points on the outline of scanned analog font and join the points using lines, arcs or curves. The tools would then generate descriptions for that font automatically, using PostScript or other font specification languages.

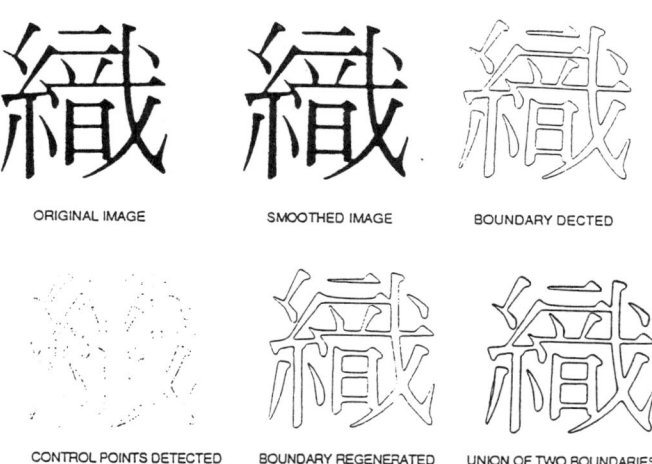

Figure 6. Automatic outline tracing based on cubic splines [Moon & Hui 89]

A recent report [Riley 89] shows that a designer can produce, on the average, 20 to 30 fonts per day. The quality of the manually prepared fonts depends on the skills and consistency of the designers. For the large number of Chinese fonts, a lot of experienced designers would be required. Unfortunately, such designers are not abundant in the Orient. As a result, the progress of this manual approach is slow. Moreover, insufficient understanding of the mathematical and computing background of font technology also prevents these font developers from any advancements beyond those provided by the tools suppliers.

3.1.2.2 Automatic Outline Tracing

To combat the slow and inconsistent manual outline tracing method, Moon and his colleagues have attempted to automate the outline tracing method using computer vision techniques [Moon & Hui 89] [Moon & Szeto 88]. The entire process is illustrated in figure 6, while some sample characters thus generated are shown in figure 7 and 8. In brief, the automatic outline tracing process is performed in three steps.

i. Automatic tracing of the edges of a bitmap font of size at least 200 x 200.
ii. Computation of the slopes and curvatures for the discrete points on the edges, thereby producing the corner points and tangent points.
iii. Joining the corner points by lines, arcs or curves to fit the edges. Whenever no good approximation can be obtained, control points in between the corner points are generated and the fitting step is repeated.

The merit of Moon's approach is, of course, efficiency. A library of 5000 commonly used Chinese characters in the form of bold Song type was successfully created in two man-months time. A lot of the effort was actually spent on the careful scanning of analog font masters to convert them into bitmaps. An average of 306 bytes is used to store the description of a font using a compact linked list. When this description is translated into PostScript, an average of 3.6 Kbytes are required.

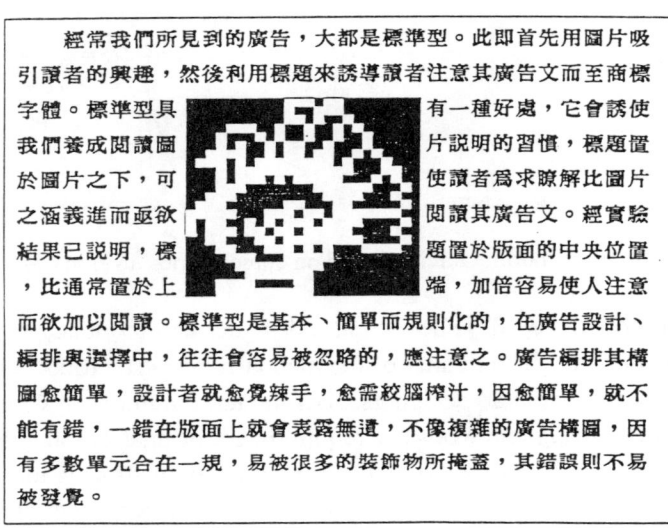

Figure 7. Characters built from Bezier, line and arc segments [Moon & Szeto 88]

Figure 8. Imperfect outlines at stroke crossings (such as rounded corners)

The automatic outline tracing method, however, has its own weaknesses. Some difficulties faced by the computer-vision based algorithm are as follows.
- The analog fonts must be scanned very accurately to reduce noise due to scanning and to make sure that analog fonts on paper are accurately oriented when the paper is placed on the flatbed scanner.
- A lot of computing time is required to fit the characters using combinations like the best-fit and first-fit heuristics. Some parameters like the discrete slopes and curvatures are very difficult to compute accurately, so that the corner points and control points are sometimes not very accurately specified.

For these reasons, degradations in quality are often encountered, such as :
- misalignment of intersecting strokes;
- unsharp corners;
- fitting a straight line by a long arc; and
- undesirable Bezier curve shapes due to inaccurate estimations of curvatures at the curve endings.

Although the fonts thus produced are already good enough for desktop publications, occasional touch-up is necessary to satisfy the toughest requirements of professional typesetters.

3.2 Composition-oriented Methods

We have previously pointed out that Chinese characters are composed of radicals and strokes in a hierarchical manner. Thus, an obvious approach to designing Chinese fonts is to compose the fonts from a finite set of outlines of strokes or radicals. Of course, the strokes and radicals must be individually transformed and scaled before being combined to form a single font character. In fact, the radical approach has received much attention in the academic world due to its storage efficiency. Only the descriptions of the strokes, radicals and their transformations are needed.

Historically, most of the previous works were carried out using MetaFont [Knuth 88] because of its suitability for specifying nested composition of radicals and strokes, and its flexibility for controlling complicated transformations. At least four groups of work have been reported.

1. *LCCD* [Dong 81]
   LCCD is a font compiler based on MetaFont. Simple affine transformations are applied to canonical strokes so that only minor variations to the strokes can be obtained. Thus, LCCD maintains many different versions for each stroke. Similarly, only simple scalings are available to adjust the radicals before combining them to form a character.

2. *Hobby and Gu* [Hobby & Gu 84]

   In this work, complicated parameterizations of strokes are supported. Only 13 strokes are provided, comparing to 108 in LCCD. A basic stroke is defined using a skeleton. Control routines then accept complicated parameters to generate strokes for different typefaces. In the case of the Song style, as many as 68 parameters are required. When joining the strokes together to form radicals, Gu and Hobby allow overlapping of the strokes. However, like LCCD, only simple transformations are applied to transform the radicals prior to combining them together to generate a character.

3. *Li* [Li 85]

   Li's work is aware of the nonlinear scalings of strokes and radicals. Nevertheless, details are unavailable.

4. *JACM* [Chan et al 88]

   This is another piece of MetaFont-based work that allows a user to combine strokes and radicals using a graphical interface. Again, very few details have been reported.

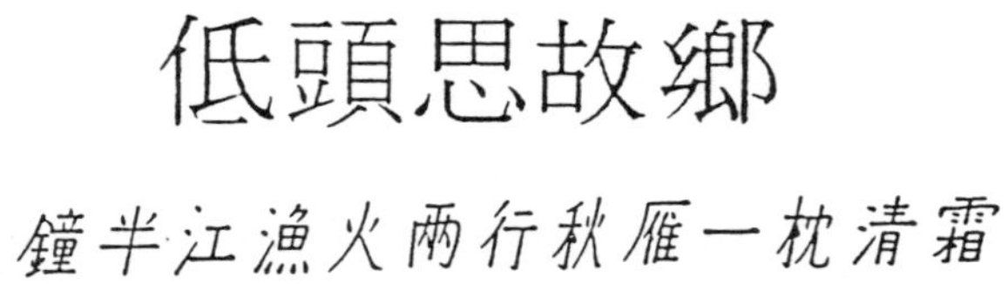

低頭思故鄉

鐘半江漁火兩行秋雁一枕清霜

Figure 9. Mis-scaling and mis-positioning of radicals [Dong 81]

All the above four pieces of work, however, have not reported the completion of any Chinese font library or even a significant number of characters. The quality of fonts thus produced are in general not satisfactory either, as illustrated in figure 9. We believe that the difficulties arise from the following factors.

- As far as font caching is concerned, the composition approach would necessitate statistical information on radical (or even stroke) usage as well. The problem is that, so far, no universally recognized set of radicals ever exists.
- MetaFont is hard to use and is basically a batch-oriented system; the resulting production efficiency is low [p.143, Rubinstein 88].
- The transformations of the strokes and radicals are very complicated, especially if they are performed in a trial-and-error manner on a batch system. The same radical may be rendered in a totally different manner in different characters, as illustrated in figure 10.

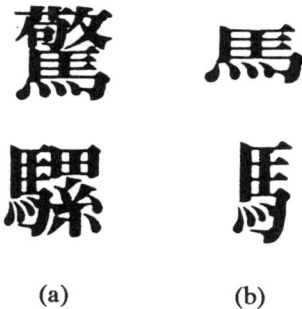

(a) (b)

Figure 10. The same radicals (b) rendered differently in two characters (a)

4 Future Research

The character-oriented approach, though very efficient in terms of human labour, suffers from some intrinsic difficulties due to discrete errors and machine weakness like scanning errors. For this reason, no single algorithm can be claimed as a panacea. Instead, continuous engineering efforts are required to refine the heuristics for polishing the output fonts. In fact, we believe that different typefaces actually require different refinement strategies.

On the other hand, the economical radical approach has not produced any truly fruitful result yet. We envisage that the following works must be done in order to make the radical approach feasible for generating font libraries in the future.

A. Experimental work must be performed to identify the set of strokes and radicals. Needless to say, such standardization must be accompanied by corresponding sets of mathematical transformations that can be applied to the strokes and radicals prior to combining them to form character fonts.

B. An interactive editor must be developed to enable designers to combine the radicals to form characters in an ad hoc manner. The editor must also support storage of the font libraries in a hierarchical manner.

5 Conclusions

It is clear that not much work can be done in the bitmap font area. Nevertheless, development of general-purpose rasterization techniques for converting outline into small bitmap font for display purpose is quite urgent.

Producing high-quality digital Chinese fonts will remain to be a very difficult task.[1] At present, the character-oriented approach dominates in the real world production shops. However, in the foreseeable future, we project that the radical approach would eventually overtake the leadership position. The reason is not merely due to economization of font storage. Rather, design effort can be concentrated in creating the relatively small number of radicals or strokes. The ways to combine the strokes to form radicals, which in turn combine to form character fonts are, to our thinking, not very different from one typeface to another, so that the experience or even work done are transferable.

Font specification languages have evolved continuously. Besides PostScript which is well known, other languages for font specification have emerged almost simultaneously lately. These include Apple's Royal Format [Apple 89], HP's Intellifont format [Hewlett 89] and SUN's F3 format [SUN 89]. Some of them support quadratic B-splines and some use lines and circular arcs only. Refitting the outlines of the Chinese fonts using different sets of primitives are very expensive and time consuming. Therefore, work must be done for automatic conversions of Chinese fonts from one font description into another.

Finally, we must point out that the availability of analog font masters is the biggest obstacle to overcome in designing a *complete* Chinese digital font libraries. No matter whether we are developing bitmap or outline fonts, paper font masters must be used as templates. This is, however, a very difficult problem to solve in the near future.

Font development is both a cultural and scientific matter. The old ideographical fonts are just in their infancy stages for digitization. The road is long but we must begin our journey now.

---

[1] Little has been mentioned about the digital fonts experience in China. In fact, most of the Chinese developments are state supported, closely linked to the development of their own typesetting machines. In the 70's and early 80's, much work had been devoted to compacting large bitmap fonts for use on phototypesetters [Xie & Suen 84] as well as to improving the rasterization speeds of vector-based outline fonts [Wang et al 84]. However, these works were very hardware dependent and details were not widely available. Up-to-date, brief surveys can be found in [Wang 90] and [Xie 90]. With the recent wide acceptance of desktop laser printers, we believe that popular font description tools such as PostScript, Royal Format, etc. will soon be used in the production of new digital fonts in China.

References

[Adobe 85] Adobe Systems Incorporated, *PostScript Language Reference Manual*, Addison Wesley, Reading, Massachusetts, 1985.

[Altsys 89] Altsys Corporation, *Fontographer User's Guide - a Professional Font Editor*, Plano, Texas, 1989.

[Apple 89] Apple Computer Inc., *Macintosh System Software Release 7.0 Outline Fonts - Preliminary Developer Note*, 1989.

[Bei et al 88] Bei, Chang, & Jiang, *Statistics of Chinese Character Usage*, Electronic Industry Publishing Ltd., Beijing, 1985.

[Bigelow 85] C. Bigelow, *Font Design for Personal Workstations*, Byte, Vol. 10, No. 1, January 1985, pp.255-270.

[Casey et al 82] R.G. Casey, T.D. Friedman and K.Y. Wong, *Automatic Scaling of Digital Print Fonts*, IBM Journal of Research & Development, Vol. 26, No. 6, June 1982.

[Chan et al 88] K.M. Chan, K.P. Chow & W.M. Lo, *JACM - Just Another Chinese Metafont*, Proceedings of the International Conference on Computer Processing of Chinese and Oriental Languages, 1988, pp.311-315.

[Dong 81] Y.M. Dong, *LCCD - a Language for Chinese Character Design*, Software, Practice and Experience, Vol. 11, 1981, pp.1273-1292.

[Fuchs & Knuth 85] D.R. Fuchs & D.E. Knuth, *Optimal Prepaging and Font Caching*, ACM Transaction on Programming Languages & Systems, Vol. 7, No. 1, January 1985, pp.62-79.

[Hewlett 89] Hewlett Packard Inc., *Creating Intellifont-compatible Fonts using the AGFA Compugraphic FAIS Standard*, 1989.

[Hobby & Gu 84] J. Hobby & G. Gu, *A Chinese Meta-Font*, TUGBoat, Vol. 5, No. 2, 1984, pp.1-136.

[Knuth 88] D.E. Knuth, *MetaFont*, Addison Wesley, Reading, Massachusetts, 1989.

[Li 85] J. Li, *Generation of some Chinese Characters with Metafont*, Proceedings of the First European Conference TEX for Scientific Documentation, ed. D. Lucarella, Addison Wesley, 1985, pp.161-170.

[Lin 76] S. Lin, *A Statistical Study on Chinese Character Set for Computer Use*, Technical Report CC-601, National Chiao Dong University, Hsinchu, Taiwan, 1976.

[Moon & Szeto 88] Y.S. Moon & Y.P. Szeto, *Efficient Construction of high-quality Chinese Font Libraries*, Proceedings of the 1988 International Conference on Computer Processing of Chinese and Oriental Languages, 1988, pp.262-265.

[Moon & Cheang 89] Y.S. Moon & S.M. Cheang, *Deficiencies of Postscript in Displaying and Printing Chinese Fonts*, Internal Report, Department of Computer Science, The Chinese University of Hong Kong, 1989.

[Moon & Hui 89] Y.S. Moon & W.K. Hui, *High-quality Chinese Font Generation for Desktop Publishing - a Computer Vision Approach*, Pattern Recognition Letters, Vol. 9, 1989, pp.147-151.

[PRC-NS 81] The People's Republic of China National Standard, *Code of Chinese Graphic Character Set for Information Interchange Primary Set GB 2312-80*, Technical Standards Press, Beijing, 1981.

[Riley 89] J. Riley, *Ideographic Fonts Come of Age*, Special Report, South China Morning Post, Hong Kong, November 21, 1989.

[Rubinstein 88] Richard Rubinstein, *Digital Typography - An Introduction to Type and Composition for Computer System Design*, Addison Wesley, Reading, Massachusetts, 1988, 440 pages.

[SUN 89] SUN MicroSystems Inc., *TypeMaker Reference Manual*, 1989.

[Taipei 88] Taipei Computer Industry Association, *Computer Chinese Fonts*, 1988.

[Wang et al 84] X. Wang, Z. Lu & Z. Chen, *Augmentation and Reduction for Chinese Character Images with High Resolution*, Chinese Journal of Computers, Vol. 7, No. 6, 1984, pp.418-426.

[Wang 90] X. Wang, *Development of Chinese Electronic Publishing Systems*, Proceedings of the International Conference on Computer Processing of Chinese and Oriental Languages, 1990, pp.272-278.

[Warnock 80] J.E. Warnock, *The Display of Characters using Gray Level Sample Arrays*, Report CSL-80-6, Xerox Palo Alto Research Center, May 1980.

[Xie & Suen 84] K. Xie & C.Y. Suen, *Design of Chinese Character-Generating System and Compression of Chinese Character Image Data*, Chinese Journal of Computers, Vol. 7, No. 6, 1984, pp.451-457.

[Xie 90] K. Xie, *Standardization Problems in Chinese Font Information Processing*, Proceedings of the International Conference on Computer Processing of Chinese and Oriental Languages, 1990, pp.308-310.

[Yeung & Cham 87] C.S. Yeung & W.K. Cham, *Stroke Extraction, Scaling and Transformation of Chinese Character Patterns*, IEEE Asian Electronics Conference, 1987, pp.182-187.

[Zhao & Xu 87] P.Z. Zhao & L. Xu, *Jisuanji Zhongwen Xinxi Chuli, (Computer Processing of Chinese Information)*, Beijing, 1987.

Documents as User Interfaces

Eric A. Bier[†] and Aaron Goodisman[‡]

[†]*Xerox Palo Alto Research Center*
3333 Coyote Hill Rd.
Palo Alto, CA 94304

[‡]*Massachusetts Institute of Technology*
Department of Electrical Engineering and Computer Science
Cambridge, MA 02139

ABSTRACT: Each year the electronic documents community produces better tools for creating and changing document elements, including text, illustrations, tables, equations, video, voice, hypertext links, and animation. At the same time, the user interface community is working to build interfaces that improve the quality of interaction by effectively presenting information to the user and making it easy to act on and manipulate that information. These efforts can be combined by using documents as user interfaces. This paper describes a prototype architecture, EmbeddedButtons, that allows arbitrary document elements to behave as buttons. Using examples from EmbeddedButtons, we enumerate some of the reasons that user interfaces should be documents and documents should be user interfaces.

KEYWORDS: active documents, user interfaces, buttons, EmbeddedButtons

1 Introduction

Each year, electronic documents and their editors are becoming more powerful and more widely available. The term *electronic document* has come to encompass a wide variety of media including text, illustrations, tables, equations, scanned images, video, voice, hypertext links, and animation. The electronic documents community is producing software to create, edit, lay out, and navigate multimedia documents.

At the same time, the user interface community is working to build interfaces that improve the quality of interaction by effectively presenting information to the user and making it easy to act on and manipulate that information.

These two efforts are intertwined in many ways. In the first place, they depend on each other for success: good user interfaces are crucial to the construction of successful multimedia editors, and the effective presentation of a variety of media is crucial to the development of successful user interfaces. They also depend on the same presentation technologies, including raster displays, voice, and video. Finally, pointing devices such as the mouse and stylus enable both the direct manipulation of document elements and access to user interface elements such as buttons, menus, property sheets, and dialog boxes.

In this paper, we propose that electronic documents and user interfaces should be combined in a very intimate way. Documents should *be* user interfaces. User interfaces should *be* documents. By removing the boundary between the two, we can:

- empower users by allowing them to turn their skills for creating documents into skills for creating and using user interfaces,

- include in the document itself the functionality that is most often needed when that document is read, allowing the user to stay focused on the task that the document represents rather than on desktop tools,

- send user interfaces through electronic mail,

- provide a new way to customize document editors, and

- allow users to copy and combine parts of application control panels to make new customized control panels.

As a first step towards merging documents and user interfaces, we have implemented EmbeddedButtons, an architecture that allows document objects in any participating editor to behave as buttons. These buttons perform many of the functions needed to build application control panels: when clicked, they can call an application function, pop up a menu, or change state (e.g., from on to off). Any document object, be it a text string, a spline curve, or part of an equation, can become a button. When a document is stored, the attributes of each button are written to the document file as a text string, so buttons persist from session to session and can be mailed to any workstation that runs our document editors.

Documents that contain buttons are an example of a larger set of documents, which we call *active documents*, that exhibit dynamic behavior. While the work reported here focuses on buttons, it is part of an effort to understand active documents and their applications.

Section 2 describes related work that has brought documents and user interfaces closer together. Section 3 describes the advantages of using documents as user interfaces by presenting some of the applications that we have constructed using EmbeddedButtons and some that we envision. Section 4 describes the appearance and use of buttons from the user's point of view. Section 5 describes the document editors that currently participate in our architecture and how that architecture responds when a button is pressed. Section 6 describes some early experiences with EmbeddedButtons. Finally, section 7 presents our conclusions and plans for future work.

The EmbeddedButtons architecture has been implemented in the Cedar programming environment [Swinehart et al. 1986], which runs on Xerox Dorado and SUN workstations. EmbeddedButtons works together in the same documents with other active document systems in Cedar, including Active Tioga [Terry & Baker 1990], in which document activity is triggered by scrolling or editing the document; Scripted Documents [Zellweger 1989], in which activity is triggered at a document site when the user arrives at that site via an electronic path; and CaminoReal [Arnon 1988], in which mathematical equations embedded in a document are re-evaluated in response to document redisplay.

2 Related work

EmbeddedButtons draws on work in electronic documents, user interfaces, and systems that combine the two. In particular, EmbeddedButtons takes advantage of the tradition of mouse-based WYSIWYG editors such as Bravo [Xerox 1979], Tioga [Beach 1985; Swinehart et al. 1986], Star [Johnson et al. 1989], Grif and pedtnt [Furuta et al. 1988], Andrew [Morris et al. 1986], and others. The mouse allows buttons to be pressed, and WYSIWYG systems interpret the attributes of document elements during editing, rather than waiting until the document is to be printed. This is essential to the use of document elements as buttons.

Because we wish to make it easier to define user interfaces, we share many of the concerns of user interface toolkits and layout tools such as NextStep [Webster 1989], FormsVBT [Avrahami et al. 1989] and Cardelli's user interface editor [Cardelli 1988].

Other systems that have included user-definable buttons as a technique for customizing user interfaces include Xerox Lisp Buttons [MacLean et al. 1990], CUSP buttons [Xerox 1988], and Hypercard [Goodman 1987].

EmbeddedButtons is closely related to the Symbolics Presentation Manager [McKay et al. 1989] and CUE Forms [Kaczmarek 1984], which also combine buttons and documents in an intimate way. Like Symbolics presentations, our buttons can be arbitrary document objects, even non-rectangular elements such as indented paragraphs and graphical shapes, and can have state. CUE Forms is a language for describing hierarchically-organized office forms, where any form element can be a button. Like CUE forms, our buttons are persistent, user-editable, and can have state.

EmbeddedButtons differs from previous work in that it is not a particular system for investigating active elements in documents, but rather an architecture for including such facilities in any document editor. EmbeddedButtons is also an attempt to unify the advantages of previous systems, providing buttons that can be normal objects in persistent, user-editable, exchangeable multimedia documents, using whatever hit-testing methods the document editors provide. With this framework, we are trying to broaden the set of applications for which active documents are used.

3 Taking advantage of documents

The Introduction lists five benefits that derive from merging documents and user interfaces. This section describes these benefits in more detail.

3.1 Document skills become user interface skills

Document editors contain functions to create, select, move, copy, delete, store, retrieve, search for, scroll through, change the style of, selectively display, and print document information. When documents are user interfaces, all of these capabilities become available both for creating and employing user interfaces.

The familiar layout capabilities of document editors can be used to compose control panels. Graphical editors can be used to create borders and icons. Text editors can be used to lay out lines or tables of buttons with appropriate colors, fonts, underlining and so forth. Such control panels inherit the ability of text editors to reformat text for different page sizes and scaling factors.

When a user interface is a document, document editors provide ways to navigate through it. If users build large documents containing many active elements to aid them in a variety of tasks, they can take advantage of scrolling, level-clipping (e.g., seeing header names only), fish-eye views [Furnas 1986], and textual search to find user interface components.

Textual search-and-replace and graphical search-and-replace [Kurlander & Bier 1988] can be used to quickly make user interfaces from existing documents. For instance, a document of names, addresses, and phone numbers can be turned into an active document by searching for strings that look like phone numbers and turning them into buttons that dial the phone number.

3.2 Staying focused on the task

Often when we read an electronic document, we are searching for information that we intend to put to use immediately. When we type a command to list the files in a directory, we often want to read, rename, or delete some of the files in the list. In most current interfaces, we move our eyes from the list to a command shell or file tool to open an editor window on one of the listed files. If the file names are buttons, we can perform these operations directly on the file list, without moving our attention from the list.

3.3 Buttons in electronic mail

The sender of an electronic mail message may wish to include buttons that help recipients act on the information in the message. For instance, a message describing a software release, a phone number, or a file can contain a button to install the software, dial the number, or open the file, respectively.

3.4 Customizing document editors

Buttons can be used in several ways to enhance document editors. For instance, users can create button collections that perform tedious or complicated editor operations, including searches and style changes. For instance, each line in figure 1 is a button that transfers its dash pattern or line width to a selected graphical object such as the object shown at the right. As another example, a text string that is to be used repeatedly in a document can be turned into a *stuffer* button, which copies the string to the current text editor insertion point.

Figure 1. Graphical Style Macros. These buttons transfer their dash patterns and stroke widths when the cursor, a circle with a black dot in its center, clicks near them.

Buttons can also be used to improve document navigation. One example, inspired by the Symbolics Presentation Manager [McKay et al. 1989], is the ability to hide a portion of a document behind a button. With each button press, the text is alternately revealed and hidden. Such *hider* buttons allow the user to browse through a document using screen space only for document parts of interest. A document with hider buttons can be used as a layered control panel.

Buttons can be used to directly alter the behavior of a graphics editor. If we wish to play with different colorings of circles as shown in figure 2, we could use graphics editor commands to select each circle in turn and apply a color to it, taking several mouse clicks per color change. If instead we turn each circle into a two-state button that is, say, black when on and white when off, we need only one mouse click per color change. When we are done, we can turn off button activity, leaving a recolored picture that can once again be edited normally.

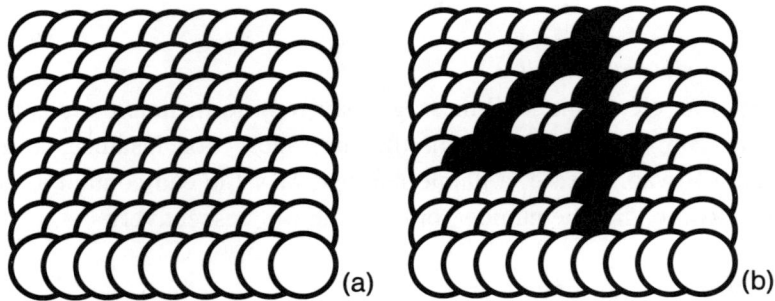

Figure 2. (a) A pattern of circles. (b) The recolored pattern.

3.5 Reusing control panels

Sets of buttons can be linked to a pane of an application window, allowing button-containing documents to act as control panels. Once control panels are documents, document editors can be used to navigate through them, modify them, copy them, and combine parts of them into customized control panels for special tasks. To test this idea, we are in the process of replacing the control panel of the Gargoyle graphics editor [Pier *et al.* 1988], currently implemented using Cedar window system widgets, with a button-containing document.

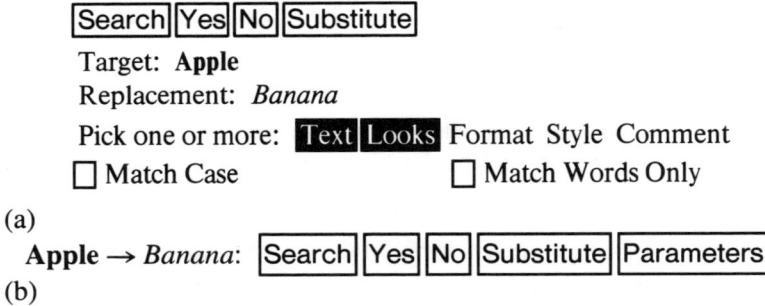

Figure 3. Text Search Tool (a) The dialog box. (b) A special-purpose version.

Documents can also be used to replace dialog boxes. Figure 3(a) shows a text search tool. It is set to search for the bold word **Apple** and replace it with the italic word *Banana*. The Search, Yes, No, and Substitute buttons provide functions for performing replacements either one by one or all at once. A user who will need to perform this replacement frequently may wish to copy this control panel *with its current settings* into another document as shown in figure 3(b). To save space, a hider button, Parameters, has been used to encapsulate the details of the search pattern. If desired, the user can click on Parameters to expose the hidden fields.

4 Buttons in documents

Section 3 described many types of user support that become possible when buttons are tightly integrated with documents. Fortunately, achieving this support requires only a small number of types of buttons. We have found three button classes to be useful: *pop-up*, *multi-state*, and *radio*. In this section, we describe the appearance and use of each of these button classes from the user's point of view.

4.1 Pop-up buttons

When the user holds down a mouse button over a document object that has been made into a pop-up button, a pop-up menu appears, with one of its entries centered on the cursor. When the user makes a selection, the pop-up button sends a command to the application indicated by the button. For instance, in figure 4, the user has clicked on the text string "Alphabet." The pop-up menu offers to change the alphabet of the currently selected text string in some other document (not shown). The rectangle below the menu displays documentation for the currently selected menu entry. The pictures on the left edge of the menu indicate which of the three mouse buttons can be used as an accelerator for future button presses. If the user clicks quickly on the button with one of these mouse buttons, no pop-up menu appears; the action is performed immediately. This pop-up menu facility, but not its use from active documents, has been previously described [Pier *et al.* 1988].

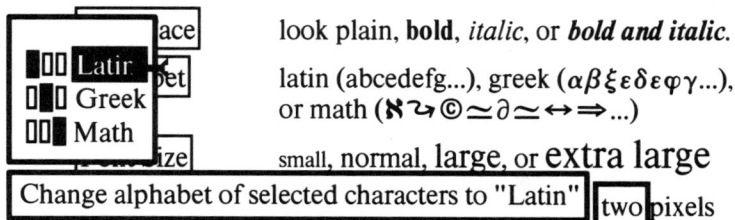

Figure 4. A pop-up button that performs text editor macros.

4.2 Multi-state buttons

Multi-state buttons respond to mouse clicks by modifying the contents of an internal variable, Value. Value cycles through a set of strings that are provided by the interface designer. For instance, if the strings are on and off, the button will switch between on and off. If the strings are apple, banana, and grapefruit, the button cycles through these names.

The interface designer decides how each state is displayed. The state of a textual button could be shown by changing the font (figure 5(a)), the relative color of text and background (figure 5(b)), or the text contents of the button (figure 5(c)). In fact, any document editor operation can be used to achieve highlighting.

(a)   Grid   →   **Grid**

(b)   Grid   →   Grid

(c)   Grid: on   →   Grid: off

Figure 5. Button Highlighting. (a) Font change. (b) Video reverse. (c) Text change.

Multi-state buttons can be used to control an application. An application can read and write the value of a button by providing its name and parent document to routines that EmbeddedButtons provides. The application does not need to know where the button is placed in the document or what the class of the button is. A button can be programmed to ask an application for permission before it changes state. This protocol allows button clicks in an active document to be synchronized with other user actions received by the application.

4.3 Radio buttons

A radio button is a member of a group of buttons, only one of which may be on at a time. As with multi-state buttons, the designer decides how the button will change appearance to reflect its state. Our radio buttons refer to their group by name rather than by document locality; they need not be positioned near each other. Each arrow in figure 6 is a radio button. Clicking on one arrow makes it black and turns all of the other arrows white.

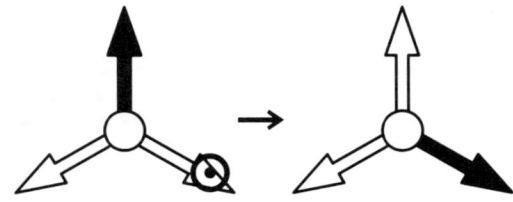

Figure 6. Graphical Radio Buttons.

5 Implementation

Our button architecture consists of a language, Poppy, that is used to represent button behavior and a software package, the EmbeddedButtons kernel, that handles the document-independent aspects of responding to button presses. Two Cedar editors, the Tioga text editor and Gargoyle illustrator, currently participate in the architecture. Their participation depends both on existing features of these editors and on extensions made specifically to support EmbeddedButtons. In this section, we describe the participating editors, the Poppy language, and the behavior of the kernel.

5.1 Tioga and Gargoyle

Tioga is a multi-font WYSIWYG galley editor used to edit program text, high-quality documents, and the fields of dialog boxes and other tools [Beach 1985; Swinehart et al. 1986]. Tioga documents are tree-structured to express document logical structure such as sections, subsections, and paragraphs. Nodes or characters can have associated properties. The values of these properties may be text strings or Cedar data structures. Built-in node properties include the *format* property, which determines formatting parameters such as leading, indentation, and typeface. Built-in character properties include *looks*, which specify local changes to typeface, superscripts, etc. Properties can be viewed and changed using a dialog box. The set of properties is extensible. Tioga preserves properties and their values even if it doesn't recognize them.

Gargoyle is a structured graphics editor [Pier et al. 1988]. Any Gargoyle object can have a set of associated properties like those supported by Tioga. Gargoyle uses a gravity function, which is part of the *snap-dragging* drawing technique [Bier & Stone 1986], to allow the user to point to objects that are near the cursor. EmbeddedButtons uses gravity to allow users to point to objects, like the lines in figure 1, that have little area.

Tioga and Gargoyle can both be driven by an interpreted language consisting of a sequence of editing commands and their arguments. In fact, all user input from mouse and keyboard is translated into strings in these input languages before being passed to these editors. By including these strings in buttons, we can take advantage of the full power of these editors for displaying button feedback.

5.2 The Poppy language

Each document element that is to have button behavior is associated with a text string called its *button attribute* that describes its behavior. Users can apply this attribute using a dialog box or they can click on a *buttonizer* button. We provide a document containing buttonizer buttons that create a variety of common types of buttons. Button attributes are written in a language called Poppy that was inspired by CUE Forms [Kaczmarek 1984]. Users can modify button behavior by textually editing the button attribute. Here is the button attribute for a button in a Tioga document:

```
Class: PopUpButton
MessageHandler: Colorizer
Menu: (
  ((SetColor Red) "Red" "Makes selected objects red")
  ((SetColor Blue) "Blue" "Makes selected objects blue"))
Feedback: (
  Enter: <SetCursor bullseye>
  Down: (SelectButton Bold ApplyLook RestoreSelection)
  EndActivity: (SelectButton Bold RemoveLook RestoreSelection))
```

This pop-up button sends commands to an application called the Colorizer. The message it sends is either (SetColor Red) or (SetColor Blue) depending on which menu option the user selects. Its menu entries, labeled Red and Blue, display the documentation string shown when the cursor enters them. The cursor changes to a bull's-eye pattern when the cursor enters it. This button makes its text bold when clicked and restores the plain font face when its activity is finished by sending Tioga a string in Tioga's input language: (SelectButton ... RestoreSelection).

Multi-state buttons and radio buttons have two additional fields, Name and Variables, expressed in Poppy as, for example:

```
Name: Fruit
Variables: (Value: {orange, apple, banana} = orange).
```

Here, Value may take on the values orange, apple, or banana. Its current value is orange. Applications refer to this value, to read or write it, using the button's name, Fruit.

If several buttons have the same name, the value of this name could become ambiguous. We currently force all buttons with the same name to have the same value; changing the value of one causes all of the others to change. However, we also foresee the utility of looking up the value of a given name in a particular subpart of a hierarchically structured document. For instance, if a button, A, refers to a value named N, the system could look for N first in buttons near to A

in the document tree. This would allow multiple copies of a paragraph containing interrelated buttons to be used in the same document without requiring renaming.

5.3 The EmbeddedButtons kernel

When a participating editor receives an input action from the mouse, it must look to see if this action occurs near a document element that has an associated button attribute. If so, and if the user has activated button activity for the current document, then the editor does not process the input action itself, but passes the event to the EmbeddedButtons kernel.

Figure 7 shows the communication paths between EmbeddedButtons, the editors, and the applications during the handling of a button event. The editor passes EmbeddedButtons the event and the button attribute associated with the button that was pressed. The kernel parses the attribute to determine what action to take. If this event requires that the button change its appearance, the kernel sends an edit string to the editor. Next, EmbeddedButtons determines which application should be notified of this button click and sends a command string to that application, by calling a procedure that the application registered with EmbeddedButtons when the application was loaded. When the command has completed, EmbeddedButtons may send a final edit message to the document editor to provide feedback that the command is finished.

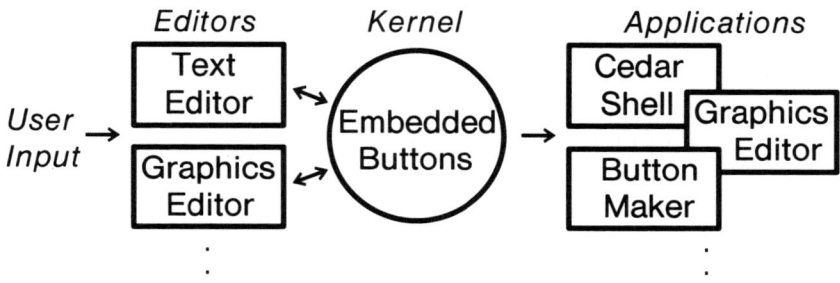

Figure 7. EmbeddedButtons communication paths.

6 Early experiences with EmbeddedButtons

EmbeddedButtons became available for use in September of 1989. Early applications have included online documentation and programming tools. For instance, buttons in a document are used, like buttons in hypertext, to create windows that display related documents and to start application programs that are described in that document. One online help document created by an administrative assistant includes buttons that open forms and graphics templates, start up document editing tools, perform text editing macros, and congratulate the reader on completing the task.

Buttons that encapsulate a particular text search-and-replace operation have been used for programming tasks such as updating a set of program files to use a new name for a procedure or variable.

Our experiences have also shown us that we must sometimes override the usual properties of electronic documents to employ them as user interfaces. For instance, the Tioga text editor warns the user when he or she attempts to delete a text window that has been edited but not saved. When a document is used as a control panel, EmbeddedButtons "edits" the document to provide feedback when buttons are pressed. However, the user is unlikely to be interested in saving these edits. The warning can be avoided either by telling the editor to ignore certain edits or by suppressing the warning for user interface documents.

7 Conclusions and future work

The capabilities of electronic documents are constantly being extended to include better layout algorithms, better navigational aids, a broader range of media, and tighter integration with workstation applications. By embedding active elements in our documents, we can take advantage of these new capabilities to use and build user interfaces.

The EmbeddedButtons architecture described here makes it possible for text, graphics and other elements of persistent multimedia documents to act as buttons. Buttons are a simple type of active element that serves as a foundation for a large class of active document applications. Buttons can be added to documents to lay out control panels, build collections of macros, or customize document editors. Online documents such as reference manuals, program code, telephone directories, and electronic mail can be augmented with buttons to facilitate the use of their contents. Because buttons are normal document objects, they can be copied, moved, found by search operations, created by search-and-replace, recolored, and reformatted. They can also be highlighted using any document operation, including color, font, and shape changes.

The electronic documents community can facilitate the use of documents as user interfaces. Flexible document architectures are needed so that properties like the button attribute can be added to document data structures and external document formats. Interactive document editors should be constructed to receive editing commands from both programs and users and to control applications exterior to themselves. Finally, as we broaden the range of media used in documents, we must ensure that active elements can be embedded in the new media, so that each new medium can be used actively rather than simply viewed (or heard, etc.) passively.

As this project matures, we plan to replace many of the control panels of existing Cedar applications with active documents and to revise existing text-based programs to produce active documents as output. In the long term we plan to recast our window system as a document editor; this will allow any window-based application to be included in a document.

Acknowledgments

We thank Doug Wyatt for modifications to the Tioga text editor, Ken Pier for modifications to the Gargoyle illustrator and detailed comments on the paper and Polle Zellweger for helpful comments on numerous drafts that improved the structure, readability and content of the paper. We thank our reviewers for helpful comments. Finally, we thank all of the members of the Interactive Documents Project for encouragement and for discussions that led to a better understanding of active documents.

References

[Avrahami89] Gideon Avrahami, Kenneth P. Brooks, and Marc H. Brown, "A Two-View Approach to Constructing User Interfaces," *Computer Graphics*, vol. 23, no. 3, July 1989, pp. 137-146.

[Beach85] Richard J. Beach, *Setting Tables and Illustrations with Style*, Ph. D. thesis, U. of Waterloo, Canada. Also available as Xerox PARC Technical Report CSL-85-3.

[Bier86] Eric A. Bier and Maureen Stone, "Snap-Dragging," *Computer Graphics*, vol. 20, no. 4, August 1986, pp. 233-240.

[Cardelli88] Luca Cardelli, "Building User Interfaces by Direct Manipulation," in Proceedings of the ACM SIGGRAPH Symposium on User Interface Software, October 1988, pp. 152-166.

[Furnas86] George W. Furnas, "Generalized Fisheye Views," in *Human Factors in Computer Systems,* proceedings of CHI'86, April 1986, pp. 16-23.

[Furuta88] Richard Furuta, Vincent Quint, and Jacques André, "Interactively Editing Structured Documents," *Electronic Publishing*, vol. 1, no. 1, April 1988, pp. 19-44.

[Goodman87] Danny Goodman, *The Complete HyperCard Handbook*, Bantam Books, 1987.

[Johnson89] Jeff Johnson, Teresa L. Roberts, William Verplank, David C. Smith, Charles H. Irby, Marian Beard, and Kevin Mackey, "The Xerox Star: A Retrospective," *Computer*, vol. 22, no. 9, September 1989, pp. 11-29.

[Kaczmarek84] Thomas S. Kaczmarek, "CUE Forms Description," an internal technical report of the University of Southern California Information Sciences Institute (USC/ISI), July 25, 1984.

[Kurlander88] David Kurlander and Eric A. Bier, "Graphical Search and Replace," *Computer Graphics*, vol. 22, no. 4, August 1988, pp. 113-120.

[MacLean90] Allan MacLean, Kathleen Carter, Lennart Lövstrand and Thomas Moran, "User-Tailorable Systems: Pressing the Issues with Buttons," *Human Factors in Computing Systems*, proceedings of CHI '90, April 1990, pp. 175-182.

[Morris86] James H. Morris, Mahadev Satyanarayanan, Michael H. Conner, John H. Howard, David S. H. Rosenthal, and F. Donelson Smith, "Andrew: A Distributed Personal Computing Environment," *Communications of the ACM*, vol. 29, no. 3, March 1986, pp. 184-201.

[Pier88] Ken Pier, Eric Bier, and Maureen Stone, "An Introduction to Gargoyle: An Interactive Illustration Tool," *Document Manipulation and Typography*, proceedings of EP'88, Cambridge University Press, 1988, pp. 223-238. Also available in Xerox PARC Technical Report EDL-89-1.

[Swinehart86] Daniel C. Swinehart, Polle T. Zellweger, Richard J. Beach, Robert B. Hagmann, "A Structural View of the Cedar Programming Environment," *ACM Transactions on Programming Languages and Systems*, vol. 8, no. 4, 1986, pp. 419-490. Also available as Xerox PARC Technical Report CSL-86-1.

[McKay89] Scott McKay, William York, and Michael McMahon, "A Presentation Manager Based on Application Semantics," in *Proceedings of the ACM SIGGRAPH Symposium on User Interface Software and Technology*, ACM Press, November 1989, pp. 141-148.

[Terry90] Douglas B. Terry and Donald G. Baker, "Active Tioga Documents: An Exploration of Two Paradigms," to appear.

[Webster89] Bruce F. Webster, *The NeXT Book*, chapter 7, Addison-Wesley, 1989.

[Xerox79] Xerox Corporation, "Bravo Manual," in *Alto User's Handbook*, Xerox Palo Alto Research Center, 3333 Coyote Hill Rd., Palo Alto, CA 94303, 1979, pp. 31-62.

[Xerox88] Xerox Corporation, *VP CUSP Buttons Reference*, VP Series Reference Library, Version 2.0, Xerox Viewpoint, Xerox Corporation, 1988, Xerox Product Education, 701 South Aviation Boulevard, ESCN-215, El Segundo, CA 90245.

[Zellweger89] Polle T. Zellweger, "Scripted Documents: A Hypermedia Path Mechanism," in *Hypertext '89 Proceedings*, ACM Press, November 1989, pp. 1-14.

An Extensible, Object-Oriented System for Active Documents

Paul M. English, Ethan S. Jacobson, Robert A. Morris[*], Kimbo B. Mundy, Stephen D. Pelletier, Thomas A. Polucci, and H. David Scarbro

Interleaf, Inc.
Ten Canal Park
Cambridge, MA 02141
[*]*University of Massachusetts at Boston*
Harbor Campus
Boston, MA 02125

ABSTRACT: An extensible, object-oriented system for describing and executing active documents is discussed. An existing commercial, structured document processing system was extended with a run-time bindable object system and Lisp interpreter.

1 Introduction

Object-oriented programming paradigms are now well understood to be highly productive and to contribute to re-usable code. Extensible document processing systems, even as "simple" as Emacs (Sta81), the original and one of the most widely-used extensible editors, are known to be especially powerful. This is because they permit the entire community of users to mold the underlying editor for tasks sometimes not imagined by the software architects.

The earliest computerized document processing systems reflect an understanding that portions of documents interact with each other and with outside data, events, and programs. Even such primitive internal relations as automatic number streams, cross references, tables of contents, and indices represent document objects that must be computed by the processing system based on more or less complex relations within parts of the document.

Walker (Wal81) describes mechanisms for using Emacs as both the editor and invoker for documents formatted by Scribe, as well as the invoker of related documentation tools. Recently, explorations of complex document interactions have appeared from many directions. Towner (Tow88) describes documents with sufficient indirection that they support auto-updating from an external database whose form is known in advance to the software. Chamberlin, et al. (Cha88) describe a mechanism for providing external formatting modules based on properties of the document object being formatted. Arnon, et al.(Arn88) report about a system that can send a mathematical object from a document to a symbol manipulation system and reformat the returned object, so that editing a mathematical object can cause related objects to have their content changed before reformatting. Zellweger (Zel88) has built a mechanism for documents that invokes external scripts supporting such things as voice annotation.

A theme has emerged that the document pieces might be described not by what they *are*, but rather by what they *do*. That notion may best be captured by the name "active documents," a term that seems to have originated with Brian Reid during the EP-88 conference. We are unaware of any precise definition of active documents, but we take it to mean structured documents and their processors in which the objects in the documents can be acted upon by, and can themselves act upon, other objects in the document or the outside world.

This paper describes work at Interleaf, Inc. to produce an extensible, object-oriented active document processing system. In its most static state, this system corresponds to the standard commercial software. In its most dynamic state, the software provides facilities whereby third parties, including end users, can radically change the manner in which document objects behave, as well as change the user interface, the methods by which objects are treated (e.g., the pagination and composition methods), and even what kinds of objects can be regarded as part of a document. Unlike the approaches mentioned above, what we describe requires no special advance cooperation between the system architects and the document architects. Each document object can carry its own method for interacting with its environment or for computing its content or that of other document objects.

2 Objects and Methods

The Interleaf object software is a message-passing, object-oriented system built on a Lisp interpreter embedded in the distributed software. Standard class creation and inheritance mechanisms are provided (Mey88).

Lisp programs can have access to all objects in documents, ranging from characters and graphics to the higher-level objects that give them structure, such as document *components* and other document hierarchy elements. At a minimum, each such object responds to messages that request the object to set or report its properties. Classes can be requested to create new instances and these instances can be given properties, be linked into documents, or even have their methods changed. For example, although equation objects are externally modeled on *eqn*, it is possible to introduce a new class called doc-tex-equation-class whose composition methods cause an invocation not of Interleaf composition modules, but of an external TeX engine. Sub-classes that inherit the methods of the parent class can be created and can have their methods rebound or have new methods added.

What are sometimes called "live" or "hot" links in personal computing environments are a simple kind of active document object that is easy to implement with the system described here. Two instances that have been demonstrated involve binding the edit method for particular kinds of graphics elements to an invocation of external software. In one case, selecting a CAD-CAM picture produced by AutoCad™ software causes AutoCad to begin running, permitting the recomputation of the graphics object. That object is then automatically updated by receiving messages to set its properties based on the AutoCad computation (e.g., as recorded on the file system or sent via interprocess communication mechanisms) and a message to redraw itself. In a similar application, selecting a table or data-driven chart object can cause the invocation of Lotus 1-2-3™. The resulting manipulations are reflected—without further user intervention—in the document object. The actors (AutoCad or 1-2-3 in these examples) do not need to run on the same host as the document processor, as long as they can communicate with the host either through the network file system or via various supported interprocess communication facilities that can be used by the Lisp programs. Such a capability is similar to that of CaminoReal (Arn88), but the dynamic bindings of Lisp make it possible to implement such capabilities without any special advance compiled-in arrangements in the document processor. The particular choice of AutoCad and Lotus is incidental. Any network-accessible programs that support compatible data interchange could be used just as easily; indeed, such choices could be made at run-time.

Another simple application supports document objects by indirection. At various events, such as opening, printing, or display, objects can be sent messages causing them to query external data or processes to get the current state of the data from which they are produced. Several mechanisms are in place to facilitate this. In the most straightforward, the open method for a document can examine a list of document objects that require messages to be sent to them. These objects can be located by document navigation facilities described below.

We note that the above constructions are simple but powerful instances in which the object content is computed much as, say, cross references might be in traditional systems. The lack of distinction between program and data in Lisp provides the ability to have content be the result of procedure, not data. In addition, the run-time binding of Lisp eliminates the requirement that the object architecture be determined at compile-time, as is the case for other object-oriented languages such as C++.

3 Document Objects

From its initial release, Interleaf publishing software has been object-oriented from the user's point of view. However, its objects had a fixed collection of properties chosen by the system architects. For example, components have margins, default font, leading, and similar properties; graphics objects have size and color properties, etc. Initially, this object orientation was reflected more in the user interface than in document structure.

Recently there has been further evolution of structural object orientation. By release 4.0, the current commercial release, a style sheet mechanism built on the document substrate was in place. In these style sheets, called "catalogs," master templates for components and graphics objects can contain shared content as well as form. Catalogs do not appear to be different from any other kind of document, but editing them causes corresponding changes to all associated objects in all associated documents. These associations were not programmatic but rather were based on the name space to determine object affiliation. All objects of the same name as the master object were changed when the master was changed. Geometric relationships on the desktop further restricted the scope of conflicting names in multiple masters. (An object is an instance of a master only if the corresponding catalog is in the same instance of a special container, called a "book," and if the catalog is the nearest one with that master in the geometric ordering of the documents in the book.)

There was no other class mechanism than that described above, but a mechanism was added that provided a limited way to add properties. This was called "effectivity control" (Ils88) and permitted components to be marked with numerical or textual attributes, on whose values certain actions could be modified. For example, in an aircraft maintenance manual, a particular component could be tagged with an attribute specifying the customer for the aircraft, and a specialized document printed that contained all the common maintenance documentation plus that which applied only to the planes of that customer. This kind of structure tagging mechanism was powerful enough to support an SGML-based system compliant with the CALS requirements (Cal88).

The new document object ("doc-obj") system is built on top of a Lisp-based general object system. All the "traditional" Interleaf objects (both in the document and in the user interface) are available in this system, and new ones are easily added. The pre-existing doc-objs have a hierarchy that encompasses objects as large as a directory full of documents and as small as a marker between any two characters in a document. Individuals characters may be addressed via markers, but the characters are not full-fledged objects. However, strings may be wrapped in "inline component" objects, which can be recursively nested to provide objects with which to manipulate text, much as we provide a "group" to manipulate graphics.

Doc-objs come equipped with default methods that, in some cases, are simply Lisp invocations of the underlying C code that supported them in previous versions of the system. The inheritance mechanism permits an application to add the specific intelligence it needs. Sub-classing document objects leverages on the fact that documents are a very general paradigm of communication.

A document is a heterogeneous collection of doc-objs. Due to the logical complexity needed to support a structured, revisable, WYSIWYG, formatted collection of objects, the traversal between doc-objs differs depending on the perspective of interest to the programmer. These perspectives are referred to by optional keywords in the navigation methods. Two important perspectives include *structure* and *layout*.

In the structure perspective, objects are related according to their logical dependencies: headings precede paragraphs, graphics are contained within the token that anchor them in the text flow. This is similar to how these kinds of structures are described in declarative markup languages like Scribe or LaTeX.

In the layout perspective, the relationships reflect the appearance of the printed page: pages contain columns, and columns contain lines of text or floating graphics. Normally, these objects are created and linked automatically by the composition rules built into the software. However, by giving programmers access to this information, it is possible to add composition-sensitive extensions to the editor or to the layout itself.

More than one perspective is needed because some doc-objs have meaning in multiple perspectives. For example, markers can be viewed either as being contained within a paragraph or within a line on the page; floating graphics are treated both as containers for graphics and as layout elements on a page. Thus, it is possible for Lisp programs to concern themselves as little or as much as needed with the structure or the layout, separately or in concert.

4 User Interface Configurability

Interleaf software usually provides a uniform user interface (UI) across multiple platforms, but this interface is not suitable for all users (for example, occasional MacIntosh users might prefer a more familiar "Mac-like" UI). Further, since the document processing system itself is extensible, we need to allow the UI to extend to new objects. Finally, where we seek to improve the standard user interface, we need to provide experienced users with the ability to retain a familiar interface if they wish, or to otherwise tailor it to their own needs.

These requirements are met by exposing the user interface to Lisp programs in much the same way as are document objects. In fact, document objects can *become* part of the user interface. This permits the full power of the graphics and text editing facility already in the software to be invoked to do the graphics and text parts of the interface. Lisp permits the run-time reconfiguration of the user interface, from its "look" (the graphical representation of its paradigms) to its "feel" (the actions it supports) to the text of its messages.

More than any other extension features described in this paper, Interleaf UI extensibility may be seen as evolutionary from earlier versions of the system. Release 3.0 provided a desktop "Create" popup menu. Adding files to the desktop Create cabinet caused these file names to be added to the menu. Selecting one of these names caused the file to be copied to form a new instantiation. Release 4.0 added a similar desktop-based extensible "Custom" menu. But files in the Custom cabinet contained Lisp programs to be executed upon selection. These programs had access to some internal state, but no access to objects within a document. Their effect was limited to interaction with the desktop and the underlying operating system, and to choosing from among fixed UI alternatives.

We next describe how Lisp programs access the user interface. The UI of any contemporary interactive document processing system may be said to have several components: the input event handlers, window managers, and display managers. At the lowest level, these are often handled by general software that is not of concern to us here. At the next level of abstraction, the user interface comprises things such as keyboard mapping and the menu system. It is these that we have opened to Lisp.

Keystrokes are mapped to Lisp actions, thus supporting an arbitrary collection of "keyboard macros" much as Emacs or many PC software products do. As with Emacs, these actions can be arbitrary procedures and potentially have access to entire documents and more.

For example, Figure 1 contains a key binding, the invocation of which "tells" the current insertion point to insert the text output of a date routine:

```
(kbd–define–key doc–kbd–map (fcn–key "F1")
  '(tell (doc–point–marker) mid:insert (get–date :usa–format)) )
```

Figure 1: Defining a key to insert the current date

The extensibility of the menu system provides more novel possibilities. For example, property sheets can be implemented as a special case of active documents. An ordinary document with graphics looking like "buttons," "sliders" or other "widgets" can have Lisp procedures tied to the graphics objects. Selecting these objects invokes the procedure and the desired action takes place. Even dialog in such sheets can be parsed by the Lisp program.

Interrupt messages, which post a dialog box with which the user must deal before continuing, have simple access from Lisp. The corresponding objects have text properties (the message text) and a list of buttons. When a button is selected, the button object is returned to the Lisp caller, which then executes the procedure that is mapped to that button. This procedure need not be specified at compile time, although for pre-existing dialogs the default binding is simply the C code that previously was called when the process was controlled in C (we say more about our C to Lisp interface below).

We plan ultimately to recode the entire UI using doc-objects, including graphics objects. Some of this has already been done. In release 5.0, the entire UI will be exposed to Lisp to facilitate our, or third-party, replacement of the UI with doc-obj based interfaces. This could be used to change the UI to one that behaves and looks like any of a number of popular user interface paradigms.

5 Lisp Environment

With one exception, the Lisp interpreter we implemented has no features unique to document processing environments. The exception arises from the requirement to deal with the 16-bit characters required in Interleaf documents to support large multi-language character sets. These characters are externally represented with 8-bit character sequences, but within Lisp strings they are not treated differently from 8-bit characters. Lisp symbols are restricted to 8 bits to promote portability of the interpreter (the software runs on a wide variety of platforms and operating systems, including several variants of Unix, DOS, VAX VMS, and IBM mainframe operating systems).

To assist migration from C to Lisp implementations, the Lisp system provides in-house programmers with the ability to call C from Lisp and Lisp from C. The principal goal of this arrangement is to facilitate an object-oriented interface to existing C code and data structures. Lisp programs need not distinguish between data and procedures defined in the underlying C code and those defined purely in Lisp, and thus they may be freely mixed. We do not provide arrangements whereby Lisp programs can call C code not defined at compile time because not all platforms support the required dynamic linking of the resulting executable code. However, below we describe supported interprocess communication methods that permit our system to become part of composite environments with no advance arrangements required between Interleaf and the authors of the other pieces of the environment. In such environments, Lisp code can be used to encapsulate IPC calls to external code written in any language environment.

As with many other Lisp systems, our Lisp objects have documentation strings among their properties, intended as on-line documentation for Lisp programmers. These strings form the data for an interactive inquiry system about the definitions and values of Lisp objects, classes, methods, functions, and symbols. Thus, arbitrary Lisp programs can be self-documenting.

6 Active Documents as Generalizations

Carrying methods with the document is very powerful. Permitting these methods to be *defined* at document execution time potentially decouples the constraints on the document architecture from those decreed by the system architects, or even by the original document architect.

Hypertext is easily implemented on such a substrate. Links are simply the execution of programs based on events, such as selection, that cause the editor to move to other objects. Since Lisp programs are data, it is straightforward to make a link editing mechanism that has the effect of generating (invisibly to the user) those links. Indeed, *hypermedia*, not merely hypertext, can be supported with no further requirements. For example, if the underlying environment supports voice I/O, objects in a suitably designed document can invoke this mechanism as desired (see "Interprocess Communication" below).

The notion of an independent filter or other document conversion program is not inherently necessary. An active document that contains a reference to a document in an alien format can carry with it as much or as little as needed of the method for interpreting that format. The user of such a document need have no concern for the existence of conversion software, nor, if the document design itself is adequate, even be aware that the object *is* in an alien format. Further, as we describe below, the document objects need not carry the actual interpretation software. Instead, they can carry a method for *accepting* or *requesting* the interpretation procedures when they are needed. Or document objects can identify themselves as a certain class of object for which methods are already known.

An object-oriented system with procedures as data and with run-time binding makes it feasible to use a document processing substrate to solve problems for which advance knowledge is unnecessary on the part of the system designers. Indeed, *document* architects can even free themselves of some of these details by making arrangements to receive them at execution time.

7 Interprocess Communication

Some applications require a document to communicate with external processes. We have provided three methods for this. The simplest of these—file system event handling—is generally useful on all supported platforms.

The Lisp *load* primitive permits an arbitrary ASCII file containing Lisp to be read and interpreted. *read* and *write* primitives permit uninterpreted stream I/O. These might be done on events such as opening or printing the document, selecting an object, or anything else that causes a Lisp procedure to execute. The modification time of a file (as well as all other file primitives useful in a programming environment) is available, so a procedure that wished to implement an invisible update or change could do so.

When the system runs interactively, the outermost event control mechanisms examine timer objects, which can be created by a Lisp procedure with arguments detailing a timeout period, and a Lisp expression to be evaluated at the timeout. Using this mechanism, document objects can schedule their own responses to external events by creating such timers.

On platforms that support it, we have also demonstrated communication with sub-processes through their own return mechanisms and communications elsewhere on the network with TCP/IP sockets. Lisp code can use IPC to communicate with a remote process, thereby adding its intelligence to the document. In the opposite direction, a Lisp *read-eval-print* loop is offered as the top-level IPC protocol, allowing the active document system to be programmatically directed from the outside. A particularly simple, but quite useful application of this mechanism is to induce the remote process to produce Encapsulated PostScript, which our underlying software knows how to display.

8 Applications

A number of interesting and important applications have been developed both in-house and externally, and we describe some of them now. Two things are especially noteworthy. First, the architecture described here supports a very broad notion of documents and even permits use of the software as *both* a back end (i.e., as a report generator) and a front end (i.e., as the user interface) to virtually any kind of software, such as data base, spreadsheet, CAD-CAM systems, or even on-line help for the system itself. We describe below a very powerful production quality, forms-management system written by the Amoco Corporation with Interleaf's assistance. Second, Lisp turns out to be a language that is easily learned by non-programmers. We describe a document-based UI editor written in Lisp by a user with minimal previous programming experience, and also some smaller but interesting applications written in-house. Finally, we sketch a document-based online help system for the end user.

Forms management. The Amoco application is a combined inventory, ordering, and documentation system for handling oil exploration equipment. It is time and cost critical that these complex equipment orders are correct for a given project. Amoco could find excellent forms-generation software to support their input design, database software to verify their constraints, and publishing software to publish purchase orders and reports. But there was no way to make these pieces cooperate invisibly to the user. Since the constraints could be programmatically specified, the solution possible with active documents is to make the form itself do the constraint computation and generate the report. This system was prototyped in three weeks and is now in production use. Because much oil exploration is cooperative, Amoco is now seeking to make the system an industry-wide solution.

User Interfaces. The popup menu system is a hierarchical collection of context-dependent menus that appear in response to particular mouse or key events. Access to this by Lisp programs permits each node in the tree to be represented by a Lisp object which, as always, can be either procedure or data—there being no essential difference in Lisp. It is possible, however, to know whether the Lisp object represents a method or a doc-obj, and when the selection is made (typically by releasing the mouse button), the popup system traverses the selection path back up the hierarchy until it encounters a method. That method is then applied with the selected child list as argument. For example, suppose the selection yielded the list "Create→Character→Math→∫." In this case, the calling Lisp program would find a method only when it reached the "Create" Lisp object, and would invoke that method on a list containing "Character," "Math," and "∫," resulting in the insertion of the integral sign at the current point.

It is incidental that the application of the create method is induced by a popup event. If it is also desired to have a keyboard event insert an integral sign, no different program is required, only a different invocation event. More importantly, in an active document such programs can be stored *with the document objects*, and these programs can be altered at run-time. Imagine this kind of program attached to a document object only a little more complex, say an entire integral expression. That program could be replaced *at run time* with, for example, a program that sends the expression to a symbolic mathematics processor for symbolic integration in much the same way that the CaminoReal software might (Arn88).

An example of the utility of traditional documents as a front end can be mentioned here. Using the popup interface described above, an Interleaf quality assurance engineer constructed a simple but useful popup editor that is manipulated as an ordinary document. The user specifies a portion of the popup tree for editing simply by inducing but not invoking it (in this case, pressing a mouse button and making appropriate mouse motion, but not releasing the button). Then, the user presses a keyboard function key, temporarily bound to "record-the-popup-tree." This causes the program to construct a text representation of the current popup tree in an ordinary document. Then a special subset of editing capabilities can be used to manipulate that tree graphically to add, delete, or rearrange nodes. Finally, the Lisp program interprets the new text tree as a popup tree and re-inserts it into *the running user interface*. In this case, the text tree document is the active document. Its content is far less important than its interpretation as a representation of a user interface component. While this scheme is roughly limited to rearrangement of existing UI pieces, such rearrangement is a task one might want to provide to users who want some UI control but do not want to learn to program to make new paradigms. Moreover, implementing this editor in Lisp took the non-programmer about a week. (We estimate that experienced Lisp programmers could accomplish it in a few hours.) This level of productivity was possible because the editing substrate was already in place and all that was necessary was to interpret a document as a UI specification in ways that *produced* the UI. Finally, this example also shows the commonality between menu arrangements and keyboard arrangements. Rearranging the popup tree is not essentially different from re-mapping keyboards.

Miscellaneous applications. Another inexperienced in-house user—a marketing writer—wrote several simple but useful programs for demonstration and personal use. One of these permits the filling in of expense forms, with appropriate minor arithmetic done by the form. In addition, filling in such a form has the side effect of updating *another* document that keeps running expenses and can generate an explanatory memo if the expenses go over budget.

A more utilitarian application is a primitive outline processor that rebinds the key normally bound to "create component of the same type." If the current component is given a particular attribute, this binding instead creates an arbitrary sequence of components of types specified by its argument list. This twenty-line program was written in about fifteen minutes, using a small library of general string manipulation procedures the user had already written to deal with attribute values (see above discussion of effectivity control).

Using the same string handling facility, the user has demonstrated documents that examine the environment for the name of the user attempting to open them, then compare that name to a "security list" in another document. Depending on the data found in the security list, the document hides some or perhaps all of its sub-objects by comparing attributes in the document to security clearances the user has in the security list.

Complex content from external objects. Using a Lisp program that interprets Lotus 1-2-3 spreadsheet files and returns lists of cell values, a demonstration program was written that correctly maintains, in a single document, three different views of the data. The demonstration displays the manufacturing costs of a bicycle. In one view, the data are presented in a table, in another in a pie chart, and in a third as line drawings of the bicycle parts, with their sizes proportional to their costs. The objects can be told to update themselves at document open time, on a menu event, or when the spreadsheet changes. Simplified key fragments of this program are shown below, in Figure 2.

```
(defun import–contents–of–diagram (diagram)
   (let (  (data–editor (doc–get–attr–value diagram "data–editor"))
           (data–file (doc–get–attr–value diagram "data–file"))
           (data–filter (doc–get–attr–value diagram "data–filter"))
           cell–list cost–list )

      ;; The data editor, file name and filter name have been
      ;;   read from the object. Now run the program
      ;;   named by data–editor on the file named by data–file...
      (proc–wait (proc–create data–editor data–file))

      ;; External edit completed and data–file rewritten,
      ;; so parse it with function named by data–filter...
      (setq cell–list (funcall (find–symbol data–filter) data–file))

      ;; Now cell–list reflects the spreadsheet.
      ;; Get the data from the row "TOTAL:"...
      (setq cost–list (make–cost–list cell–list "TOTAL:"))

      ;; Update the various doc–obj representations of data–file...
      (rebuild–chart (get–first–chart diagram) cost–list)
      (rebuild–table (get–first–table diagram) cost–list)
      (rebuild–graphic (get–first–graphic diagram) cost–list)
      (tell diagram mid:draw)))   ;Redisplay revised diagram

(defun get–first–chart (diagram)
   (let ((chart (tell diagram mid:get–child :along :structure)))
      (while (and chart (not (typep chart 'dg–chart)))
         (setq chart (tell chart mid:get–next :along :structure)))
      chart))

(defun rebuild–chart (chart cost–list)
   (let ((row 0) value)
      (while cost–list
         (setq value (cost–of–row (pop cost–list)))
         (tell chart mid:set–prop :data (list (list row 0 value )))
         (setq row (1+ row)))))
```

Figure 2: Lisp document object program to import a diagram

In this example, *data–editor* was the program name "123," *data–file* was "bicycle.wk3," the name of the spreadsheet file to be associated with this diagram, and *data–filter* was "wk3–to–list," the name of a Lisp function used to parse a Lotus wk3 file into a Lisp list. All are stored in the document as the values of the corresponding user-defined attributes of the diagram. The edit method for the diagram is bound to this procedure, so that the normal process of selecting and editing it actually results in the external software being invoked, followed by an interpretation in the document of the result. In the navigation procedure *get–first–chart*, the keywords *:along :structure* in fact denote the default perspective for diagram objects and could be omitted.

9 Implementation Experiences

We feel that most of the engineering challenges we encountered were not specific to document processing systems. They included extending the definition of important C data structures such that they can be manipulated by Lisp, and making the object system work with C, with Lisp, and with combinations of C and Lisp.

Enabling programs to change the behavior of time-critical functionality without incurring interpreter-related performance penalties was an important goal. Decisions about the granularity with which to expose internal methods and objects to Lisp were driven by engineering time constraints and the requirement to maintain current performance levels. We may need to reduce this granularity (giving more detailed access) as users' experiences give us more insight into what their Lisp programs require.

The problem most centrally related to documents is how to store Lisp data in documents that survives editing sessions. Because some of our document objects are ephemeral, only living at document edit time, the associated Lisp cannot be saved, but must be regenerated at load time.

10 Summary

We have implemented a runtime-extensible, object-oriented system for describing and executing active documents. This system sits on a substrate comprising a powerful, high performance, structured document editor and an open object architecture with an application programming interface with sufficient power to permit easy participation in cooperative software environments. The programming interface can be invoked as a side-effect of opening a document or selecting an object or almost any other event. The object-orientation facilitates application programming in which mechanisms are hidden from end users, who need only know what the objects are—the application takes care of what they do. Because document construction, editing, and interpretation are, first of all, symbol manipulation problems, Lisp is an especially suitable language for rapid, powerful implementation of a wide range of facilities.

References

(**Arno88**) Dennis Arnon, Richard Beach, Kevin McIsaac, and Carl Waldspurger, "Camino-Real: An Interactive Mathematical Notebook," *Document Manipulation and Typography,* Proceedings of the International Conference on Electronic Publishing, Document Manipulation and Typography, Nice (France) April 20-22, 1988, Cambridge University Press, 1988, pp. 1-18.

(**Cal88**) *Markup Requirements and Generic Style Specification for Electronic Printed Output and Exchange of Text,* Military Specification MIL-D-28000, CALS Policy Office, DASD(S) CALS, Pentagon, Room 2B322, Washington, D.C., 1988.

(**Cha88**) Donald D. Chamberlin, Helmut F. Hasselmeier, and Dieter P. Paris, "Defining Document Styles For WYSIWYG Processing," *Document Manipulation and Typography,* Proceedings of the International Conference on Electronic Publishing, Document Manipulation and Typography, Nice (France) April 20-22, 1988, Cambridge University Press, 1988, pp. 121-138.

(**Ils88**) Richard Ilson, "Interactive Effectivity Control: Design and Applications,"*Proceedings of the ACM Conference on Document Processing Systems, December 5-9, 1988 Santa Fe, New Mexico,* ACM Press, 1988, pp. 85-92.

(**Mey88**) Betrand Meyer, *Object-oriented Software Construction,* Hemel Hempstead, Herts., England, and Englewood Cliffs, N.J, U.S.A., 1988.

(**Sta81**) Richard M. Stallman, "Emacs, The Extensible, Customizable Self-Documenting Display Editor," *Proceedings of the ACM SIGPLAN SIGOA Symposium on Text Manipulation, Portland Oregon, June 8-10, 1981*, SIGPLAN Notices v. 16, no. 6, June, 1981, pp. 147-56.

(**Tow88**) George Towner, "Auto-Updating as a Technical Documentation Tool," *Proceedings of the ACM Conference on Document Processing Systems, December 5-9, 1988 Santa Fe, New Mexico,* ACM Press, 1988, pp. 31-36.

(**Wal81**) Janet H. Walker, "The Document Editor: A Support Environment for Preparing Technical Documents," *Proceedings of the ACM SIGPLAN SIGOA Symposium on Text Manipulation, Portland Oregon, June 8-10, 1981*, SIGPLAN Notices v. 16, no. 6, June, 1981, pp. 44-50.

(**Zel88**) Polle T. Zellweger, "Active Paths Through Multimedia Documents," *Document Manipulation and Typography,* Proceedings of the International Conference on Electronic Publishing, Document Manipulation and Typography, Nice (France) April 20-22, 1988, Cambridge University Press, 1988, pp.19-34.

The Role of a Descriptive Markup Language in the Creation of Interactive Multimedia Documents for Customized Electronic Delivery

Gil C. Cruz and Thomas H. Judd

Multimedia Communications Research Division
Bellcore
Morristown, N.J., USA 07960-1910

ABSTRACT: The emerging broadband telecommunications network promises to support a myriad of new mass-market information services that may in turn create a tremendous demand for new source material capable of exploiting the multimedia transport capability of the network. Authoring such material is presently a complex and time consuming process requiring specialized tools. We propose that a descriptive markup language, based on SGML and enhanced for interactive multimedia applications, can form the basis for a new set of authoring tools that will let experienced text authors transfer their skills to multimedia documents. Experience with a prototype version of such a language in the production of an experimental electronic magazine indicates that the approach is valid and useful. Future work includes defining text-like structure in temporal media and creating a unified set of editing and previewing tools.

KEYWORDS: authoring, hypermedia, interactive, markup, SGML

1 Introduction

The emerging digital telecommunications network will provide both increased bandwidth and enhanced flexibility, simultaneously transporting information streams in multiple formats. While such a network promises to support innovative new multimedia services, vendors of these services may be hard pressed to meet the resulting demands for new material. On the other hand, the sheer volume of information that may be created in response to these demands could overwhelm potential users unless some means for screening or selective delivery can be provided. As a part of our research aimed at understanding the needs and requirements of such a future network, we have focused on mechanisms for creating information packages we call *multimedia documents* and on the problems encountered while trying to ensure that users get only those documents that they need and want.

The same growing computer power that will control the increasingly intelligent telecommunications network could be used by service vendors to customize information streams, raising the possibility of a new type of service that delivers a customized package of information to each individual subscriber. Information in the form of multimedia documents incorporating text, graphics, audio, and still or moving images could be accessed interactively on an electronic terminal such as a high-definition television (HDTV) set enhanced with an electronic pointing device. The future network could route these documents through *customizing agents* that provide information filters, distributing particular documents only to users who want and need them.

Much R&D in networking, information filtering, and display will be needed before such information services will be possible. Even if the delivery problems are solved, however, the problem of creating appropriate multimedia documents will remain. Historically, interactive multimedia presentations have required a complex and time consuming authoring process involving a team of specialists using media-specific tools, scripts, storyboards, and computer programming languages. While this may be inevitable for complex presentations, it places too many demands on the authors who will labor to meet the demands of mass-market information services.

1.1 Existing Media-Specific Tools

Various sophisticated tools have been constructed to aid the authoring process [Hodges *et al.* 1989; Kajimoto *et al.* 1989; Tabuchi & Muracho 1989; Mackay & Davenport 1989]. While they are a step in the right direction, these tools require authors to deal with specialized hardware and with different editors for different media, and they treat different media at different levels of abstraction. Text, for example, is manipulated by sentences or paragraphs, while video is edited frame-by-frame and audio millisecond-by-millisecond. Some recent video and audio editors deal at a higher level (e.g., the video scene) but all are specialized devices intended for specific purposes.

Specialized authoring systems to handle the task of unifying various media segments for presentation [Frenkel 1989] are typically intended for (and execute only on) a specific hardware configuration. Thus while these authoring systems may help in the production of interactive programs, they contribute to the proliferation of proprietary delivery systems. The resulting lack of standardization has hindered the development of interactive systems and has made it difficult to reuse material among applications. Some system vendors have attempted to develop software that permits a degree of hardware independence among authoring systems or emulates the operation of one system while running on another platform [Magel 1989]. Such software may strengthen the position of de facto hardware standards, but it begs the question of true hardware and software independence.

1.2 The Goal of Unified Systems

One goal of our research has been to find better ways to create interactive multimedia documents, particularly ways that are independent of the characteristics of specific display devices or delivery systems. We want authors to work at a comfortable level of abstraction, ideally treating all media at the same level with the same tools. Such unified authoring tools might provide an evolutionary path for authors to transfer their text skills to the creation of interactive multimedia documents.

A key element in the creation of such unified authoring systems is a high-level document markup language that will permit an author to deal with the *structure* of a document independent of its *presentation*. If such a language can handle both the spatial structure of text and the temporal structure of audio/video, then an author could treat all media at the same level of abstraction. If all its elements are described in a complete and unambiguous way, a document can be formatted and presented automatically by computer programs that resolve the details of differing hardware systems.

Our research indicates that such a markup language is both possible and practical. In Section 2 of this paper, we present the concept of markup languages, discuss the Standard Generalized Markup Language (SGML), and present our prototype SGML-based markup language with its extensions for interactive multimedia documents. Section 3 describes an experimental application of our language—the creation of interactive multimedia articles for a prototype electronic magazine. Section 4 discusses related work in this field and outlines some thoughts for future work.

2 Markup Languages

Although the term *markup* originally referred to the process of marking manuscript copy for manual typesetting [Chicago 1982], it now generally refers to instructions included in a document to control machine processing. One comprehensive review [Coombs et al. 1987] identified six types of markup used in preparing text documents. Of the six, only two types are directly applicable to machine processing of text.

Procedural markup consists of commands indicating how text should be formatted by a specific computer program; it must be rewritten when the text is processed by a different formatter. *Descriptive* markup inserts tags to identify the various text elements (e.g., <para> for paragraph). This markup describes what the text elements are, rather than how a particular text formatter should handle them. Formatting is a separate operation, so the structure of a document (defined by tags) can be considered separately from its appearance (defined by formatter rules).

Coombs, *et al.*, concluded that descriptive markup best supports the process of document development and publication, for a number of reasons:

- Authors can focus on content and structure rather than on presentation.

- Composition assistance procedures such as alternative views (display an outline, etc.) or structure-oriented editing (delete a footnote, etc.) can be used.

- Style changes can be made without exposing document contents to corruption.

- Separation of content from presentation encourages standards that support document portability.

The first two points address document creation for mass-market information services. The others are significant for documents delivered to differing terminals on a network where the presentation will be determined by service vendors rather than by authors.

2.1 The Standard Generalized Markup Language

SGML, the *Standard Generalized Markup Language* [ISO 1986], is an international standard meta-language defining the syntax of a descriptive markup language [Barron 1989] that identifies the structural elements of a document with descriptive *tags,* each consisting of a delimited *generic identifier* (GI) with optional attributes. SGML specifies a markup syntax, not a vocabulary of specific GIs for the tags. The vocabulary of GIs and the rules for using them are described in an SGML construct known as a *document type definition* (DTD).

An SGML document is always interpreted according to a DTD that rigorously specifies the structure of the document and the element-tagging syntax. Authors can either create their own DTD or use an existing one such as the Association of American Publishers DTD for articles [AAP 1987]. Our research began with this DTD, then extended it to encompass the interactive multimedia nature of electronic documents.

Once the DTD is defined, an author can create a new document with a word processing system or with SGML-specific authoring software. The document is then processed by an SGML parser that checks for conformance with the DTD, performs tag expansions, and inserts implied tags. The parser creates an SGML-tagged document that is passed to a formatter that maps its elements onto a particular output device [Barron 1989]. The formatter operates according to a style definition that controls the appearance of its output. This definition might be represented in the Document Style Semantics and Specification Language (DSSSL) [ISO 1988] in the form of a set of rules to be adhered to in presenting a document.

There are other descriptive markup languages, each with its cadre of supporters. However, SGML is an international standard with a growing number of users. In 1987 the U.S. Department of Defense promulgated MIL-STD-1840A [White 1989], commonly known as the Computer-aided Acquisition and Logistic Support (CALS) program, requiring all defense contractors to use the military version of SGML (MIL-M-28001) for their documentation. In 1989 Federal Information Processing Standard (FIPS) 152 required that all hardware and software procurements related to text and document processing be capable of handling SGML. As with many government decrees, these may well result in SGML becoming **the** standard for document preparation, regardless of the merits of competing systems.

2.2 Extensions for Interactive Multimedia Documents

We have created a research prototype SGML markup language based on the AAP's DTD for printed articles. We added tags for temporal media elements (audio and video) and a mechanism to link these elements to text, thus providing for control of non-text media on an interactive electronic display terminal.

With our language, text defines the basal structure of an electronic document. Other media are introduced through *sidebars,* a generalized concept for constructs that interrupt the linear presentation of a document. The language provides a mechanism for creating *links* from text elements to sidebar elements defined in a separate section of the document. These links allow for interaction with the document—the "from" element in the text indicates that the link exists, while the "to" element specifies the resulting action if the user chooses to follow that link. An example of a sidebar is a timed sequence of images (with optional caption and audio) called a *slideshow*. It is the "to" element of a link and is activated when a reader triggers the "from" element, a specified text string in the body of the document.

A sidebar is created by referencing it in the body of an article, then defining it in a sidebar definition section. For example, an author might include the following in the body of an article to create a slideshow sidebar that illustrates a point:

```
<body>
   ... to <sidebar_ref [id=startup]> start the machine
         </sidebar_ref> one must first ...
         :
</body>
```

followed by this after the end of the body:

```
<sidebar_def [id=startup]>
<slideshow [type=ramp]>
<caption> Start-Up Sequence </caption>
<audio_ref [id=sound_effect1]>
<slide [id=slide1; duration=4]>
<slide [id=slide2; duration=2]>
<slide [id=slide3; duration=3]>
</slideshow>
</sidebar_def>
```

Depending on the style definition in effect at the time, a formatter might represent the "from" element of the link by highlighting the string "start the machine" in the body of the document. If the user "clicked" this highlighted string, the slideshow would be triggered; a window would pop up, sequentially displaying the images with audio and a caption. In this example, image *slide1* would appear for 4 seconds, followed by *slide2* for 2 seconds and finally *slide3* for 3 seconds. The slideshow was declared to be of type *ramp* so its images would be displayed in a diagonal array. This example shows how an author could create a slideshow by describing its spatial and temporal structure and declaring a sidebar link from within running text. Similar constructs handle audio and video clips.

If documents are to be distributed via customizing agents with information filters, those agents must be able to ascertain their contents. Descriptive markup aids this process by explicitly identifying document elements. It is straightforward, for example, to distinguish a keyword in a title from one in a paragraph, allowing context-dependent keyword matching. However, it is difficult or impossible to surmise an author's intent in matters like the degree of expertise, prerequisite knowledge, or demographics of the intended reader. Thus our prototype markup language allows an author or editor to embed explicit classification information in the source file.

If this paper were to be prepared with the prototype language, it might include *class tags* such as:

```
<class [field=computers]>
<class [area=publishing]>
<class [aspect=interactive]>
<class [aspect=multimedia]>
<class [occupation=professional]>
<class [breadth=2]>
<class [expertise=4]>
<class [prerequisite=4]>
<class [education=4]>
```

The first five tags, for which a glossary of keywords must be provided, indicate that this is a paper on computer-based publishing of interactive multimedia documents and that it was intended for professionals in the field. The other tags, with metric values on a scale of 1 to 5, indicate that the subject matter is fairly narrowly focused and is intended for users with considerable expertise, prerequisite knowledge, and a college education. Information conveyed by the first four tags could be inferred from the text, but that in the last five tags would be difficult if not impossible to extract from the text alone.

3 A Specific Instance: The Electronic Magazine

As an experiment to test our prototype markup language, we have been investigating the concept of an information service that could use the future telecommunications network to distribute information in the format of an electronic magazine containing interactive multimedia documents called articles [Judd & Cruz 1989]. The user controls viewing of these articles; two readers of the same article might access different elements in a different order.

Figure 1 shows a simple flow chart of the creation and delivery of such a magazine. Publishers (teams of authors and human editors) create articles and use the network to deposit them in a source database. A filter program matches characteristics of articles in the database against a profile of an individual user's interests. The filter selects appropriate articles from the database, packages them in a format similar to a printed magazine, creates a summary of the information, and delivers the customized package to the user's terminal.

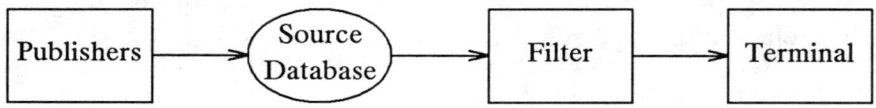

Figure 1: Electronic Magazine Flow Chart

To test the markup language, we created a set of software tools that formats, filters, and displays multimedia articles. Using these tools, we have created more than 90 articles with text, images, slideshows, audio segments, and video clips. Although our present filter has only rudimentary keyword matching capabilities, we have succeeded in automatically generating multimedia magazines for people with different interest profiles. This experience has strengthened our belief that a descriptive markup language can bring significant benefits to the creation and dissemination of multimedia articles. Specific advantages we have found include:

- A multimedia article can be created with a standard text editor, once the visual and audible elements have been created.

- Article elements are explicitly tagged so appropriate entries in the source database can be automatically created.

- Since an article's elements retain their tags in the database, it is straightforward for the filter to access those needed to create a summary of a magazine's contents.

- Because the presentation of an article is determined by a style definition (set of rules) belonging to the formatter, not to the source material, it is easy to change the appearance of an article.

4 Future & Related Work

Text presently defines the basal structure of a document; other media are introduced via links into sidebars. It may be possible to define a unique structure for each medium, and hence to create an arbitrary basal structure. We believe that there is a distinct advantage in adopting the structure of text to all media, however, at least in the particular case of authoring documents for mass-market services. Basing a multimedia editor on the familiar paradigm of a text editor could let authors apply a lifetime of acquired language skills to the less familiar world of audio and video communication. Our current work includes defining media structures that parallel that of text, and determining what computer tools might best support future authors.

4.1 Structure in Temporal Media

One possible text-related hierarchical structure for video might be:

video	text
program	document
scene	paragraph
shot	sentence
frame	word

Based on this model, a video program (document) is made up of scenes (paragraphs) containing shots (sentences) which are in turn comprised of frames (words). A text-like editor could then be used to rearrange scenes in video as easily as paragraphs in text.

Without such structure it is difficult to define links between arbitrary media; with it inter-media links could be declared freely. For example, the basal structure of a document might be defined by video, with other media introduced by sidebars. Using SGML notation, the source document could contain the following reference:

```
<video_program [id=vidprog]>
<video_scene [id=vid1]>
<sidebar_ref [id=other_medium]> <video_scene [id=vid2]>
</sidebar_ref>
<video_scene [id=vid3]>
</video_program>
```

If the reader "clicked" on the image while viewing scene *vid2* of program *vidprog*, the video would be suspended and sidebar *other_medium* would be activated. At its conclusion, *vid2* would resume, followed by *vid3*.

An audio program could be handled similarly. For speech, which can be viewed as another manifestation of text, the parallel structure would be nearly identical, given the addition of some sense of time. Although music also has structure, it may require more of a leap of faith to reduce it to a text-like representation. An effort has been made by the Music in Information Processing Standards (MIPS) committee of ANSI to apply SGML structure to the development of SMDL, the Standard Music Description Language [Newcomb & Goldfarb 1989]. The HyTime subset [Goldfarb & Talbot 1989] of that language contains a model for the duration and synchronization of events. Although developed for describing music, the SMDL time model is applicable to multimedia and time-sequenced documents in a more general sense; HyTime could be used as a language for the creation of such documents. Because of the differences in goals, SMDL and HyTime are quite different from our prototype markup language, with its strongly text-oriented approach. Our language is suited to the needs of text authors who wish to expand into multimedia documents. SMDL, on the other hand, has a sophisticated and flexible notion of time and synchronization that is presently missing from our language.

4.2 Unified Editor/Previewer Environment

Encoding the structure of all media with SGML tags provides the necessary "hooks" for the arbitrary inter-media links needed for true multimedia documents. Beyond providing these multimedia hooks, encoding an explicit structure for all elements of a document could support the creation of a unified media editor. Text elements would be designated with conventional tags delineating text tokens represented by character strings. Temporal elements, on the other hand, would be designated by tags with generic identifiers reflecting the nature of the medium. Audio or video tokens would be represented by surrogates, graphical icons or other symbols within the lexicon of the editing computer. Based on the text paradigm, such an editor could manipulate the various elements of a document much as text is now manipulated by a word processor. Since it can be created on the same system that manipulates it, text will always enjoy an inherent editing advantage; audio and video tokens must be created elsewhere and merely rearranged or truncated by the editing system. Nevertheless, such a unified editor could be a powerful tool in the hands of an author who needed to manipulate all the elements of a multimedia document.

To complete such a system, the author needs a previewer that displays output from the unified editor on a terminal. The previewer (a particular instance of a formatter) would take the document elements as delineated by SGML tags and map them into representations appropriate for a terminal. To do this, it would employ a set of rules that define the style and design of the presentation on a given terminal. By loading different sets of rules, the previewer could emulate different terminals. With such a previewer and unified media editor, an author could refine multimedia documents by iteratively editing and viewing them.

4.3 From Here to Hypermedia

We have been considering links between elements of self-contained interactive documents. More generally, links from one document could refer to elements of another, leading to *hypermedia* systems in which documents are specific instances of multimedia elements drawn from a database of information. Hypermedia is a generalization of hypertext, a database technology typically characterized by small fragments of text interconnected by machine-supported links [Conklin 1987].

In a hypermedia system, information elements would be encoded by descriptive markup, but the "chunks" of information would be smaller than the self-contained documents of the prototype electronic magazine. Authors would create individual elements in various media and define links with attributes for external use. The user would determine the order of presentation, or *path* through a hypermedia document, by selecting links between elements. If link selection is unconstrained, the presentation may become confusing and disorienting to the user. One way to constrain link selection is to create a *script*, defined as "an active directed path through one or more documents that need not follow the linear order of the documents" [Zellweger 1988]. Rather than being a text document with links to other elements, an article might be a menu of scripts, each specifying a path through a collection of hypermedia elements. Each path might define a user experience that was the result of the efforts of multiple authors.

A descriptive markup language could be used in the preparation of such scripts. If they included our concept of class tags, the scripts could capture the author's intentions in writing them, and a customizing agent could select an appropriate script for an individual user. This procedure would preserve the flexibility and power of hypermedia systems, while ensuring that individuals received only suitable material.

5 Conclusion

The future broadband telecommunications network promises to support interactive multimedia presentations. For such presentations to become routine offerings of mass-market information service vendors, they must be much easier to create than present-day interactive video applications. Providing powerful authoring tools is an important step toward simplifying the creation of multimedia documents.

By explicitly defining the structure of a document, a descriptive markup language supports the creation of unified media editors and document previewers. Imposing the structure of text on temporal media such as audio or video permits the development of editing tools that are familiar and comfortable to authors of text documents. Such tools could help these authors transfer their skills to multimedia document production. SGML, an established international standard syntax with a growing list of applications, is a reasonable basis for such a markup language. Although most SGML applications have historically been for processing text, extensions to handle audio, video, and slideshows are straightforward and extend the benefits of descriptive markup to these media.

Documents created with descriptive markup are inherently suited for processing by database-driven information filters and can be formatted for different output devices without changing source material. Extensions to the language allow the creation of links between elements of arbitrary media and ultimately allow the creation of full hypermedia links among arbitrary elements of an information space.

The research reported here is just the beginning of the work needed to realize the goal of unified tools to ease the creation of full hypermedia presentations. Our progress, along with the work of other researchers, indicates that SGML forms a solid basis for this work.

References

[AAP 1987] *Standard for Electronic Manuscript Preparation and Markup,* Electronic Markup Series, Association of American Publishers, Washington, D.C., August 1987.

[Barron 1989] David Barron, "Why use SGML?," *Electronic Publishing,* vol. 2, no. 1, April 1989, pp. 3-24.

[Chicago 1982] *The Chicago Manual of Style,* University of Chicago Press, 1982, 13th Edition.

[Conklin 1987] J. Conklin, "Hypertext: An Introduction and Survey," *IEEE Computer,* vol. 20, no. 9, September 1987, pp. 17-41.

[Coombs, *et al.* 1987] T. Coombs, A. Renear, and S. DeRose, "Markup Systems and the Future of Scholarly Text Processing," *Communications of the ACM,* vol. 30, no. 11, November 1987, pp. 933-947.

[Frenkel 1989] Karen A. Frenkel, "The Next Generation of Interactive Technologies," *Communications of the ACM,* vol. 32, no. 7, July 1989, pp. 872-881.

[Goldfarb & Talbot 1989] C. Goldfarb and A. Talbot, "Standard Music Description Language (SMDL) Part Two: Hypermedia/Time-Based Document Subset (HyTime)," *X3V1.8M/SD-6 Journal of Development,* Fifth draft, August 11, 1989.

[Hodges *et al.* 1989] M. Hodges, B. Davis, and R. Sasnett, "Investigations in Multimedia Design Documentation," in Edward Barrett (ed.), *The Society of Text,* MIT Press, 1989, pp. 79-89.

[ISO 1986] *Information Processing—Text and Office Systems—Standard Generalized Markup Language (SGML)* (ISO 8879), International Standards Organization, 1986.

[ISO 1988] *Information Processing—Text and Office Systems—Document Style Semantics and Specification Language (DSSSL),* International Standards Organization (ISO/IEC JTC 1/SC 18/WG 8 N606), July 1988.

[Judd & Cruz 1989] T. H. Judd and G. C. Cruz, "Customized Electronic Magazines: Electronic Publishing for Information Grazing," *Advanced Printing of Paper Summaries, Electronic Imaging '89,* October 1989, pp. 504-509.

[Kajimoto et al. 1989] K. Kajimoto, F. Nakayama, T. Nonomura, Y. Imai, S. Isoda, and Y. Kushiki, "New-Media Document (NewDoc) and Dynamic Navigation on the BTRON Specification," in *Digest of Papers,* COMPCON Spring '89, March 1989, pp. 40-42.

[Mackay & Davenport 1989] W. Mackay and G. Davenport, "Virtual Video Editing in Interactive Multimedia Applications," *Communications of the ACM,* vol. 32, no. 7, July 1989, pp. 802-810.

[Magel 1989] Mark Magel, "Springtime for System Integrators," *AV Video,* April 1989, pp. 48-53.

[Newcomb & Goldfarb 1989] S. Newcomb and C. Goldfarb, "Standard Music Description Language (SMDL) Part One: Objectives and Methodology," *X3V1.8M/SD-6 Journal of Development,* Fifth draft, August 11, 1989.

[Tabuchi & Muracho 1989] M. Tabuchi and Y. Muracho, "MeSOD: the Metric Spatial Object Data Model for a Multimedia Application: Hyperbook," in *Digest of Papers,* COMPCON Spring '89, March 1989, pp. 396-401.

[White 1989] William White, "'Til The CALS Come Home," *Electronic Publishing & Printing,* vol. 4, no. 9, December 1989, pp. 54-55.

[Zellweger 1988] Polle T. Zellweger, "Active Paths Through Multimedia Documents," in C. C. vanVliet (ed.), *Document Manipulation and Typography,* Proc. Int'l. Conference on Electronic Publishing, Document Manipulation and Typography, Cambridge University Press, 1988, pp. 19-34.

Colophon

These EP90 proceedings were prepared from camera-ready masters submitted by the authors (page numbers were added by hand). Each author received a set of formatting guidelines, based on the Cambridge University Press house style, and were told how to obtain copies of a set of LaTeX macros and **troff** macros that implemented the style. As a reflection of the power of the concept of generic coding (and of these two formatting systems), almost all of the published papers were produced with one or the other of these macro sets. Another interesting trend, since the earlier EP86 and EP88 conferences, is the increasing prominence of PostScript printers as the output device of choice. Three of the papers were produced from electronically-transmitted source, as described below.

Listed below are the specifics for each of the papers for which we received formatting information:

- Brian W. Kernighan: Originally produced with an experimental version of the **troff** cup macros. Because of difficulties with them, the paper was hand-translated into LaTeX and printed on a phototypesetter.

- Vincent Quint, Marc Nanard, and Jacques André: Produced with LaTeX and electronically transmitted to the University of Maryland, where it was printed on an Apple LaserWriter.

- Donald D. Chamberlin: Edited and formatted by the Janus experimental formatter at IBM Research and printed on an Autologic APS-5 photocomposer.

- Allen L. Brown, Jr. and Howard A. Blair: Prepared with LaTeX and printed at 600 dpi on a Xerox 4650.

- Anne-Marie Vercoustre: Produced with LaTeX and electronically transmitted to the University of Maryland, where it was printed on an Apple LaserWriter.

- Giovanni Guardalben and Mosé Giacomello: Prepared with Winword (the Windows version of Microsoft Word) and printed on a 300 dpi Hewlett-Packard LaserJet IIP. The fonts are Bitstream Times Roman, produced with Bitstream Fontware for Microsoft Windows. Pictures were produced with Freelance and CorelDraw.

- Anthony P. Wolfman and Daniel M. Berry: Prepared with **troff** and printed on a Linotronic 300 at 1270 dpi.

- Paul Kahn, Julie Launhardt, Krzysztof Lenk, and Ronnie Peters: Preparation environment was not specified.

- B. N. Rossiter and M. A. Heather: Preparation environment was not specified.

- Pekka Kilpeläinen, Greger Lindén, Heikki Mannila, and Erja Nikunen: Prepared with $\LaTeX$ and printed on an Apple LaserWriter II. One figure was produced with `fig` and the other by the `snapshot` utility of the XView environment.

- José Valdeni De Lima and Henri Galy: The original version was prepared with Microsoft Word 4.0 on the Macintosh. Because of difficulties with linespacing, we hand-translated the Word source into $\LaTeX$ at the University of Maryland and printed it on an Apple LaserWriter.

- David F. Brailsford, David R. Evans, and Geeti Granger: Prepared with the `cup` **troff** macros.

- John Handley and Stuart Weibel: Prepared with $\LaTeX$ and printed on an Apple LaserWriter at 300 dpi.

- A. Lawrence Spitz: Produced using FrameMaker 2.0 on a Sun SPARCstation 1 and printed on an Apple LaserWriter II. Figure 3a and the text portions of figure 4 were scanned at 300 dpi on a Sharp greyscale scanner. Figure 3b and the remainder of figure 4 were captured as Sun rasterfiles.

- Gary E. Kopec and Steven C. Bagley: Prepared using the $\LaTeX$ macros on a Sun 4/60 and printed on an Apple LaserWriter II at 300 dpi.

- Sten F. Andler: Prepared with Janus and printed on the Autologic APS-5.

- Y. S. Moon and T. Y. Shin: Preparation environment was not specified.

- Gil C. Cruz and Thomas H. Judd: Prepared with **troff**, **tbl**, and **pic**, and using an augmented version of the `cup` macros. Printed on an Imagen 7320 printer.

- Paul M. English, Ethan Jacobson, Robert A. Morris, Kimbo B. Mundy, Stephen D. Pelletier, Thomas A. Polucci, and H. David Scarbro: Prepared with Interleaf publishing software and output on a Linotronic 300.

- Eric A. Bier and Aaron Goodisman: Prepared using the Tioga WYSIWYG text editor, which runs in the Cedar programming environment at PARC. Tioga produced an Interpress master, which was then printed on the Platemaker experimental 1200 spot per inch laser printer at PARC.

- Front and backmatter was prepared with LaTeX and printed on an Apple LaserWriter. The keyword index was produced using the keywords supplied by the authors.

We would like to thank the RIDT'89 organizers for providing us with the statement of formatting guidelines, which were adopted in essentially unchanged form for EP90. The LaTeX and **troff** macros have a long history of their own. The LaTeX macros are a modification of the standard "article" style. I produced the initial version of these modifications for the book *Structured Documents*, published by Cambridge University Press in 1989. Richard Southall improved the macros for publication of that book and subsequently again with Ph. Louarn for publication of the RIDT'89 proceedings in May of 1989. A variant of these macros is now being used for LaTeX articles published in the journal *Electronic Publishing: Origination, Dissemination and Design*.

David Brailsford provided us with the **troff** macros. I asked him to describe their history. David tells us that "the **troff** cup macros started life as a macro set, developed by Mike Lesk and Brian Kernighan, to model the layout of the journal *Software—Practice and Experience*. The user interface to the macros is very similar to that of the well-known ms set. Over the last two years these macros have seen further adaptation to form the ep macros for the journal *Electronic Publishing: Origination, Dissemination and Design*. The ep set has, in turn, been further modified to create the cup set for RIDT and EP90."

RICHARD FURUTA

List of authors

ANDLER, STEN F.	221
ANDRE, JACQUES	17
BAGLEY, STEVEN C.	207
BERRY, DANIEL M.	93
BIER, ERIC A.	277
BLAIR, HOWARD A.	47
BRAILSFORD, DAVID F.	169
BROWN, ALLEN L., JR.	47
CHAMBERLIN, DONALD D.	31
CRUZ, GIL C.	249
DE LIMA, JOSE VALDENI	153
ENGLISH, PAUL M.	263
EVANS, DAVID R.	169
GALY, HENRI	153
GIACOMELLO, MOSE	79
GOODISMAN, AARON	277
GRANGER, GEETI	169
GUARDALBEN, GIOVANNI	79
HANDLEY, JOHN	183
HEATHER, M. A.	125
JACOBSON, ETHAN	263
JUDD, THOMAS H.	249
KAHN, PAUL	107
KERNIGHAN, BRIAN W.	1
KILPELAINEN, PEKKA	139
KOPEC, GARY E.	207
KRZYSZTOF LENK	107
LAUNHARDT, JULIE	107
LINDEN, GREGER	139
MANNILA, HEIKKI	139
MOON, Y. S.	235
MORRIS, ROBERT A.	263

MUNDY, KIMBO B. 263
NANARD, MARC 17
NIKUNENM, ERJA 139
PELLETIER, STEPHEN D. 263
POLUCCI, THOMAS A. 263
QUINT, VINCENT 17
RONNIE PETERS 107
ROSSITER, B. N. 125
SCARBRO, H. DAVID 263
SHIN, T. Y. 235
SPITZ, A. LAWRENCE 193
VERCOUSTRE, ANNE-MARIE 65
WEIBEL, STUART 183
WOLFMAN, ANTHONY P. 93

Index

abstract syntax notation one 183
access, remote file 169
active documents .. 263, 277
analysis, document structure .. 183
anchor 65
authoring 249
automatic generation 221

binding, run-time 263
bitmap editing 207
buttons 277

character recognition 193
complex objects ... 125, 153
computer aided refereeing system 169

databases 125, 153
Ditroff 93
document description language 47
document modelling 125
document processing 183
document recognition .. 193, 207
document structure analysis 183
document systems 31
documents, active .. 263, 277
documents, scripted 65
documents, structured ... 153
DOEOIS 153

editing, structured 65
editors, syntax directed ... 65
editors 31
EmbeddedButtons 277
extensibility 31, 263

file access, remote 169
flowcharting 93
fonts, outline 221
full-text retrieval 183
functional models 153

graphic design 107
gridfitting hints 221

hypermedia 107, 249
hypertext 263
hypertext 65

inheritance 31
interactive 249
Intermedia 107

journal production 169

layout processing 47
layout, page 79
Lisp 263
logic grammar 47
logical structures 153

markup 31, 249
models, functional 153
multilingual 193

object-oriented 263
objects, complex 153
ODA 79, 153
ODIF 153
ORACLE 153
outline fonts 221

page layout 79
Pic 93
production, journal 169
professional publishing ... 79
programmability 263
properties 31
publishing, professional .. 79

remote file access 169
retrieval, full-text 183
run-time binding 263

scripted documents 65
segmentation 193
SGML 249
structured documents ... 153
structured editing 65
structures, logical 153
syntax directed editors ... 65

text editing 207
typesetting 93

user interfaces 277

vectorization 193